WINES
OF SLOVENIA

Dr Julij Nemanič • Dr Janez Bogataj

WINES
OF SLOVENIA

Dr Julij Nemanič • Professor Dr Janez Bogataj

Photography
Janez Pukšič

Designer
Žare Kerin

Editor
Nina Žibert

Assistant
Nana Ahčin

Translated by
Darja Sunesko

Language editor
Robert Whitelock

Desktop publishing
Marko Pekolj/Camera

Printed by
Gorenjski tisk

First edition: first printing
Number of copies: 3,000

Company representatives: Lili Mistral, Rok Kvaternik

Ljubljana, October 2004

Copyright © 2004, Rokus Gifts, Ltd. All rights reserved.

No part of this publication may be reproduced, stored in a retrieval system, or transmitted in any form or by any means - electronic, photocopying, recording, or otherwise - unless the written permission of the publisher has been obtained beforehand. This book may not be lent, resold, hired out or otherwise disposed of by way of trade in any form of binding or cover other than in which it has been published, without the prior consent of the publisher.

Rokus Gifts, Ltd.
Gosposvetska cesta 2, SI-1000 Ljubljana, Slovenia, Europe
Phone: +386 1 234 97 20, Fax: +386 1 234 97 30
Email: darila@rokus.com, Website: www.darila.com

CIP - Kataložni zapis o publikaciji
Narodna in univerzitetna knjižnica, Ljubljana

663.2(497.4)

NEMANIČ Julij
Wines of Slovenia / Julij Nemanič ; [introduction] Janez Bogataj ; [photographs Janez Pukšič ; translated by Darja Sunesko]. - 1st ed., 1st printing. - Ljubljana : Darila Rokus, 2004

Prevod dela: Vina Slovenije

ISBN 961-6531-06-9

215759616

Dear lovers of good wine!

I have long been working towards the publication of the book you are holding today. The whole idea of it, and the fact that the popularity of Slovene wines simply cried out for some kind of publication, have occupied me constantly for the past five years. Recently the business of publishing has rarely afforded me the peace and other means to fulfil this wish, so that now I finally have the book in front of me it is all the more a moment to celebrate.

During the last year especially, in my numerous meetings with people from other countries, the subject of wine has quickly found its way into conversation. I am convinced of the pride that Slovenes take in describing the greatness of their wine culture, whether at home or abroad. Sometimes, if circumstances allow, our guests are lucky enough to attend a tasting at one of the 386 wine-growing premises included in this book. All are surprised at the quality of the produce from the various Slovenian wine regions, and foreign visitors usually suggest or even demand — greater promotion of Slovene wines.

I will not forget the enthusiasm in the eyes of some true wine connoisseurs — foreign friends whom I met while they were travelling around Slovenia and discovering our wines: the American, vice-president of a large corporation, on first discovering the world of Slovenian wine, which he continues to admire to the present day; Japan's first female sommelier, who was thrilled to give advice to one of the best Slovene vintners (to his utmost surprise); or the German businessman, who places Slovene wines above all others and regularly purchases them when he visits.

The overview of Slovenian wine growers provided by this book is a necessary tool for any wine lover, whether from Slovenia or abroad. I am sure it will surprise you with its diversity, comprehensiveness, clarity, layout and, especially, the words of Dr Julij Nemanič, whose hard work and considerable expertise have produced superb descriptions of the high-quality Slovene wines selected for inclusion. I hope that growers, as well as wine lovers, will make the book their own and spend the ensuing months in the company of this oenological bible until 2006, when a revised edition should be published.

Unfortunately there is as yet no suitable guide to the world of Slovene restaurants and inns, such as the Michelin (Red Guides), Zagat or GaultMillau. So let us make *Wines of Slovenia* the first building block in the story of Slovene oenological and gastronomical identity, a story that the world is only now just beginning to explore.

Rok Kvaternik, Publisher

There are Three Good Things in the World: The Three Wine Regions of Slovenia

There is a Slovene saying that a wine is not happy alone, and the Slovenes' long association with wine has an impressive heritage, as well as a rich variety of contemporary manifestations. This cultural wealth all derives from the diversity of the soil and climate in a geographically small area, and from the hundreds of years of experience accumulated by creative wine growers and vintners, who have learnt how to produce high-quality wines in these varied, but often strenuous, natural conditions. At the meeting-point of the European Alps, the Mediterranean and the region of Pannonia, people have grown vines and produced wine for over two millennia. Throughout history wine has moulded the many and diverse customs and festivities, and the whole way of life — both the differences and local characteristics — in the three wine-growing regions of Slovenia: **Primorska** (6,500 ha), **Posavje** (7,500 ha) and **Podravje** (10,200 ha), and within these regions another fourteen wine-growing districts.

Viticulture and the wine trade are commercial ventures, although in their diverse forms they have a significant influence in all areas of human endeavour — not just the material, but social interaction, creativity and spirituality. Thus, in a discussion of viticulture and the wine trade, and the product that unites them — the wine itself — we can speak of a web of cultural forms. This embodies not only our knowledge of wine growing and the yearly cycle of production, but also our whole interaction with wine: our ability to distinguish different varieties, to enjoy, mix, taste and so on. In sum, it embodies all the dimensions, meanings and modes of expressing the positive nature of our relationship with wine, whereby it is viewed as man's noble companion, beneficial to health and life; it has nothing to do with the negative perception that has predominated for centuries: wine as the cause of alcoholism, and by extension of social evils such as bankruptcy, domestic violence and, ultimately, self destruction. In the context of this negative perception the abundance of sayings and proverbs deriving from folk philosophy on 'wise' drinking comes as no surprise. On one hand we have nature's beautiful gift to us, the drink of the gods, the spring of sparkling thoughts and positive companionship, which, on the other, can lead all too quickly to a life of sadness, mistakes — even decay. As one typical Slovene proverb, loosely translated, puts it:

Wine says 'I am good, as long as you're in charge; but when I'm in charge — you're in trouble!'

In spite of a great effort to promote and develop wine culture, to a large extent we still associate the drinking of wine simply with the stimulation of merriment. From merriment to melancholy is usually a short step, and in a social situation the first can quickly change to the second.

THERE ARE THREE GOOD THINGS

Wine brings negative and positive elements into our everyday lives, so in the modern day we try to promote the latter: there is much to be said about knowing, tasting, appraising wines; the relationship between other forms of nourishment and wine (which itself must be treated as a foodstuff); the common choice of wine as a personal or business gift; the practice of toasting with the sparkling varieties; wine collection; the organization of cellars; and, of course, a significant wine trade.

But that is not the end of it. We should understand the rich culture that surrounds wine growing on all levels: not just the tacky kitsch of the barrels turned into chairs in breweries, or tables in the wine cellars, but also the wine barrel as the motivic symbol of a rich culture that in continually evolving to express itself in new ways. These contemporary manifestations — the individual elements, the regionalised terminology of our heritage — are bound up with the present-day division of winemaking Slovenia into three distinct regions. The differences between these three regions and, within them, even between individual wine-growing districts, have a bearing upon many aspects of wine making and culture, as well as upon the wines themselves. We can trace these differences throughout their historical development; many of them have survived to the present day, some are radically transformed, and others we know of only through writings or other forms of historical evidence.

The diversity of viticultural Slovenia can be seen primarily in the **culture of the individual wine-growing regions**, a direct consequence of vine cultivation, although through history the cultural landscape has changed, especially during the second half of the twentieth century. By the end of the sixties some people, among them a number of architects, were already warning of the destruction of the wine-growing landscape. We should talk of change rather than destruction, however: just as cultivation methods gradually developed, so the landscape itself was bound to alter. Naturally part of this change was down to the newly built wine cellars, holiday accommodation and blocks of flats that sprang up next to the vineyards, but the so-called 'traditional' viticultural landscape remained unchanged in the wine-growing region of Primorska — the geographical meeting-point of the sunny Mediterranean with the contrast of the Alps — thanks to the coexistence of viticulture with orchards (growing such fruit as cherries, apricots and olives) and other forms of agriculture.

In the Karst region, trees were frequently planted on wooden frames among the vines as a second support for the grapevine. In the region of Posavje, with its sub-Alpine climate and a rather complex soil make-up based on limestone and dolomite, small vineyards with wine 'rooms' and 'cottages' are typical. In the sixteenth century people began to live in them, and since then the vineyards of this area have always been inhabited. Influenced by the Pannonian climate, the region of Podravje has its own distinctive-looking vineyards on the slopes of the hilly landscape, where the vines were planted in rectangular formation along the tops of the hills and the cellars were mostly constructed of wood, or covered with straw. In among the wine cellars overlooking the slopes of the vineyards they planted tall poplars — a regional characteristic — which also functioned as natural lightning conductors. And it's not just the positioning of the vineyards that differed; cultivation methods varied too. The accepted method of planting vines in Karst and Brda was completely different from the practice, common in Podravje for instance, of tying the vines to poles. As early as the second half of the fifteenth century, Paolo Santonino, secretary to the patriarch of Aquileia, wrote that this was the region where 'the vines are tied to poles according to the Roman tradition'.

The **wine cellars** are the basic environment for man's wine-growing endeavours, and these also differ from one region to another, primarily by their very names: in different areas one hears of **wine cellars**, **wine rooms**, and **wine cottages.** Apart from these three key terms the Slovene language also has *gora, gorca* (denoting a cellar or vineyard), *vrh, kevder, kelder* (all denoting some form of cellar), and other dialect words. A study of terminology by region shows that in Primorska, for example, wine cellars were never used as single-purpose buildings, and were often used, at least partially, as housing or farm buildings; this remains the case today. The wine cellars would form part of a farmhouse, a castle, or even a town dwelling. There are a few cases of dedicated wine cellars above the Vipava valley, but questions about the manner of their development remain unanswered. In the region of Posavje, like Podravje, the dedicated wine cellar is a familiar site as a building at the edge of the vineyard. In Posavje there are two distinct expressions used to refer to these buildings: those made of wood are 'wine rooms' and those of brick 'wine cottages'. In Posavje, more precisely on the left bank of the Sava river, there are also cellars that form part of the basement in people's houses. Such cellars are even more common in Podravje, where the wine cellar is most commonly an independent building, often on top of a hill planted with vineyards, and always some distance from the main residential area.
Further differences between the wine regions are seen in the basic natural material used for construction, something considered only by social historians and museum curators. In Primorska this was exclusively stone. Exceptionally well-preserved examples of older cellars, with arches and details carved into the stone, testify to the

coexistence of man, stone, and wine for centuries. The Posavje region is a kind of intermediate stage in the use of building materials for wine cellars; a combination of stone and wood can be seen even in the two distinct types mentioned previously — the wine room and the vineyard cottage. The latter term is so widely used that even some wooden wine rooms are referred to as cottages. In Podravje wood is the basic building material and was in the past accompanied by clay, sometimes mixed with straw and, of course, brick, from the nineteenth century onwards. If the wine-keeper — or vintner — in Primorska always kept his wine at home, the vintner in Posavje or Podravje would go to cultivate his vines and savour his wines at a separate vineyard. The wine cellars of these areas also became occasional, seasonal residences for the vintners and their families, in similar fashion to the stockbreeders in the Alpine world who, during the summer months, moved with their cattle to the Alpine meadows.

The diversity of the three Slovene wine regions is also to be seen in the **methods of cultivation** used, and the range of vineyard **tools and implements** to have evolved from our great wine-growing tradition. Different soil composition dictated different shapes of **hoe** for vineyard cultivation. Short-handled and broad hoes were used in Haloze, for instance, to till the vineyards on the steep slopes, where one must be careful to keep the soil from running down the hill. In the Karst region, which is mostly flat with only the occasional slope, the nature of the cultivation work, and hence the tools involved, were completely different. There are at least three different types of wooden wine press, each particular to one of the three wine regions; made of oak or chestnut, they were masterpieces of the local, self-taught craftsmen. These days they're no longer used for their original purpose, so we tend to see them as rather tacky ornaments in wine cellars, bars, and shops. There were also differences in the construction of the **barrels**, not only

in the wood they were made of (oak or acacia), but also in their shape. In Primorska long, narrow barrels continue to be used, whilst in the neighbouring regions the barrels are more rounded or oval. We should not overlook another distinctive vineyard implement, historically indigenous only to the Podravje region, although over the last two decades it has spread to Posavje. Beside some of the native wines it is the most distinctive feature of Slovene viticulture: the *klopotec,* designed to scare the birds away from the ripening grapes. Its birth, in spite of less educated speculations to the contrary, has been placed by historians during the last years of the eighteenth century, when the state began to educate the peasantry in the science of viticulture with a view to increasing crop success. Made of two (in Prlekija and Slovenske Gorice) or three (in Haloze) thin wooden plates attached to the top of a wooden pole in a windmill-like formation, it was put in motion by the wind, causing a loud banging noise as the plates rotated and struck against the pole, and the singing of these bird-scarers announced the approaching grape harvest. The *klopotec* is an invention of Slovene wine-growers and has spread from Podravje to the neighbouring Austrian wine regions, taking one of its Slovene names along with it.

Particularly multifaceted is the relationship between wine and local **diet** and **culinary culture** in each of the wine regions. This aspect of wine's heritage offers a rich seam for exploration but also opens the window on a darker side of man's past, when wine — of lesser quality — often provided his only daily sustenance. Of course, this is true only in certain areas: primarily Posavje and Podravje, where subordinate positions such as that of the vine dresser (who trimmed and tended the vines) were common. There is an interesting inscription to be found on a Roman oil lamp excavated at Ptuj:

'Bread, wine and a radish make the poor man's dinner.'

In the present day we cannot conceive of Slovenia's wine culture without its surrounding culinary traditions, which bind all together into a complete blend of regional flavours. Wine and cooking also combine in the local manner of **receiving guests**, when it is customary, following various forms of greeting (for instance a welcome might be offered verbally or in song) to accompany a glass of wine with a taste of traditional local food. In Primorska it is still customary to receive guests in the wine cellar; in Posavje in front of or inside the vineyard cottage; and in Podravje once again in the cellar, or the accommodation within it. In Podravje some innkeepers of the 'old school' are still in the habit of bringing their guests' chosen wine to the table, together with an extra glass. The innkeeper then toasts his guests with this glass before leaving them to enjoy the rest of the wine with their food.

Today it is the Primorska region that offers the most interesting and, in terms of modern diet, the **most positive heritage**. The wines of this region are served accompanied by a wide variety of vegetables and vegetable dishes (fennel, aubergines, asparagus, artichoke, garlic, tomato), pies, Karstic prosciutto and seafood. The locals excel in their preparation of poultry and venison, as well as a number of types of pasta: particularly noted are a hand-made variety known as *fuži*. The food here is typically prepared using olive oil and various local herbs. Among the various everyday dishes and side dishes that accompany the basic meat and wine sauces (called *toč*), yellow and white varieties of polenta feature prominently. Other specialities include baked meat sausages and the sweet and savoury varieties of *krvavice*, or 'blood sausages'. The Primorskans make an excellent type of stuffed pastry roll (*štruklji*), similar to strudel but boiled rather than baked, whilst among the most popular casseroles are *mineštra* (known in English by its Italian name, *minestrone*) and *jota* (a dish comprising sauerkraut, smoked ham and beans). Another local speciality is *frtalje*, or *fritaje* — frittatas: omelettes with herbs, sausages, and prosciutto. Among sweet dishes, walnut dumplings (*štruklji*), *fritole* (a type of doughnut) and *kroštole* (a kind of fried pastry) particularly stand out.

Posavje's culinary character is something of a synthesis of the Alpine and Pannonian traditions. A variety of roast meats and poultry make an excellent accompaniment to the main speciality wine of this region — the red *Cviček*. The locals cook a wonderful roast duck with *mlinci* ('flat cake': a type of salted, baked pancake) and red cabbage, lots of different *štruklji* with different stuffings, and more floury flat cake (such as *Belokranjska povitica* or *prosta potica*: festive breads and cakes with a variety of fillings such as nuts, cheese or poppy seeds). In Bela Krajina, the cooks are masters of grilled and roast lamb and of fine poultry dishes, poultry also being a speciality of Bizeljsko. In the last couple of decades Posavje has developed an initiative to raise the profile of salamis and sausages, and in a number of places annual salami and sausage festivals are held to select the best products. Especially good are the various meat rolls, stuffed pork chops, and poultry and rabbit stews served with buckwheat mash. The local speciality of Dolenjska in Posavje is *matevž* — a side dish of mashed, buttered beans and potatoes served with meat and stewed cabbage.

The Pannonian influence is even stronger in the cuisine of Podravje. Here traditional cooking revolves particularly around flour, with an exceptional variety of breads and sweet or savoury pies. Best known among these are *Prekmurska*, *Prleška gibanica* and *ajdovi krapci*. Also of note is the range of foods produced following the annual pig slaughter: all kinds of fresh sausages or blood sausages, Prekmurje ham, and *kisla juha* — 'sour soup' made from the legs, tail and entrails of the pig with white wine — are the most notable dishes encountered when sampling the wine culture of this region. Next in importance are the poultry dishes, which as early as the Middle Ages were written about in chronicles of the period, whilst another speciality of the area is *Prleška tunka* — roast pork preserved in minced lard. Prekmurje is also known for its excellent dairy and pasta dishes.

The cultivation, production and consumption of wine have, throughout history, been linked with particular **crafts**, **trades** and **skills**. First, there are the many tools and implements traditionally made either in the home by self-taught craftsmen or professionally for trade; blacksmiths and woodworkers manufactured hoes, mattocks and other tools for cultivating and nurturing the vines. The making of the wooden wine presses, equipped with one or sometimes two screws hand-carved out of wood, was the territory only of master carpenters, especially skilled in this particular art. Whereas the wine presses in Posavje

and Podravje are made entirely of wood, those of Primorska also comprise some stone parts (such as the bucket that collects the freshly pressed grape juice); these were the work of local stonemasons and were often decorated with various ornaments. All three wine regions saw the widespread development of **basketry** using willow and other materials, wicker-covered wine bottles and grape-juice strainers, all of which have their own local variations and technical innovations specific to region.
The same is true of **cooperage**, which supplies the wine growers and vintners with barrels. Moving beyond the regionally based innovations of self-taught craftsmen, the activity developed into a high-quality trade. The wares of Slovene coopers, such as those from Tacen near Ljubljana, were appreciated abroad even before the Second World War. Forest 'glasshouses', or *glažutas*, evolved during the nineteenth century into a fully fledged industry supplying the wine market with glassware, whilst the potters in all the former Slovene pottery areas produced a broad range of wine and beer jugs, cups, and baked clay 'glasses', both for everyday use and for festive occasions. Two styles of festive wine jug are especially noteworthy. The first, from Posavje, is shaped like a rooster, and is known today as the *Šentjernejski petelin* (the **rooster of St Bartholomew**). It is the particular emblem of the Dolenjska region or, more precisely, the town of Šentjernej and its surroundings. The second represents the southeast and has the Slovene **devil** or **screech owl**, depicted in the stylized decorations around the rim. The twentieth century saw the spread of another style of wine jug, its name, *majolika*, a sign of foreign influence and, in fact, an indication of the way it is fashioned; it has no other connection with the Slovene pottery tradition.

A significant influence in the development of Slovenian wine culture is the practice of the wine trade itself, which has been conducted for centuries in this area, key to trade routes. The area surrounding Ptuj, Maribor and other towns in Styria represents a trading district of particular importance, and there are numerous records to be found containing extensive reports of the Styrian wine trade, although certain wines of Primorska too — *Rebula* for example — were known in places such as Carinthia, Upper Styria, and Salzburg; as early as the second half of the fifteenth century, Paolo Santonino remarked on the fine taste of Rebula. We still have numerous stories and documentary sources that speak of the exceptional worth of particular Primorskan specialities such as *Teran*, which was also believed to be beneficial to health. Some excellent wines of the Podravje region — in particular those from Slovenske Gorice, Prlekija and Haloze — have been

sold since the Middle Ages out of Maribor, Ptuj, Radgona and Slovenska Bistrica. The wine trade represented a major interest, and so by the fourteenth century conflicts were beginning to arise between the towns; Maribor and Ptuj were literally engaged in a wine war that lasted until the seventeenth century, caused by disputes over the use of roads to transport the wine, the right to transport wine through towns, payment of tolls and similar matters. Wine was sold and transported in barrels; the practice of returning the barrels (which were themselves worth a considerable sum) did not begin until the nineteenth century.
During the nineteenth century, the wine trade experienced a major geographical spread. Numerous larger trading entities appeared both at home and abroad, with many of them growing directly from former tradesmen's families. The centre-point of the wine trade was Ljubljana, with numerous trade paths running through it from the south into the north and west. For centuries the Primorskan wines dominated, with those of Posavje and Podravje slowly beginning to establish themselves in the nineteenth century. During the 1920s Ljubljana became recognized as a centre for large-scale wine fairs, so Slovene wines were guaranteed a permanent place among the wares on display. International exhibitions of Slovene wines go back even further: as early as 1857 they were shown in Vienna and, in 1903, at the first exhibition of Carniolan wines in Prague. At the end of Second World War the first international wine exhibition took place, with an international tasting in 1954 in Ljubljana. This continues to the present day and is the oldest international wine tasting event in the world.

The evolution of wine culture was necessitated not only by trade, but also by the development of professional viticulture and education in the field; the development of professional viticulture dates far back into history and is connected in particular to the work of the Cistercian and Carthusian monastic orders in Slovenia. Alongside general and agricultural development, viticulture also experienced growth in the eighteenth and nineteenth centuries; an important role was played at this time by farmers' associations, as well as by some exceptional individuals who produced the first Slovene literature on the subject in the nineteenth century. In the second half of the century Slovene vineyards were affected by various diseases and pests such as the fungal diseases peronospora and oidium, as well as phylloxera, the wine louse, and there followed a complete renewal, which gave way to further growth in the field of professional viticulture. Most of the affected vineyards were restored by the time of the First World War.
The cultural diversity of all three Slovene wine regions was further influenced by the heritage of **social status** and **class relations**, these being closely connected to the social structure of land ownership and employment in the vineyards. In the region equating to modern Primorska a system similar to that of the roman 'colonate', whereby agricultural workers were permanently attached to the land

and dependent on the landowners, was the typical form of tenancy for all kinds of property, including the vineyard. The tenant farmer in this case was a freeman, his employment by the owner governed by a short-term contract that could be terminated. Tenants paid rents and taxes in harvests and labour. The Podravje region is historically linked with a particular social group of vineyard and farm labourers known as vine dressers, who were allotted the cultivation of a vineyard by their employers — typically wealthier farmers, tradesmen and townsmen — as well as a house, and often even cattle. The vine dresser was required to serve in his master's vineyard and other properties, cultivate the wine crop, harvest it, and work in the forest, yet for all this he could barely feed himself or his family, which would usually be large. Employment conditions were very harsh; although either party could cancel the contract, up to the Second World War vine dressing embodied one of the worst forms of worker exploitation in the vineyard, and it is in the hard lives of the vine-dressing population that we see the darker side of humanity and the winemaking way of life. Not surprisingly, vine dressing became associated with alcoholism and failed to keep pace with social developments in other professions, and people often had to depend on refermented poor-quality wines and brandies made from grapeskins for their basic nourishment.

The Posavje region represents a compromise between the two extremes: it never developed any form of 'colonate' or vine-dressing system, practices which reached full swing in the nineteenth century and ended in 1945. In Posavje the vineyards were smaller and of lesser quality, so the interests of the town owners were accordingly smaller, and for a long time the traditional miners' statutes were enforced and prevented the development of vine dressing. These statutes represent something of a local social phenomenon; the practice of joint decision making on vineyards and wine meant that all members of all social strata sat together, peasants alongside gentry. Traces of these old wine-growing communities remained longest in Bela Krajina.

The heritage of the three wine regions merges with modern practices in **customs and traditions.** In some cases we can see a genuine continuity with the past, whilst others are, in reality, modern inventions that have nevertheless become part of an invented tradition. In the ceremonial customs that celebrate life's key events — births, weddings and funerals — wine generally assumes a ritual significance. In Podravje it is the common tradition to propose a toast in church as part of the wedding ceremony, and even today it is customary for a bottle of wine, suitably decorated with fresh greenery, to be carried in as part of the wedding procession and placed upon the altar for the priest to bless before toasting the newly-weds. Many wedding customs

incorporate **written toasts** and **songs**, which lend a certain rhythm to the enjoyment of the wine and enhance the atmosphere. A similar practice, though less noisy and more informal, is the raising of a glass to the peace of the departed at the meal following a funeral, today inappropriately referred to as the wake (which means more accurately an overnight period of vigil or prayer). This incorrect use of the term is a good illustration of the way customs and traditions evolve over time.

The annual calendar is punctuated by a number of **holidays** and other occasions on which wine plays a part in ritual or ceremony. The annual **harvest** is just such an occasion, when work and festivities combine and participants not only observe the traditions, but feel themselves an integral part of the whole ritual of the wine-production process. Similar to the harvest both in symbolic meaning and manner of observance is the **celebration of the pig slaughter** (*koline, furež*). Today, of course, grape harvesting and the whole practice of wine making are far more technological in nature, so their associated festivals embrace modern practices, whilst the events of the modern wine-making calendar may even occur at different times. In Podravje and Posavje most of the inherited harvest customs and traditions are observed alongside the modern ones, and Podravje is famous for its especially high-spirited **late** and **special** harvest festivals, which perhaps came about also because harvests are difficult to predict, dependent as they are on weather and temperature conditions. The key elements of the harvesting ritual are merrymaking and festive meals comprising meat courses, desserts and, of course, wine.

Less associated with wine are the many **carnivals**, or *šagra* as they are called in Primorska. That isn't to say that there is no wine at all at such events, but it is beer that dominates, except at 'themed' events that are based on a wine motif. One of the biggest, requiring the most organization, must be the Spring Wine Festival known as the *Vinska Vigred* held in Metlika, with a high standard of wines on offer and a wide-ranging accompanying programme of cultural events. The wines included are quality-checked. Another traditional festival is the *Cvičkarija* which in past years has also been held in some other Slovenian places and not just in the Dolenjska region. There are also large turnout for the festival of Teran and prosciutto in Dutovlje, the festival of Refosk in Marezige, and numerous others. These days the traditional festivals have one major *raison d'être* — merrymaking. Some can last several days and involve a plethora of sporting, cultural, oenological and social events, as well as shows and concerts. Wine is available at all these festivities as well as on various **visitor days** and **weeks,** when particular local culinary ingredients are promoted, and where farmers' wives' societies and wine-growing associations play an important role. The sign of a forthcoming festival is usually a maypole, not just on May Day, but at many other festivals too. A piece of ham and/or a bottle (or even a barrel) of wine is hung at the top of the pole, and the first to climb it wins the prize. This custom is especially popular in Podravje and Posavje.

Among the most important and widespread customs in Slovenia involving wine is the **builders' treat** — *likof* — a celebration held at the completion of building work. This feast for the workers isn't just for finishing houses, flats or other buildings, but also for the opening of roads, bridges and tunnels. Another custom, and one that forms part of a ceremony performed all over the world, is the breaking of a bottle of champagne at the launching of a ship to ensure safe voyage.

Finally there are all the **national** and **religious holidays**, scattered throughout the year in all three wine regions. Almost following an unwritten rule, all these holidays became connected with wine. Not only was wine always on offer at the feast tables, but there were also holidays specifically dedicated to the vine and to the drink it produced. In this way people showed their devotion to this delicate plant, which each year might bring them good or poor wine. The tradition still plays a central part on certain dates today: particularly associated with wine and the vine are the feast days of **St Urban** (25 May), **St Martin** (11 November) and **St John the Evangelist** (27 December). Besides these, other dates also have a certain association with wine, especially religious feast days such as those of **SS Peter and Paul** (there is a traditional Slovene rhyme that translates as 'St Peter and St Paul shared some wine; Peter poured, and Paul drank'), **St Vincent** — especially in Posavje — and others. Wine has a ritual significance at the **Easter** service, as a bottle of wine is one of the things that people bring to church for Easter blessing. At **Christmas** and **New Year** wine is always present at table.

But let's return to the three main 'wine' feast days. Up to the Second World War **St Urban's day** was celebrated mainly in Podravje, whilst **St Martin's day** was celebrated in the regions of Primorska and Posavje. People are especially pleased to have St Martin's day fall in the middle of the week, so that they can celebrate two St Martin's Saturdays and Sundays and the celebration lasts for the entire week. The St Martin's festivities are extremely varied, but on St Urban's day there are comparatively few celebrations. The day is marked most notably by the honorary members of the wine conventions and

THERE ARE THREE GOOD THINGS

societies, who strive for the 'clear conscience of Slovene wine'. They work in Maribor, Ljubljana and Koper, and arrange all kinds of festive social events. The members of the Ljubljana convention, for example, gather to celebrate beside the offshoot of the oldest vine in Maribor, which thrives to this day at Ljubljana Castle, where they enjoy a range of local dishes and taste a selection of Slovene wines.
St Martin's day has, in recent decades, broadened its scope, and almost every year the media call for it to become a national holiday. Of course, the St Martin's celebrations have borrowed from neighbouring countries — particularly from the region of Graz in Austria — both in practice and in understanding of exactly what is being celebrated. As a result St Martin's day in Podravje and Posavje, rather than building on the regions' own rich heritage, has turned into a kind of fancy-dress carnival touring wine cellars and even hotels, offering entertainment to hotel guests in the form of this supposedly traditional St Martin's 'custom'. The feast is celebrated in much more ingenious fashion in Primorska, where traditional elements are incorporated into the modern-day St Martin's experience in an exemplary manner. In the Brda area, for instance, a *martinc* (an apple with herbs) is placed on a barrel, and the tap is hung with a *trcent* or *šperonc* (a wreath made of thirteen vine twigs to reflect the thirteen letters in the Slovene saying that translates as 'Martin, guard it!'). The events that surround the new wine in Medana in Brda also represent a model celebration of this particular feast day.

The third 'wine holiday' is **Šentjanževo** or just **Janževo**, the feast day of St John the Evangelist. It is the day on which the wine is blessed, and is popularly referred to as 'the St John's' (the Church itself instituted the blessing of the wine, and John is also the patron saint of vintners). Some wine-growers choose the best wine of the year specially for this purpose, which is then earmarked for the most important celebrations the following year, such as weddings and funerals. St John's day had more significance, and correspondingly more was made of its celebration, prior to the Second World War, especially in the region of Podravje. Wine blessed on St John's day was tasted by every family member, and doing so was believed to ensure good health. The wine was also used to spray the vineyard so that the next year it would produce a good crop, and some drops would be poured into the barrels, thus symbolically concluding the blessing of the crop.

The rich heritage surrounding wine and viticulture is further reflected in the **visiting of inns, restaurants and other taverns**. In some individual cases the practice of this particular custom might be viewed as a ritual in itself, as there is a whole tradition of particular groups always gathering at the same table, meeting on certain days and participating in a particular inn's festivities. The inns of all three wine regions have come a long way in the last couple of decades in the effective combining food and wine, recognizing wine's full potential.

THERE ARE THREE GOOD THINGS

The observation of '**under the branch**' wine trading — known as *osmica* (literally 'ivy branch') or *vinotoč* (a rudimentary wine shop) — has lately re-emerged from the oblivion of the past and is starting to take place again in Primorska, especially in the Karstic area, where it has become a regular form of wine offer. According the vintner the privilege of selling his own wine in his own cellar (or some other makeshift place), possibly accompanied by his own produce (bread, cheese, smoked meat), dates back to Emperor Charles V and his descendants, who allowed an eight-day period of wine pouring at the inn, marked with an ivy branch over the door. After the Second World War this form of wine selling was banned, but it was restored in the eighties. The privilege of pouring the wine 'under the branch' was once also familiar in the regions of Posavje and Podravje, but with a different kind of branch. Whilst ivy (or sometimes juniper) was the custom in Primorska, pine branches would have represented the *vinotoč* in Podravje, and spruce or a sprig of pine whittlings in Posavje: another example of the cultural diversity of the three Slovene wine regions.

A brief glance at the role of wine in the heritage and contemporary life of the three Slovene wine regions reveals numerous forms of cultural expression; through wine we learn of the impressive diversity of the regions and of the people who live and work in them to produce this precious commodity. With the individual characteristics and idiosyncrasies of each region we enrich not only our own lives, but also the viticulture and trade of Slovenia's wider surroundings — the world. Of course, for a truly rounded view we shouldn't forget the less positive side of social wine drinking in Slovenia. This too manifests itself in a vast array of traditional and contemporary forms, reminding us, as we mentioned earlier, of the effort still needed to make the relationship between man and wine a wholly positive one. Wine can be so much more than a mere drink; rather than a means of drowning one's sorrows, first and foremost it should be a wonderful friend and companion.
It can only become that if we realize the noble role wine has to play in all man's material, social and spiritual endeavours.

Text & photography: Professor Dr Janez Bogataj

Introduction

What were the criteria used in selecting the wines included in the present edition? Originally, the idea was to narrow down the vast range of possibilities to 100 top-quality wines. Convenient though this number may be, however, this would have entailed serious discrimination against some fascinating and delicious wines that could not have appeared in this book; it is true to say that the range of wines that Slovenia has to offer is incredibly broad and reaches a number well in excess of 100 varieties. The initial selection was therefore enriched sufficiently for the reader to gain a clear and comprehensive picture of the unique and marvellous world of wines that makes up one of the most cherished treasures of Slovenia. We wish we could widen the selection even further.

The majority of wines presented here are top-quality varieties: they make up the Slovenian Olympic team, so to speak, and are certainly worthy of being launched on the international wine-market. But as we know, in an Olympic team there is room for only a limited number of members, and sometimes great and accomplished athletes do not make the team.

This edition aims to offer the opportunity to all vintners operating on the Slovenian wine-market to get their wines promoted in both Slovenian and English. In preparing the book we invited contributions from a number of vintners who have participated in various local, national and international wine tastings.

We wanted to offer vintners the chance to promote their own wines, so that they could become known to a wider circle of wine lovers and buyers. In our survey of the vintners we advanced several suggestions as to which wines are most representative of our country, but the vintners were also invited to describe a variety of their own choice if they wished, and a minority went for this option. Some of the wines had to be rejected, either because of an insufficient range of quality or the obscurity of regional varieties. The aim was not to write a critique of different wines, but to reveal the abundance of wines on offer in the three Slovene wine-growing regions.

I was given the unique opportunity of tasting all these wines myself. I was aware of the great responsibility this task carried along with it, so I dedicated a lot of time and attention to every one. During the tasting phase, I realised that Slovenia has an exquisite variety of wines of very different characters within its relatively small area. In this sense Slovenia might be seen as a 'miniature Europe', and I am certain that Slovenian wine can attract many wine lovers and connoisseurs to the country. Translated into English, I hope this book will enable many vintners to shed their anonymity.

Organoleptic complexity and quality in a particular wine are guarantee that its description will be varied and colourful as well. I have become convinced that wine diversity depends not only upon questions of variety, location, cultivation and tradition, but also upon human resourcefulness, knowledge and originality. Despite the fact that the term terroir is not very familiar to Slovenian vintners, I would readily classify some Slovenian wines 'terroir wines'. The French–Slovenian dictionary explains the term as earth or soil; in the wine grower's terminology, however, terroir means much more than that. It might be described as a wine's 'formula': a combination of topographical and geological influences — the influences of geology, soil, grape variety, climate and experience — upon the quality and character of a particular wine. The wines, whose characters accurately reflect the natural environments from which they originate, are proof enough that many Slovenian vintners already follow the 'terroir' philosophy. Such an approach to wine growing will certainly strengthen the competitiveness of Slovenian wines on the European market. I am well aware that in many wine-growing countries it would be counter-productive to demand such high standards of wine production, simply because the European market has not attained a high level of wine awareness and culture.

I dedicated a lot of time to performing an in-depth sensory analysis of every wine I tasted. With an appropriate working environment I could work in peace and quiet, so I was able to concentrate and experience all the hidden treasures that wine has to offer the attentive taster. Working in standard eight-hour shifts, I aimed to taste and rate four to six wines a day. I used different-shaped glasses depending on the type of wine. The wines had rested for a long period of time at appropriate temperatures. During the tasting period I made sure that I was always fully fit, both mentally and physically. The wines are all rated descriptively as I did not follow any of the accepted rating methods that involve points. The descriptions I offer result from my sensory findings, but also from my knowledge and many years of experience in the art of rating Slovenian wines and others. I tried to put into words what I felt the wines had communicated to me. Concentrating on the contents of the glass, I gave descriptions of the wine's appearance, smell and taste. Wine-rating methods that award points are only understandable to a small circle of experts, who are familiar with all the points systems. Pure description, on the other hand, includes a wider audience. None of the wines I tasted had yet reached their peak and they were still at the maturing stage, so I have recommended cellarage. My specific recommendations are added to the descriptions. All the wines are accompanied by suggestions for combining them with appropriate dishes.

The editorial board wanted me to rate the overall quality of the wines by assigning them up to three stars. Three stars are definitely not enough to give an accurate rating in terms of quality. I therefore opted for four stars on five occasions when the wines in question not only proved of exceptionally high quality and distinctive character, but also reflected the grape variety, terrain and soil, and the skill or good fortune of the vintner. All the wines described in this book, however, have attained a certain level of excellence, even if they have not been awarded stars.

Each of the 'great' wines of the world has its 'father': one who dedicated a lot of love, who gave it his soul, formed its character and shaped its beauty. It is well known that vintners all around the world, no matter how big and successful, pride themselves on their wine. Even if the primary purpose of a wine is to bring in profit, the vintner will always strive for its fame and dignity, the qualities which, in reality, bring him true happiness. The enthusiasm and drive of Slovenia's vintners contribute to the steady growth of the wine-growing industry and to the ever-improving quality of Slovenian wines, despite many economic drawbacks and natural disadvantages. What are the main contributing factors to wine quality? Location of the vineyard, soil, grape variety, vintage and, we must not forget, a wise and responsible and vintner. All that is not enough, however, if the vine yields too high a crop and the juice is too watery. It is no secret that the best wines are produced when the yield of grapes is low; grapes cannot mature fully when there is a high crop load. The technical minimum-required maturity, prescribed by law, is based on chemical measurements, but that alone is not enough to guarantee a top-quality wine. The grapes should mature physiologically as well, in terms of feel and taste; only then can the wine achieve its highest possible quality. Just as we are likely to refuse fruit that is not yet ripe, so we do not like the taste of wine made from under-ripe grapes.

In conceiving, writing and bringing this book together, I had in mind a wide readership, consisting of wine lovers — regular but moderate consumers who daily accompany their meals with a glass of their chosen wine — as well as collectors, connoisseurs and professional colleagues. Wine must be the drink most compatible with human sociability. It calls for conversation and stimulates it during meals. People want to learn the correct way to taste and describe wine because educated drinking enables them to enjoy and experience wine fully. Wine cannot simply be described as something that eases our thirst, although there are certainly varieties that are excellent thirst quenchers and stimulate geniality. These are simple table wines of regional quality, however, which reveal little of interest besides the pleasure of drinking them. When wine becomes a topic of conversation or discussion, it gains a new cultural dimension: the artistic value of a masterpiece, having an individual history. The history of wine reaches back to the origins of human civilization and to the ancient peoples who nurtured the cult of wine alongside other art forms.

The current generation of Slovenian vintners continues to thrive, and is writing the next chapter in the history of our wines. All the wines described here form an important part of this success story. They are all very respectable ambassadors for the Slovenian wine-growing regions and the varieties they represent and, of course, they also promote their vintners. I have tried to describe these wines as I truly experienced them in a relaxed and pleasant atmosphere. Some wines, though not all, have more to say than people. Some make easy and flowing conversation, others are brief and to the point, but when one is completely relaxed they are remarkably unforgettable. In this, you will notice, they bear a certain similarity to people. Quality is not the only decisive factor in wines; character, when it reflects the natural conditions that formed the wine, is extremely important too. Cviček and Teran are protected on the basis of internationally established traditional nomenclature (PTP). These two — Cviček in particular — got their name and reputation solely as a result of their character, and not so much for their quality.

In describing these wines I have endeavoured to remain completely unbiased and to judge them objectively, depending solely on my knowledge and on my senses. No pressure was exerted either by the vintners or by my publisher. More than half of the wines I was tasting for the first time, and I am acquainted with the majority of the vintners. It often occurred to me that there was a slight similarity between the character of the wine and that of the vintner, but nevertheless I tried to remain objective throughout the process. Among the vintners previously unknown to me I discovered some incredibly attractive wines of irresistible quality and unique character, but I think I can safely say that I stuck to my guns and managed to remain objective and professional in every way. I have also remained indifferent to the fashionable trend for highly scientific techniques and modern technologies that has resulted in the production of 'technological' wines, which have, unfortunately, spread extensively into the market thanks to their easy affordability for the ordinary consumer. Naturally, the economizing involved has caused a reduction in quality and individuality.
In my opinion, vintners should stick to producing wines with a minimum of harmful artificial interference, and ideally none at all. Wines produced naturally are able to mature without interruption for as long as they need to develop all their exquisite natural characteristics.

I spent a lot of time thinking how to present these wines properly in my own words. It is quite possible to express quality using only professional terminology: sugar-free extract, acidity, alcohol, residual sugar, phenol level etc., and that is by far the easiest and most accurate way. Wine is not an artificial drink put together in a laboratory using a precise formula, however. It invites emotional expression, poetry is permissible, but not without an accompanying clear-headed note of professionalism to balance imagination with reality. Wine is a unique drink, worshipped by the gods of Greek mythology and by poets of every nationality of the globe throughout literary history. Wine is a gift of god, said the Chinese poet Li Tai Po. This gift accordingly deserves a godlike and hedonistic description, emphasizing the pleasures it has to offer. This book also tries to alert readers when encountering a distinguished wine, so that they will readily appreciate its quality, and not baulk at the price. Among the wines described there may be some that will not be fully understood by beginners, but which are very interesting nonetheless, deserving of respect, attention and consumer demand.

During Slovenia's short history of independence, several vintners have established wines and brand-names produced naturally and independently, without artificial interference. The period has also brought progress in wine culture as a result of proper education in this direction by sommeliers. Progress can be seen from a commercial viewpoint as well as from the sociological one of wine-growing associations, clubs, conferences and wine lovers. Many of the festivities surrounding viticulture have nowadays reached an impressively professional level, their development stimulating the emphasis of quality over quantity in wine consumption, preferring moderation and pleasure over excess. The improvement in the quality of wine is accelerating, and Slovenians seem to welcome it. The Slovenians' emotional attachment to their wines is almost proverbial. International trading and imported wines are enabling us to become familiar with wines from other parts of the globe; comparison with them will be interesting and useful for consumers and producers alike.

The influence of globalization is reflected in the quality and character of international wines. Homogeneity is noticeable, especially in the countries of the New World. Industrial processes and identical recipes play an important part in this, as they result in standardization of wines, lack of complexity and relatively easy adaptability to consumer taste. These processed wines, produced using a common formula, will definitely find their way to the Slovenian consumer as well, as they are cheap.

We must be aware of the perils of globalization, however. Wine production based on uniformity endangers the individuality and identity of the typical Slovenian wine. Over-emphasis on such a philosophy would be harmful to the great diversity of Slovenian wines, therefore pushing them into the anonymous mass of 'global wines' where the deciding factor is low price and not the character of the wine. In a world where production outstrips demand, these wines are easily replaced and interchangeable.

Most Slovenian vineyards are planted in locations exclusively devoted to wine growing, on steeply hilly terrain that requires a lot of manual work. As yet there is no vineyard in Slovenia where mechanized grape-picking would be possible. This is a strong advantage in promoting and advertising Slovenian wines, as the label 'hand-picked grapes' adds a certain value and credibility to the wine, automatically putting it into the higher price bracket. A bright future for Slovenian viticulture is therefore possible only if based on maintaining its unique identity. This book includes several wines that confirm they can maintain a distinctive and recognizable character that also ranks highly on an international level. The individuality and identity of Slovenian wines can contribute a great deal to the recognition and high standing of Slovenia in the world today. The younger generations need an injection of self-confidence, and we therefore ought to reward them with wines of distinguished quality and prestige. Our attitude towards our cultural heritage as represented by the wines, as well as our inherent respect for wine itself, will leave an important patriotic mark on the next generation of Slovenes. One of the aims of this book is also to encourage genuine love of one's motherland.

Dr Julij Nemanič

GLOSSARY

BELO VINO	WHITE WINE
Beli pinot	Pinot Blanc
Dišeči traminec	Fragrant Traminer
Furlanski tokaj	Tokay Friulano
Laški rizling	Italian Riesling
Malvazija	Malvasia
Muškat ottonel	Muscat Ottonel
Pikolit	Picolit
Rumena rebula	Ribolla (Italian: Ribolla Gialla)
Renski rizling	White Riesling
Rizvanec	Rieslaner
Rumeni muškat	Muscatel
Sauvignon	Sauvignon Blanc
Sivi pinot	Pinot Gris
Traminec	Traminer
Zeleni silvanec	Sylvaner
RDEČE VINO	RED WINE
Modra frankinja	Blue Franconian
Modri pinot	Pinot Noir
Portugalka	Blue Portuguese
Refošk	Refosco
Šentlovrenka	St Laurent
PREDIKATNO VINO/VINO POSEBNE KAKOVOSTI	PREDICATE WINE
Izbor	Selection/Auslese
Jagodni izbor	Grape selection/Beerenauslese
Ledeno vino	Ice wine
Pozna trgatev	Late harvest
Suhi jagodni izbor	Dry grape selection/Trockene Beerenauslese
Arhivsko vino	Archive wine
Odprto vino	Wine on tap
Penina	Sparkling wine
Posebno vino iz sušenega grozdja	Special wine produced from dried grapes
PTP - priznano tradicionalno poimenovanje	Traditionally accepted nomenclature (used for Cviček and Teran)

KEY

RATINGS

★★★★ EXCEPTIONAL WINE
★★★   EXCELLENT WINE
★★   TOP-QUALITY WINE
★   QUALITY WINE
WITHOUT PLEASANT FOR DRINKING

KEY TO FOOD SYMBOLS

BREAD

CHEESE

DISHES WITH MUSHROOMS

EGG DISHES

PASTA

VEGETABLE DISHES

MEAT DISHES

POULTRY DISHES

GAME DISHES

SALAMIS AND SAUSAGES

FISH DISHES

SEAFOOD DISHES

SWEET DISHES

FRUIT DISHES AND COMPÔTES

APERITIF

Maribor Wine-Growing District
Podravje Wine-Growing Region

MARIBOR WINE-GROWING DISTRICT

Franc in Borut Anderlič

Meljski hrib 37, si-2000 Maribor
Phone: +386 (0) 2 251 92 24, Fax: +386 (0) 2 251 92 24
Email: borut.anderlic@volja.net, Website: www.slovino.com/anderlic

Wine selling ❧ Wine tasting
Production of wine and food ❧ Wine cellar tours
Wine route ❧ Sales material

Wines on offer

Sauvignon, Renski Rizling, Sivi Pinot, Chardonnay, Traminec, Rumeni Muškat, Muškat Ottonel, Modri Pinot and predicate wines (*Izbor*, *Jagodni Izbor*, *Suhi Jagodni Izbor* and *Ledeno Vino*).

Boštjan in Franc Bračko

Spodnje Hlapje 22, si-2222 Jakobski dol, Phone: +386 (0) 2 644 94 47, (0) 31 533 703
Website: www.dv-jakob.00server.com

Wine selling ❧ Wine tasting for announced groups
Wine route ❧ Sales material
❧ Wine cellar tours for announced groups

Mix of wines on offer

52% blend, 14% Rumeni Muškat, 12% Renski Rizling, 9% Chardonnay, 7% Sivi Pinot, 5% Laški Rizling, 1% Laški Rizling *Jagodni Izbor*.

Brglez — Šparovec

Jože Brglez, Brezje pri Oplotnici 9, si-2317 Oplotnica
Phone: +386 (0) 2 801 94 59, (0) 31 579 011, Fax: +386 (0) 2 801 94 47
Email: b_brglez@yahoo.com

Wine selling ❧ Wine tasting for announced groups
Wine route ❧ Sales material
Wine cellar tours for announced groups ❧ Wine and food for announced groups

Mix of wines on offer

50% 'Pristavčan' blend, 10% Modra Frankinja, 8% Sauvignon, 8% Sivi Pinot, 8% Beli Pinot, 3% Kerner, 13% Laški Rizling.

Milan Celcer

Brdo 18a, si-3210 Slovenske Konjice, Phone: +386 (0) 3 575 54 71, (0) 31 399 442
Email: milan.celcer@slovenskekonjice.si

Wine selling ❧ Wine tasting for announced groups
Wine cellar tours for announced groups ❧ Wine route

Mix of wines on offer

30% Chardonnay, 10% Chardonnay *Pozna Trgatev*, 32% white blend (Laški Rizling and Rumeni Muškat), 8% Rumeni Muškat, 15% Kerner, 5% Modra Frankinja.

MARIBOR WINE-GROWING DISTRICT

ČRNI KOS

Andrej Kos, Rošpoh 25c, si-2000 Maribor
Phone: +386 (0) 2 250 24 73, Fax: +386 (0) 2 250 24 74
Email: andrej.kos@crnikos.com, Website: www.crnikos.com

❧ Wine selling

MIX OF WINES ON OFFER
70% Rumeni Muškat and 30% Sauvignon.

DOBAJ

Ivan in Tomaž Dobaj, Jurski vrh 22, si-2201 Zgornja Kungota
Phone: +386 (0) 2 656 28 81, (0) 40 549 512, Email: tomazd1@volja.net

Wine selling ❧ Wine tasting for announced groups

MIX OF WINES ON OFFER
35% Chardonnay, 20% Renski Rizling, 18% Laški Rizling, 12% Sauvignon,
9% Sivi Pinot and 6% Rumeni Muškat.

IVAN DREISIEBNER

Špičnik 1, si-2201 Zgornja Kungota
Phone: +386 (0) 2 656 00 40, (0) 2 656 07 77
Email: majda.777@email.si

Wine selling ❧ Wine tasting
Production of wine and food ❧ Wine cellar tours
Wine route ❧ Accommodation

MIX OF WINES ON OFFER
19% 'Dreisiebner' blend, 10% Traminec, 10% Laški Rizling, 10% Sivi Pinot,
9% Rumeni Muškat, 9% Kerner, 9% Renski Rizling, 8% Sauvignon,
8% Beli Pinot and 8% Chardonnay.

DVORSKO VINO

Jana Sever, Pesniški dvor 18, si-2211 Pesnica pri Mariboru
Phone: +386 (0) 2 654 35 06, (0) 41 662 071
Email: dvor@siol.net, Website: www.dvorsko-vino.com

Wine selling ❧ Wine tasting for announced groups
Wine cellar tours ❧ Sales material

MIX OF WINES ON OFFER
65% Rumeni Muškat, 25% Dišeči Traminec and 10% Renski Rizling.

MARIBOR WINE-GROWING DISTRICT

ČRNKO

Silvo Črnko, Jareninski vrh 5, si-2221 Jarenina
Phone: +386 (0) 2 640 73 51, (0) 41 767 117, Fax: +386 (0) 2 640 73 51
Email: silvo@crnko.net, Website: www.crnko.net

Wine selling ❧ Wine tasting for announced groups
Sales material ❧ Tasting for groups of up to 55 persons
Wine cellar tours for announced groups ❧ Production of wine and food for announced groups

The Črnkos have been in wine growing since 1967 and their first wine labels were printed in 1985. They mostly grow quality 'Jareninčan', a blend of several varieties. They are proudest of their Rumeni Muškat, which merits the farm's reputation just on its own. Their highest expectations are for the better-known wines such as Chardonnay, Sivi Pinot and predicates. The cellar also holds a range of other wines, including Renski Rizling, Sauvignon, Traminec, Muškat Ottonel and some sparkling varieties. Still available are the 2000 Sauvignon *Pozna Trgatev*, the 2001 Laški Rizling *Suhi Jagodni Izbor* and the 2002 Renski Rizling.

Mix of wines on offer

40% 'Jareninčan' blend, 15% Rumeni Muškat, 10% Chardonnay, 10% Sivi Pinot, 7% Renski Rizling, 7% Sauvignon, 5% Traminec, 5% Muškat Ottonel, 5% sparkling wines and 1% predicate wines.

Awards

Since 1989 the Črnkos have continued to win awards both at home (Ljubljana) and abroad (Paris, Montreal, San Francisco, Madrid).

Culinary recommendations

Their wines — in particular the Rumeni Muškat — go well with cheese cake or cottage-cheese *gibanica*.

2003 Renski Rizling
11.08% vol., semi-sweet, ★

This pale yellow wine with some green lights has a vibrant, glowing appearance. Its fresh flavour and bouquet of vine blossoms, lime, meadow flowers, grapes and vineyard peaches are pleasant and soothing. The freshness of the young Riesling lingers on the palate so that the grape variety is still clearly recognizable. The flavour, light and sweet, shows a medium structure, has complexity and maintains a lovely balance right through to the finish.
Recommended dishes: This is an aperitif wine and makes a welcome accompaniment to cottage-cheese *gibanica* or pancakes stuffed with walnuts.

MARIBOR WINE-GROWING DISTRICT

2003 Renski Rizling

MARIBOR WINE-GROWING DISTRICT

Diona

Mihaela Krsnik Kopše, Dolnja Počehova 35, si-2211 Pesnica pri Mariboru
Phone: +386 (0) 2 653 11 61, (0) 2 654 32 02, Fax: +386 (0) 2 654 32 00
Email: diona@siol.net

Wine selling ❧ Wine tasting for announced groups
Production of wine and food ❧ Wine cellar tours
Wine route ❧ Sales material
❧ Tennis, squash, sauna, fishing

The beginings of wine growing and selling here reach back to the early date of 1938, the 1983 vintage being the first to bear its own label. The most commonly grown grape varieties in the vineyards are Laški Rizling and Renski Rizling, with Sauvignon and Traminec as the two that grow most successfully. The choice specimens of the winecellar are the dry wines: Sauvignon, Laški Rizling and Muškat Ottonel.
The best vintages are 2000 Traminec and the 2002 Laški Rizling *Suhi Jagodni Izbor*.

Wines on offer
'Mariborčan', blend; Renski Rizling, Sauvignon, Muškat Ottonel, Traminec, Chardonnay, sparkling Chardonnay and Laški Rizling *Suhi Jagodni Izbor*.

Awards
They take pride in their numerous gold medals from Gornja Radgona and a silver from the Ljubljana fair for their 1997 Sauvignon.

Culinary recommendations
They are pleased to offer aperitif and digestive wines with their mushroom dishes, both hors d'oeuvres and mains. Their homemade *tunka* meat or *štruklji* with different fillings provide the best accompaniments to their wines.

2000 Traminec
11.63% vol., semi-sweet, ★★

The golden yellow colour simply glows in the glass, promising a rich composition. The abundant aroma of the Traminer grape is complex in make-up and resembles yellow peaches, violets, withered roses, dried apricots and almonds. The mild palate seems more solid than fresh, typically for a mature Traminer. The rich body delivers a complex experience that lingers and leaves a firm impression of the flavour and its bouquet. The fundamental aroma of the variety can still be detected as well, even though the wine is already four years old. In the finish, the bouquet of Traminer prevails over other flavours, which subside somewhat.
Recommended dishes: sweet pies, grilled back of veal with rosemary, aromatic fresh fruit salads.

MARIBOR WINE-GROWING DISTRICT

2000 Traminec

MARIBOR WINE-GROWING DISTRICT

Karl Fabijan

Zgornje Hlapje 18, si-2222 Jakobski dol
Phone: +386 (0) 2 644 93 45, (0) 41 636 486, Fax: +386 (0) 2 644 93 58
Email: karl.fabijan@vino-fabijan.com
Website: www.vino-fabijan.com

Wine selling ❧ Wine tasting for announced groups
Wine cellar tours for announced groups ❧ Sales material

Wines on offer

Sivi Pinot, Rumeni Muškat, Traminec, Muškat Ottonel, Renski Rizling, Chardonnay, Sauvignon, 'Fabijanova Penina' (produced in the classical way), Beli Pinot and Ranina.

Viktor Hajšek

Zrkovska cesta 81, si-2000 Maribor, Phone: +386 (0) 2 471 34 35

Wine selling ❧ Wine tasting for announced groups

Wines on offer

Renski Rizling, Rumeni Muškat, Traminec, Sauvignon, Sivi Pinot and Modri Pinot.

Dušan Hlade

Šober 15, si-2351 Kamnica, Phone: (0) 2 623 14 64

Wine selling ❧ Wine tasting for announced groups
Wine cellar tours for announced groups ❧ Wine route
❧ Production of wine and food for announced groups

Mix of wines on offer

40% blend, 16% Rumeni Muškat, 11% Kerner, 9% Renski Rizling, 9% Zeleni Silvanec, 8% Chardonnay and 6% Sauvignon.

Jurij Hlupič

Kamniška ulica 9a, si-2000 Maribor, Phone: (0) 2 250 88 46

Wine selling ❧ Wine tasting
Production of wine and food ❧ Wine cellar tours
❧ Sales material

Mix of wines on offer

20% Chardonnay, 30% Renski Rizling, 10% Modri Pinot, 10% sparkling 'H Classic', 10% Sauvignon, 5% Rumeni Muškat, 10% 'Jurjevina' and 5% Laški Rizling.

MARIBOR WINE-GROWING DISTRICT

Alojz Hojnik

Ogljenšak 20a, si-2314 Zgornja Polskava
Phone: +386 (0) 2 803 66 03, (0) 41 644 373, Fax: +386 (0) 2 803 66 03

Wine selling ❧ Wine tasting
Wine cellar tours ❧ Wine route
❧ Sales material

Mix of wines on offer

25% Renski Rizling, 25% Laški Rizling, 25% Chardonnay, 12,5% Beli Pinot and 12,5% Zeleni Silvanec.

Jakob Horvat

Počehova 29, si-2000 Maribor
Phone: +386 (0) 2 251 78 72, (0) 41 266 231, (0) 41 359 565, Fax: +386 (0) 2 251 78 72
Email: vino.horvat@siol.net

Wine selling ❧ Wine tasting
Wine cellar tours ❧ Sales material
❧ Production of wine and food for announced groups

Mix of wines on offer

30% Renski Rizling, 25% Chardonnay, 16% Sauvignon, 12% Traminec, 9% Sivi Pinot, 4% Laški Rizling and 4% Rumeni Muškat.

Ignac Jamnik

Svečina 13, si-2201 Zgornja Kungota, Phone: +386 (0) 2 656 49 31

Wine selling ❧ Wine tasting
Wine cellar tours ❧ Wine route
Accommodation ❧ Sales material

Wines on offer

Rumeni Muškat, Kerner (also *Izbor*), Traminec, Renski Rizling and Chardonnay.

Maksimilijan (Milan) Jarc

Slatina 10, si-2201 Zgornja Kungota, Phone: +386 (0) 2 656 49 61, (0) 41 771 954

Wine selling ❧ Wine tasting for announced groups
Wine route ❧ Wine cellar tours for announced groups
❧ Production of wine and food for announced groups

Mix of wines on offer

5% Renski Rizling, 5% Rumeni Muškat, 5% Sauvignon, 5% Chardonnay, 50% 'Svečinčan' blend and 30% wine on tap.

MARIBOR WINE-GROWING DISTRICT

Faust

Blaž Železnik, Meljski hrib 47, si-2000 Maribor
Phone: +386 (0) 2 480 58 00, (0) 2 251 75 28, (0) 2 228 12 20, (0) 41 614 678
Email: blaz.zeleznik@expobiro.si

Wine selling ❧ Wine tasting
Wine cellar tours ❧ Wine route
❧ Sales material

Železnik can take pride in a wine-growing tradition that stretches back 270 years. The composition of the vineyards, where the Laški Rizling is most impressive, is identical to the wines on offer. All the wines here promise something special, especially the dry and semi-dry varieties.
The 1997 Chardonnay *Izbor*, 2000 Laški Rizling, and 2000 Laški Rizling *Ledeno Vino* represent just a few of their best vintages, still available from their cellar for some time to come.

Mix of wines on offer
35% Renski Rizling, 25% Chardonnay, 20% Laški Rizling, 15% Kerner and 5% Rumeni Muškat.

Awards
A gold medal at the Ljubljana fair and two grand gold medals from Gornja Radgona and Split attest to their high standards.

Culinary recommendations
They serve the house speciality, barley porridge with beans (*ričet*), with their wines, as well as any other dish eaten with a spoon.

2000 Laški Rizling
11.8% vol., semi-sweet, ★★

A pale yellow wine, glowing in appearance. The bouquet is discreet but candid, redolent of dried flowers, a whiff of tobacco and dried fruit, and seems to have a calming effect. The palate at first delivers an interesting range of sensations that, despite the fact that the wine is semi-sweet, still come alive, underwriting a definite quality and style. The balance between sweet and sour is perfect, and maintains the wine's vivacity. Such is the final impression also, giving us a sense of length, continued freshness and a bouquet of light spices.
Recommended dishes: veal ragout, *prleška gibanica*, pancakes with walnuts, apricot cake, fruit cakes.

MARIBOR WINE-GROWING DISTRICT

2000 Laški Rizling

MARIBOR WINE-GROWING DISTRICT

Gaube

Špičnik 17, Svečina, si-2201 Zgornja Kungota
Phone: +386 (0) 2 656 35 11, (0) 41 747 151, Fax: +386 (0) 2 656 35 11
Email: vinarstvo.gaube@siol.net

- Wine selling
- Wine tasting
- Wine cellar tours
- Wine route
- Sales material
- Walk along the Austrian—Slovenian border with wine tastings on either side
- Production of wine and food for announced groups

The tradition of wine growing and trading goes back to the end of the nineteenth century here, and their first wine labels were printed as early as 1939. Chardonnay and Renski Rizling dominate in the vineyards, but the grapes that bring the most pleasure are Rumeni Muškat, Sivi Pinot and Zeleni Silvanec. They take great pride in their fruity, ready-to-drink wines, kept in a completely dry cellar.

Wines on offer

Sivi Pinot, Renski Rizling, Laški Rizling, Zeleni Silvanec, Modri Pinot, Rumeni Muškat, Kerner, Chardonnay and Muškat Ottonel.

Awards

In Slovenia they have won gold medals at the Gornja Radgona fair and silvers in Ljubljana. They have also brought back silver medals from Slovakia and Croatia and a grand gold medal from Austria.

Culinary recommendations

Guests can wash down the homemade cold cut Kibelfleisch with Modri Pinot, and the sommelier tells us that the Laški Rizling goes particularly well with asparagus.

2003 Sivi Pinot

12.5% vol., dry, ★

With its pale yellow, straw-like appearance it produces lots of tiny bubbles when poured, promising a vibrant wine. Pinot Gris is known for its reticent bouquet, but the ripeness of the grape can be perceived nevertheless, with fragrances of yellow fruits such as peach, apricot and melon. The first impression on the tongue is extremely fresh. The structure of the wine is medium-rich, and as the palate develops it is still quite youthful, making the wine drinkable and attractive.
Recommended dishes: Veal ragout, asparagus dishes, soured beef with onions.

MARIBOR WINE-GROWING DISTRICT

2003 SIVI PINOT

MARIBOR WINE-GROWING DISTRICT

Zlatko Kauran

Sladki Vrh 11k, si-2214 Sladki Vrh, Phone: +386 (0) 2 645 91 20, (0) 41 675 936
Email: zlatko@kauran.com, Website: www.kauran.com

Wine selling ❧ Wine cellar tours for announced groups
Sales material ❧ Production of wine and food for announced groups

Mix of wines on offer

35% 'Sladkogorčan' blend, 7% Renski Rizling, 10% Zeleni Silvanec, 10% Laški Rizling, 8% Rumeni Muškat, 16% Laški Rizling Predicates (10% *Pozna Trgatev*, 3% *Jagodni Izbor*, 3% *Ledeno Vino*), 10% Kerner *Pozna Trgatev*, 4% Kerner *Izbor*.

Ivan in Tomaž Kren

Plač 12, si-2201 Zgornja Kungota,
Phone: +386 (0) 2 656 43 61, (0) 41 880 673, Fax: +386 (0) 2 656 43 61

Wine selling ❧ Wine tasting for announced groups
Wine cellar tours for announced groups ❧ Sales material

Mix of wines on offer

25% Renski Rizling, 20% Chardonnay, 15% Kerner, 15% Sauvignon, 10% Laški Rizling, 5% Sivi Pinot, 5% Modri Pinot and 5% Rumeni Muškat.

Klet Kropec - Sonce 'spod Pohorja

Vinko Kropec, Kovača vas 83, si-2310 Slovenska Bistrica
Phone: +386 (0) 2 843 15 86, (0) 41 645 182, Fax: +386 (0) 2 843 15 88
Email: kropecvi@siol.net, Website: www.slovenka.net/kropec

Wine selling ❧ Wine tasting
Production of wine and food ❧ Wine cellar tours
Wine route ❧ Sales material

Mix of wines on offer

30% 'Ritoznojčan' blend, 10% 'Bistriško' blend, 8% Laški Rizling, 8% Renski Rizling, 9% Traminec, 15% Modri Pinot, 12% Sivi Pinot and 8% Sauvignon.

Kraner — Plateis

Peter Kraner, Zgornje Hlapje 13, si-2222 Jakobski dol,
Phone: +386 (0) 2 644 93 47, (0) 41 278 279

Wine selling ❧ Wine tasting
Wine cellar tours ❧ Sales material

Mix of wines on offer

15% Traminec, 15% Kerner, 15% Renski Rizling, 15% Sivi Pinot, 15% Sauvignon, 10% Rumeni Muškat, 10% Chardonnay and 5% Zeleni Silvanec.

MARIBOR WINE-GROWING DISTRICT

Košaki

Anton Kaloh, Stolni vrh 30, si-2000 Maribor
Phone: +386 (0) 2 251 73 11, (0) 41 579 463, Email: danica.kaloh@s5.net

Wine selling ❧ Wine tasting
Production of wine and food ❧ Wine cellar tours for announced groups
Wine route ❧ Accommodation

Wines on offer

Rumeni Muškat (*Pozna Trgatev, Izbor* and *Jagodni Izbor*), Sauvignon (*Pozna Trgatev, Jagodni Izbor, Suhi Jagodni Izbor* and *Ledeno Vino*), Traminec (*Izbor* and *Suhi Jagodni Izbor*), Beli Pinot (*Izbor*) and Renski Rizling (also *Pozna Trgatev, Jagodni Izbor* and *Ledeno Vino*).

Gregor Kebrič

Spodnji Jakobski dol 23b, si-2222 Jakobski dol, Phone: +386 (0) 2 644 94 97,
(0) 31 644 581, (0) 41 727 694, Email: gregor.kebric@dem.si,
Website: www.vinogradnistvo-kebric.00server.com

Wine selling ❧ Fruit and herbal brandies; liqueurs

Wines on offer

Rumeni Muškat, Sauvignon *Pozna Trgatev*, Laški Rizling *Jagodni Izbor*, blend and Sauvignon.

Jakob - Igor Leber

Podigrac 19, si-2201 Zgornja Kungota, Phone: +386 (0) 2 651 30 71, (0) 31 559 896

Wine selling ❧ Wine tasting
Production of wine and food ❧ Wine cellar tours
❧ Wine route

Mix of wines on offer

25% Laški Rizling, 20% Chardonnay, 15% Renski Rizling, 10% Beli Pinot, 7% Sivi Pinot, 7% Rumeni Muškat, 7% Sauvignon, 5% Traminec and 3% Kerner.

Vlado Mak

Vodole 3a, si-2000 Maribor. Phone: +386 (0) 2 473 20 06

Wine selling ❧ Wine tasting
Production of wine and food ❧ Wine cellar tours
Wine route ❧ Sales material

Wines on offer

Renski Rizling, Laški Rizling, Beli Pinot, Rumeni Muškat, Sivi Pinot, Modri Pinot and Dišeči Traminec.

MARIBOR WINE-GROWING DISTRICT

Klet Bistrica

Škofija Maribor, Vinarska ulica 3, si-2310 Slovenska Bistrica
Phone: +386 (0) 2 805 08 20, Fax: +386 (0) 2 805 08 29
Email: info@klet-bistrica.com, Website: www.klet-bistrica.com

Wine selling Wine tasting
Production of wine and food Wine cellar tours for announced groups
Wine route

Although Klet Bistrica has been in the wine-growing business for only a decade, their diverse range of wines sets them alongside many longstanding growers. Besides Chardonnay, the best wines from their vineyards are Renski Rizling, Laški Rizling, Sauvignon, Sivi Pinot, Kerner and Rumeni Muškat. The wines are sold under three brand-names: *Mašno Vino, Klet Bistrica* and *Crependium*. In one of the most beautifully arched wine cellars in Slovenia visitors can still enjoy the 1997 Laški Rizling *Suhi Jagodni Izbor* and 1999 Laški Rizling *Ledeno Vino*.

Wines on offer

'Andrejevo Vino', Chardonnay, Rumeni Muškat, Renski Rizling (also *Ledeno Vino*), Laški Rizling (also *Suhi Jagodni Izbor and Ledeno vino*), 'Rajska Penina', 'Bistričan' blend, 'Ritoznojčan' blend, Sivi Pinot, Kerner, Modri Pinot, Modra Frankinja, Sauvignon and Beli Pinot.

Awards

Since 1996 Klet Bistrica has been participating in wine appraisals. They can be justly proud of their nine grand gold medals and thirteen gold medals from Slovenia, as well as ten top prizes from various European locations.

Culinary recommendations

They serve mushroom soup with Sivi Pinot and pohorska bunka with Modra Frankinja or Ritoznojčan. They guarantee to find a wine from their abundant selection to suit any dish.

2003 Chardonnay

12.5% vol., semi-dry, ★★

The yellow, straw-like, glowing appearance, accompanied by tiny bubbles, foretells freshness, and this is the first aspect of the nose to strike us; we encounter floral and fruit fragrances. They remind us of pears and nuts, with some undertones of withered blossoms. A sense of the variety's identity is convincingly and pleasantly delivered on the palate. The wine is well-structured, coming across as full-bodied and well-rounded. There is an easily perceptible sweetness, smoothed and freshened by the acidity. The wine's youthful character is still clearly present. This wine is still maturing and needs more time to reach its peak.
Recommended dishes: asparagus dishes, veal ragout, seafood dishes, strongly flavoured pork dishes, fruit cakes.

MARIBOR WINE-GROWING DISTRICT

2003 Chardonnay   2003 Rumeni Muškat 'Mašno Vino'

2003 Rumeni Muškat 'Mašno Vino'

11.0% vol., semi-sweet, ★★★

A pale yellow and crystal-clear wine. The bouquet of the variety is candid, offering a complex range of floral (blossom, withered roses) and fruit (grapes, lemons, lychees, exotic fruit) fragrances. The palate senses sweet flavours at first, and these prevail for some time. This sweet character is not dull, but shows a beautiful versatility, reflecting several different shades of sweetness, deriving from the complex flavours of different sugars and alcohols contained in the wine. The acidity is slightly backward, but fulfils its role in the overall balance. The bouquet remains constant throughout, and assets the identity of the wine from the first impression to the finish.

Recommended dishes: Buckwheat pie, grilled veal back with rosemary, tender and aromatic desserts, and fruit salads of pears and peaches.

MARIBOR WINE-GROWING DISTRICT

Meranovo

Univerza v Mariboru, Fakulteta za kmetijstvo, Vrhov Dol 14, si-2341 Limbuš
Phone: +386 (0) 2 250 58 00, Fax: +386 (0) 2 229 60 71
Email: fk@uni-mb.si

Wine selling ❧ Wine tasting
❧ Wine cellar tours for announced groups

They began growing and trading in wine in 1994, with their first labels appearing in 1995. The terroir of the vineyards is considered best suited for Sauvignon, so it is no coincidence that this is their primary grape variety and a winner at that. They also produce Chardonnay, Renski Rizling, Laški Rizling, and Sivi Pinot.
The 1997 Sauvignon *Pozna Trgatev* will continue to be available for some time.

Mix of wines on offer
50% Sauvignon, 15% Chardonnay, 20% Renski Rizling and 15% 'Merančan' blend.

Awards
The exceptional quality of the Sauvignon is confirmed by a gold medal from the Czech Republic (the Sauvignon Forum of 1998), as well as many titles won at home: Slovene champion of its variety (Ljubljana) and overall champion (Gornja Radgona, 2002 and 2003).

Culinary recommendations
Sauvignon goes best with fish dishes.

1997 Sauvignon *Pozna Trgatev*
11.5% vol., semi-sweet, ★★★★

Its golden-yellow colour has a gem-like sparkle, enticing and pleasing to the eye. Dried flowers, tealeaves, spices and undertones of honey can be clearly identified in the complex nose. The wonderful flavour of this grape develops on the palate, though not straightaway. The bouquet, though full, does not give away the grape variety, which first becomes apparent in the tongue. This wine repays full attention, slowly unlocking its delicious secrets. It does not radiate power or energy, but has a lot more to offer in terms of character, complexity, quality, distinction and beauty. Finally, there is a mineral aftertaste (a product of the local soil and terrain) and a short whiff of smoke: a fine finish to a mature, high-quality Sauvignon.
Recommended dishes: Fish dishes (lobster with vanilla), stuffed pears, apple tart, blue cheese.

MARIBOR WINE-GROWING DISTRICT

1997 SAUVIGNON *Pozna Trgatev*

Maribor Wine-Growing District

Roman Mulec

Ročica 40, si-2222 Jakobski dol, Phone: +386 (0) 2 644 94 57, (0) 31 374 416, (0) 41 342 528
Email: korentatjana@hotmail.com

Wine selling ❧ Wine tasting for announced groups
Wine cellar tours ❧ Wine route
Accommodation ❧ Production of wine and food for announced groups
❧ Tennis, cycling, deers

Mix of wines on offer

20% Renski Rizling, 16% Modri Pinot, 13% Rumeni Muškat, 13% Sauvignon, 12% Traminec, 12% Sivi Pinot and 6% Chardonnay.

Janko Papež

Morje 27, si-2313 Fram, Phone: +386 (0) 2 608 92 93, (0) 41 279 713
Fax: +386 (0) 2 608 92 94, Email: janko.papez@volja.net

Wine selling ❧ Wine tasting
❧ Wine route

Wines on offer

Blend and predicate wines: Sauvignon *Jagodni Izbor*, Laški Rizling (*Pozna Trgatev, Jagodni Izbor, Suhi Jagodni Izbor*), Renski Rizling *Pozna Trgatev*, Sivi Pinot (*Pozna Trgatev* and *Jagodni Izbor*), Beli Pinot (*Pozna Trgatev* and *Suhi Jagodni Izbor*) and Chardonnay (*Izbor* and *Jagodni Izbor*).

Mira in Franc Pečnik

Grušce 26, si-3222 Dramlje
Phone: +386 (0) 3 579 82 24

Wine selling ❧ Wine tasting

Mix of wines on offer

25% Laški Rizling, 10% Chardonnay, 10% Sauvignon, 15% Rumeni Muškat, 30% blend and 10% Modra Frankinja.

Anton in Marjeta Perko

Spodnja Velka 59, si-2213 Zgornja Velka, Phone: +386 (0) 2 644 35 61, (0) 31 501 934

Wine selling ❧ Wine tasting

Mix of wines on offer

66% blend, 12% Chardonnay, 12% Sivi Pinot and 10% Rumeni Muškat.

MARIBOR WINE-GROWING DISTRICT

Alojzij Plečko

Vilenska cesta 54, Radizel, si-2312 Orehova vas
Phone: +386 (0) 2 604 04 60, (0) 2 604 04 61, (0) 31 395 372
Email: alenka.plecko@siol.net

Wine selling ❧ Wine tasting

Mix of wines on offer

8% Sauvignon, 6% Chardonnay, 6% Renski Rizling, 5% Laški Rizling and 75% 'Radizelčan' blend.

Daniel Prosenc

Drankovec 8, si-2222 Jakobski dol
Phone: +386 (0) 2 644 92 45, (0) 2 649 02 01

Wine selling ❧ Wine tasting
Wine cellar tours ❧ Wine route

Mix of wines on offer

50% blend, 15% Sauvignon, 15% Chardonnay, 10% Laški Rizling, 5% Renski Rizling, 3% Kerner and 2% red blend.

Protner

Bojan Protner, Dragučova 65, si-2231 Pernica
Phone: +386 (0) 2 473 03 92, Fax: +386 (0) 2 473 03 92

Wine selling ❧ Wine tasting
Production of wine and food ❧ Wine cellar tours
Wine route ❧ Sales material

Mix of wines on offer

5% Chardonnay, 5% Sivi Pinot, 4% Kerner, 4% Sauvignon, 4% Renski Rizling, 2% Laški Rizling, 1% Muškat Ottonel, 1% Sparkling 'Protner', 50% 'Protner' blend and 24% wine on tap.

Matjaž Ramšak

Medvedova 6, si-2000 Maribor
Phone: +386 (0) 2 252 71 81, (0) 41 816 514

Wine selling ❧ Wine tasting for announced groups
❧ Wine cellar tours for announced groups

Mix of wines on offer

80% high-quality wine (15% Zeleni Silvanec, 45% Sivi Pinot, 30% Chardonnay and 10% Rumeni Muškat) and 20% quality wine.

MARIBOR WINE-GROWING DISTRICT

Očkerl

Sokolska ulica 5, si-2212 Šentilj
Phone: +386 (0) 2 651 05 81, (0) 31 223 380, Fax: +386 (0) 2 651 05 81

Wine selling ❧ Wine tasting
Wine cellar tours for announced groups ❧ Wine route
❧ Wine and food for announced groups

The Očkerl family inherited a 200-year-old tradition of wine growing and trading in 1963, and decided to start labelling their wines in the early nineties. The vineyards predominantly grow Rumeni Muškat and Laški Rizling, their sunny position also favouring varieties such as Traminec, Sauvignon, Chardonnay, Šipon, Modri Pinot, Modra Frankinja and Rizvanec. The family are delighted with the high demand for Muscatel. Still available are the 1997 and 2000 Rumeni Muškat, the 1997 Šipon *Pozna Trgatev* and 1998 Šipon *Ledeno Vino*, the 1997 Chardonnay *Izbor* and 1998 Laški Rizling *Suhi Jagodni Izbor*.

Mix of wines on offer

50% 'Šentiljčan' blend, 10% Rumeni Muškat, 5% Sauvignon, 5% Chardonnay, 5% Traminec, 5% Sivi Pinot, 5% Kerner, 5% Laški Rizling, 5% Modri Pinot and Modra Frankinja and 5% predicate wines (Laški Rizling and Šipon).

Awards

Two hundred years of dedication to wine growing have borne fruit, as confirmed by numerous medals from international sources (Zagreb, Kutjevo, Split) and more than ten medals at home.

Culinary recommendations

They recommend their wine as an accompaniment to *bograč* (a casserole with three kinds of meat), *žganci* (corn mash) and goulash or *potica*.

1998 Šipon *Ledeno Vino*

9.3% vol., sweet, ★★★

The sunny, golden colour glows makes the glass seem to glow with promise. The nose brings an initial impression of freshness, and conjures up the autumn chill in which the harvest of the frozen grapes took place. The scent of peaches is revealed, followed by dried pears, figs, beeswax, caramel, grapes with noble rot and tea blossom — altogether a parade of fine fragrances. The palate is continually sweet, but allows other things to make their mark. The wine is simultaneously full-bodied and tender, sweet and fresh, and all can be sensed very clearly. This is a fine wine, which pleasantly occupies the senses over dessert and thus provides the crowning point of a meal, but it can soothe both body and soul at any time, over a chat among wine lovers.
Recommended dishes: Goose liver pâté, buckwheat pie, breads with olive oil, walnut *potica*, pancakes with walnuts.

MARIBOR WINE-GROWING DISTRICT

1998 ŠIPON *Ledeno Vino*

MARIBOR WINE-GROWING DISTRICT

Joannes

Boštjan Protner, Vodole 34, si-2229 Malečnik
Phone: +386 (0) 2 473 21 00, (0) 41 654 305, (0) 41 345 707
Fax: +386 (0) 2 473 21 02, Email: joannes@siol.net
Website: www.slovino.com/joannes

Wine selling ❧ Wine tasting for announced groups
Wine cellar tours for announced groups ❧ Wine route
Accommodation ❧ Sales material
❧ Wine and food Fridays and Saturdays and for announced groups

It is over three decades since the Protners began growing and trading in wine; their first labels date back to 1987. On the Šempeter hill they grow varieties such as Renski Rizling, Chardonnay, and on the Vodole Sivi Pinot and Sauvignon, which represent the best and most rewarding varieties of this cellar. There are still some bottles available of 1997–2002 Renski Rizling, 2001 Chardonnay and 2001 Sivi Pinot.

Mix of wines on offer

20% Renski Rizling, 15% Chardonnay, 10% Modri Pinot, 10% Sivi Pinot, 10% Sauvignon, 10% Beli Pinot, 5% Zeleni Silvanec, 5% Rumeni Muškat and 10% 'Sparkling Joannes'.

Awards

The 1995 Laški Rizling proudly bears the title of Champion of the Fair.

Culinary recommendations

You will be served grilled sausages in wine accompanied by Chardonnay at the Protnerjeva Hiša Joannes, whilst their selection of cold cuts (homemade salami, meat preserved in *tunka* (a kind of lard) and different spreads) goes well with Renski Rizling. With such a vast range of flavours their wines suit any dish.

2001 Sivi Pinot

13% vol., dry, ★★★

The intense yellow colour of the Chardonnay with its golden reflections is seductive and enticing. The complex fruit bouquet is redolent of peaches and apricots, with a distinct scent of smoke, forest undergrowth and spices — all an indication of a good structure and a level of maturity. The palate is full-bodied, vibrant and complex; as the alcohol warms up, a full-flavoured, playful acidity balances the alcohol in an interesting contrast. We imagine that its unique character can be traced to the terrain and soil of the vineyard. The long finish is again accompanied by spices, ripe fruits and an undertone of smoke.
Recommended dishes: Cold selection — homemade salami, meat preserved in tunka, spreads, veal ragout, roast pork, beef steak.

MARIBOR WINE-GROWING DISTRICT

2001 SIVI PINOT

MARIBOR WINE-GROWING DISTRICT

Dušan Savič

Rošpoh 38a, SI-2000 Maribor
Phone: +386 (0) 2 251 23 22

Wine selling ❧ Wine tasting
Production of wine and food ❧ Wine cellar tours
Wine route ❧ Sales material

Mix of wines on offer

21% Renski Rizling, 20,2% Chardonnay, 20,2% Beli Pinot, 16,1% Sauvignon, 8,1% Laški Rizling, 8,1% Sivi Pinot, 6,5% Traminec and blend.

Ivo Senekovič

Spodnji Jakobski dol 64
SI-2222 Jakobski dol
Phone: +386 (0) 2 640 47 11, (0) 41 514 422
Email: vino_vrhunsko@volja.net
Website: http://users.volja.net/vino_vrhun/

Wine selling ❧ Wine tasting
Wine cellar tours for announced groups ❧ Wine route

Mix of wines on offer

15% Rumeni Muškat, 15% Sauvignon, 15% Chardonnay, 10% Traminec, 10% Beli Pinot, 5% Sivi Pinot, 5% Renski Rizling and 25% 'Vino iz Jakoba' blend.

Marko Šebart

Lormanje 18, SI-2230 Lenart v Slovenskih goricah
Phone: +386 (0) 41 441 809, (0) 31 496 694
Email: sebart72@yahoo.com

Wine selling ❧ Wine tasting

Mix of wines on offer

50% Sauvignon *Pozna Trgatev* and 40% Chardonnay *Pozna Trgatev*.

Dušan Šfiligoj

Kmetija Šfiligoj - Kočevar, Hrastje 84, SI-2341 Limbuš
Phone: +386 (0) 2 613 32 00

Wine selling ❧ Wine tasting for announced groups
Wine cellar tours for announced groups ❧ Wine route

Mix of wines on offer

50% Renski Rizling and 50% Sauvignon.

MARIBOR WINE-GROWING DISTRICT

Srečko Šumenjak

Spodnje Hlapje 23, si-2222 Jakobski dol, Phone: +386 (0) 2 644 94 45, (0) 41 277 794
Email: sumenjak@volja.net

Wine selling ❧ Wine tasting for announced groups

Wines on offer

Sivi Pinot, Chardonnay, Modri Pinot, Renski Rizling, Rumeni Muškat, Sauvignon, Laški Rizling and Kerner.

Miroslav Trojner

Vinogradništvo - vinarstvo Trojner M&M,
Zgornji Jakobski dol 7, si-2222 Jakobski dol
Phone: +386 (0) 2 644 90 04, (0) 41 806 675, (0) 41 809 005
Email: tmitja@siol.net

Wine tasting for announced groups ❧ Wine cellar tours for announced groups
❧ Production of wine and food for announced groups

Mix of wines on offer

35% 'Trojner' blend, 20% Renski Rizling, 20% Sauvignon, 10% Traminec, 10% Rumeni Muškat and 5% Sivi Pinot.

Uroš Valcl

Zgornja Kungota 34, si-2201 Zgornja Kungota, Phone: +386 (0) 2 656 19 11, (0) 31 467 143
Email: uros@valcl.com, Website: www.valcl.com

Wine selling ❧ Wine tasting for announced groups
Wine cellar tours for announced groups ❧ Wine route

Mix of wines on offer

65% blend, 9% Chardonnay, 7% Sivi Pinot, 7% Renski Rizling, 7% Laški Rizling *Pozna Trgatev*, 3% Chardonnay *Jagodni Izbor* and 2% Chardonnay *Ledeno Vino*.

Alojz Valentan

Vodole 36, si-2229 Malečnik, Phone: +386 (0) 2 473 05 18, (0) 31 532 462

Wine selling ❧ Wine tasting
Production of wine and food ❧ Wine cellar tours
Wine route ❧ Sales material
❧ Guided tastings

Mix of wines on offer

40% 'Valentan' blend, 30% Renski Rizling, 20% Kerner and 10% Sauvignon.

MARIBOR WINE-GROWING DISTRICT

Milan Šiker

Močna 47, SI-2231 Pernica
Phone: +386 (0) 2 720 62 39, (0) 41 755 932
Email: sasa.siker@volja.net

Wine selling ❧ Wine tasting
Wine cellar tours ❧ Wine route
Sales material ❧ Production of wine and food for announced groups

The beginnings of wine growing here date back to the 1870s, and the first bottles were labelled in 1983. They grow numerous varieties, and among them thrives the Rumeni Muškat which, with Renski Rizling, shows the most promise. Best among the vintages still available are the archival 1985 and 1986 Laški Rizling and the 2003 Rumeni Muškat *Pozna Trgatev*.

Mix of wines on offer

18% Rizvanec, 16% Rumeni Muškat, 15% Laški Rizling, 11% Beli Pinot, 10% Modra Frankinja, 9% Chardonnay, 9% Šipon, 6% Renski Rizling and 6% Muškat Ottonel.

Awards

Numerous gold and silver medals from fairs in Ljubljana and Gornja Radgona testify to the quality of the wines.

Culinary recommendations

A tried and tested recipe for the gourmet is the homemade dessert *šarlota*, accompanied by Rumeni Muškat.

2003 Rumeni Muškat *Pozna Trgatev*

10.97% vol., semi-sweet, ★★

With its pale yellow colour and the host of tiny bubbles released on pouring, this wine has a youthful character and promises a fresh flavour. The grape variety is full on the nose, the pure tones opening up to a rich bouquet of aromas comprising acacia blossoms, anise, the Muscat grape, lemon and peaches: a noble feast for lovers of aromatic wines. The palate is light and pleasant. The sugar content has beautifully enhanced the body and helps tone down the inevitable bitterness, giving this unique wine a truly sinful sweetness.

Recommended dishes: Seafood, *šarlota*, pancakes filled with walnuts.

MARIBOR WINE-GROWING DISTRICT

2003 Rumeni Muškat *Pozna Trgatev*

MARIBOR WINE-GROWING DISTRICT

Valdhuber

Janez in Bogomir Valdhuber, Svečina 19, si-2201 Zgornja Kungota
Phone: +386 (0) 2 656 49 21, (0) 41 346 895, (0) 40 557 199, Fax: +386 (0) 2 656 49 21
Email: valdhuber@siol.net

Wine selling ❧ Wine tasting
Wine cellar tours ❧ Sales material

The Valdhubers have been synonymous with wine growing and trade since 1931, and in 1990 they first printed their own labels. Their biggest successes are their Renski Rizling and the dry Traminec. They also grow a young wine, 'Falot'. Abroad they aspire to success with fruity, dry wines, such as Sauvignon, Renski Rizling and Rumeni Muškat.

Mix of wines on offer
15% 'Falot' blend, 20% Renski Rizling, 15% Sauvignon, 10% Rumeni Muškat, 10% Traminec, 10% Sivi Pinot, 10% Chardonnay and 10% Laški Rizling.

Awards
Their 1992 Sauvignon earnt the title of dry white wine champion in Graz in 1992, and at the Ljubljana wine fair their 1995 Traminec was declared the Slovene champion of its variety. Other wines are also frequently chosen as champions among the dry wines.

Culinary recommendations
Creek crab or trout are well complemented by the Sauvignon; stuffed chicken thigh or young beef with Renski Rizling.

2002 Sauvignon
13.0% vol., dry, ★★★

With its bright, straw-like appearance this glowing wine looks lively from the outset, and it instantly delivers a strong bouquet. A background of flowers discreetly supports that distinctive Sauvignon nose of elder flowers, tomato leaves, wild asparagus, lemon, gooseberry, green apples and pears, and it is Sauvignon that continues to prevail. Inhale before every mouthful to appreciate its richness to the full. The Sauvignon character opens up beautifully on the palate. A pleasant, herbaceous character accompanies other complex flavours, which remain ever fresh and juicy. An attractive structure engages the taste buds and compels enjoyment of the wine's personality and balance. The nose, good and long, confirms that this is quality.
Recommended dishes: Soured beef with onions, asparagus dishes, Idrija's ravioli-like speciality *žlikrofi* with *bakalca*, crayfish, trout served in Trieste fashion.

MARIBOR WINE-GROWING DISTRICT

2002 SAUVIGNON

MARIBOR WINE-GROWING DISTRICT

Vilko Vesenjak

Pekel 22, si-2211 Pesnica pri Mariboru
Phone: +386 (0) 2 653 90 11

Pokušnja vin za deset let nazaj Wine tasting for announced groups

Vesenjak has been in viticulture and the wine trade since 1947, and first labelled his bottles in 1988. His vineyards are best suited to the Muškat Ottonel and Laški Rizling varieties. He swears by the quality of the latter, especially its late harvest.
His cellar still holds Laški Rizling from 2000–3, and 2001 Muškat Ottonel, both of which are available for purchase.

Mix of wines on offer
30% Laški Rizling, 30% Muškat Ottonel, 10% Sauvignon, 10% Rizvanec and all varieties in vintages spanning the last fifteen years.

Awards
Vesenjak has received more than thirty commendations in Gornja Radgona for his dedication to wine growing.

Culinary recommendations
Whenever a piglet is grilled at the Vesenjaks', the housekeeper will serve you a dry Laški Rizling; with cheese strudel or gingerbread a semi-sweet Laški Rizling.

2003 Laški Rizling
10,0 vol.%, semi-sweet, ★★

A pale yellow coloration with some green notes and lots of tiny bubbles give the wine a youthful appearance and promise a fresh palate. On the nose it is pleasant and gentle, redolent of dried flowers, ripe pears, honey and sweet spices. The palate is mild and charming. The sweet flavour resembles caramel, supported and freshened by a pleasant acidity and accompanied by diverse flower and fruit overtones. The bouquet has a long, beguiling finish.
Recommended dishes: Cheese strudel, gingerbread, apricot cake.

MARIBOR WINE-GROWING DISTRICT

2003 Laški Rizling

MARIBOR WINE-GROWING DISTRICT

Vinag

Trg svobode 3, si-2000 Maribor
Phone: +386 (0) 2 220 81 15
Website: http:www.vinag.si

❧ Wine selling
❧ Wine tasting for announced groups
❧ Wine cellar tours for announced groups

The Vinag wine cellar was established in 1846. It had operated under various owners until 1960, when Vinag took over and printed his first label. Among the dozen grape varieties that have been grown in the vineyards, the exceptional fruit of the Laški Rizling and Renski Rizling varieties cause these wines to prevail. They expect the Rieslings, Traminec, Sauvignon, Chardonnay and Modri Pinot to be especially lucrative. It is noteworthy that Vinag cellars quite a few of his best wines, and in enviable quantities: 1986 and 1989 Sauvignon, 1989 Chardonnay, 1986 and 1989 Sivi Pinot, 1976 and 1977 Renski Rizling, 1958 and 1981 Laški Rizling and 1981 Rumeni Muškat.

Wines on offer

'Mariborčan' blend, 'Lisičkino vino' blend, Laški Rizling, Renski Rizling, Beli Pinot, Chardonnay, Zeleni Silvanec, Traminec, Rumeni Muškat, Kerner, Sivi Pinot, Sauvignon, Modri Pinot and Sparkling Royal (dry and semi-sweet).

Awards

The Vinag company hold real gold — they have won a total of 465 medals and have been awarded ten championship titles from Ljubljana and Gornja Radgona. They have also come away with gold medals from England, France and the USA, and from Croatia they have more than ten medals plus three championship titles.

Culinary recommendations

Their wines make a lively companion to freshwater fish: carp with dry Laški Rizling, trout with Sauvignon, and perch with Renski Rizling. 'Lisičkino vino' and styrian pork and sausages also make an excellent match. The Modri Pinot is recommended as an accompaniment to roast duck, or to goose with chestnuts or red cabbage.

MARIBOR WINE-GROWING DISTRICT

2001 Laški Rizling
13.5% vol., dry, ★★★

A magnificent yellow the colour of sunbeams is the first thing our senses register about this appealing wine, and one cannot fail to notice the numerous, well-formed legs that slide down the glass and predict a full body. This wine has an intense bouquet for an Italian Riesling (honey, acacia, camomile and dried apricots). The palate brings greater complexity and demonstrates the wine's breadth. It is full-bodied and juicy, fruity and mineral, full of energy, but remains perfectly composed. This is altogether a successful creation, comprising many elements of merit to attain quality and character. We get the impression that harvest took place just before the grapes became over-ripe, which is demonstrated clearly in the length of the bouquet. A challenge for the gourmet trying to find the perfect dish to accompany an informal gathering, or for a wine collector wishing to see this wine develop in his or her own cellar.

Recommended dishes: Freshwater edible carp, pâté, *tunka* meat, sour pork soup, Carniolan sausage, *Prekmurje* ham.

MARIBOR WINE-GROWING DISTRICT

2003 Mariborčan Lisičkino Vino

12.5% vol., semi-dry, ★

This pale yellow wine with green reflections is crystal-clear. The rich and fine fragrances open up on the nose like a rainbow, offering a floral and fruity bouquet typical of this grape: we get violets, withered roses, peaches, pears and lychees. A well-thought-out balance of different grapes is reflected in a complex palate, aromatic, fruity, vibrant and well-tuned. The fundamental flavours develop beautifully from the first impression of sweetness to one of freshness that shows a light mineral touch — the sign of good terrain and ripe grapes. This wine will be very appealing to all wine lovers as well as to the connoisseur in search of the complex mosaic of fragrances and flavours that this wine has to offer. The finish remains full of pleasant things, which linger on and delight our senses.

Recommended dishes: Serve as an aperitif or with sweet pies, shrimps with balsamic vinegar, grilled veal back with rosemary or aromatic fresh fruit salads.

MARIBOR WINE-GROWING DISTRICT

2000 ROYAL

11.5% vol., semi-dry, ★★

The first impression is of a pale yellow colour with golden reflections and tiny bubbles that maintain a full circle around the rim of the glass. The scents of dried flowers, dried fruit and rusk seem fresh and pleasant. Initially the palate is mild, the freshness of the bubbles pleasing. The sensations that follow, characterizing the basic composition of the wine, demonstrate a good balance between sweet and sour; the acidity is just enough to refresh, and lends vivacity. The structure is pleasantly mild, and the finish brings with it a taste of dried figs.
Recommended dishes: Serve as an aperitif, with strawberries or with fruit cakes.

MARIBOR WINE-GROWING DISTRICT

Franc Vrezner

Grušena 12b, si-2201 Zgornja Kungota
Phone: +386 (0) 2 656 77 41

Wine selling ⚜ Wine tasting

The beginnings of wine growing date back to 1968, and in the mid eighties they produced their first labels. The predominant variety here is Sauvignon, which along with Renski Rizling is the most exciting crop. Mostly they produce the 'Veteran' and 'Grušenčan' blends.
Why not come to the cellar yourself to discover just why the Renski Rizling, Sauvignon and Laški Rizling are counted as their best varieties.

Mix of wines on offer
20% Sauvignon, 15% Renski Rizling, 15% Beli Pinot, 15% Rumeni Muškat, 2% Laški Rizling *Pozna Trgatev*, 2% Sauvignon *Pozna Trgatev*, 1% Laški Rizling *Izbor* and 25% 'Veteran' and 'Grušenčan' blends.

Awards
Vrezner has received eight gold medals, six silver medals and one grand gold medal in Ljubljana.

Culinary recommendations
The dishes that particularly complement the characteristics of Vrezner wine are buckwheat bread with walnuts, cheeses, salami, meat dishes, venison, fish and *potica*.

2002 Renski Rizling
12,6 vol.%, semi-dry, ★★

This wine is bright yellow with some green lights and a glow that feels like chasing sunbeams. The beautiful and complex floral and fruit bouquet immediately strikes the nose, and it is easy to pick out the scent of lime blossom. The gentle fruit aromas of ripe peaches and apricots complete it to perfection. On the tongue the bouquet penetrates the entire oral and nasal cavity and nearly overshadows the palate, rendered subtle at first by residual sugar. Quite soon a delicious acidity asserts itself and distinguishes the wine with a liveliness we expect only of the best young White Rieslings. There is an interesting balance between the sugar, which seems to surround the palate, and this vivacious acidity, acting as a second backbone. This wine will interest the general enthusiast and connoisseur alike.
Recommended dishes: Buckwheat bread with walnuts, meat preserved in *tunka*, chicken and veal ragout, smoked sweet cabbage with beef.

MARIBOR WINE-GROWING DISTRICT

2002 Renski Rizling

MARIBOR WINE-GROWING DISTRICT

Zlati grič

Stari trg 29a, si-3210 Slovenske Konjice
Phone: +386 (0) 3 758 03 50, (0)3 758 03 60, (0) 41 636 957, Fax: +386 (0) 3 758 03 78
Email: info@zlati-gric.si, Website: www.zlati-gric.si

Wine selling ❧ Wine tasting
Production of wine and food ❧ Wine cellar tours
Sales material ❧ Announcing the harvests with
the St Martin's golf tournament

The fairly young Zlati grič company has counted traditional wine growing and selling among its concerns since the post-war era began. Most of the vineyards grow Laški Rizling and Renski Rizling, both of which thrive on the terrain of Balant and Jamna. The wine exhibits on offer are Chardonnay (dry, semi-dry), Renski Rizling (semi-dry), special labels and sparkling wines. The Chardonnay *Izbor*, White Riesling *Izbor*, sparkling wines and *Ledeno Vino* are among the best of the wines that await you here.

Mix of wines on offer

74% 'Beli Konjičan' blend, 8% 'Rdeči Konjičan' blend, 8% high-quality wines (Renski Rizling, Chardonnay, Traminec, Sauvignon, Laški Rizling), 5% predicate wines ('Viteško Vino', *Pozna Trgatev*, *Izbor*, *Ledeno Vino*) and 5% sparkling wines (white and rosé, produced in the classical way).

Awards

Year after year they have won gold medals in both Ljubljana and Gornja Radgona. They have also convinced connoisseurs abroad: in Zagreb, Novi Sad, Sarajevo and Spain.

Culinary recommendations

The house speciality, *škalska pogača*, is served with predicate wines *Izbor* or *Pozna Trgatev*.

2003 Renski Rizling

12.2% vol., semi-dry, ★★

This wine has a pale yellow colour with green notes. Floral and fruit fragrances prevail on the nose (dried flowers, apples, pears, lemon peel). The palate is gentle, fresh and distinctive of this variety. The medium structure opens up on the palate and shows its youth. The residual sugar is barely noticeable, with acidity dominating and providing backbone that guarantees successful maturity. It needs at least a year to show its hidden potential.
Recommended dishes: Shrimp in balsamic vinegar, beef with smoked sweet cabbage, chicken or veal ragout.

MARIBOR WINE-GROWING DISTRICT

2003 Renski Rizling

MARIBOR WINE-GROWING DISTRICT

Marjan Zupan

Celestrina 3, si-2229 Malečnik
Phone: +386 (0) 2 471 60 55, Fax: +386 (0) 2 471 60 51

Wine selling

The beginnings of wine growing and selling here date back to 1971, and a decade later the first bottles were labelled. On unfertilized soil they grow Laški Rizling, Kerner, Beli Pinot, Renski Rizling and Chardonnay; they see greatest potential in the last three. Their best vintage is 2001: Chardonnay (dry and *Izbor*), Renski Rizling (dry and *Izbor*), Kerner *Jagodni Izbor* and Beli Pinot *Jagodni Izbor*.

Mix of wines on offer

18% Chardonnay, 15% Chardonnay (*Izbor* and *Pozna Trgatev*), 11% Beli Pinot, 10% Beli Pinot (*Jagodni Izbor* and *Pozna Trgatev*), 5% Kerner, 8% Kerner *Jagodni Izbor*, 16% Renski Rizling, 9% Renski Rizling *Izbor* and 8% Laški Rizling *Izbor*.

Awards

They have entered the wine fair in Gornja Radgona with great success, as shown by 25 gold and even more silver medals. They are the proud holders of the grand gold medal from Split.

2001 Chardonnay

14% vol., dry, ★★★

This is a pale yellow wine, glowing in appearance, with a multitude of tiny bubbles that quickly evaporate in the glass. The pleasant fruit bouquet is quite mature and is typical of this variety. Flowers (lime) present themselves to the nose, but are overshadowed by yellow fruit. Even the hints of honey are almost undetectable, indicating that this vineyard gets lots of sun all year round. The rich body proves both subtle and lively. The promise of the bouquet is delivered on the palate, and the fruitiness puts a special seal on the finish. The high alcohol content is well integrated, barely noticeable within the entire structure, but plays an important part for sure in keeping the balance of the wine.

Recommended dishes: Smoked cold cuts, fried veal liver, roast pork, medallions of hare in dough with red cabbage.

MARIBOR WINE-GROWING DISTRICT

2001 CHARDONNAY

MARIBOR WINE-GROWING DISTRICT

Vina Orešič

Tine Orešič, Metava 55, si-2229 Malečnik
Phone: +386 (0) 2 473 03 11, (0) 41 789 367
Fax: +386 (0) 2 473 24 06, Email: nadja.oresic@guest.arnes.si

Reservation required for wine tastings. ❧ Every tasting includes lectures on various aspects of wine culture. This cultural feast is accompanied by classical music.

Mix of wines on offer

20% blend, 20% Rosé, 14% Renski Rizling, 11% Chardonnay, 8% Muškat Ottonel, 8% Sauvignon, 8% Laški Rizling, 6% Traminec and 5% Beli Pinot.

Vinogradništvo Čerič

Trčova 270, si-2229 Malečnik
Phone: +386 (0) 2 473 04 64, (0) 41 333 629

Wine selling ❧ Wine tasting
Wine cellar tours for announced groups ❧ Sales material
❧ Tour of the vineyards, maintained using manual labour and light machinery because of a sheer slope

Mix of wines on offer

80% blend (Rumeni Muškat, Sauvignon, Traminec, Laški Rizling and Renski Rizling) and 20% high-quality wine.

Vinogradništvo Mlaker

Pesnica pri Mariboru 50e, si-2211 Pesnica pri Mariboru
Phone: +386 (0) 2 653 15 81

Wine tasting ❧ Wine cellar tours for announced groups

Mix of wines on offer

10% Chardonnay and 90% blend.

Radgona-Kapela Wine-Growing District

Podravje Wine-Growing Region

RADGONA-KAPELA WINE-GROWING DISTRICT

Danijela Borko

Partizanska cesta 47, si-9250 Gornja Radgona
Phone: +386 (0) 2 561 13 94, (0) 2 561 13 79, (0) 41 730 093
Email: jernej_borko@siol.net

Wine selling ❧ Wine tasting for announced groups
Wine cellar tours ❧ Production of wine and food for announced groups

Wines on offer

Chardonnay, Laški Rizling, Sauvignon, Traminec, Beli Pinot, Sivi Pinot, Renski Rizling, Šipon and red blend.

Branislav in Terezija Brus

Vrazova ulica 5, si-9250 Gornja Radgona, Phone: +386 (0) 41 575 965

Wine selling ❧ Wine tasting
Wine cellar tours for announced groups ❧ Wine route

Wines on offer

Chardonnay, Chardonnay *Pozna Trgatev*, Laški Rizling (*Pozna Trgatev* and *Izbor*) and Sauvignon.

Dušan Cvetko

Mihovci 19, si-2274 Velika Nedelja
Phone: +386 (0) 2 719 86 86, (0) 41 610 117
Fax: +386 (0) 2 719 86 96, Email: cvetko.dits@siol.net

Wine selling ❧ Wine tasting
Wine cellar tours for announced groups ❧ Wine route
Sales material ❧ Wine and food for announced groups

Mix of wines on offer

20% Kerner, 20% Renski Rizling, 9% Rumeni Muškat, 50% white blend and 1% Laški Rizling *Ledeno Vino*.

Zvonko Fleisinger

Spodnji Ivanjci 31, si-9245 Spodnji Ivanjci,
Phone: +386 (0) 2 560 11 54, (0) 41 942 132, (0) 31 736 063
Email: zvonko.fleisinger@siol.net

Wine selling ❧ Wine tasting
❧ Production od wine and food

Mix of wines on offer

50% 'Ivanjčan' blend, 10% Rumeni Muškat, 10% Sivi Pinot, 10% Sauvignon, 10% Traminec, 10% Renski Rizling and Modra Frankinja.

RADGONA-KAPELA WINE-GROWING DISTRICT

Štefan in Jernej Frangež

Prežihova 10, si-9250 Gornja Radgona,
Phone: +386 (0) 2 561 12 45, (0) 41 716 527

Wine selling ❧ Wine tasting for announced groups
Wine cellar tours ❧ Sales material
❧ Production of wine and food for announced groups

Mix of wines on offer

90% sparkling wines and 10% Chardonnay, Modri Pinot and Kerner.

Branko in Zdenka Kaučič

Ivanjševski vrh 56, si-9245 Spodnji Ivanjci
Phone: +386 (0) 2 560 10 11, (0) 41 951 639

Wine selling ❧ Wine tasting
Wine cellar tours for announced groups ❧ Sales material
❧ Production of wine and food for announced groups

Mix of wines on offer

50% 'Jager' blend, 25% Chardonnay, 10% Renski Rizling and 15% Modri Pinot.

Jakob Kocuvan

Sovjak 30, si-9244 Sv. Jurij ob Ščavnici, Phone: +386 (0) 2 568 10 17

Wine selling ❧ Wine tasting
Production od wine and food ❧ Wine cellar tours
❧ Sales material

Mix of wines on offer

20% Renski Rizling, 15% Sauvignon, 15% Laški Rizling, 15% Traminec, 15% Muškat Ottonel, 10% Sivi Pinot and 10% Šipon.

RADGONA-KAPELA WINE-GROWING DISTRICT

Kapela

Paričjak 22a, si-9252 Radenci, Phone: +386 (0) 2 520 42 50

Wine selling   Wine tasting for announced groups
　　　　　　　Wine cellar tours for announced groups

This company has been dedicated to wine growing and the wine trade since 1945. Chardonnay and Laški Rizling are its two most promising varieties. They concentrate on developing quality wines such as Laški Rizling, Rizvanec and Kapelčan, and this last, alongside Renski Rizling, Sauvignon and Traminec, is one of their best assets in a fiercely competitive market. Some of their finest vintages are still available: 1993 and 2002 Traminec, 1997 Laški Rizling *Ledeno Vino*, 1999 Chardonnay *Ledeno Vino* and 2000 Chardonnay.

Wines on offer

Kapelčan, Laški Rizling and Rizvanec, Chardonnay, Renski Rizling, Sauvignon, Traminec and predicates. The remainder is represented by regional wines.

Awards

They have already won several gold medals at the Ljubljana wine fair for their Traminec *Izbor* and Chardonnay (*Izbor* and *Ledeno Vino*). For the latter they have been awarded several grand gold medals in Gornja Radgona and Split.

Culinary recommendations

Their wines are best when complemented by sour soup, the Ormož feast, meat preserved in *tunka*, *bujta repa* (turnip), walnut *potica* and *kvasenice*.

1993 Traminec

14.0% vol., semi-sweet, ★★★

The golden-yellow glittering colour simply fascinates, along with voluptuous, declicately shaped legs. As you raise your glass, you are immediately greeted by Traminec's luxurious aroma. The attentive taster will encounter a series of colourful and enticing scents on the nose, ranging from withered roses and overly ripe nectarines and peaches to ginger and cinnamon. However, maturity of bouquet and plentiful flower and fruit essences predominate. The fascination does not end here of course, but continues and even escalates on the palate. The wine must have reached its maturity in the most favourable conditions: it has a superbly rich structure. The bouquet, coming to life on the tongue, only reaffirms the nose: a mild but rich palate with a rounded and succulent foundation, combining strength and complexity. The sugar, nicely integrated into the body, plays an important role, creating a lovely final impression after swallowing. The sugar does not overshadow the complex palate however, and this wine delivers prolonged pleasure.
Recommended dishes: Warm duck pâté with dried apple, smoked salmon, fish spiced with saffron (spices such as ginger, cinnamon and pepper work equally well, as do walnuts and honey), Styrian *gibanica*, pancakes with walnuts.

RADGONA-KAPELA WINE-GROWING DISTRICT

1993 Traminec

RADGONA-KAPELA WINE-GROWING DISTRICT

KOGL

Zlatka in Franci Cvetko, Velika Nedelja 23, si-2274 Velika Nedelja
Phone: +386 (0) 2 713 60 60, Fax: +386 (0) 2 713 60 61
Email: kogl@siol.net, Website: www.kogl.net

Wine selling ⚜ Wine tasting for announced groups
Wine cellar tours for announced groups ⚜ Sales material

Since as far back as 1542 the Cvetko family have grown many grape varieties in their vineyards: Šipon, Chardonnay, Auxerrois, Samling, Renski Rizling, Kerner, Muškat Ottonel, Sauvignon, Rumeni Muškat, Laški Rizling, Sivi Pinot, Traminec, Ranina, Modri Pinot and Syrah. 'Kogl' is the label of their various red and white wines, predicate wines, white and red (barrique) blends, and classically produced sparkling wine.
Some of their best vintages, including 1987, 1995, 1997, 1999 and 2000 are still available.

Wines on offer

Šipon, Chardonnay, Auxerrois, Samling, Renski Rizling, Kerner, Muškat Ottonel, Sauvignon, Rumeni Muškat, Laški Rizling, Sivi Pinot, Traminec and Ranina, predicates (*Pozna Trgatev, Izbor, Jagodni Izbor, Suhi Jagodni Izbor, Ledeno Vino*), white blends, red blends (barrique), Modri Pinot, Syrah barrique and sparkling wine (produced in the classical way).

Culinary recommendations

All these wines are enjoyable with dishes from the Prlekija area.

2003 Auxerrois

12.5% vol., dry, ★★

A bright yellow, straw-like colour and a vigorous effervescence when the wine is poured reveal the vivacity of Auxerrois. The fresh, fruity nose, reminiscent of lemon, apples and pears, is moderately intense, but pure and open nonetheless. This wine has quite a full, complex and bold palate. The vaguely bitter aftertaste in no way detracts from the overall harmony and fullness, but adds a masculine note. This basic characteristic, giving the wine a surface liveliness, is perhaps even a welcome addition as long as it doesn't become too exaggerated, since it is not explicitly acidic. All in all, Auxerrois by far exceeds its classification as a 'regional wine'.
Recommended dishes: Meat preserved in *tunka*, Prlekija local cuisine, fried veal liver, plaice fillet cooked with butter and lemon.

RADGONA-KAPELA WINE-GROWING DISTRICT

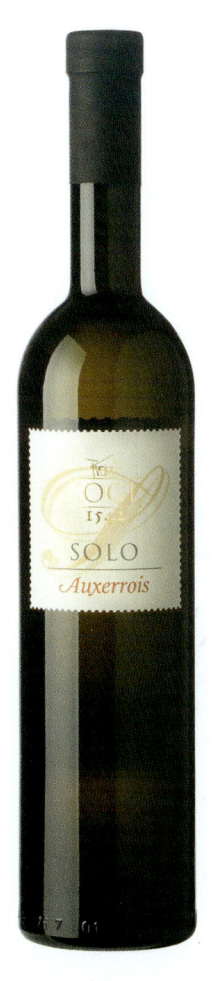

2003 AUXERROIS   2002 MAGNA DOMINICA RUBER RED

2002 Magna Dominica Ruber Red

12.5% vol., dry, ★★

The highly intense, almost opaque ruby red colour is entrancing; rarely do we see wines so generous in appearance. The bouquet delivers with equal intensity and yields cooked red fruit on the nose with spicy notes of vanilla and pepper, a touch of oak and a faint waft of roasting. The palate is interesting but is yet to be completely tamed; the tannins are a touch too loud and their duet with the acidity is not yet perfectly tuned. Nevertheless Magna Dominica is a very interesting wine, and the connoisseur will find much enjoyment in its lavish assortment of aromas and the consequent wildness aroused on the palate.

Recommended dishes: Dried meats, grilled sausage and blood sausage with sauerkraut, roast pork.

RADGONA-KAPELA WINE-GROWING DISTRICT

Radgonske Gorice

Jurkovičeva 5, si-9250 Gornja Radgona
Phone: +386 (0) 2 564 85 11, (0) 2 564 85 13, Fax: +386 (0) 2 561 10 39
Email: kms.radgonske.gorice@siol.net
Website: www.radgonske-gorice.si

Wine selling   Wine tasting for announced groups
Wine cellar tours for announced groups   Wine route
Sales material

The Radgonske Gorice have been involved in the wine-growing industry since 1852, which is also the year when they started producing 'Zlata Radgonska Penina' sparkling wine. Their vineyards are planted with Traminec and Radgonska Ranina, but also with Chardonnay and Laški Rizling, which occupy the largest share in terms of quantity. 'Janževec' blend is their major product.

Mix of wines on offer

48,7% 'Janževec' blend', 22,5% 'Srebrna Radgonska Penina' sparkling wine, 9,4% 'Zlata Radgonska Penina' sparkling wine, 3,9% Traminec, 2,9% 'Radgonski Biser' sparkling wine, 0,8% Radgonska Ranina and Laški Rizling, Renski Rizling, Sivi Pinot and Chardonnay.

Awards

Between 1996 and 1999 they won several gold and silver medals at tastings in Brussels, Ljubljana and Bordeaux, and in the new millennium alone their wines have already won championship titles in Ljubljana, G. Radgona, Zagreb and Split.

Culinary recommendations

Sparkling wine makes a marvellous aperitif which, accompanied by meat preserved in *tunka* can be replaced by 'Janževec' or Laški Rizling.

2003 Renski Rizling

12.0% vol., semi-dry, ★★

Although a young vintage, this wine has a very pleasing appearance, distinguished by a beautiful, intense yellowish colour. Ripe floral fragrances of dried wild flowers merge with white-fleshed fruits on the nose. On the tongue, its sharp character immediately comes to the fore. The sharpness develops into full-blown acidity, despite residual sugar and a decent structure. Wines of diverse character can be developed from Renski Rizling, and the present wine is just one example. Although it is labelled only semi-dry it seems closer to dry on the palate. But it is too early as yet for this wine to yield all it is capable of; this takes time, and Rieslings are wines that 'know' how to mature. Time smoothes away all the palate's rough edges and brings out yet further complexity in a fascinating bouquet. This wine is an excellent candidate for cellarage.
Recommended dishes: Meat preserved in *tunka*, shrimp with balsamic vinegar, sauerkraut dishes (such as sarma — mince rolled in sauerkraut leaves).

RADGONA-KAPELA WINE-GROWING DISTRICT

2003 Renski Rizling   Zlata radgonska penina

Zlata Radgonska Penina

12.5% vol., dry, ★★★

The golden-yellow colour matches the name given to this famous sparkling wine. Medium-sized bubbles stubbornly push towards the surface, preserving the 'necklace' at the rim of the glass and spreading a long-lasting bubbly veil over the surface of the wine. After the first impression, reminiscent of fresh flowers and lemon scent, fruity aromas of fully ripe pears and peaches come to life on the nose, and the whole is spiced with a smoky tinge, completing the complex bouquet. The palate reveals a beautiful structure. The balance between its fresh character and body tends to veer towards overall freshness. Finally, to complete this interesting gustatory experience, you can pick out a vague hint of toast and hazelnuts.
Recommended dishes: Served as an aperitif with salmon spreads or caviar.

RADGONA-KAPELA WINE-GROWING DISTRICT

STEYER

Danilo Steyer, Plitvica 10, si-9293 Apače
Phone: +386 (0) 2 569 14 56, (0) 41 768 026, Fax: +386 (0) 2 569 14 56
Email: steyer.vina@siol.net

Wine selling ❧ Wine tasting
Wine cellar tours Sales material ❧ Sales material
Tours and harvesting in the ampelographical garden ❧ Production of wine and food for announced groups

Steyer has been growing and producing wine since 1989. His leading variet is Dišeči Traminec as it enables him to offer a wide range of different wines. Other varieties are also grown in his vineyards, however: Chardonnay, Renski Rizling, Sivi Pinot and Sauvignon. They are very confident here of the market stability of Dišeči Traminec, Steyer Mark Cuvée and *Ledeno Vino* made from Dišeči Traminec.
The best vintages of these wines are still available: 1999 'Kraljevo Vino' Dišeči Traminec *Ledeno Vino*, 1999 and 2000 Dišeči Traminec Exclusive and 2001 Steyer Mark Cuvée.

Mix of wines on offer

40% Dišeči Traminec, semi-sweet, 10% 'Steyer Mark Cuvée' white, 10% Chardonnay, 10% Renski Rizling, 5% Sivi Pinot, 5% Sauvignon, 5% Dišeči Traminec, dry, 5% Dišeči Traminec, semi-dry, 5% 'Steyer Mark Cuvée' red and 5% Dišeči Traminec predicates.

Awards

In Ljubljana, Dišeči Traminec has twice been made Slovenian champion of the Traminec variety. It is also the Slovenian champion in the white wine category and champion of the northern hemisphere. In Ljubljana, Gornja Radgona and Split the Stever vineyard have won several gold and grand gold medals.

Culinary recommendations

Dišeči Traminec comes to life when accompanied by home-baked Styrian *gibanica*.

RADGONA-KAPELA WINE-GROWING DISTRICT

2001 STEYER MARK CUVÉE
13.5% vol., dry, ★★★

The golden-yellow colour reflects the generous autumn sunshine captured within the grapes. It immediately yields many of the scents that predominate in this blended variety, produced from three different grapes. The Traminec bouquet, redolent of dried flowers, fruit, and spices, is open, delivering fully on the nose, and has a soothing effect on all our senses. The initial impression on the palate is just pleasantly vinous, but the full body quickly expands and we experience the complexity that is to be found only in strong-flavoured wines, the basic flavours being finely balanced. This fullness is tempered by a decent level of acidity, making a very pleasant drink. The bouquet has a prolonged persistence on the palate: the sure sign of a carefully structured character.

Recommended dishes: Smoked salmon, Styrian *gibanica*, pancakes with walnut filling, bread made with dried fruits.

RADGONA-KAPELA WINE-GROWING DISTRICT

Vinar Kupljen

Franc in Vlado Kupljen, Okoslavci 2a, si-9244 Sv. Jurij ob Ščavnici
Phone: +386 (0) 2 568 90 77, (0) 41 681 698, Fax: +386 (0) 2 568 90 76
Email: irena.kupljen@siol.net

Wine selling ❧ Wine tasting
Wine cellar tours ❧ Accommodation
Organising the St Lucy's day harvest ❧ Production of wine and food for
(13 Dec) and Epiphany (6 Jan) announced groups

The Kupljen family have been in the winegrowing industry since 1950. Among the dozen or so grape varieties they grow, the largest share is divided among Laški Rizling, Šipon and Renski Rizling. Their vineyards offer most potential for Chardonnay, Beli Pinot and Traminec. Since 1988 they have marketed their bottled wines under their own brand-names and labels. They are most proud of their Traminec and Renski Rizling. Many varieties from their best vintages are still available: 2000 Renski Rizling *Pozna Trgatev*, 2000 Traminec *Ledeno Vino*, 1993 Beli Pinot *Izbor*, 1994 Chardonnay *Pozna Trgatev*, 1995 Laški Rizling *Pozna Trgatev*, 2000 *Ledeno Vino* and 2000 Šipon *Ledeno Vino*.

Mix of wines on offer

15% Laški Rizling, 10% Šipon, 10% Renski Rizling, 8% Chardonnay, 8% Beli Pinot, 7% Traminec, 6% Sivi Pinot, 6% Sauvignon, 6% Rumeni Muškat, 6% Rizvanec, 5% Modri Pinot, 4% Ranina, 4% Zeleni Silvanec and 3% Muškat Ottonel.

Awards

In all they have won 34 silver medals, 38 gold medals and 5 grand gold medals in Ljubljana and Gornja Radgona.

Culinary recommendations

Prlekija *tunka* is served with Šipon, and Prlekija *gibanica* with Traminec, but these wines are sure to make an excellent accompaniment to most Slovenian dishes.

2001 Laški Rizling *Ledeno Vino*

12.5% vol., sweet, ★★★

The wine exudes a sunny glow, like that of gemstones, with strong legs that drizzle down the wall of the glass. The nose is initially very flowery, becoming reminiscent of herbs, dried lemon peel, mint tealeaves and a variety of fresh and complex scents. The complexity continues on the palate and, despite high sugar levels, the wine is light, fruity and juicy, and so very drinkable. This is a very good vintage for ice wines, bursting with freshness as if wanting to preserve the freezing winter air in which the grapes were picked.
Recommended dishes: Prlekija *gibanica*, apricot cake.

RADGONA-KAPELA WINE-GROWING DISTRICT

2001 Laški Rizling *Ledeno Vino*

2000 Laški Rizling *Pozna Trgatev*
('Wine Queen's' wine)

2000 Laški Rizling *Pozna Trgatev* ('Wine Queen's' wine)

10.13% vol., semi-sweet, ★★

A bright yellow hue gives a pleasing shine to this wine, which initially delivers a nose of discreet but noble nature. When the wine is swirled in the glass, pure floral and peachy fragrances emerge, as well as a hint of grapes affected by noble rot, all finished with a vaguely spicy aroma. The palate confirms the character anticipated by the bouquet; the structure is not magnificent, but it is perfectly proportioned nevertheless. Throughout the tasting we are rewarded with a succession of pleasing sensations, concluding with a complex and likeable finish. A wine for people of aesthetic sensibilities!
Recommended dishes: Prlekija *gibanica*, apricot cake.

RADGONA-KAPELA WINE-GROWING DISTRICT

Milan in Margita Kolarič

Norički vrh 35, SI-9250 Gornja Radgona, Phone: +386 (0) 2 564 17 13

Wine selling ❧ Wine tasting
Wine cellar tours ❧ Wine route
❧ Tour of the wine route by train

Mix of wines on offer

10% Sauvignon, 10% Sivi Pinot, 10% Ranina, 5% Rumeni Muškat and 65% blend.

Slavko Kolbl

Okoslavci 5a, SI-9244 Sv. Jurij ob Ščavnici, Phone: +386 (0) 2 568 17 84

Wine selling ❧ Wine tasting for announced groups
Wine cellar tours for announced groups ❧ Wine route
❧ Production of wine and food for announced groups

Mix of wines on offer

30% Beli Pinot, 30% Renski Rizling, 20% Rumeni Muškat, 10% Laški Rizling and 10% white blend.

Edvard Missia

Kocjan 8, SI-9244 Sv. Jurij ob Ščavnici
Phone: +386 (0) 2 565 13 66, (0) 3 541 41 71, (0) 31 455 021, Fax: +386 (0) 3 491 19 22

Wine selling ❧ Wine tasting for announced groups

Mix of wines on offer

55% Chardonnay, 25% Renski Rizling and 20% Sauvignon.

Anton Roškar

Lastomerci 25, SI-9250 Gornja Radgona, Phone: +386 (0) 2 564 95 18

Wine selling ❧ Wine tasting for announced groups
Wine cellar tours for announced groups ❧ Wine route

Wines on offer

White blend and Sauvignon *Pozna Trgatev*.

RADGONA-KAPELA WINE-GROWING DISTRICT

Milan Senekovič

Lomanoše 25, si-9250 Gornja Radgona
Phone: +386 (0) 2 564 14 90, (0) 2 561 19 62, (0) 31 848 967, Fax: +386 (0) 2 564 14 90
Email: maja.krajnc1@guest.arnes.si

Wine selling ❧ Wine tasting
Wine cellar tours ❧ Wine route

Mix of wines on offer

60% 'Radgončan' blend, 10% Radgonska Ranina, 5% Chardonnay,
5% Sauvignon and Modri Pinot, Muškat Ottonel, Renski Rizling, Sivi Pinot,
Traminec, Laški Rizling and Rizvanec.

Vino Kolmanič

Slavko Kolmanič, Rožički vrh 86, si-9244 Sv. Jurij ob Ščavnici
Phone: +386 (0) 2 568 11 17, (0) 41 526 471, Fax: +386 (0) 2 568 11 17
Email: vino.kolmanic@volja.net, Website: http://users.volja.net/vinokol

Wine selling ❧ Wine tasting
Wine cellar tours ❧ Wine route
Sales material ❧ Production of wine and food for
announced groups

Mix of wines on offer

15% Renski Rizling, 20% Sauvignon, 20% Chardonnay, 15% Traminec
and 30% blend.

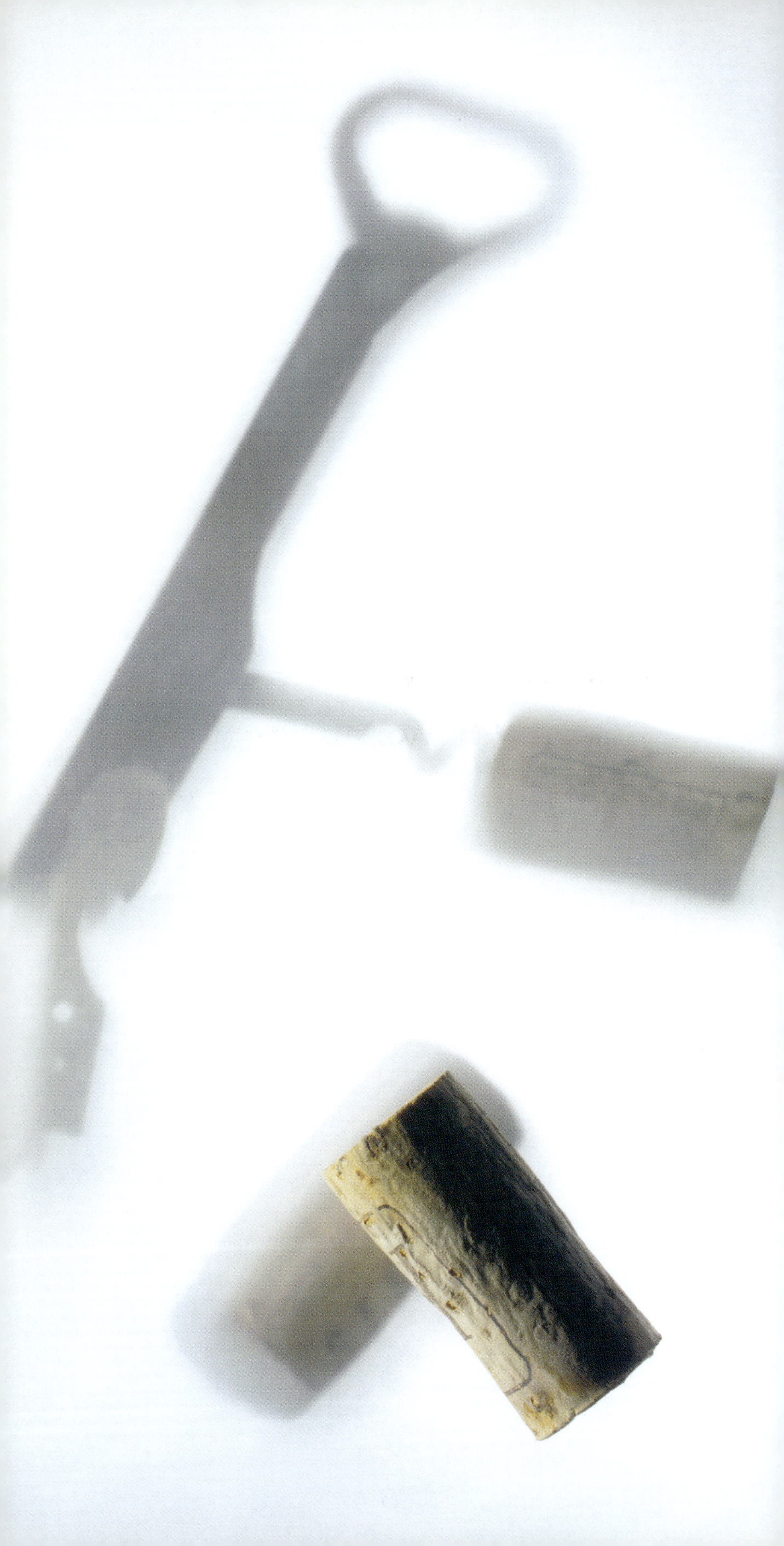

Srednje Slovenske Gorice Wine-Growing District
Podravje Wine-Growing Region

SREDNJE SLO.GORICE WINE-GROWING DISTRICT

Ptujska klet

Vinarski trg 1, si-2250 Ptuj
Phone: +386 (0) 2 787 98 10, Fax: +386 (0) 2 787 98 13

- Wine selling
- Wine tasting
- Wine cellar tours
- Sales material
- Multimedia presentation
- Open cellar day

The origins of the Ptuj wine cellar date back to 1239, when the Minorite monastery was established; the first Wiber Švab label was printed in 1790. Today, this company mainly engages in the production side of the wine industry, and their main product is 'Haložan', along with several other grape varieties: Šipon, Laški Rizling, Sauvignon, Beli Pinot, Renski Rizling and Rizvanec. Younger wines are sold under the 'Noblesse' brand, the 'Noble' label comprises culinary wines and 'Royal Red' represents the cream of their red varieties. Besides the oldest wine in Slovenia — 1917 Zlata Trta — they also store their finest vintages: 1983 Renski Rizling *Pozna Trgatev*, 1983 Sauvignon, 1993 Chardonnay *Izbor*, 1993 Renski Rizling *Pozna Trgatev* and 2001 Laški Rizling *Ledeno Vino*.

Wines on offer

'Haložan', 'Vitez', Laški Rizling, Modra Frankinja, 'Royal White' Renski Rizling, Šipon, 'Noblesse' Sivi Pinot, 'Noblesse' Cuvée, 'Noblesse' Rumeni Muškat, 'Noblesse' Muškat Ottonel, 'Noblesse' Chardonnay, 'Noblesse' Renski Rizling, 'Noblesse' Sauvignon, 'Noblesse' Beli Pinot, 'Noblesse' Zeleni Silvanec, 'Royal Red' Žametno Rdeče, 'Royal Red' Modri Pinot, 'Royal Red' Modra Frankinja and sparkling wines Grand Cuvée.

Awards

They are the proud possessors of two gold medals from the Ljubljana fair, and two golds and a championship title from the Gornja Radgona fair. They also participate successfully at international wine tastings such as those held in San Francisco, London, Bordeaux and Kutjev, where they have won several prizes.

Culinary recommendations

Pork, ham and sauerkraut go well with 'Haložan', and Traminec is a great accompaniment to *potica*.

SREDNJE SLO.GORICE WINE-GROWING DISTRICT

2003 Haložan

12.5% vol., semi-dry, ★

This pale yellow wine with its green notes is glowing and vibrant in appearance. The bouquet is reminiscent of flowers and fruit (e.g. lemon), and is agreeably fresh. This freshness continues on the palate, hiding for a second the full body of the wine, but we soon perceive that the freshness is due to a pleasing acidity, built wonderfully into the body and playing its role perfectly. The palate is predominantly one of fruitiness, accentuating the full variety of flavours. A mild bitterness that becomes detectable shortly after swallowing does not diminish the wonderful palate, and remains well concealed by the residual sugar.

Recommended dishes: sour pork soup, Prlekija *tunka*, veal ragout.

SREDNJE SLO.GORICE WINE-GROWING DISTRICT

2003 Sivi Pinot
11.5% vol., semi-dry, ★★★

The pale, straw-like colour with pink notes is in keeping with the Rulander's traditional appearance. On pouring the wine we spot fresh bubbles indicative of freshness, whilst the abundant legs predict a full body.
    Gentle, not particularly intense floral and fruit (apricot) fragrances hint at grapes of rich content. The palate is similarly mild, but we soon become aware of an 'oily' and 'muscular' body, which nevertheless manages to remain silky and tender. The acidity is barely present, and the wine seems juicy and somewhat spicy. This prompts us to savour it for longer, and we are soon rewarded with a bouquet released by the rich body even after swallowing.
Recommended dishes: offal dishes, white meat in gravy or grilled sausage.

SREDNJE SLO.GORICE WINE-GROWING DISTRICT

1983 Renski Rizling *Izbor*

★★★★

The sight of this crystal-clear, golden wine pouring into the glass is magnificent, and calls our attention to a fine quality that has been maturing for several years. The mature bouquet opens up its complex fragrances, and it is as though we were holding a posy of dried flowers or a bowl of dried fruit, nuts and honey. Finally we perceive the mineral character so typical of a good White Riesling: a variety that shows its finest in a good vintage when produced from over-ripe grapes. This wine, from a fine vintage, fully emerges on the palate and shows its vivacity. The mature bouquet simply gushes out, and the acidity is as good as it can be in any food or drink. It seems fresh and youthful; it still retains some residual sugar, but it is hard to pick out, wonderfully hidden as it is in the body. On the tongue this wine entertains our taste buds just as it did our nostrils, and it is a hard wine topart with. Once we swallow it, however, it simply does not go away. This is a really fine wine, a masterpiece for the vintner who harvested the grapes and the oenologist who preserved the quality and brought it to such perfection.
Recommended dishes: caviar, smoked salmon, sweet pies, fruit cakes.

SREDNJE SLO.GORICE WINE-GROWING DISTRICT

Robert Hafner

Krivi vrh 13, si-2233 Sv. Ana v Slovenskih goricah
Phone: +386 (0) 2 703 22 17, (0) 31 665 596
Email: vinarstvo.hafner@volja.net

Wine selling ❧ Wine tasting
Wine cellar tours ❧ Sales material
❧ Sightseeing tours of the vineyards while enjoying the magnificent natural surroundings.

Mix of wines on offer

30% Chardonnay, 20% Renski Rizling, 15% Traminec, 10% Rumeni Muškat, 5% Sivi Pinot, 5% Sauvignon, 5% Ranina and 5% Modri Pinot.

Marjan Lah

Remčeva 5, si-2250 Ptuj, Phone: +386 (0) 41 728 940

Wine selling ❧ Wine tasting
Wine cellar tours ❧ Sales material

Mix of wines on offer

30% Šipon, 25% Renski Rizling and 45% blend.

Zoran Petkoski

Ulica kneza Koclja 7, si-2250 Ptuj, Phone: +386 (0) 41 579 489
Email: petkoski@volja.net

Wine selling ❧ Wine tasting
❧ Wine cellar tours for announced groups

Mix of wines on offer

60% Renski Rizling (20% dry, 70% semi-sweet, 10% *Pozna Trgatev*), 20% Rumeni Muškat and 20% Traminec.

Ljutomer-Ormož Wine-Growing District
Podravje Wine-Growing Region

LJUTOMER-ORMOŽ WINE-GROWING DISTRICT

ČURIN

Hiša kakovosti Čurin — Praprotnik, Kog 14-15, si-2276 Kog
Phone: +386 (0) 2 719 60 46, (0) 2 719 62 77, (0) 41 620 573 Fax: +386 (0) 2 713 70 24
Website: www.curin.net

- Wine selling
- Wine tasting
- Wine cellar tours
- Wine route
- Sales material

They have been growing and selling wine since 1962, and their wines have borne labels since 1972. From vines growing on ten hectares of land they produce mainly extraordinary 'Vodnar' blend. Their most promising wines are those of the highest quality and all those from vines that have produced a low crop load: Traminec, Sauvignon, Renski Rizling (their best of their wines on sale), Rumeni Muškat and Sivi Pinot. Their wine cellar is well-supplied and offers these top vintages, all available as semi-dry, semi-sweet and sweet: 1975 — 2003 Šipon, 1980 — 2003 Renski Rizling, 1990 — 2003 Sivi Pinot, 1990 — 2003 Traminec and 1975 — 2003 Sauvignon.

Mix of wines on offer

20% Renski Rizling, 15% Sauvignon, 5% Šipon, 5% Laški Rizling, 7% Sivi Pinot, 5% Chardonnay, 4% Rumeni Muškat, 3% Muškat Ottonel, 8% Traminec and 28% 'Vodnar' blend.

Awards

Since their wines first appeared at the Ljubljana fair in 1973, they have won 21 silver, 74 gold, and 41 grand gold medals in Slovenia alone. At fairs abroad — Croatia, Belgium, Turkey, Spain — they have been awarded with many — over 500 — medals and championship titles. and 13 silvers, 14 golds, 1 grand gold and 12 championship titles.

Culinary recommendations

They recommend two combinations in particular: smoked *tunka* meat with a semi-dry Šipon, and walnut *potica* with *Ledeno Vino* or a *Suhi Jagodni Izbor*. Their wines liven up a buckwheat flat cake, walnut *potica* or any type of cake.

LJUTOMER-ORMOŽ WINE-GROWING DISTRICT

2000 ŠIPON

10.77% vol., semi-sweet, ★★★

The pale yellow, crystal-clear colour simply shines. The first, discreet aroma soon yields up a variety of floral and fruit characteristics (meadow flowers and dried apricots), spiced by a sweetness on the nose. The first impression on the tongue is one of sappiness, but it quickly opens up to reveal a subtle and complex character. Its mild palate brings out some barely noticeable sweet overtones that are wonderfully tamed by the acidity: a well-structured wine that offers a distinctively balanced and harmonious blend of flavours. One might think of Šipon as the king of the vineyards in the Ljutomer-Ormož district, and this wine proves that Šipon can be produced in original forms in all categories.

Recommended dishes: Dishes containing asparagus, buckwheat flat cake, bread with olive oil, walnut *potica*.

LJUTOMER-ORMOŽ WINE-GROWING DISTRICT

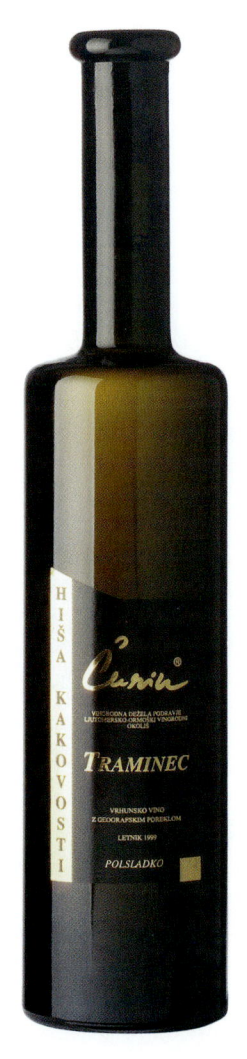

1999 Traminec

11.75% vol., semi-sweet, ★★★

This yellow wine, tinged with sunny, golden nuances, is immediately enticing. The distinctive bouquet of the blend seems almost to glow the very instance we raise the glass. The eyes instinctively close and the complex nose ranges from flowers (violets, withered roses) and fruit (e.g. peaches) to spices (e.g. mint). This individual bouquet continues on the palate, and is further developed by warming the wine on the tongue, wonderfully complementing the full flavour.
In spite of its full body this wine is light and vibrant, thanks to a masterly balancing of the basic flavours. Finally there is a bitterness, so characteristic of a Traminec, but only just noticeable enough to mark it as one of its kind.
Recommended dishes: Serve as an aperitif, and as an accompaniment to grilled shoulder of veal with rosemary or walnut *potica*.

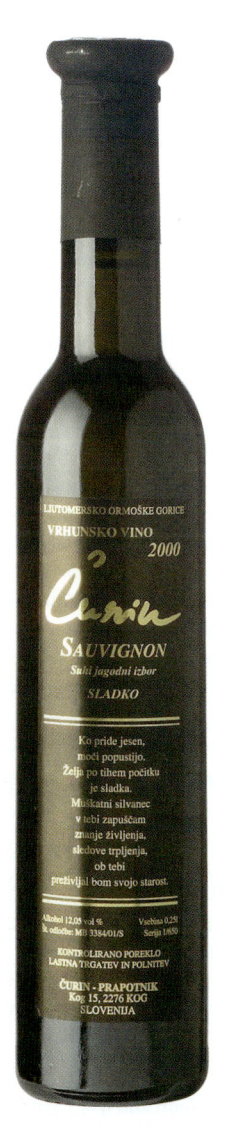

2000 Sauvignon *Suhi Jagodni Izbor*
12.05% vol., sweet, ★★★★

The pouring of this wine feels like the ceremonial entrance of a VIP guest on a red carpet — slow and dignified. Yellow, straw-like colours, with interestingly shaped legs on the side of the glass, beguile the eyes and excite the senses. The ripe nose flaunts itself and resembles roasted fruit, sweet spices, dried apricots and figs, honey and beeswax: all the fragrances of noble rot. The palate is in harmony with the nose; the senses have to work their hardest to keep up with the abundance of the flavours that wash over the tongue, and the bouquet continues to linger long after it has started to subside. A rich and lengthy wine: a feast for the senses.

Recommended dishes: Goose-liver pâté, lobster with vanilla, blue cheese.

LJUTOMER-ORMOŽ WINE-GROWING DISTRICT

Milan Hlebec

Kog 108, si-2276 Kog
Phone: +386 (0) 2 713 70 60, (0) 2 713 70 61, (0) 31 867 464, (0) 41 689 229
Email: hlebec@mp-ptuj.si
Website: www.hlebec-kog.com

Wine selling ❧ Wine tasting
Production of wine and food ❧ Wine cellar tours
Wine route ❧ Accommodation
❧ Sales material

The Hlebec family has been in the wine-growing business and the wine trade since 1985. On the hard, clay soil of their vineyards the most impressive grape varieties are Šipon, Chardonnay, Sauvignon and Renski Rizling. They produce high-quality wines, with the most promising being Šipon and the predicates. They still have some of the best vintages of Šipon and Chardonnay in store.

Wines on offer

Renski Rizling (also *Pozna Trgatev*), Chardonnay (also *Izbor* and barrique — dry), Zweigelt (also barrique), Šipon (also *Izbor* and *Ledeno Vino* — barrique), Traminec (also *Pozna Trgatev*), Rumeni Muškat, Sauvignon (also *Izbor* and *Suhi Jagodni Izbor*), Zeleni Silvanec, Rizvanec and Muškat Ottonel.

Awards

Their wines have been successfully presented in numerous places — in Ljubljana and Gornja Radgona as well as further afield in Croatia and Austria.

Culinary recommendations

For a St Martin's day feast, Miran, the sommelier, recommends a dry Šipon, a dry Sauvignon or a semi-sweet Chardonnay.

2003 Šipon

11.9% vol., semi-dry, ★

The wine ranges from colourless to pale yellow, and is glowing in appearance. The simple, fresh, fruit-and-flowers fragrance reminds us of hawthorn blossoms and lemon scent. The freshness continues on the palate and the wine's youth is reflected in a lively and pleasing flavour, the main characteristic of the wine.
Recommended dishes: Meat preserved in *tunka*, offal, the St Martin's day feast.

LJUTOMER-ORMOŽ WINE-GROWING DISTRICT

2003 ŠIPON

LJUTOMER-ORMOŽ WINE-GROWING DISTRICT

Jeruzalem Ormož

Kolodvorska cesta 11, si-2270 Ormož, Phone: 741 57 00, Fax: +386 (0) 2 741 57 07
Email: info@jeruzalem-ormoz.si
Website: www.jeruzalem-ormoz.si

- Wine selling
- Wine tasting
- Wine cellar tours
- Wine route
- Tour of the Malek vineyard cottage (museum, chapel, traditional wine-pressing, wine cellar)

The beginnings of the company date back to 1898, when the cellar society was established; the first wine labels date back to 1946. Their most important trademark is 'Jeruzalemčan', a wine blend made from five different varieties. Besides dry and semi-dry sparkling wines they also produce high-quality wines; a line of wines for the catering business, 'Holermuos'; and predicate wines. The company is looking to a bright future for a number of wines in particular: Šipon, Renski Rizling, Sauvignon, Traminec, Laški Rizling and some blends. The best vintages are all on offer from their cellars: 1971 Beli Burgundec (Beli Pinot), 1983 (Renski Rizling, Laški Rizling, Chardonnay), 1993 (Chardonnay, Šipon, Laški Rizling), 1997 Sauvignon, 1999 Traminec, 2000 (Laški Rizling and Renski Rizling) and 2001 (Renski Rizling *Ledeno Vino*, Traminec *Ledeno Vino* and Laški Rizling *Pozna Trgatev*).

Mix of wines on offer

70% litre bottles (of which 60% are 'Jeruzalemčan', 15% 'Prlek', 5% Šipon and 20% Laški Rizling), 20% bottles with the region's well-known yellow label (Šipon, Renski Rizling, Sauvignon, Chardonnay, Traminec, Laški Rizling, Sivi Pinot, Beli Pinot, Muškat Ottonel, Rumeni Muškat and Rizvanec), 5% sparkling wines (Chardonnay, Beli Pinot, Šipon, Muškat Ottonel), 4% 'Holermuos' brand (Šipon, Renski Rizling, Sauvignon, Chardonnay and Traminec) and 1% predicates.

Awards

In all they have won twelve championship titles for sparkling wines and Traminec in Ljubljana and Gornja Radgona. In Brussels they were awarded gold medals for their 1996 and 1997 Sauvignon, their 2001 Renski Rizling *Ledeno Vino*, their 2001 Traminec *Ledeno Vino* and their 1983 Šipon *Suhi Jagodni Izbor*. They have returned from Montreal with the jury award on three occasions. Among their many awards the grand gold medal they won for their 2000 Renski Rizling at the Brussels international wine tasting stands out.

Culinary recommendations

Tunka-preserved meat is perfectly complemented by Šipon, breads with pumpkin oil and garlic by Sauvignon, and St Martin's goose by Renski Rizling. Anywhere in Slovenia you can wash down a walnut *potica* with Chardonnay *Pozna Trgatev*.

LJUTOMER-ORMOŽ WINE-GROWING DISTRICT

2003 ŠIPON

13% vol., dry, ★★

This wine has a yellow hue with green notes, which, when the glass is held up against natural light, seems almost colourless. The wine's youth seems to waft from the glass and manifests itself in floral, herbal and fruit fragrances that blend into a harmonious nose. The first impression on the tongue is one of intensity, presenting a good, solid structure. The palate is fresh, complex and vibrant with a mineral quality: a good basis for the ageing and development of the wine, which over a few years will become even milder and finer.

Recommended dishes: Bread with olive oil, mushroom soup, *tunka*-preserved meat, Carniolan sausage, oven-baked turkey

LJUTOMER-ORMOŽ WINE-GROWING DISTRICT

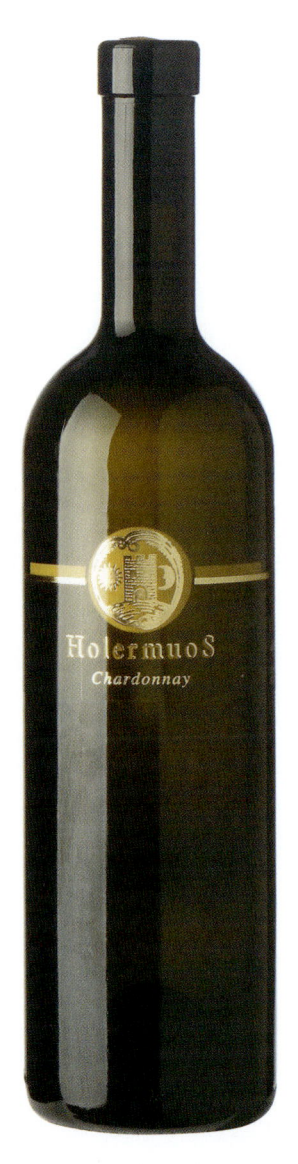

2002 Chardonnay Holermuos

13.5% vol., dry, ★★★

A pale yellow wine with green reflections. Beautiful and thick legs suggest a full-bodied wine. On the nose, one discovers floral aromas and fruit fragrances. The wine is simultaneously full-bodied, gentle and vibrant — the essence of freshness — and accentuates the fruitiness and innate character of the blend. A certain mineral character, derived from the local soil and terrain, enriches the wine. The beautiful composition of this wine creates vibrancy and gently lingers.
Recommended dishes: Thick soup with truffles, asparagus dishes, soured beef, fried veal liver, pork dishes, hard cheeses.

LJUTOMER-ORMOŽ WINE-GROWING DISTRICT

2003 Renski Rizling

12% vol., semi-dry, ★

A pale yellow wine with a few green notes, a unique glow and tiny bubbles — the heralds of a fresh taste. The nose, with its characteristics of wild flowers, is like a June meadow in full bloom. It is accompanied by a less distinctive fragrance of lemon maramalade and, with continued swilling of the wine in the glass, even a hint of grapefruit and withered blossoms. At first it is very mild on the palate, with a medium structure. This slowly opens out, livening up the wine's character, and a fruitiness with a unique scent of peaches emerges. The acidity contributes to the wine's freshness and lingers for a few seconds after drinking.

Recommended dishes: *Tunka*-preserved meat, chicken and veal ragout, smoked sweet cabbage with beef, goat's cheese.

LJUTOMER-ORMOŽ WINE-GROWING DISTRICT

Franc Kolbl

Cven 48c, si-9240 Ljutomer, Phone: +386 (0) 2 584 98 76, (0) 41 340 589
Email: vinoteka2000@email.si, Website: www.geocities.com/vinoteka2000

Wine selling ❧ Wine cellar tours for announced groups
Wine route ❧ Accommodation
Sales material ❧ Production of wine and food for announced groups

Mix of wines on offer

20% Zeleni Silvanec, 20% Rumeni Muškat, 10% Renski Rizling, 10% Laški Rizling, 10% Šipon and 30% 'Hruškovo vino', a pear wine.

Mitja Kos

Ključarovci 66, si-9242 Križevci pri Ljutomeru
Phone: +386 (0) 2 588 82 33, (0) 41 620 568, Fax: +386 (0) 2 588 82 34
Email: kovinogalvanadoo@siol.net
Website: www.kovinogalvana.si

Wine selling ❧ Wine tasting
Production of wine and food ❧ Wine cellar tours
Wine route ❧ Sales material

Wines on offer

Šipon, Laški Rizling, Kerner, Chardonnay, Sauvignon, Sivi Pinot, Rumeni Muškat and Rizvanec (half from normal harvest and half special-quality wines).

Edi in Anica Kosi

Radomerščak 34, si-9240 Ljutomer, Phone: +386 (0) 2 581 16 33

Wine selling ❧ Wine tasting
Production of wine and food ❧ Wine cellar tours

Wines on offer

Laški Rizling, Šipon, Renski Rizling and Chardonnay.

Mirko Krajnc

Veliki Brebrovnik 83, si-2275 Miklavž pri Ormožu. Phone: +386 (0) 2 719 70 65

❧ Wine selling

Wines on offer

Laški Rizling and Sauvignon.

LJUTOMER-ORMOŽ WINE-GROWING DISTRICT

Tanja in Zlatko Korpar

Oslusevci 49, si-2273 Podgorci
Phone: +386 (0) 2 713 00 06, (0) 2 713 00 07, (0) 41 611 247, (0) 41 516 689,
Fax: +386 (0) 2 713 00 05
Email: tanja.korpar@stajerles-trade.si, zlatko.korpar@stajerles-trade.si

Wine selling ❧ Wine tasting
❧ Production of wine and food for announced groups

WINE ON OFFER
Renski Rizling.

Štefan Krampač

Kopriva 1, si-9240 Ljutomer, Phone: +386 (0) 2 589 11 57
Fax: +386 (0) 2 589 11 57, Email: natalija.krampac@siol.net

Wine selling ❧ Wine tasting
Wine cellar tours for announced groups ❧ Wine route
❧ Production of wine and food for announced groups

Mix of wines on offer
15% Beli Pinot, 15% Chardonnay, 15% Renski Rizling, 15% Laški Rizling, 10% Sauvignon, 10% Traminec, 10% Sauvignon, 5% Muškat Ottonel and 5% Šipon.

Rado Lesjak

Vuzmetinci 22, si-2275 Miklavž pri Ormožu
Phone: +386 (0) 2 719 71 16, (0) 31 246 725, Fax: +386 (0) 2 740 21 81

Wine selling ❧ Wine tasting
Wine cellar tours ❧ Wine route
❧ Tradicional press

Mix of wines on offer
25% Rumeni Muškat, 14% Muškat Ottonel, 14% Sivi Pinot, 14% Dišeči Traminec, 14% Sauvignon, 9% Laški Rizling and 9% Šipon.

Angela in Viktor Munda

Prerad 7, si-2257 Polenšak, Phone: +386 (0) 2 755 57 91

Wine selling ❧ Wine tasting
Production of wine and food ❧ Wine cellar tours

Mix of wines on offer
40% blend, 25% Laški Rizling, 20% Sauvignon and 15% Zeleni Silvanec.

LJUTOMER-ORMOŽ WINE-GROWING DISTRICT

Milan Krajnc

Lahonci 50, si-2259 Ivanjkovci
Phone: +386 (0) 2 719 41 26, (0) 41 518 285, Fax: +386 (0) 2 719 41 26
Email: vino.krajnc@email.si

Wine selling ❧ Wine tasting
Wine cellar tours ❧ Wine route
❧ Sales material

He has been growing wine for the last fifteen years and is most pleased with his Chardonnay, which gives good results in all its forms from dry wine to *Suhi Jagodni Izbor*. He says we can expect a lot from the Šipon, a speciality in this county.
Still available for some time to come are: Chardonnay *Pozna Trgatev* from 1995, 1996 and 2001; 1997 Renski Rizling; 2000 Chardonnay *Suhi Jagodni Izbor*; and 2001 Sauvignon.

Mix of wines on offer
50% ´Lahončan´ blend, 10% Renski Rizling, 9% Sauvignon, 7% Chardonnay, 7% Sivi Pinot, 6% Modri Pinot, 6% Traminec and 5% different predicates.

Awards
They have returned from Gornja Radgona with two grand gold and five gold medals, and from Ljubljana with five gold and five silver medals.

Culinary recommendations
The cellared predicate wines go well with dried fruit.

2002 Renski Rizling
12.8% vol., dry, ★★★

The vibrant, pale colour has an especially attractive glow. The floral-fruit bouquet expresses the grape variety, and yields fragrances in an open and pure form, resembling dried flowers (lime, acacia) and fruit (vineyard peaches, dried lemon peel). The first impressions on the palate are delightful: for content, for Riesling characteristics, for complexity. The wine has a superb foundation in all four basic flavours: first sweetness, soon refreshed by tasty acidity, then a mineral touch to confirm the grape variety and finally a good solid foundation. The final, pleasant bitterness contributes to the overall palate and character of the wine. Renski Rizling can be a pleasant surprise in its diverse forms, and this is a fine example indeed of a dry Renski Rizling.
Recommended dishes: Prlekija *tunka*, sour pork soup, sarma, grilled chicken.

LJUTOMER-ORMOŽ WINE-GROWING DISTRICT

2002 Renski Rizling

LJUTOMER-ORMOŽ WINE-GROWING DISTRICT

Ljutomerčan

Kidričeva ulica 2, si-9240 Ljutomer
Phone: +386 (0) 2 585 88 00, (0) 2 584 98 10, (0) 41 747 530, Fax: +386 (0) 2 585 88 10
Email: info@ljutomercan.si, Website: www.ljutomercan.si

Wine selling ❧ Wine tasting for announced groups
Wine cellar tours for announced groups ❧ Sales material
❧ Wine and food for announced groups

The company was founded in 1954. The blend after which the company was named is composed of six individual varieties. They believe that their best grapes come from the Laški Rizling and Chardonnay vines, which provide a good basis for sparkling wines. For the future they have particularly high expectations of Šipon, an indigenous grape variety mentioned as early as 1678, and 'Ljutomerčan', which maintains its quality and tradition, as well as Laški Rizling and predicate wines, both of which have the right conditions to thrive.

Mix of wines on offer

41% 'Ljutomerčan' blend, 22% Laški Rizling, 13% Šipon, 4% Chardonnay, 5% Renski Rizling, 4% Sauvignon and Traminec, Sivi Pinot, Ranina, Rumeni Muškat, Muškat Ottonel, sparkling wines and predicates.

Awards

At the GAST fair of 2004 they won the grand gold commendation for their 2003 Ranina, and the gold medal for their 2004 Laški Rizling, sparkling 'Philippus Primus' and 'Philippus'. They left Gornja Radgona with the grand gold medal for their 1999 Laški Rizling *Ledeno Vino* and the gold medal for their 2000 Laški Rizling. At the Ljubljana wine fair their 2001 Traminec was awarded the gold medal.

Culinary recommendations

The Šipon goes best with Prlekija *tunka*; the semi-dry Laški Rizling with buckwheat *krapci*. Do not turn down the chance of trying 'Ljutomerčan' with Styrian sour soup, or a Sauvignon, either with roast duck or with duck and *mlinci*. There are also some good dessert wines: try pancakes and custard with a semi-sweet Ranina or walnut *potica* with a semi-sweet Traminec.

2002 Philippus Primus

12.0% vol., dry, ★

The wine has a yellow coloration with some green notes. Numerous small-to-medium bubbles are released for some time and form a complete circle at the surface. The first fragrance is intense, resembling fresh flowers, lemon, grapefruit and ripening apples. Freshness prevails on the palate as well; the wine shows a lovely, rich backbone, but seems youthful, refreshing, and particularly suitable as an aperitif.
Recommended dishes: As an aperitif, with bread with spreads (bakalah).

LJUTOMER-ORMOŽ WINE-GROWING DISTRICT

2002 Philippus Primus   2003 Laški Rizling

2003 Laški Rizling

13.5% vol., dry, ★

This is a crystal-clear wine, pale yellow in colour with intense green notes, promising freshness. On the nose, the first thing is a floral, pleasant fruitiness, redolent of meadow flowers, fresh grapes, ripe apples and lemon peel. The wine has a full palate and is quite complex. There is a good balance between the warming alcohol, the residual sugar and the freshness of the wine, which has a pleasantly rounded finish.

Recommended dishes: Spreads with pâté, dishes with sauerkraut (such as sarma — a cabbage roll stuffed with mince), Carniolan sausage.

LJUTOMER-ORMOŽ WINE-GROWING DISTRICT

Bojan Lubaj

Kajuhova 3, si-2325 Kidričevo, Phone: +386 (0) 2 796 18 11

Wine selling 🍖 Wine tasting

The Lubajs have been in winegrowing and the wine trade since 1993 and added labels to their bottles four years later. Their vineyards grow Renski Rizling and Sauvignon, and their main grape varieties are Šipon and Laški Rizling, which offer the highest quality grapes. The best vintages in their cellar are the 2000 Šipon *Suhi Jagodni Izbor*, the 2000 and 2001 Laški Rizling *Suhi Jagodni Izbor* and the 2002 Šipon *Ledeno Vino*.

Mix of wines on offer

60% Laški Rizling *Suhi Jagodni Izbor*, 20% Šipon *Suhi Jagodni Izbor*, 10% Laški Rizling *Izbor* and *Jagodni Izbor* and 10% dry and semi-dry wines, Šipon, Laški Rizling, Renski Rizling and Sauvignon.

Awards

Numerous accolades and medals testify to the continued quality of their work. Many are from Gornja Radgona, alongside a gold medal from the Ljubljana fair, two grand golds from Split and the championship title from Novi Sad.

2002 Laški Rizling *Suhi Jagodni Izbor*
11.1% vol., sweet, ★★★

Sunny gold in appearance, this wine practically glows in the glass. The wonderful bouquet offers itself in an abundance that can only be attained from grapes with noble rot. One can pick out fragrances of very ripe fruit (peaches, apricots, baked apples), spices (vanilla, cinnamon), honey and caramel. Every mouthful is full-bodied and virile; the firm backbone, characterised by ethanol, tones down the effect of the sugar and preserves the complexity of the palate. The length of the wine is complemented by the lovely consistency of the bouquet, which lasts long after drinking.
Recommended dishes: Goose liver pâté, Prlekija *gibanica*, pancakes with walnuts, apricot cake.

LJUTOMER-ORMOŽ WINE-GROWING DISTRICT

2002 LAŠKI RIZLING *Suhi Jagodni Izbor*

LJUTOMER-ORMOŽ WINE-GROWING DISTRICT

Magdič

Cesta na Vilo 1a, si-9240 Ljutomer, Phone: +386 (0) 2 581 19 72, (0) 41 518 148

Wine selling ❦ Wine tasting
Wine cellar tours ❦ Wine route
Modern tastings with expert commentary ❦ Production of wine and food for announced groups

Janko Magdič has been a vintner for a quarter of a century, and today he tends 16,000 grapevines of the Laški Rizling and Renski Rizling, Chardonnay, Sauvignon, Sivi Pinot and Šipon grape varieties. They produce high-quality and quality wines here, the latter sold under the trademark 'Lotmeržan'. The unbottled wine, in stainless-steel barrels, is intended for gastronomy. As he is drawn to red wine varieties, Janko Magdic has succumbed to Modri Pinot, Zweigelt and Cabernet Sauvignon. The local market is growing rapidly, so his cellars are rather low in stock.

Wines on offer

Modri Pinot, Renski Rizling, Chardonnay, Sauvignon, Sivi Pinot, Šipon and Laški Rizling.

Awards

Although he rarely attends wine tastings and fairs, he has won a gold medal in Gornja Radgona and champion of its variety for his Modri Pinot.

2003 Modri Pinot

12.0% vol., dry, ★★

The medium-intense colour is ruby red with a typical crimson tone. The nose is distinctly fruity, with the smell of red berries — typically raspberry, black cherry and cherry — all in a very open and fresh mix. This fruitiness continues on the palate and is similar to the popular characteristics of young red wines made by maceration in the carbon dioxide of the atmosphere. The tannins are mild and sparse, normal for a wine of this variety. The balance is centred on the fruitiness, which compensates if the wine is a little lacking some other fundamental qualities. The palate fully engages the tastebuds, it abounds in the characteristic traits of Modri Pinot, the sensations experienced are wholly pleasant and this wine deserves a top rating.
Recommended dishes: Roasted chestnuts, blood sausages with cabbage, goose breast with beans, roast veal.

LJUTOMER-ORMOŽ WINE-GROWING DISTRICT

2003 Modri Pinot

LJUTOMER-ORMOŽ WINE-GROWING DISTRICT

MiroVino

Miro Munda, Jastrebci 36, si-2276 Kog
Phone: +386 (0) 2 719 75 30, (0) 2 719 76 30, (0) 41 474 935, Fax: +386 (0) 2 719 76 30
Email: miro.munda@email.si
Website: www.slovino.com/mirovino

Wine selling Wine tasting
Wine cellar tours Wine route
 Sales material

This young international company has been in wine growing and the wine trade since 1992. More than half the vineyards are devoted to the Laški Rizling grape, with the remainder growing other varieties, among which Beli Pinot, Renski Rizling, Sauvignon and Šipon do particularly well. They also produce blended wines: 'Špargelj'; a young wine named 'Junior'; and a blend comprising three varieties named 'Kog 3', a light, dry wine. They have the highest expectations of their Sauvignon, Beli Pinot, Šipon and 'Kog 3'.
Some fine vintages are still available: 1993 Laški Rizling, 2000 Renski Rizling, 2000 Beli Pinot and 2002 Sauvignon réserve.

Mix of wines on offer

30% Laški Rizling, 10% Sauvignon, 10% Chardonnay, 10% Beli Pinot, 20% 'Kog 3' blend, 7% 'Junior' young wine, 7% 'Špargelj' blend and 6% Šipon.

Awards

In Gornja Radgona the Laški Rizling was named champion of its variety. In Ljubljana the Beli Pinot won a gold medal and the Chardonnay likewise in Split.

Culinary recommendations

If *tunka* meat with the 2002 Sauvignon or home-style roast chicken with the 2002 Renski Rizling do not persuade you, then fresh cow's cheese with homemade bread and the 2002 Chardonnay Classic definitely will!

2002 Sauvignon Réserve

13% vol., dry, ★★★

The wine is pale yellow in colour with barely perceptible hints of green. The wine's characteristic scent is very immediately distinctive on the nose. It comprises the fragrances of garden plants: tomato leaves, currant bushes and box tree, with the scent of lime in the background. The wine is lively and fresh, and quite bold on the tongue. There is a certain mineral character, probably deriving from the soil. It does not hide its herbaceous character, which beautifully accentuates the essence of the variety without being excessive. It has a fresh finish, again very characteristic of the variety: another good attribute.
Recommended dishes: Meat preserved in *tunka*, classic goulash, tarragon *potica*, fish dishes with asparagus.

LJUTOMER-ORMOŽ WINE-GROWING DISTRICT

2002 SAUVIGNON RÉSERVE

LJUTOMER-ORMOŽ WINE-GROWING DISTRICT

Franci Plajnšek

Kočice 54, Potni vrh, si-2287 Žetale, Phone: +386 (0) 2 769 29 11, (0) 41 557 021

Wine selling ⁂ Wine tasting
Wine cellar tours ⁂ Production of wine and food for announced groups

Wines on offer

Sauvignon (high-quality, *Izbor* and *Jagodni Izbor*), Rumeni Muškat (high-quality and semi-sweet), Renski Rizling (high-quality and semi-sweet), blend (semi-dry), Sivi Pinot (dry) and Chardonnay (semi-dry).

Vinko Ratek

Mali Brebrovnik 33, si-2259 Ivanjkovci
Phone: +386 (0) 2 719 60 40, (0) 31 225 009, (0) 31 638 271, Fax: +386 (0) 2 719 60 40

Wine selling ⁂ Wine tasting
Production of wine and food ⁂ Wine cellar tours
Wine route ⁂ Sales material

Mix of wines on offer

30% Renski Rizling, 30% Sauvignon, 25% Rumeni Muškat and 15% Modri Pinot.

Jakob Svenšek

Sela 29, si-2324 Lovrenc na Dravskem polju, Phone: +386 (0) 2 781 12 01, (0) 41 778 435

Wine selling ⁂ Wine tasting
Production of wine and food ⁂ Wine cellar tours
Accommodation ⁂ Sales material

Mix of wines on offer

30% Sivi Pinot, 15% Laški Rizling, 15% Rumeni Muškat and 40% blend.

Emil Trop

Lahonci 36a, si-2259 Ivanjkovci, Phone: +386 (0) 2 719 42 42, (0) 31 373 001
Email: perot@email.si

Wine selling ⁂ Wine tasting
Wine cellar tours ⁂ Wine route
Sales material ⁂ Production of wine and food for announced groups

Mix of wines on offer

44% Chardonnay, 22% Sauvignon, 22% Laški Rizling and 12% Renski Rizling

LJUTOMER-ORMOŽ WINE-GROWING DISTRICT

Avgust Šadl

Viktorja Kukovca 2, si-9240 Ljutomer, Phone: +386 (0) 2 581 10 47

Wine selling ❦ Wine tasting
❦ Wine cellar tours

Mix of wines on offer

20% Sauvignon, 40% Chardonnay, 18% Renski Rizling, 8% Sivi Pinot, 3% Rumeni Muškat, 6% Muškat Ottonel and 5% Traminec.

Miran – Ferdo Trop

Runeč 65, si-2259 Ivanjkovci, Phone: +386 (0) 2 719 40 74, (0) 41 919 090

Wine selling ❦ Wine tasting
Wine cellar tours ❦ Wine route
❦ Production of wine and food for announced groups

Mix of wines on offer

50% Renski Rizling, 10% Chardonnay, 15% Rumeni Muškat, 10% Sauvignon and 15% Laški Rizling.

Ivo – Janez Trstenjak

Stročja vas 46, si-9240 Ljutomer
Phone: +386 (0) 2 584 84 45, (0) 41 413 663, Fax: +386 (0) 2 581 13 84
Email: janez.trstenjak@siol.net

Wine selling ❦ Wine tasting for announced groups
❦ 100% pure grape juice sold

Mix of wines on offer

30% blend, 30% Sauvignon *Pozna Trgatev*, 10% Šipon *Pozna Trgatev*, 10% Muškat Ottonel, 10% Kerner and 10% Laški Rizling.

Vid Vincetič

Litmerk 44, si-2270 Ormož, Phone: +386 (0) 2 740 16 43, (0) 2 740 16 73, (0) 31 636 762
Email: videk44@volja.net
Website: http://users.volja.net/videk44

Wine selling ❦ Wine tasting
Wine cellar tours ❦ Wine route
❦ Production of wine and food for announced groups

Wines on offer

Rumeni Muškat (also *Pozna Trgatev* and *Izbor*), Sauvignon (also *Pozna Trgatev* and *Izbor*), Chardonnay, Muškat Ottonel, Šipon, 'Ljutomerčan' and Renski Rizling.

LJUTOMER-ORMOŽ WINE-GROWING DISTRICT

Jože Slavinec

Mihalovci 45, si-2259 Ivanjkovci
Phone: +386 (0) 2 719 41 11, (0) 2 719 48 88, (0) 41 626 822, Fax: +386 (0) 2 719 41 11

Wine selling ❧ Wine tasting
Wine cellar tours ❧ Wine route
Accommodation ❧ Sales material

The tradition of viticulture and selling wine dates back to 1914 here but it was in the early eighties that they first produced their own labels. The Laški Rizling grape predominates in the vineyards, as it can produce the most quality and high-quality wines, as well as predicates. Šipon, Renski Rizling, Rumeni Muškat, Chardonnay, Muškat Ottonel and Sivi Pinot are the wines for which the Slavinec family is famous and on which their reputation rests.
The best vintages still available are: 1988 Renski Rizling *Pozna Trgatev*, 1989 Chardonnay *Pozna Trgatev*, 2000 Laški Rizling *Jagodni Izbor* and 2001 Renski Rizling.

Mix of wines on offer

30% Laški Rizling, 18% Šipon, 12% Renski Rizling, 12% Rumeni Muškat, 9% Chardonnay, 3% Muškat Ottonel, 6% Sivi Pinot and 10% Chardonnay *Pozna Trgatev*, Renski Rizling *Pozna Trgatev* and Laški Rizling *Jagodni Izbor*.

Awards

They have won several gold medals in Gornja Radgona as well as having their wines declared variety champions, and in Ljubljana their Laški Rizling was named the chivalric wine.

Culinary recommendations

They say that their dry wines are suitable for all occasions, while their predicates make splendid aperitifs and are also good dessert wines. *Tunka*-preserved meat, *zaseka* (minced lard) and homemade bread complement the flavour of their wines.

2002 Renski Rizling

10.74% vol., semi-sweet, ★

This is a pale yellow wine with green notes, and glows crystal clear in appearance. The fresh bouquet, typical of the variety, delivers vine blossom, lime, meadow flowers and grapes, and is pleasantly enticing. The characteristic freshness of the young Riesling continues on the palate, where one can perceive the variety's pleasing aroma. A medium structure and the wine's youth make it highly drinkable and a light, pleasurable experience.
Recommended dishes: An aperitif wine and a welcome companion to a medium-sweet *potica*.

LJUTOMER-ORMOŽ WINE-GROWING DISTRICT

2002 Renski Rizling

LJUTOMER-ORMOŽ WINE-GROWING DISTRICT

Stanovščak

Frančišek Alojzij Lah, Podgorci 26, si-2273 Podgorci
Phone: +386 (0) 2 719 21 13, (0) 41 311 408

Wine selling ❧ Wine tasting
Wine cellar tours for announced groups ❧ Wine route
❧ Sales material

In 1970 Lah became a grower and seller of wine and opted for labels twelve years later. Laški Rizling and Šipon predominate in the vineyards, the latter being the main ingredient of Lah's blended label. The cream of what's on offer are the Šipon, grown and cared for according to the standards of the 'Klub Šipon' association, as a bottled wine, or Šipon as high-quality dry wine. The best vintages of the latter pairing — 1999 and 2002 — are still available.

Mix of wines on offer
69% blend, 8% Šipon, 7% Renski Rizling, 7% Sauvignon, 6% Laški Rizling and 3% Rumeni Muškat.

Awards
Lah successfully presents his wines in Gornja Radgona, Rogaška Slatina and Ptuj, as well as at the Podgorca wine festival.

Culinary recommendations
Tunka meat or, even better, home-prepared roast duck or goose, complement a dry or semi-dry Šipon or Laški Rizling.
In general Šipon is best with all meat dishes.

2002 Šipon
13.17% vol., dry, ★★★

This is tempting with its glowing yellow colour and golden notes. Heavy legs slip down the glass and attest to the firm backbone. The bouquet immediately opens up and yields fragrances of dried flowers (lime), peaches, dried fruit and more, and the abundant richness of the body continues on the palate. The complexity of the palate is exceptional, with white fruit prevailing, accompanied by a constant freshness. In this it matches the bouquet, reflecting the wine's balance. The distinctive character of the variety is equally exceptional and contributes to this Šipon's reputation. A fine example of high-quality Šipon.
Recommended dishes: *Tunka* meat, fried veal liver, home-prepared roast duck or goose and cold cuts of smoked Slovenian meat.

LJUTOMER-ORMOŽ WINE-GROWING DISTRICT

2002 ŠIPON

LJUTOMER-ORMOŽ WINE-GROWING DISTRICT

Jože Šnajder

Ulica dr. Hrovata 12, si-2270 Ormož, Phone: +386 (0) 2 740 05 89

Wine selling ❧ Wine tasting
❧ Wine cellar tours for announced groups

For over fifty years Šnajder has been tending his vineyards and producing wines, and in 1988 he labelled his bottles for the first time. The Laški Rizling and Kerner grape thrive in his vineyards, but the pride of the cellar are his Renski Rizling and Šipon.
There are still some excellent wine samples on offer: 1971 Laški Rizling, 1983 Chardonnay, 1986 Kerner, 1997 Laški Rizling *Pozna Trgatev* and 1997 Laški Rizling *Ledeno Vino*.

Mix of wines on offer

50% Laški Rizling, 30% Kerner, 10% Šipon and 10% Renski Rizling.

Awards

Their wines have achieved fourteen gold medals (including one grand) in Gornja Radgona, and a gold medal for the 1991 Laški Rizling at the Vino forum.

Culinary recommendations

Pheasant stew with the Laški Rizling, or the Renski Rizling with Easter ham, horse-radish and apples are two of Šnajder's culinary recommendations.

2000 Laški Rizling *Pozna Trgatev*

12.01% vol., semi-sweet, ★★★

The pale yellow wine with golden reflections is crystal clear. The mineral fragrance suggests more maturity than one would expect from the wine's appearance. The fragrances of dried flowers, dried apricots and beeswax complete the nose of this splendid wine — a fully developed personality. The rich structure unfolds with complexity on the palate, despite a powerful sweetness. A character of noble rot and sun-scorched grapes lends the wine liveliness; it is full of energy and rounded in the true meaning of the word. To finish, there is a full bouquet that completes the fine impression made by this particularly successful, late-harvest wine.
Recommended dishes: Pheasant stew, Prlekija *gibanica*, walnut-filled pancakes.

LJUTOMER-ORMOŽ WINE-GROWING DISTRICT

2000 Laški Rizling *Pozna Trgatev*

LJUTOMER-ORMOŽ WINE-GROWING DISTRICT

Saško Štampar

Kajžar 43, si-2275 Miklavž pri Ormožu
Phone: +386 (0) 2 713 70 30, (0) 41 386 037, Email: jerno1@email.si

Wine selling   Wine tasting
Wine cellar tours   Wine route
Sales materials   Harvest and wine pressing using a wooden press.
Production of wine and food for announced groups

The Štampars began wine growing and trading in 1966, with 1990 bringing their first wine labels. They produce high-quality and quality wines from Laški Rizling and Renski Rizling, Šipon and Kerner grapes. The micro-climate of their vineyards is best suited to Šipon which, along with Renski Rizling, is their show wine.
Šipon and Renski Rizling predicates are still available from the 2000 vintage.

Mix of wines on offer

40% Laški Rizling, 25% Renski Rizling, 20% Šipon and 15% Kerner.

Awards

They are proud of a string of successes in Gornja Radgona: four grand gold medals, eight gold medals and a variety champion.

Culinary recommendations

Tunka-preserved meat or Prlekija *gibanica* will bring out the best in their wines.

2000 Šipon *Suhi Jagodni Izbor*

10.7% vol., sweet, ★★★

A wine with a glowing, golden-yellow colour. The candid and intense bouquet is complex and rich in composition, resembling over-ripe peaches, quince, fresh figs, walnuts and dried flowers. The aroma of noble rot can be detected as sizzling veal fat in a frying pan. The high sugar level contributes to the wine's full flavour — authoritative, with a pronounced taste of grapes and caramel, but with just enough freshness for the character of this particular wine.
In spite of overwhelming sugar, the wine creates diverse impressions on the palate, which linger on, slowly subsiding, and leave a wholly pleasant effect. On drinking this wine the imagination opens up like a flower and one senses the autumn, when these grapes were awaiting harvest.
Recommended dishes: blue cheeses, Prlekija *gibanica*, pancakes with walnuts, stuffed pears, apricot cake, fruit cakes.

LJUTOMER-ORMOŽ WINE-GROWING DISTRICT

2000 ŠIPON *Suhi Jagodni Izbor*

LJUTOMER-ORMOŽ WINE-GROWING DISTRICT

Vino Kupljen

Jože Kupljen, Veličane 59 in Mihalovci 41, si-2259 Ivanjkovci
Phone: +386 (0) 2 719 41 28, (0) 2 719 40 01, Fax: +386 (0) 2 719 46 15, (0) 2 719 44 44
Email: vino-k@t-online.de, Website: www.vino-kupljen.com

Wine selling ❧ Wine tasting
Production of wine and food ❧ Wine cellar tours
Wine route ❧ Accommodation
Sales material ❧ 1st National Wine Bank of Slovenia

Jože Kupljen entered the wine trade in 1972 and soon filled his first bottles. On carefully selected terrain he has planted the most suitable grape varieties: Chardonnay, Modri Pinot, Sivi Pinot, White and Laški Rizling, Sauvignon, Kerner, Traminec, Rumeni Muškat and Šipon. They are especially proud of their Chardonnay, Sauvignon, Modri Pinot and Sivi Pinot.
The Kupljen wine cellar can still offer you 2002 Chardonnay; Modri Pinot (also barrique), from 2001, 2002 and 2003; Renski Rizling from 2001, 2002 and 2003; and their speciality — the archive of the first national wine bank.

Mix of wines on offer

30% Chardonnay (dry, *Pozna Trgatev*, *Izbor*, *Suhi Jagodni Izbor*, barrique), 30% Modri Pinot (dry, barrique), 20% Renski Rizling (dry and predicates), 10% Sauvignon (dry) and Traminec, Rumeni Muškat and Šipon.

Awards
They attend tastings in Ljubljana and Paris.

Culinary recommendations
At the Taverna inn they serve home cooking with their high-quality wines.

2002 Renski Rizling

12% vol., dry, ★★

This crystal-clear, pale yellow wine with mild green notes simply seems to chase the light. The first impression is of the fresh aroma of grass and wild flowers. Fruits such as lemons and green apples with a tang of peaches follow on the nose; they suggest both sternness and freshness, interesting characteristics in a Riesling. The wine is also lively on the palate: the aromas assert themselves and show their fresh side. A tasty acidity comes out, playing its part in the full body, and contributes to the fresh character of this dry wine. The palate is fully matched by the lingering finish: a sweet farewell.
Recommended dishes: Meat preserved in *tunka*, dishes with sauerkraut (such as sarma), grilled sausage with cabbage.

LJUTOMER-ORMOŽ WINE-GROWING DISTRICT

2002 Renski Rizling   2001 Modri Burgundec (Modri Pinot)

2001 Modri Burgundec (Modri Pinot)

12% vol., dry, ★★★

The ruby red wine with cherry tones is medium-coloured. Gradually the mature bouquet sets in, redolent of black cherries, mulberries, blackcurrants, leather and coffee. Similar aromas come through on the palate, enriched with vanilla and scents of roasting. The light and straightforward flavour reflects the medium structure. The wine's herbaceous character (oak) is barely detectable and gives it its backbone. The tannins do not seem fully softened, and together with a half-sensed acidity contribute to the wine's vivacity. After swallowing one continues to sense that the essential character of the variety has been well-preserved. Here is proof that it is possible to produce mature Modri Pinot wines of high quality.

Recommended dishes: Smoked meat, steak tartare, shoulder of lamb with onions, stuffed hare with broad beans.

LJUTOMER-ORMOŽ WINE-GROWING DISTRICT

Vinska Klet Püklavec

Franček Püklavec, Zasavci 21, si-2275 Miklavž pri Ormožu
Phone: +386 (0) 31 549 311, (0) 31 868 908, (0) 41 916 543, Fax: +386 (0) 2 719 65 00,
Email: puklavec@volja.net
Website: http://www.slovino.com/puklavec/index.html

Wine selling ❦ Wine tasting
Production of wine and food ❦ Wine cellar tours
Wine route ❦ Accommodation
❦ Sales material

The Püklavec family have worked on their eight hectares of vineyards since 1975, and have produced wine in labelled bottles since 1985. Among the varieties grown, Chardonnay, Renski Rizling, Sauvignon and Muškat Ottonel do particularly well. The terroir is especially well-suited to Šipon, which is the best crop in this wine county. Some of the finest vintages are still available: 1996 Sivi Pinot, 2001 Šipon *Ledeno Vino* and 2002 Šipon *Jagodni Izbor*.

Wines on offer

Šipon (barrique, *Izbor*, *Jagodni Izbor*, *Ledeno Vino*), Chardonnay (*Pozna Trgatev* and *Izbor*), Renski Rizling (also *Pozna Trgatev*), Sauvignon, Sivi Pinot (also *Izbor*), Muškat Ottonel, Modri Pinot, Traminec, Rizvanec and Laški Rizling *Izbor*.

Awards

Since 1994 Gornja Radgona has awarded the Püklavec wines 2 grand gold medals, 21 gold medals and 2 silvers, as well as 2 championship titles. In 1998 they received the gold medal at the Vino forum tasting.

Culinary recommendations

Roast turkey from the baker's oven accompanied by a glass of Šipon or Sauvignon is sure to stimulate your senses. Try the, semi-dry Renski Rizling *Pozna Trgatev* with St Martin's goose.

2003 Muškat Ottonel

11.49% vol., ★

This wine is pale yellow in colour with soft green notes. The wonderful Muscat aroma, medium-intense and candid, is rich with the fragrance of flowers (acacia, lime, carnations), fruit (lemons, exotic fruit), and spices (anise), and is soft and likeable — a romantic feast. Softness is the signature of this wine, and continues on the tongue, signifying its slender body. The relationship between the residual sugar and mild acidity is interesting, not fully succeeding in freshening the palate. The finish is gentle and pleasant, but fades rapidly. This wine is currently at its best and will remain appealing for several years.
Recommended dishes: Buckwheat flat cake, mushroom soup, light desserts and fruit salads with pears or peaches.

LJUTOMER-ORMOŽ WINE-GROWING DISTRICT

2003 Muškat Ottonel

LJUTOMER-ORMOŽ WINE-GROWING DISTRICT

Vino Plemenič

Miran Plemenič, Kog 93, si-2276 Kog, Phone: +386 (0) 2 719 63 86, (0) 41 896 876
Email: matej.plemenic@s5.net

Wine selling ❧ Wine tasting
❧ Wine route

Wines on offer

Renski Rizling, Muškat Ottonel, Chardonnay, Šipon, Laški Rizling, Beli Pinot, Zeleni Silvanec and blend.

Vinogradništvo Janežič Vinski Vrh

Gustek Janežič, Veliki Brebrovnik 5, si-2275 Miklavž pri Ormožu
Phone: +386 (0) 2 719 61 17, (0) 41 316 077

Wine selling ❧ Wine tasting
Wine cellar tours ❧ Wine route
❧ Sales material

Mix of wines on offer

30% open blend (Šipon and Laški Rizling), 28% litre bottles of Laški Rizling and Šipon, 8% Chardonnay, 7% Sauvignon, 5% Šipon, 7% Laški Rizling *Pozna Trgatev*, 7% Šipon *Pozna Trgatev*, 6% Chardonnay *Izbor* and 2% Laški Rizling and Šipon *Ledeno Vino*.

Jožefa Zabavnik

Jastrebci 39, si-2276 Kog, Phone: +386 (0) 2 719 63 00, (0) 2 740 10 96, (0) 41 341 918
Email: markozabavnik@hotmail.com

Wine selling ❧ Wine tasting

Wines on offer

Chardonnay, Laški Rizling and Šipon.

Franc Žličar

Vrtna 13, si-9240 Ljutomer, Phone: +386 (0) 2 581 11 74

❧ Wine tasting for announced groups

Mix of wines on offer

70% Renski Rizling, 15% Sivi Pinot, 5% Sivi Pinot *Izbor*, 5% Laški Rizling and 5% Šipon.

Haloze
Wine-Growing District
Podravje Wine-Growing Region

HALOZE WINE-GROWING DISTRICT

Anton Skaza

Vide Alič 41, si-2250 Ptuj
Phone: +386 (0) 2 773 38 51, (0) 41 403 710

Wine selling ❧ Wine tasting
❧ Wine cellar tours

In 1997 Skaza entered the wine-growing trade and began labelling his own wine; his vineyards comprise the same varieties as the wine he offers. He is particularly happy with his Renski Rizling, which he grows in three different variants. Renski Rizling and Sivi Pinot are his wines of choice and he plans to continue offering them for some time to come.

Mix of wines on offer
43% Renski Rizling, 20% Sivi Pinot, 17% Chardonnay, 7% Rumeni Muškat, 7% Sauvignon and 6% Traminec.

Awards
Although he has been in this area of expertise for only a decade, he has already won six gold medals in Gornja Radgona, a track record that speaks for itself.

2001 Renski Rizling
10.8% vol., sweet, ★★★

The bright yellow, golden colour of this wine immediately seduces with its soft nuances, and the noiseless flow of the wine pouring into the glass is proof of its nobility. The first impression on the nose is of meadow flowers and camomile, followed by fragrances of dried apricots, honey and noble, mature grapes. This explosion of aromas continues on the tongue, where the fresh and vivid nature of the Riesling palate comes into its own. Grape sugar on the one hand and fresh acidity on the other work in harmony to juicy effect. This wine's excellence is proof enough that no other special-quality wines can compete when it is produced from grapes with noble rot. Its interesting personality is probably a result of the terrain and soil specific to the vineyards' location. The wine's complexity and the length of the sweet, spicy bouquet certainly won't leave you indifferent.
Recommended dishes: Goose liver pâté, walnut *gibanica* from Haloze, pancakes filled with walnuts, stuffed pears.

HALOZE WINE-GROWING DISTRICT

2001 Renski Rizling

HALOZE WINE-GROWING DISTRICT

Jožef Šmigoc

Repišče 48a, si-2285 Zgornji Leskovec
Phone: +386 (0) 41 704 447, Fax: +386 (0) 2 763 04 70

🍇 Wine selling

Jožef Šmigoc has been in the wine-growing industry for twenty years now, and in 1998 he started to label his own wines. His vineyards are planted with four different kinds of grape, among which Laški Rizling thrives to its maximum potential, given the conditions of the rough terrain. The predicates are expected to do best in the future.

Mix of wines on offer
80% blend and 20% predicates (Laški Rizling, Šipon, Sauvignon and Chardonnay).

Awards
He regularly takes part in wine tastings in Gornja Radgona, where he has won nine gold medals over the last four years.

Culinary recommendations
His wines are excellent when accompanied by meat preserved in *tunka*, home-baked *gibanica* or home-baked bread, as well as by cheese and smoked meats.

2000 Laški Rizling *Izbor*
12,87 vol.%., semi-sweet, ★★

The Laški Rizling has a glittering yellow colour with soft green notes and an intense nose of over-ripe grapes. It is accompanied by a wide range of scents: white and yellow fruits, toasted caramel and honey.
The palate is full and complete. The body is generously structured, with the relationship of individual flavours creating a colourful balance.
The length of the bouquet after swallowing is lovely, with a pleasant aftertaste.
Recommended dishes: Home-baked bread, home-baked *gibanica*, pancakes with walnuts.

HALOZE WINE-GROWING DISTRICT

2000 Laški Rizling *Izbor*

HALOZE WINE-GROWING DISTRICT

Turčan

Konrad Janžekovič, Turški vrh 65, si-2283 Zavrč
Phone: +386 (0) 2 766 00 81, (0) 2 761 12 61, (0) 2 778 24 61, (0) 31 638 801, (0) 41 638 801
Fax: +386 (0) 2 766 00 81
Email: turcan@siol.net
Website: www.vinoturcan-janzekovic.si

Wine selling Wine tasting
Wine cellar tours Wine route
Sales material Production of wine and food for announced groups

In 1972, the first thousand vines were planted on the steep slopes of Turški Vrh. To begin with wine growing was just a hobby, but today this area is covered by more than seventeen hectares of vineyards, planted with more than a dozen grape varieties. They have great hopes here for the future of Laški Rizling, predicates, Sauvignon, Renski Rizling, Traminec and Sivi Pinot. They believe that the high-quality semi-dry varieties, ecologically cultivated and produced and distinguished by their harmonious character, are the wines of the future. Some of the finest vintages are still available: 2001 Sivi Pinot, 2002 Renski Rizling, 2002 Sauvignon and 2002 Rumeni Muškat.

Mix of wines on offer

45% blend, 10% predicates, 7% Rumeni Muškat, 7% Sauvignon, 6% Laški Rizling, 5% Renski Rizling, 4% Traminec, 4% Chardonnay, 3% Rizvanec, 2% Muškat Ottonel, 2% Beli Pinot, 3% Sivi Pinot and 2% Modri Pinot.

Awards

Their wines have been awarded a silver medal in Ljubljana, whilst in Gornja Radgona they have received grand gold medals and the title of variety champion.

2002 Sauvignon

13.0% vol., semi-sweet, ★★

A bright yellow, soft golden colour, with abundant, finely shaped legs. The nose is subtle but beautifully structured. Pear and peach aromas predominate, expressing the wine's noble and mature character. There are smoky nuances - a feature characteristic of Sauvignons grown in good locations on the favourable soils that are stimulating for this variety. It delivers a rich and complex palate. A vivacious acidity dominates despite the residual sugar and the powerful alcohol, making the wine very lively and fresh.
Recommended dishes: Tuna, dishes with asparagus and sweetish gravy, local-style Haloze, walnut *gibanica*.

HALOZE WINE-GROWING DISTRICT

2002 SAUVIGNON

HALOZE WINE-GROWING DISTRICT

Jurij Cvitanič

Gorišnica 62, si-2272 Gorišnica, Phone: +386 (0) 2 740 83 34, (0) 2 740 83 35, (0) 41 710 257
Email: jurij.cvitanic@email.si

Wine selling ❧ Wine tasting
Wine cellar tours ❧ Wine route
❧ Sales material

Mix of wines on offer

50% Šipon (also predicates), 35% Renski Rizling (predicates), 5% Laški Rizling (predicates), 5% Muškat Ottonel and 5% Traminec.

Viktorin

Viktor Šprajc, Zamušani 70, si-2272 Gorišnica
Phone: +386 (0) 2 713 01 40, (0) 41 920 486

Wine selling ❧ Wine tasting
Production of wine and food ❧ Wine cellar tours

Mix of wines on offer

30% 'Kručan' blend, 30% 'Viktorin' sparkling wine, 5% Sauvignon, 5% Rumeni Muškat, 5% Renski Rizling and 5% Traminec.

Vinoreja Bezjak Haloze

Dušan Bezjak, Gorišnica 54/58, si-2272 Gorišnica
Phone: +386 (0) 2 740 86 40, (0) 40 220 356
Email: d.bezjak@siol.net, Website: www.slovino.com

Wine selling ❧ Wine tasting
❧ Wine cellar tours

Wines on offer

Blend, Sauvignon, Renski Rizling, Laški Rizling.

Prekmurje Wine-Growing District

PODRAVJE WINE-GROWING REGION

PREKMURJE WINE-GROWING DISTRICT

Matija Gjerkeš

Fikšinci 49, si-9262 Rogašovci
Phone: +386 (0) 2 558 86 20, (0) 2 720 02 05, (0) 41 632 657, (0) 41 623 125, Fax: +386 (0) 2 720 02 03
Email: info@vina-gjerkes.com
Website: www.vina-gjerkes.com

Wine selling ❧ Wine tasting for announced groups
Wine cellar tours for announced groups ❧ Wine route
Sales material ❧ Guided tours of Prekmurje
and the Goričko wine trail. Wine
tasting in our cellar is included.

In 1992 they first went into the business of viticulture and wine trading, and two years later they labelled their own wines and put them on the open market. They mostly grow Chardonnay and Laški Rizling, while Renski Rizling, Sivi Pinot and Rumeni Muškat also feature but in small quantities. They produce high-quality wines.

Mix of wines on offer

30% Chardonnay, 25% Laški Rizling, 17% Renski Rizling, 13% Sivi Pinot and 15% Rumeni Muškat.

Awards

At the Gornja Radgona fair they have been awarded four gold medals and several silvers.

2002 Renski Rizling

10% vol., semi-sweet, ★

The bright yellow colour, with green undertones and a slight sparkling quality when poured, foretell a liveliness on nose and palate. The fresh bouquet of lemon, green apples and lime trees is very pleasing. This fresh character, typical of the young Riesling, continues on the palate and the grape variety is distinctly recognizable. The structure of the wine is light and gentle, making it a very pleasant drink. The finish is similarly soft and pleasurable.
Recommended dishes: Aperitif, dishes with white meat sauces, apricot cake.

PREKMURJE WINE-GROWING DISTRICT

2002 Renski Rizling

PREKMURJE WINE-GROWING DISTRICT

Drago Apatič

Pot ob Črncu 3a, si-9231 Beltinci, Phone: +386 (0) 2 541 21 37

❦ Wine selling

Wines on offer
Laški Rizling, Renski Rizling and Šipon.

Jožef Balažek

Velika Polana 189b, si-9225 Velika Polana
Phone: +386 (0) 2 571 17 35, (0) 41 357 451

❦ Wine tasting for announced groups

Wines on offer
Laški Rizling, Renski Rizling and blend.

Štefan Barbarič

Ulica Štefana Kovača 98, si-9224 Turnišče, Phone: +386 (0) 2 572 10 64
Email: boris.barbaric@email.si

Wine selling ❦ Wine tasting for announced groups

Wines on offer
Laški Rizling, Chardonnay and Traminec.

Ludvik Cuk

Kmetija z nastanitvijo "Hiša vin", Lendavske gorice 248, si-9220 Lendava
Phone: +386 (0) 2 577 12 86, (0) 41 611 681, Fax: +386 (0) 2 577 12 86
Email: eva.c@email.si

Wine selling ❦ Wine tasting
Production of wine and food ❦ Wine cellar tours
Wine route ❦ Accommodation
❦ Sales material

Mix of wines on offer
41% 'Hadikova Kri' blend, 13% Beli Pinot, 13% Sauvignon, 10,5% Renski Rizling, 10,5% Traminec, 9% Laški Rizling and 3% Rumeni Muškat.

PREKMURJE WINE-GROWING DISTRICT

Janez Erniša

Suhi vrh 103, si-9208 Fokovci. Phone: +386 (0) 2 548 18 59

Wine selling ❦ Wine tasting
Production of wine and food ❦ Wine cellar tours for announced groups
Wine route ❦ Accommodation
❦ Sales material

Wines on offer

Chardonnay, Renski Rizling, Kerner, Traminec, Zweigelt, Modri Pinot, Modra Frankinja and Zeleni Silvanec.

Miran Erniša

Suhi vrh 131, si-9208 Fokovci, Phone: +386 (0) 2 548 12 47, (0) 2 538 15 50, (0) 31 621 111

Wine selling ❦ Wine tasting
Production of wine and food ❦ Wine cellar tours
Wine route ❦ Sales material

Wines on offer

Blend, Renski Rizling *Jagodni Izbor*, Chardonnay *Pozna Trgatev*, Sauvignon *Izbor*, Kerner (*Pozna Trgatev* and *Jagodni Izbor*) and Laški Rizling *Jagodni Izbor*.

Franc Flegar

Gerlinci 15, si-9261 Cankova, Phone: +386 (0) 2 540 10 36

Wine selling ❦ Wine tasting for announced groups
Wine route ❦ Sales material
Wine cellar tours for announced groups ❦ Production of wine and food for announced groups

Mix of wines on offer

35% blend, 30% Chardonnay, 20% Laški Rizling and 15% Rizvanec.

Jožef Gjuran

Kidričeva 29, si-9220 Lendava, Phone: +386 (0) 2 575 12 18, (0) 41 208 215
Email: josu.gjuran@email.si

❦ Wine route

Mix of wines on offer

72% Laški Rizling, 25% Sauvignon and 3% Traminec.

PREKMURJE WINE-GROWING DISTRICT

Grajska klet Lendava

Kmetijsko gospodarstvo Lendava, Kolodvorska ulica 1, si-9220 Lendava
Phone: +386 (0) 2 577 64 30, (0) 2 574 18 70, Fax: +386 (0) 2 577 64 36

Wine selling ❧ Wine tasting
Wine cellar tours ❧ Wine route
❧ Sales material

The company has been in the wine trade since 1997. Their leading product is 'Lendavčan', which is made from high-quality grape varieties from other suppliers. It is a blended, dry white wine, made from Laški Rizling, Chardonnay, Renski Rizling, Beli Pinot and Sivi Pinot. The rest of the wines on offer are semi-dry: Chardonnay, Renski Rizling, Laški Rizling and Sivi Pinot. Some of their finest vintages are still available: 1997 Laški Rizling archive wine, 2001 Renski Rizling, 2001 Chardonnay and 2002 Sivi Pinot.

Mix of wines on offer

40% 'Lendavčan' blend, 10% Laški Rizling, 20% Chardonnay,
20% Renski Rizling and 10% Sivi Pinot.

Culinary recommendations

Bograć is best when served with 'Lendavčan', *tunka* meats are good with 1997 Laški Rizling, and Prekmurska *gibanica* tastes its sweetest when accompanied by 2001 Renski Rizling.

1997 Laški Rizling

10.8% vol., semi-dry, ★

A crystal-clear wine of slightly yellow hue. The mature fragrance is reminiscent of dried white fruit and flowers. The nose is further intensified by swilling the wine in the glass, and there is an accentuated fruitiness. The first mouthful presages complexity, and the wine's medium structure yields a fullness beyond all expectations: the palate is beautifully harmonious. Despite the vintage — the wine is now in its seventh year — it has kept its freshness, giving continued pleasure even after swallowing.
Recommended dishes: *Tunka*-preserved meat, chicken or veal ragout.

PREKMURJE WINE-GROWING DISTRICT

1997 Laški Rizling

PREKMURJE WINE-GROWING DISTRICT

Janez in Nada Grabar

Selo 34, si-9207 Prosenjakovci, Phone: +386 (0) 2 544 14 33

Wine selling ❧ Wine tasting for announced groups
Wine route ❧ Production of wine and food for announced groups

Mix of wines on offer

45% blend, 20% Chardonnay, 15% Modra Frankinja, 15% Laški Rizling and 5% Rizvanec.

Peter Gruškovnjak

Na Kamni 8, si-9231 Beltinci, Phone: +386 (0) 2 542 18 95

❧ Wine selling

Mix of wines on offer

20% Renski Rizling, 30% Chardonnay and 50% blend.

Hani

Jožef Hančik, Dobrovnik 238, si-9223 Dobrovnik
Phone: +386 (0) 2 579 91 03, Fax: +386 (0) 2 579 91 04

Wine selling ❧ Wine tasting for announced groups
Production of wine and food ❧ Wine cellar tours for announced groups
Wine route ❧ Sales material

Wines on offer

Blend, Renski Rizling, Renski Rizling *Ledeno Vino*, Laški Rizling, Beli Pinot, Beli Pinot (*Pozna Trgatev* and *Izbor*), Sivi Pinot and Rumeni Muškat.

Martin Jerič

Ulica Štefana Kovača 4, Rakičan, si-9000 Murska Sobota
Phone: +386 (0) 2 527 17 49, (0) 41 603 698, (0) 31 703 612

Wine selling ❧ Wine tasting
Wine cellar tours ❧ Wine route

Mix of wines on offer

30% Chardonnay, 12% Renski Rizling, 6% Sivi Pinot, 4% Beli Pinot, 5% Traminec, 5% Modra Frankinja, 15% Laški Rizling and 23% blend.

PREKMURJE WINE-GROWING DISTRICT

Franc Jošar

Prosenjakovci 19, si-9207 Prosenjakovci, Phone: +386 (0) 2 544 10 18

Wine selling ❧ Wine tasting
Production of wine and food ❧ Wine cellar tours
❧ Wine route

Mix of wines on offer

30% Laški Rizling, 25% white blend, 25% Modri Pinot, 15% Chardonnay and 5% Rizvanec.

Vladimir Kelenc

Lendavske gorice 325e, si-9220 Lendava, Phone: +386 (0) 2 577 12 92, (0) 41 580 223

Wine selling ❧ Wine cellar tours
❧ Wine route

Mix of wines on offer

16% Laški Rizling, 50% blend, 12% Renski Rizling, 5% Renski Rizling *Pozna Trgatev*, 12% Sauvignon and 5% Sauvignon *Pozna Trgatev*.

Štefan Kepe

Kratka ulica 6, Gaberje, si-9220 Lendava
Phone: +386 (0) 2 574 18 07, Email: stefan.kepe@varstroj.si

❧ Wine selling

Mix of wines on offer

50% Renski Rizling, 25% Laški Rizling and 25% Beli Pinot.

Štefan Kulčar

Cankarjeva 5, si-9220 Lendava, Phone: +386 (0) 2 575 17 64

Wine selling ❧ Wine tasting for announced groups

Wines on offer

60% Laški Rizling, 10% Chardonnay, 10% Renski Rizling, 10% Sauvignon and 10% Šipon.

PREKMURJE WINE-GROWING DISTRICT

Ernest Novak

Vaneča 15c, si-9201 Puconci
Phone: +386 (0) 2 526 17 52, (0) 2 545 15 70, (0) 31 703 607
Email: ernest.novak@siol.net

Wine selling Wine tasting for announced groups
Wine cellar tours for announced groups

Novak has been in the wine-growing trade for thirty years. His vineyards contain a whole spectrum of varieties, from which he produces high-quality wines. His main product is the quality wine 'Goričanec', but the wines he offers have been extended by predicates of Laški Rizling and Sauvignon. Novak prides himself on his special-quality wines which, in fifteen years, have exceeded a formidable fifty in number. Laški Rizling *Ledeno Vino* from the 1999 vintage, 2001 Renski Rizling *Ledeno Vino*, 2003 Sauvignon and 2003 Laški Rizling are just a few examples.

Mix of wines on offer

70% 'Goričanec' blend, 10% Sauvignon, 5% Chardonnay, 5% Renski Rizling, 5% Sivi Pinot and 5% Laški Rizling, Sauvignon *Izbor*, Chardonnay *Izbor*, Laški Rizling *Ledeno Vino* and Renski Rizling *Ledeno Vino*.

Awards

His wines have been awarded four variety champion titles, seventeen grand gold medals, eighteen gold medals and four silvers in Gornja Radgona, Ljubljana, Ptuj and Maribor.

Culinary recommendations

Bograč will go well with 'Goričanec', while Sauvignon or Chardonnay are perfect with Prekmurska *gibanica*.

1999 Laški Rizling *Ledeno Vino*

10.16% vol., sweet, ★★★

The wine is a sunny yellow colour, already imbued with a ripe amber hue, and pours noiselessly, immediately commanding respect and attention. The wine looks and smells mature; on the nose it is reminiscent of over-ripe grapes, dried white fruit, honey and dried flowers. The nose is intensified by swilling the wine in the glass, though without acquiring further complexity. The character is open. The rich variety of aromas continues to be delivered on the palate, where the balance between them and the residual sugar, which wants to dominate, is nicely maintained. The strong structure of the wine is improved still further after a period of maturing, when the palate and aroma will be developed to perfection. The persistence of the bouquet in the finish confirms the high potential of this wine.
Recommended dishes: Liver pâté, Prekmurska *gibanica*, apricot cake.

PREKMURJE WINE-GROWING DISTRICT

1999 Laški Rizling *Ledeno Vino*

PREKMURJE WINE-GROWING DISTRICT

Bela Küzmič

Lendavska 37a, si-9000 Murska Sobota, Phone: +386 (0) 2 522 15 55, (0) 41 265 107

Wine selling ❧ Wine tasting for announced groups
❧ Wine route

Mix of wines on offer

55% Laški Rizling, 25% Chardonnay and 20% Sauvignon.

Marijan Levačič

Tomšičeva 3, si-9220 Lendava, Phone: +386 (0) 2 575 14 45, (0) 41 773 581

Wine selling ❧ Wine tasting
Wine cellar tours for announced groups ❧ Wine route
❧ Production of wine and food for announced groups

Mix of wines on offer

60% high-quality wines and 40% predicates (Beli Pinot, Sivi Pinot and Sauvignon).

Ivan Lunežnik

Mladinska 34, si-9000 Murska Sobota, Phone: +386 (0) 2 527 16 73

Wine selling ❧ Wine tasting
Wine cellar tours ❧ Wine route
❧ Sales material

Mix of wines on offer

48% blend (Laški Rizling, Kraljevina, Sauvignon), 32% Chardonnay and 20% Modra Frankinja.

Stanko Nerad

Žižki 50a, si-9232 Črenšovci, Phone: +386 (0) 2 570 11 62

❧ Wine tasting

Wines on offer

Blend, Chardonnay, Kerner and Muškat Ottonel.

PREKMURJE WINE-GROWING DISTRICT

Ivan Panker

Bratonci 93, si-9231 Beltinci, Phone: +386 (0) 2 541 23 55

Wine selling ❧ Wine tasting

Wines on offer

Laški Rizling, Šipon, Chardonnay, Rumeni Muškat and Sauvignon.

Alojz Režonja

Prešernova 42a, si-9000 Murska Sobota, Phone: +386 (0) 41 617 672

Wine selling ❧ Wine tasting
Wine cellar tours ❧ Wine route
❧ Sales material

Mix of wines on offer

50% Laški Rizling, 25% Renski Rizling and 25% Sauvignon.

Štefan Rožman

Dolgovaške gorice 131, si-9220 Lendava
Phone: +386 (0) 2 575 19 56, (0) 41 804 584, Fax: +386 (0) 2 575 19 56
Email: rozmanwine@siol.net
Website: www.slovino.com/rozmanwine

Wine selling ❧ Wine tasting
Wine cellar tours ❧ Wine route
Accommodation ❧ Sales material
❧ Production of wine and food for announced groups

Wines on offer

Laški Rizling (*Pozna Trgatev, Izbor, Suhi Jagodni Izbor*), Chardonnay, Renski Rizling *Pozna Trgatev* and Sivi Pinot.

Jože Šumak

Vaneča 84a,, si-9201 Puconci, Phone: +386 (0) 2 545 15 73, (0) 41 237 241

Wine selling ❧ Wine tasting for announced groups
Wine cellar tours ❧ Wine route
❧ Sales material

Mix of wines on offer

70% 'Goričanec' blend, 10% Renski Rizling, 6% Chardonnay, 6% Sauvignon, 4% Muškat Ottonel and 4% Chardonnay (predicates).

PREKMURJE WINE-GROWING DISTRICT

Mihael Tremel

Bokrači 28, si-9201 Puconci, Phone: +386 (0) 2 545 10 17

Wine selling ❦ Wine tasting
Production of wine and food ❦ Wine cellar tours
Wine route ❦ Accommodation
Sales material ❦ Tourist farm

Wines on offer

Modra Frankinja and 'Goričanec' white blend.

Sigfrid – Zmago Urisk

Dobrovnik 204b, si-9223 Dobrovnik
Phone: +386 (0) 2 579 90 26, (0) 41 411 714, Fax: +386 (0) 2 579 90 27
Email: urisk@siol.net

Wine selling ❦ Wine tasting
Wine cellar tours ❦ Wine route
❦ Sales material

Wines on offer

Laški Rizling (also *Pozna Trgatev, Izbor, Jagodni Izbor, Ledeno Vino*), Šipon, Beli Pinot (*Pozna Trgatev, Izbor, Jagodni Izbor, Ledeno Vino*) and Modri Pinot (*Pozna Trgatev, Izbor, Jagodni Izbor, Suhi Jagodni Izbor, Ledeno Vino*).

Vinarstvo Kisilak

Liškova 55, Černelavci, si-9000 Murska Sobota
Phone: +386 (0) 2 534 17 46, (0) 31 201 963
Email: akisilak@volja.net

Wine selling ❦ Wine tasting for announced groups
❦ Wine cellar tours for announced groups

Wines on offer

Chardonnay, Renski Rizling, Sauvignon, Laški Rizling, Sivi Pinot, Modri Pinot, Modra Frankinja, Šipon and Muškat Ottonel.

Vinotoč Lipič — Passero

Nada Passero, Tešanovci 17a, si-9226 Moravske Toplice
Phone: +386 (0) 2 548 12 36, (0) 41 531 577

Wine selling ❦ Wine tasting
Production of wine and food ❦ Wine cellar tours
Wine route ❦ Sales material

Mix of wines on offer

Blend, Renski Rizling, Laški Rizling, Chardonnay, Sivi Pinot and Sauvignon.

Šmarje-Virštanj Wine-Growing District
Podravje Wine-Growing Region

ŠMARJE-VIRŠTANJ WINE-GROWING DISTRICT

Amon

Stanislav in Greta Amon, Olimje 24, si-3254 Podčetrtek
Phone: +386 (0) 3 818 24 80, Fax: +386 (0) 3 582 90 26
Email: info@amon.si, Website: www.amon.si

Wine selling ❧ Wine tasting
Production of wine and food ❧ Wine cellar tours
Wine route ❧ Sales material
❧ Geological tours, harvest, lectures

They have been in wine growing and the wine trade since 1970. Their vineyards are planted with both white and red varieties. They produce high-quality wines, blends and predicates, marketed under the brand name 'Amon'. Their best-sellers are Sauvignon and Modra Frankinja. These vintages continue to be available until stock-clearance: 2000 Modra Frankinja *Pozna Trgatev*, 1996 and 1998 Sauvignon, 1994 Laški Rizling and 1994 Renski Rizling *Pozna Trgatev*.

Wines on offer

Sauvignon, Chardonnay, Renski Rizling, Beli Pinot, Sivi Pinot, Laški Rizling, Modra Frankinja, Gamay, white and red 'Virštanjčan' blend.

Awards

They have received prizes in Ljubljana, Gornja Radgona, Zagreb, Verona, Graz and Paris.

Culinary recommendations

Sauvignon is good as an accompaniment to trout with almonds, roast duck in Modra Frankinja sauce goes well with Modra Frankinja, venison fillet is served with Gamay. 'Virštanjčan' white blend is excellent when accompanied by styrian sour soup and so is Sauvignon combined with tarragon *potica*.

2003 Sauvignon

11.5% vol., semi-dry, ★

A pale yellow colour with a slight touch of green is an indicator of the wine's youth. It has a well-preserved, fresh aroma, much appreciated by lovers of young Sauvignon. The grapes were definitely picked before full maturity and the alcohol fermentation was kept at low temperatures in order to produce a fresh, flowers-and-fruit quality: on the nose we get jasmine, elder blossom, acacia, currants and grapefruit. The character of the variety comes through on the palate too, where the aroma is still very distinct. The residual sugar is very obvious, reaffirming the style of the wine, and merges nicely with the fundamental characteristics of the grape variety. The body seems light and slim, an impression that remains after swallowing.
Recommended dishes: Aperitif, trout with almonds, dishes with asparagus, tarragon *potica*.

ŠMARJE-VIRŠTANJ WINE-GROWING DISTRICT

2003 SAUVIGNON

ŠMARJE-VIRŠTANJ WINE-GROWING DISTRICT

Urbajs

Aci Urbajs, Rifnik 44b, si-3230 Šentjur
Phone: +386 (0) 3 749 23 73, (0) 41 786 428
Email: aci.urbajs@siol.net, Website: www.info-urbajs.si

Wine cellar tours for announced groups ❧ Sales material
❧ Visit to Rifnik, a site of archaeological interest, and to the restored farmhouses, granaries and cellars

Aci Urbajs has been in the wine industry since 1987; he decided to take up a biodynamic approach to vineyard cultivation and cellaring. has 1,000 Chardonnay, Kerner and Sivi Pinot vines, and a further 800 Laški Rizling, Modri Pinot and Renski Rizling. He produces wines of special quality, various predicates from organic grapes, and organic wines. Neither the must nor the wine is treated using artificial oenological methods; the wine matures on yeast for a period of a year. It does not get sulphurated until it is bottled. He is the proud owner of a descendant from the oldest Slovenian grapevine. Still available: 1997 Kerner *Pozna Trgatev* archived, 1997 Chardonnay *Pozna Trgatev*, 2000 Chardonnay *Izbor*, 2000 Kerner *Pozna Trgatev* and 2000 Sivi Pinot.

Wines on offer

Kerner (also archive wine and *Pozna Trgatev*), Chardonnay (also archive wine and *Izbor*), Sivi Pinot and Laški Rizling.

Awards

Urbajs has been awarded two silver medals from Ljubljana and a bronze medal from the Chardonnay du Monde wine tasting.

Culinary recommendations

The house speciality is dandelion with boiled potatoes, served with a dressing of homemade apple vinegar with a dash of water, and cold-pressed organic olive and pumpkin oil. It is best accompanied by dry wines.

ŠMARJE-VIRŠTANJ WINE-GROWING DISTRICT

2000 KERNER *Pozna Trgatev*

12.3% vol., semi-sweet, ★★★

A bright yellow colour with slight nuances of green and the noiselessness with which it can be poured are one's first impressions of this high-quality wine. The ripe nose is different from what we are used to in most Slovenian late-harvest wines. It is complex and broad-ranging: plant fragrances keep to the fore, redolent of dried mown grass, green beans, spices and tarragon. Perhaps this is a result of organic cultivation techniques. This plant-like character dominates on the palate as well, and there is also a vague smell of smoke or something burnt. The subtle sugar is just perceptible, as it should be in all good semi-dry wines. The bouquet lingers even after swallowing, and we are left with a feeling of sheer pleasure at new discovery: always welcome in a sea of uniformity.
Recommended dishes: Mushroom soup, dishes with asparagus, tarragon *potica*.

ŠMARJE-VIRŠTANJ WINE-GROWING DISTRICT

Jožef Čebular

Sladka gora 27, SI-3240 Šmarje pri Jelšah
Phone: +386 (0) 3 582 42 34, (0) 3 582 44 18, (0) 41 709 163, Fax: +386 (0) 3 582 42 34

Wine selling ❧ Wine tasting
Production of wine and food ❧ Wine cellar tours
Wine route ❧ Accommodation
❧ Sales material

Mix of wines on offer

10% Laški Rizling, 7% Sauvignon, 7% Kerner, 6% Renski Rizling, 6% Traminec, 6% Šipon, 6% Chardonnay, 6% Rumeni Muškat, 6% Sivi Pinot, 3% Zeleni Silvanec, 1% Kraljevina, 36% 'Sladkogorčan' blend and predicates Laški Rizling, Sauvignon and Chardonnay.

Franc Janković

Aškerčeva 5, SI-3250 Rogaška Slatina, Phone: +386 (0) 3 819 23 53, (0) 31 650 156,
Fax: +386 (0) 3 819 23 54, Email: franc.jankovic@siol.net

Wine selling ❧ Wine tasting
Wine route ❧ Sampling of *grenčica* (a bitter herb liqueur)

Mix of wines on offer

35% Modri Pinot, 30% Chardonnay, 25% Renski Rizling
and 10% Modra Frankinja.

Šolski Center Šentjur

Cesta na Kmetijsko šolo 9, SI-3230 Šentjur
Phone: +386 (0) 3 746 29 00, Fax: +386 (0) 3 746 29 20
Email: solski.center-sentjur@guest.arnes.si, Website: www2.arnes.si/~sscekg1s

❧ Wine selling

Mix of wines on offer

40% Sauvignon, 15% Sivi Pinot, 5% Rumeni Muškat
and 40% white blend.

Vjekoslav Kralj

Črešnjevec ob Bistrici 4, SI-3256 Bistrica ob Sotli, Phone: +386 (0) 3 580 41 11, (0) 51 307 166
Email: vino_kralj@email.si, joze_kralj@hotmail.com

Wine selling ❧ Wine tasting for announced groups
Wine cellar tours for announced groups ❧ Production of wine and food for announced groups

Wines on offer

White blend, red blend, Laški Rizling, Sauvignon, Modra Frankinja, Renski Rizling, Chardonnay, Beli Pinot, Sivi Pinot, Zeleni Silvanec and Modri Pinot.

ŠMARJE-VIRŠTANJ WINE-GROWING DISTRICT

KLET IMENO

Kmetijska zadruga Šmarje z.o.o., Obrtniška ulica 2, si-3240 Šmarje pri Jelšah
Phone: +386 (0) 3 818 18 00, (0) 3 582 91 38. Fax: +386 (0) 3 818 18 42
Email: tajnistvo@kz-smarje.si

Wine selling ❧ Wine tasting
Wine cellar tours for announced groups ❧ Sales material

MIX OF WINES ON OFFER

70% white varieties (Chardonnay, Sauvignon, Renski Rizling, Laški Rizling) and 30% red varieties (Žametna Črnina and Modra Frankinja).

KLET KREGAR

Drago Kregar, Cerovec pod Bočem 10, si-3250 Rogaška Slatina
Phone: +386 (0) 3 581 40 14, (0) 41 600 333
Email: kletkregar@volja.net

Wine selling ❧ Wine tasting for announced groups
Wine cellar tours for announced groups ❧ Wine route
❧ Sales material

MIX OF WINES ON OFFER

38% Chardonnay, 38% Sauvignon and 24% Renski Rizling.

IVAN MIJOŠEK

Zgornje Negonje 4b, si-3250 Rogaška Slatina, Phone: +386 (0) 41 386 510, (0) 3 819 21 51

Wine selling ❧ Wine tasting
Production of wine and food ❧ Wine cellar tours
Wine route ❧ Accommodation
❧ Sales material

WINES ON OFFER

'Afrodita' sparkling wine (produced in classical way) and predicates Renski Rizling, Chardonnay and Sivi Pinot (*Ledeno Vino* and *Jagodni Izbor*).

IVAN MLAKER

Bodrišna vas 27, si-3231 Grobelno, Phone: +386 (0) 3 582 11 78

Wine selling ❧ Wine tasting for announced groups
Wine cellar tours for announced groups ❧ Wine route
Sales material ❧ Production of wine and food for announced groups

MIX OF WINES ON OFFER

60% Laški Rizling, 20% white blend and 20% red blend.

ŠMARJE-VIRŠTANJ WINE-GROWING DISTRICT

Rajko Pečnik

Sedlarjevo 21, si-3255 Buče
Phone: +386 (0) 3 580 80 42, Fax: +386 (0) 3 809 81 07

Wine selling ⁂ Wine tasting
Production of wine and food ⁂ Wine cellar tours
⁂ Wine route

The Pečnik wine farm has been in existence since 1983. They have had their own wine labels since 1994. Their vineyards are planted mostly with Traminec and Laški Rizling, the latter being particularly abundant. They pride themselves on being able to offer a range of varieties: Laški Rizling and Renski Rizling, Traminec, Rumeni Muškat, Sauvignon and Modri Pinot.
Their best vintages are still available: 2001 Traminec, 1994 and 2001 Laški Rizling, 2000 Sauvignon *Pozna Trgatev* and 1994 Sauvignon.

Mix of wines on offer

50% 'Virštajnčan' white blend, 15% Traminec, 10% Laški Rizling, 7% Sauvignon, 5% Renski Rizling, 5% Modri Pinot, 5% red blend, 2% Rumeni Muškat and 1% Muškat Ottonel.

Awards

They have won several gold and silver medals in Ljubljana and Gornja Radgona, and they have successfully presented their wines in Zagreb, Novi Sad, Split and Kutijevo.

Culinary recommendations

Their white wines are served with *ocvirkovka* (a savoury version of *potica*, filled with pork crackling), the Modri Pinot is served with salami and cheese platters, and the predicates with 'lavish' *potica* (stuffed with a combination of different fillings). Dry and semi-dry wines are recommended with appetizers and main courses; the predicates are best with desserts.

2001 Traminec

12.86% vol., semi-dry

This is a crystal-clear, bright yellow wine. The nose is uncomplicated with a dominant note of fruitiness, but developing in the direction of spices and tea. The wine is clearly recognizable by its palate. This wine has reached its peak of development and is currently at its best.
Recommended dishes: Pickled asparagus, goose liver pâté, 'lavish' *potica*, apple cake.

ŠMARJE-VIRŠTANJ WINE-GROWING DISTRICT

2001 Traminec

ŠMARJE-VIRŠTANJ WINE-GROWING DISTRICT

Sekirnikova Gorca

Franc Sekirnik, Kamence 5, si-3250 Rogaška Slatina
Phone: +386 (0) 3 581 44 95, (0) 41 993 043
Email: sekirnikovagorca@email.si

Wine selling ❧ Wine tasting
❧ Wine route

Mix of wines on offer

25% Rumeni Muškat, 25% Chardonnay, 25% Renski Rizling and 25% Modri Pinot.

Vino Vrhovšek

Franc Mlaker, Linhartova 18, si-3250 Rogaška Slatina
Phone: +386 (0) 3 581 37 15, (0) 41 654 485
Email: mares@volja.net

Wine selling ❧ Wine tasting
❧ Wine route

Mix of wines on offer

80% Sivi Pinot and 20% Sauvignon.

Bizeljsko-Sremič Wine-Growing District
POSAVJE WINE-GROWING REGION

BIZELJSKO-SREMIČ WINE-GROWING DISTRICT

Aleš Balon

Drenovec 3, si-8259 Bizeljsko
Phone: +386 (0) 7 495 12 18, (0) 31 245 238
Email: alesbalon@hotmail.com
Website: www.slovino.com/balon

Wine selling ❧ Wine tasting
Wine cellar tours ❧ Wine route
Sales material ❧ Tour of the vineyard

Viticulture and the wine trade have been part of the Balon family ever since 1915. In the vineyards, which are in the immediate vicinity of their home, the best crops are Chardonnay, Rumeni Plavec and Laški Rizling. They produce mainly blended wines, such as white and red 'Bizeljčan', which also hold the most potential for them.

Mix of wines on offer

50% white 'Bizeljčan' blend, 30% red 'Bizeljčan' blend, 5% Modra Frankinja, 5% Sauvignon and 10% predicates from Chardonnay, Sivi Pinot and Laški Rizling.

Awards

Their Chardonnay has been awarded a gold medal on several occasions in Gornja Radgona.

2003 Bizeljčan, white

dry, ★

A pale yellow wine with distinctive green notes. The mild, floral-fruit fragrances indicate a vibrant palate. A medium-full wine with tasty, prominent acidity. The finish is pleasant, but soon forgotten.
Recommended dishes: Risotto with poultry, sweet and sour cabbage with part-smoked meat, sarma, carniolan sausage.

BIZELJSKO-SREMIČ WINE-GROWING DISTRICT

2003 Bizeljčan, white

BIZELJSKO-SREMIČ WINE-GROWING DISTRICT

Blažova Gorca

Martin Kovačič, Vidova pot 46, si-8259 Bizeljsko
Phone: +386 (0) 7 495 17 18, (0) 41 869 137

Wine selling ❧ Wine tasting
Wine cellar tours ❧ Accommodation
Wine route ❧ Sales material
❧ Production of wine and food for announced groups

Kovačič has been in wine growing and the wine trade since 1970, and filled his first bottle seven years ago. In the main produces high-quality dry and semi-dry wines, mostly Sauvignon.
The best specimens in Kovačič's wine cellar are 1997 Sauvignon *Pozna Trgatev*, 2001 Traminec *Ledeno Vino*, 2003 Modri Pinot and 2003 Modra Frankinja, and will remain available for quite some time.

Mix of wines on offer

30% Sauvignon, 18% Beli Pinot, 17% Modri Pinot, 14% Chardonnay, 12% Modra Frankinja, 5% Sauvignon *Jagodni Izbor*, 2% Traminec *Jagodni Izbor* and 2% Traminec *Ledeno Vino*.

Awards

They take part in wine appraisals in Gornja Radgona, Ljubljana, Zagreb and Verona.

Culinary recommendations

With a roast accompanied by bread dumplings or cheese strudel they will serve you a Modra Frankinja or Modri Pinot. They suggest trying pork and sausage with red wine, and buckwheat *potica* with Sauvignon.

2003 Modri Pinot

12.4% vol., dry, ★★★

A beautiful, youthful, ruby red colour of above-average intensity for a Pinot. Very open aromas of fruit: red fruits such as raspberries, strawberries and cherries stand out. The distinctive nose of a young Modri Pinot — the scent of oxtail soup — is quite hidden in this wine with the fruit fragrances prevailing, but it is still present in the undertones. On the palate the wine is full, quite rounded and expressive of its rich, complex and well-balanced content. The tannins are well-defined, even abundant for a Modri Pinot; they are still rough and show their youth, but guarantee continuing development in quality.
Recommended dishes: Cold cuts of smoked meats (salami), cooked beef, medium-strong red-meat pastry- and flour-based dishes, duck with flat cake and red cabbage, roast meats.

BIZELJSKO-SREMIČ WINE-GROWING DISTRICT

2003 Modri Pinot

BIZELJSKO-SREMIČ WINE-GROWING DISTRICT

Istenič

Miha Istenič, Celovška 72, si-1000 Ljubljana, Phone: +386 (0) 1 515 78 85
Telefaks:+ 386 1 515 78 80, Email: office@istenic.si, Website: www.istenic.si

Wine selling ❧ Wine tasting
Production of wine and food ❧ Wine cellar tours
Wine route ❧ Accommodation
❧ Sales material

Since 1968, when the Istenič family bought the vineyard in Bizeljsko, they have produced sparkling wines. Their basic component is Chardonnay. They have high hopes for their mature dry sparkling wines, which rest on yeast germs for a minimum of three years. The cellar still holds their best vintages: the sparkling wines Prestige barrique (2000), Gourmet Brut (2000) and Gourmet Rosé Brut (2002); and Modri Pinot barrique (2002).

Mix of wines on offer

32% 'Desiree' sparkling wine, 30% 'Barbara' sparkling wine, 12% 'No.1 Cuvée Speciale' sparkling wine, 7% 'Michelle' sparkling wine, 5% 'Miha' sparkling wine, 5% 'Cuvée Princesse' sparkling wine, 2% red 'Bizeljčan' blend, 2% Modri Pinot, 1% 'Tisočletje' sparkling wine, 1% 'Gourmet Rosé Brut' sparkling wine, 1% 'Desiree Light' sparkling wine, 0,5% 'Prestige barrique' sparkling wine, 0,5% 'Prestige Brut' sparkling wine and 0,5% Sauvignon.

Awards

The Istenič family has received numerous awards at international tastings since 1991, especially for their sparkling wines Barbara and No. 1 Cuvée Speciale.

Culinary recommendations

They offer house specialities: goose liver à la maison and smoked duck breast.

2000 Prestige Barrique

12.0% vol., dry, ★★★

The pale yellow colour shines from the glass like gold, while myriad tiny bubbles sparkle and gather in a gorgeous necklace at the rim. The fresh nose instantly brings us flowers and fruit (vineyard peaches). Roasting fragrances follow, resembling fresh bread and nuts, all beautifully and delicately in harmony. A pleasing vivacity plays gently on the tongue; the beautiful structure manifests itself quickly and is well-adjusted. The balance between sweetness, acidity, and tannins is harmonious and complex, favouring freshness. The fragrances that develop on the palate recall spices, fresh almonds and smoke.
The impressions that remain after swallowing are wholly pleasant, and confirm the good structure behind this fine palate. A sparkling wine to be drunk not only as an aperitif, but also as a good accompaniment to foods with strong flavour.
Recommended dishes: Drink as an aperitif, or with smoked salmon, goose liver, chargrilled tenderloin or hard cheeses.

BIZELJSKO-SREMIČ WINE-GROWING DISTRICT

2000 Prestige Barrique   2002 Modri Pinot Barrique

2002 Modri Pinot Barrique

12.0% vol., dry, ★★★

Ruby red in appearance with some brick tones. The predominant aroma is of fruit, especially red berries — raspberries, strawberry jam, cherries — rounded off with sweet, spicy fragrances. This wine presents itself lightly on the palate thanks to a modest tannin content, but still seems very full-bodied. Still, in a Modri Pinot we cannot expect the tannic character of some other Mediterranean wines. The tannins are clearly present in this wine, but as an undertone, sensed as tiny grains, not so much bitter as velvety. Production in oak barrels has not overshadowed the generic characteristics of the Modri Pinot; the complexity of the nose is ever present on the palate and adds to the wine's sense of identity. Finally, it gives off a fresh, juicy, pleasant aftertaste, the bouquet lingering beautifully.

Recommended dishes: Cold cuts from homemade salami and ham, goose breast with beans, roast veal, duck with flat cake and red cabbage, grilled tenderloin.

BIZELJSKO-SREMIČ WINE-GROWING DISTRICT

Matjaž Jenšterle

Sremič 32, si-8270 Krško, Phone: +386 (0) 41 719 138

Wine selling ❧ Wine tasting
Wine cellar tours ❧ Wine route
❧ Sales material

Matjaž Jenšterle has been devoted to the wine trade since 1980, and is focusing more and more on predicates while trying not to neglect the high-quality wines. He is most pleased with varieties such as Chardonnay, Kerner and Laški Rizling, which have proved the best suited to the conditions of the vineyards and the wine cellar.
Some of his best wines will be available for some time to come: 1999 Laški Rizling *Ledeno Vino*, 2000 Chardonnay and Kerner *Suhi Jagodni Izbor*.

Mix of wines on offer

60% high-quality wine and 40% predicates (Rumeni Muškat, Modri Pinot, Kerner, Sauvignon, Chardonnay, Modra Frankinja, Laški Rizling and Portugalka.

Awards

He has won gold and bronze medals in Ljubljana; the grand gold, gold and bronze in Kutjevo; a silver at Ptuj, and the vast majority of his other medals in Gornja Radgona (grand gold, gold and silver).

Culinary recommendations

They recommend their predicate wines with all desserts, especially cheese strudel with raisins, and any of their other wines with meat dishes.

1990 Kerner *Suhi Jagodni Izbor*
10.5% vol., sweet, ★★★

This golden-yellow wine glows in the glass like the evening sun. The abundance of the bouquet is sensed straightaway on the nose, and reminds one of raisins, sun-scorched grapes, dried pears and figs, honey, caramel, and stewed oranges, but above all of the fine aroma of grapes with noble rot. Beauty and harmony continue on the palate. Sweetness wants to prevail, but there is a tasty acidity to smoothe the rough edges and create harmony. The bouquet simply explodes on the palate and remains a faithful companion throughout the tasting. Its length is exceptional: it lingers on and by doing so confirms its excellence.
In spite of its age the wine maintains its juiciness;
it may yet have even more up its sleeve.
Recommended dishes: Walnut and sweet tarragon *potica*, pancakes with walnuts, fruit desserts, blue cheeses.

BIZELJSKO-SREMIČ WINE-GROWING DISTRICT

1990 KERNER *Suhi Jagodni Izbor*

BIZELJSKO-SREMIČ WINE-GROWING DISTRICT

Keltis

Marjan Kelhar, Vrhovnica 5, si-8259 Bizeljsko
Phone: +386 (0) 7 452 00 60, (0) 31 807 862
Email: keltis@siol.net

Wine selling ❧ Wine tasting for announced groups
Wine route ❧ Production of wine and food for
announced groups

Kelhar began to grow and sell wine 21 years ago. He produces mostly Traminec and Chardonnay. The latter is, in his opinion, the best suited to all categories of wine (dry, semi-sweet, predicates, sparkling wines). The semi-dry Traminec, sweet and semi-sweet Rumeni Muškat or Sauvignon, dry Chardonnay and dry Sivi Pinot are the wines that hold the greatest promise for Kelhar. 1994 and 1997 Chardonnay, 2001 Traminer and 2001 Rumeni Muškat are his best vintages still available.

Mix of wines on offer
30% Chardonnay, 30% Traminec, 15% Sivi Pinot (Rulandec), 10% Sauvignon, 10% Rumeni Muškat and 5% Laški Rizling.

Awards
Several gold medals from Gornja Radgona and Ljubljana attest to the high quality of their wines.

Culinary recommendations
They are organizing an evening of 'slow food' to promote their wines, and until then they leave you with this tip: spicy mashed potatoes with smoked pork ribs are beautifully complemented by a dry Sivi Pinot or a dry Chardonnay.

2000 Sauvignon with Predicate
11% vol., sweet, ★★★

The yellow hue with its glowing, golden reflections is most enticing. The basic aroma of the variety is accompanied by an array of flowers (elder, lime, violets) and ripe fruit (dried apricots, pears, figs) on the nose, and promises a palate of rich complexity. The beauty of the initial bouquet is joined on the palate by the fine odour of ripe grapes, and here the pleasure continues, the palate, the wine proving rich and balanced in body, employing all the taste buds. Final impressions are wholly pleasant and last well. This is an exceptional wine both in qualitative and aesthetic terms, and deserves special attention, which should be given only when we have the necessary time to experience it, when we feel dissatisfied after a long day, or when we wish to heighten other pleasures.
Recommended dishes: A subtle dessert, such as *kremšnita* (a type of cream cake), pancakes with honey and walnut filling, fruit salad with peaches, melon and ice-cream.

… BIZELJSKO-SREMIČ WINE-GROWING DISTRICT

2000 Sauvignon with Predicate

BIZELJSKO-SREMIČ WINE-GROWING DISTRICT

Lojze Kunej

Cesta prvih borcev 40, si-8280 Brestanica, Phone: +386 (0) 7 497 92 30

Wine selling ❧ Wine tasting for announced groups
Wine cellar tours for announced groups ❧ Vinska klet
Sales material ❧ Tour of the grapevine (production of vine plants)

The traditions of wine growing and selling have been in the Kunej family since 1964, and they printed their first wine labels in 1991. Their vineyards produce mainly Žametna Črnina, with the smallest areas going to Chardonnay and Beli Pinot. Both in the vineyards and in the wine cellar, Laški Rizling, Sauvignon and Modra Frankinja are most impressive. They sell their wines when they reach their optimal maturity.

Mix of wines on offer

45% red blend, 15% Laški Rizling (also predicates), 15% Sauvignon (also predicates), 15% Modra Frankinja and 10% white blend.

Awards

They have won several gold medals in Gornja Radgona and have taken part in the chivalric tournament and various tastings in Croatia.

Culinary recommendations

In view of the diversity of the wines they have on offer, they are sure that they can provide a suitable wine for any dish.

2003 Bizeljsko — Sremiško Vino, red

10.4% vol., dry, ★

A medium-intense ruby red wine with vibrant violet tones. The warm fruit bouquet delivers very ripe red grapes on the nose, and forest berries, prunes and scents of baking bread soon follow. The palate is light, yet full. It slips smoothly down the throat and leaves pleasant tannic sensations in the mouth. The tannins, acidity and sweetness are well-balanced and confirm the successful retention of the characteristics typical of the variety. The wine is very drinkable, but does not leave us indifferent thanks to an interesting structure.
A new, interesting, and promising red wine from the Bizeljsko-Sremič district.
Recommended dishes: Homemade salami cold cuts, Carniolan sausage, blood sausages, roast veal.

BIZELJSKO-SREMIČ WINE-GROWING DISTRICT

2003 Bizeljsko — Sremiško Vino, red

BIZELJSKO-SREMIČ WINE-GROWING DISTRICT

Vino Brežice

Cesta bratov Cerjakov 33, si-8250 Brežice, Phone: +386 (0) 7 466 84 00

Wine selling ❧ Wine tasting
Wine cellar tours ❧ Sales material

The company has been in business since 1946, and their most important products are the red and white blend 'Bizeljčan' as well as Dolenjskan red wine. They also produce red and white sort wines, sparkling wines and wines of special quality. Their speciality is the Muscon Towny. The best vintages are 1986 Laški Rizling *Izbor*, 1995 Chardonnay *Izbor*, 1995 Sauvignon *Izbor*, 1998 Sipon *Ledeno Vino* and 2001 Laški Rizling *Ledeno Vino*.

Mix of wines on offer

20% white 'Bizeljčan' blend, 30% red 'Bizeljčan' blend, 10% red 'Dolenjsko' blend, 10% white varieties, 10% red varieties, 5% predicates, 10% sparkling wines and 5% special wine 'Muscon Towny'.

Awards

Since 1991 the company has won 374 awards: 8 championship titles, 59 grand gold medals, 128 gold medals, 100 silver medals, 10 champions of blends or mixed wine varieties, and 69 other prizes.

Culinary recommendations

They guarantee to find a suitable wine to accompany any Slovene dish.

2001 Laški Rizling *Ledeno Vino*
11.5% vol., sweet, ★★★

This golden-yellow wine resembles the waning evening sun; the legs slip quietly down the wall of the glass and promise a delicious wine. The fresh floral-fruit fragrances are a typical characteristic of the successful *Ledeno Vino*: vineyard peaches, orange zest, quince cheese, dried figs, vanilla, anise — all offer similiar fragrances to this rich wine. The first impression on the palate is fruity and fresh. The richness of the wine is easily discernible and it delivers a clear, beautifully harmonious and candid array of sensory experiences. Powerful aromas are released on the palate and simply stay there, as if intending to remain forever. The finish is like a peacock's tail — long, with a mosaic of beautiful colours — and similarly vivid is the perception of this wine that lingers in the memory.
Recommended dishes: Walnut *potica*; pancakes filled with a mix of chocolate, oranges, dried apricots and vanilla; fruit salad with peaches, melon and ice-cream.

BIZELJSKO-SREMIČ WINE-GROWING DISTRICT

2001 Laški Rizling *Ledeno Vino*

BIZELJSKO-SREMIČ WINE-GROWING DISTRICT

Vino Graben

Janez in Mihela Šekoranja, Kumrovška 6, SI-8259 Bizeljsko
Phone: +386 (0) 7 455 10 06, (0) 70 611 010, (0) 70 611 011
Email: sekoranja_janez@yahoo.com
Website: www.vino.com/graben_winery, www.enakup.si

Wine selling ❧ Wine tasting
Wine cellar tours ❧ Wine route
Sales material ❧ *Repnicas* — underground wine cellars in silicate sands. A unique offer for Slovenia and this part of Europe.

The tradition of wine growing and selling goes back several centuries here; their first labels, dating from 1950, were hand-painted. Over 25 grape varieties are grown in their vineyards. They predominantly produce blends (Traminec, Rumeni Muškat, Sivi Pinot, Renski Rizling, Chardonnay, Gamay, Modra Frankinja, Modri Pinot and Rumeni Plavec), which ripen in the *repnica*, some 12 metres below the surface. They still hold 130 different wines dating back to 1946 along with the cellared wines that they offer for sale.

Mix of wines on offer

10% open red wine, 10% open white wine, 80% mixed varieties (20% Modra Frankinja, 10% Žametna Črnina, 10% Gamay, 3% Modri Pinot, 3% Laški Rizling, 3% Chardonnay, 3% Rumeni Plavec, 15% Renski Rizling, 8% Sivi Pinot , Rulandec, 5% Traminec, 5% Rumeni Muškat, 5% Sauvignon, 5% Neuburger and 5% Zeleni Silvanec).

Awards

In their many years of expertise in the business they have received over 100 grand gold and gold medals, as well as championship titles.

Culinary recommendations

They recommend the original corn flat cake *prga* to go with a red or white table wine: perhaps a red barrique. Buckwheat *prosti kolač* (cake) is nicely accompanied by Sivi Pinot Barrique, Chardonnay Barrique or a dry Traminec Barrique, while Traminec goes especially well with desserts containing walnuts.

BIZELJSKO-SREMIČ WINE-GROWING DISTRICT

1999 RUMENI PLAVEC *Pozna Trgatev*
11.8% vol., dry, ★★★

The yellow, straw-like appearance looks almost colourless when the glass is held up to daylight. Although labelled '*Pozna Trgatev*', this is a beautiful dry wine, clear and vibrant. Closer study reveals a sense of balance on the palate between the wine's delicious dryness and its fresh fullness. The fruitiness remains discreet, but on warming the wine in the glass, lemon peel and ripe pears release themselves on the nose and are redelivered on the palate. The quality is also the result of an excellent vintage, which has enabled Rumeni Plavec (Zinfandel) to present itself in an even more splendid form than usual. So far all the wines we have had the opportunity to experience have been pale yellow examples of this variety, but nonetheless this is a welcome wine for everyday drinking, with lunch.
Recommended dishes: Fried poultry and frog's legs, turkey steaks, mild roast veal, trout cooked Trieste-style, shark fillet with butter and lemon, fried cheese.

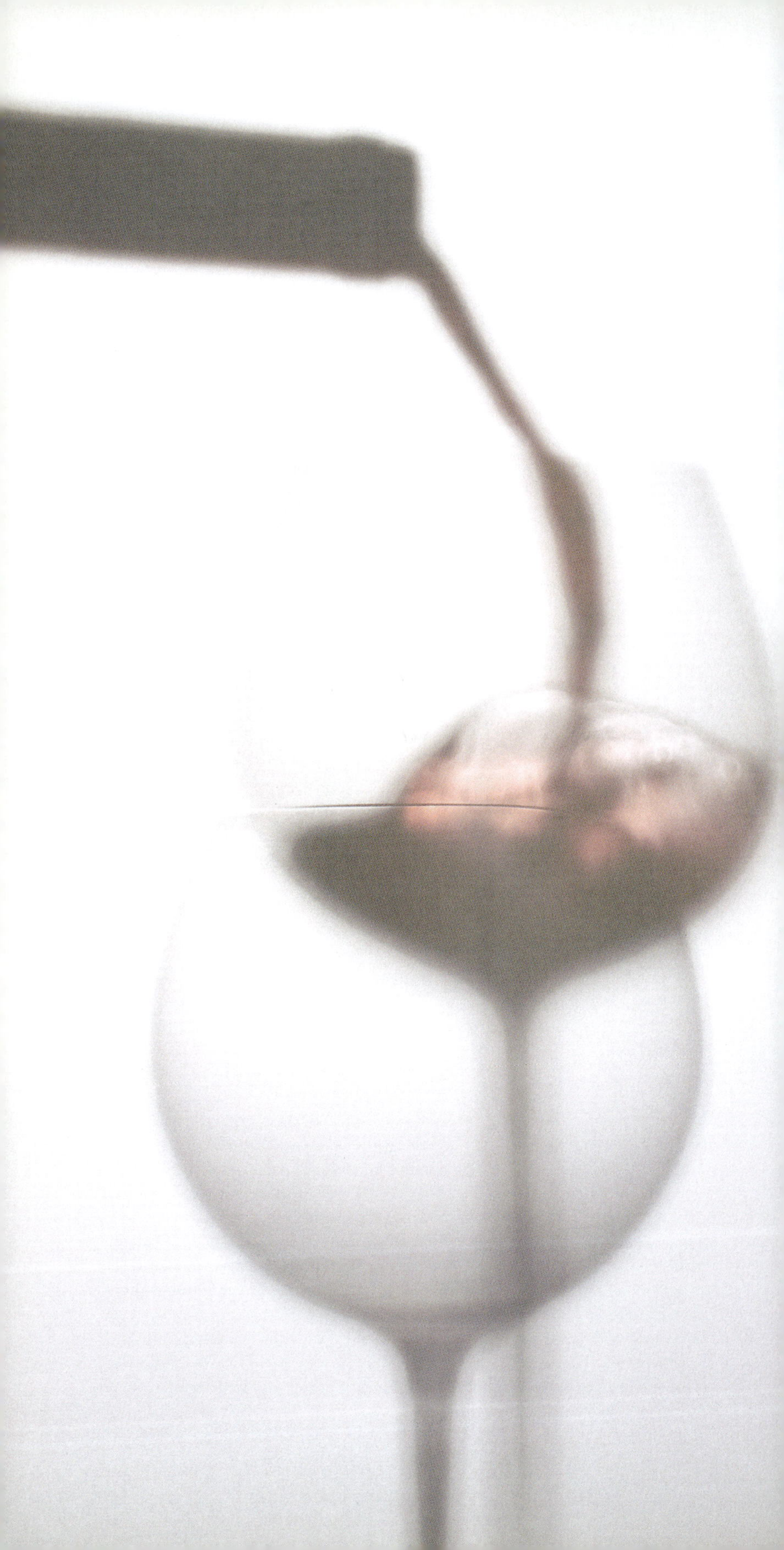

Dolenjska Wine-Growing District
Posavje Wine-Growing Region

DOLENJSKA WINE-GROWING DISTRICT

Bajnof

Cvelbar Marko, Sevno 1, si-8000 Novo mesto
Phone: +386 (0) 7 307 56 33, (0) 41 358 176, Fax: +386 (0) 7 307 56 33
Email: bajnof@yahoo.com

Wine selling ❦ Wine tasting
Wine cellar tours ❦ Sales material

Cvelbar inherited the winegrowing business in 2002 from his father, who has been a devoted vintner for a decade. They concentrate most of their attention on Cviček and it is predominantly (85%) this that they produce. Their best vintage is 2000 (the Modra Frankinja barrique *Ledeno Vino*, Chardonnay, Kerner) and 2002 sparkling wines.

Wines on offer
Cviček PTP, Modra Frankinja, Kerner, Chardonnay, Laški Rizling and sparkling wine.

Awards
Their 2000 Cviček PTP has been declared the champion of its variety, and the predicates and sparkling wine have each been awarded a gold medal.

Culinary recommendations
You can serve Cviček to accompany any Slovene dish without hesitation.

2003 Cviček PTP
10.0% vol., dry

A light, red wine, ruby in appearance and some violet reflections. The nose is pleasant and fruity, resembling red grapes and berries. Very lively and vivacious on the palate. The acidity is youthfully vibrant, as are the tannins.
Recommended dishes: Cold cuts of salami and sausage, blood sausages, Carniolan sausages, lighter roast meats, especially when accompanied by Dolenjska's famous side-dish speciality — *matevž*.

DOLENJSKA WINE-GROWING DISTRICT

2003 Cviček PTP

DOLENJSKA WINE-GROWING DISTRICT

Bojan Brcar

Hom 62, si-8232 Šentrupert, Phone: +386 (0) 7 304 01 76

Wine selling ❦ Wine tasting
Wine cellar tours for announced groups ❦ Wine route

Brcar began growing and trading in wine in 1971 and first labelled his bottles in 1993. He produces high-quality and predicate wines, Laški Rizling and Modra Frankinja. He is primarily focused on Cviček PTP (traditionally accepted nomenclature), which also exceeds his other wines in quantity.
The Žametna Črnina *Pozna Trgatev* and Laški Rizling *Izbor*, both from 1999 New Year's harvest, are the best specimens still available.

Mix of wines on offer
60% Cviček PTP, 10% Modra Frankinja, 10% Laški Rizling
and 20% high-quality and predicate wines.

Awards
He has won three gold and three silver medals at the wine tasting in Gornja Radgona.

Culinary recommendations
Cviček is good with pork and sausage and with *potica* filled with pork crackling; white wine goes well with cheese *štruklji*.

2002 Cviček PTP
10% vol., dry, ★

A light, ruby red wine with violet notes. The fresh and simple fragrance resembles red, ripe berries. The palate is light at first impression and remains pleasant throughout the tasting. Freshness, owing to a pleasant acidity — the basic trait of a Schilcher — is a characteristic. There are some tannins to liven up the wine on the tongue, and these combine well with the acidity. The finish is pleasant, and this wine has preserved a lot of its youthful freshness, although it is not from the most recent vintage.
Recommended dishes: Mushroom soup, light meat dishes, soft salami cold cuts, blood sausages and lighter roasts, especially if accompanied by *matevž* — a well-known specialty of Dolenjska.

DOLENJSKA WINE-GROWING DISTRICT

2002 Cviček PTP

DOLENJSKA WINE-GROWING DISTRICT

Jože Frelih

Šentrupert 35, si-8232 Šentrupert
Phone: +386 (0) 7 304 00 26, Fax: +386 (0) 7 304 04 43

Wine selling ❦ Wine tasting
Production of wine and food ❦ Wine cellar tours
Wine route ❦ Accommodation
Sales material ❦ Visit to the vineyard cottage, the vineyards and surroundings

Frelih has been devoted to winegrowing and the wine trade since 1945, becoming more serious in 1992 when he first added labels to his wine bottles. 'Cviček Od Fare' — which makes up more than half the wine on offer — and Cviček PTP represent the cream of the wine cellar, along with Cviček and Modra Frankinja barrique. Be sure to obtain the best specimens: 1999 Modra Frankinja barrique, 1999 sparkling Rosé 'Penina Od Fare' and 2000 sparkling 'Beal' (Šentruperška Penina and Kappelman'.

Mix of wines on offer

52% 'Cviček Od Fare' blend, 3% 'Penina Od Fare', 3% Zeleni Silvanec, 2% Modra Frankinja barrique, 2% 'Šentruperška Penina', 2% sparkling 'Kappelman' and 36% Cviček PTP.

Awards

They hold numerous gold and silver medals from tastings held in Ljubljana and Gornja Radgona, as well as two championship titles — one for Cviček PTP and the other for Modra Frankinja.

Culinary recommendations

They recommend a Cviček with homemade salami and home-baked bread, and a Zeleni Silvanec with tarragon *potica*.

1999 Penina Od Fare

11% vol., semi-dry, ★★★

The wine is pink in colour with lively violet notes and abundant bubbles, persistently rising to the surface. After the first impression a fresh fruit fragrance opens up, complex in composition and resembling the ripe aromas of smaller red berries with hints of jam. At first the palate is mild — the wine 'melts' beautifully — but freshness soon prevails and introduces a livelier quality on the tongue. The main fundamental flavours are easily detectable as they wash over the palate. The basis is pleasant and contributes a large proportion of the wine's character. A light bitterness pleasantly rounds it off and identifies this wine as a suitable companion for the right dishes.
Recommended dishes: Cold cuts of smoked meats, asparagus in balsamic vinegar with clams, fruit salads with raspberries, blueberries and strawberries.

DOLENJSKA WINE-GROWING DISTRICT

1999 Penina Od Fare   1999 Modra Frankinja Barrique

1999 Modra Frankinja Barrique
11.7% vol., dry, ★★★

An intense ruby red colour, almost opaque and with a vibrant purple quality. Scents of baking and roasting (bread crusts, coffee beans) immediately strike the nose, with spices, undergrowth and tobacco to follow, making a vast stock of aromas, delivered clearly and straightforwardly. In spite of a fine maturity on the nose, the palate seems younger. Its liveliness can be attributed to the acidity, which keeps the tannins young and promises further development to come. In spite of a long period in barrels, the wine has kept the distinctive characteristics of its variety, especially in the taste.
Recommended dishes: Dolenjskan ham, Karstic prosciutto, grilled neck of various meats, grilled pork, turkey, duck with flat cake and red cabbage.

DOLENJSKA WINE-GROWING DISTRICT

Franc Planinc

Dolenje Grčevje 31, si-8222 Otočec, Phone: +386 (0) 7 307 54 90, (0) 31 289 812

Wine selling ❦ Wine tasting
Wine cellar tours for announced groups ❦ Sales material
❦ Production of wine and food for announced groups

Franc Planinec has already been in the wine trade for twenty years. Like most vintners in the Dolenjska region he concentrates his efforts on Cviček. In his opinion the velvet grape gives best results on this soil. He will still have the following in stock for some time: Renski Rizling *Pozna Trgatev*, Laški Rizling *Pozna Trgatev*, Chardonnay *Izbor* and Zeleni Silvanec.

Mix of wines on offer

90% Cviček PTP and 10% Renski Rizling, Laški Rizling and Chardonnay.

Culinary recommendations

He recommends his wine as an accompaniment to trout fillet in sauce.

2003 Renski Rizling *Pozna Trgatev*
13.96% vol., semi-dry, ★★★

Pale yellow in colour, this is a lovely clear wine, fresh and youthful in appearance. The flesh floral and fruity fragrance is attributable to the variety, but it also has a youthful vibrancy of its own, resembling meadow flowers and, in particular, lemons and peaches. The distinctive characteristic of the variety is most strongly sensed at first instance, after which it opens up in complex and colourful sensations, maintaining harmony nevertheless. The range of the bouquet is released to its fullest extent on the palate and showers our senses with flowers. The character of the variety also comes out in the lively and tasty acidity, so typical of an excellent Riesling. The superb balance is maintained by the low level of residual sugar, which suits this promising wine, allowing its mineral side to come through — the signature of a true Renski Rizling. This wine proves that Dolenjska is capable of producing a high-quality Riesling, balancing the key traits of the variety with distinctive local character.
Recommended dishes: Goose liver pâté, fish pâté, *štruklji*, sarma and dishes with cabbage and smoked meat, grilled salmon.

DOLENJSKA WINE-GROWING DISTRICT

2003 RENSKI RIZLING *Pozna Trgatev*

DOLENJSKA WINE-GROWING DISTRICT

Kartuzija Pleterje

Drča 1, si-8310 Šentjernej, Phone: +386 (0) 7 308 12 25

Wine selling ❧ Wine tasting for announced groups
❧ Sales material

The wine cellar was built when the Carthusian monastery was founded in 1404, and their first wine label was printed in 1978. Their most important wine is Cviček, which is their main product.
One can still find the best vintages ensconced in their 600-year-old wine cellar: 1997 Chardonnay *Jagodni Izbor*, 2000 Chardonnay *Ledeno Vino*, 2003 Chardonnay and 2003 Kerner.

Mix of wines on offer

70% Cviček PTP, 15% 'Mašno Vino', 5% Chardonnay, 5% Kerner, 3% sparkling 'Pleter' and 2% predicate wines (*Pozna Trgatev, Ledeno Vino*).

Culinary recommendations

Smoked trout is nicely accompanied by Cviček.

2003 Cviček PTP Pletér

9.9% vol. dry, ★

Ruby, lightish red in appearance with purple and orange notes. A distinctive aroma of berries encourages an in-depth analysis of the bouquet. The palate is similarly interesting. The wine is simultaneously full and light; easy and drinkable, as one requires of a Schilcher; fresh; and offers more besides: a Cviček blends with character. I would like to see more Cviček blends of this kind of quality, which is surely due to an excellent vintage, good terrain and, of course, the vintner, who has preserved the quality of the grape all the way to the bottle.

Recommended dishes: Mushroom soup, light 'spoon' dishes, light meat dishes with *matevž*, blood sausages, Carniolan sausages, light roasts.

DOLENJSKA WINE-GROWING DISTRICT

2003 Cviček PTP Pletér   2003 Kerner Pletér

2003 Kerner Pletér

13% vol., semi-dry, ★★★

This pale yellow, near-colourless wine with its gentle green tones is like the first sight to greet an innocent youth on awakening. The somewhat reserved fragrances open themselves up slowly on the nose and deliver first flowers (blossom, violets, Muscat) and then fruit (ripe apples, white peaches). The palate is at first mild, but develops to become full and strong. The first impression is influenced by the residual sugar, which soon gives way to the rich body, the complex sensations lasting and continuing to surprise. This is a wine that still needs more time to show its full range. Do not miss the way the full make-up of the bouquet is revealed after swallowing.

Recommended dishes: Chicken and veal ragout, offal, smoked sweet cabbage with beef, grilled poultry.

DOLENJSKA WINE-GROWING DISTRICT

Matjaž Engel
Vavta vas 41a, si-8351 Straža, Phone: +386 (0) 41 684 216

Wine selling 〰 Wine tasting

Mix of wines on offer
80% Cviček PTP, 10% Modra Frankinja and 10% Laški Rizling.

Mihael Kvartuh
Koritno 12, si-8261 Jesenice na Dolenjskem, Phone: +386 (0) 7 495 77 54

Wine selling 〰 Wine tasting for announced groups
〰 Wine cellar tours for announced groups

Mix of wines on offer
75% Cviček PTP, 10% Modra Frankinja, 10% Laški Rizling,
5% other varieties and predicates.

Miloš Munih
Trška gora 262, si-8000 Novo mesto, Phone: +386 (0) 7 307 56 56, (0) 41 774 911

Wine selling 〰 Wine tasting
Sales material 〰 Production of wine and food for
announced groups

Mix of wines on offer
80% Cviček PTP, 10% Modra Frankinja and 10% Modri Pinot.

Alojz Pirc
Ravni 3, si-8270 Krško, Phone: +386 (0) 7 491 31 08, (0) 41 521 881
Email: janez.pirc@siol.net

Wine selling 〰 Wine tasting
Wine cellar tours 〰 Wine route

Wines on offer
Cviček PTP.

DOLENJSKA WINE-GROWING DISTRICT

Jože Prah

Vinogradniško-izletniška kmetija "Vitovc"
Velike Malence 16, si-8262 Krška vas
Phone: +386 (0) 7 495 93 60, (0) 51 247 550, (0) 31 492 123, Fax: +386 (0) 7 495 96 95
Email: vinogradniska.kmetija.vitovc@email.si

- Wine selling
- Wine tasting for announced groups
- Wine cellar tours for announced groups
- Wine route
- Accommodation
- Sales material
- Production of wine and food for announced groups

Mix of wines on offer

60% Cviček PTP, 15% Modra Frankinja, 10% Laški Rizling, 5% Kerner, 5% Rumeni Muškat, 2,5% Beli Pinot and 2,5% Sauvignon.

Milan Valek

Koritno 14, si-8261 Jesenice na Dolenjskem, Phone: +386 (0) 7 495 75 04

- Wine selling
- Wine tasting

Mix of wines on offer

80% Cviček PTP, 10% Modra Frankinja and 10% Laški Rizling.

Vinotrs - Klet gadova peč

Robert Jarkovič, Brod v Podbočju 23, si-8312 Podbočje
Phone: +386 (0) 7 497 80 49, (0) 41 730 155, Fax: +386 (0) 7 497 85 01
Email: r-jarkovic@volja.net

- Wine selling
- Wine tasting
- Wine cellar tours for announced groups
- Wine route

Mix of wines on offer

90% Cviček PTP and 10% Modra Frankinja.

Ivan Vovk in Franc Kržič

Hrastovica 25, si-8230 Mokronog
Phone: +386 (0) 7 349 95 96, +386 (0) 7 349 95 97, +386 (0) 40 858 733, +386 (0) 70 311 204
Email: franc.krzic@siol.net

- Wine tasting for announced groups
- Wine cellar tours for announced groups
- Wine route

Mix of wines on offer

75% Cviček PTP, 15% Kerner and 10% Beli Pinot.

DOLENJSKA WINE-GROWING DISTRICT

KZ Krško

Rostoharjeva 88, si-8270 Krško
Phone: +386 (0) 7 488 25 00, (0) 41 690 142, Fax: +386 (0) 7 488 25 15
Email: kmecka.zadruga@siol.net, janez.zivic.kzk@siol.net
Website: www.kz-krsko.si

Wine selling ❧ Wine tasting
Wine cellar tours ❧ Wine route
Sales material ❧ Production of wine and food for announced groups

In 1928, owing to the economic conditions of the time and the decay of the vineyards, the Viticultural Cooperative was organized in Kostanjevica on Krka with the aim of encouraging the restoration, sale, and promotion of Dolenjska's regional wines. They reached their prime in the early seventies, and today the wine cellar works under the authority of the Krško Agricultural Cooperative. Their most important brand is Cviček PTP, a blend of several grape varieties. It is Cviček PTP and Modra Frankinja that assure their cellar's reputation. The Modra Frankinja 1997, 2000 and 2002 vintages are the best still available.

Mix of wines on offer

85% Cviček PTP, 5% Modra Frankinja, 2% Zeleni Silvanec, 2% Beli Pinot, 2% Laški Rizling, 2% Sauvignon and 2% Modri Pinot.

Awards

They have won gold and silver medals for their predicates in Belgium and France, and at tastings in Gornja Radgona and Ljubljana they have achieved grand gold and gold medals for their Modra Frankinja.

Culinary recommendations

They recommend Cviček as the best companion to all traditional Slovene dishes, and bear pâté is recommended with Modra Frankinja.

2003 Cviček PTP

9.7% vol., ★

A ruby, light red appearance with purple and orange notes. The freshness and simplicity of the aroma suggest a drinkable and refreshing wine. It is undemanding, fresh, light and easily understood once it reaches the palate, easy to drink and very suitable for those moments of light relaxation and casual conversation. The finish is pleasant and brief.
Recommended dishes: Mushroom soup, lighter 'spoon' dishes, light meat dishes with *matevž*, blood sausages, Carniolan sausages, light roasts.

DOLENJSKA WINE-GROWING DISTRICT

2003 Cviček PTP   2002 Modra Frankinja

2002 Modra Frankinja

12.0% vol., ★★★

Intense ruby red, glowing, vividly coloured around the rim; all suggesting the youth of the wine and arousing expectations. Fruit fragrances of ripe, but not over-ripe, smaller red berries suggest the continuing development of the bouquet towards fragrances of roasting. The wine's youth comes across clearly on the palate; there are some tannins, which seem quite tamed. The body of the wine is medium-rich and the main elements are well-balanced. The maturing process is still under way, and the quality of this wine will improve for at least another year. The finish is pleasant and medium-long.
Recommended dishes: Smoked cold cuts, roast pork, fried liver, grilled pork and beef, duck with flat cake and red cabbage.

DOLENJSKA WINE-GROWING DISTRICT

Vinko Štemberger

Na Žago 1, si-8310 Šentjernej
Phone: +386 (0) 7 308 14 22, (0) 41 638 763, Fax: +386 (0) 7 308 14 24
Email: stemberger.vinogradnistvo@siol.net

Wine selling ❦ Wine tasting
Wine cellar tours ❦ Wine route
❦ Sales material

Vinko Štemberger began growing wine in 1963 but first labelled his bottles in 1987, the turning point for him towards more serious growing and selling. He grows a number of different grape varieties, but the larger part his output is Cviček. This still leaves a third comprising blended and predicate wines. He takes particular pride in the quality of the Laški Rizling (all varieties) and Modra Frankinja, produced by a process of long maceration and then aged in oak barrels. 2000 was an excellent vintage and he still has some Modra Frankinja and Laški Rizling available.

Mix of wines on offer

70% Cviček PTP, 10% Modra Frankinja, 5% Laški Rizling, 5% Sivi Pinot, 5% Kerner, 3% sparkling Rumeni Muškat and 2% predicate wines.

Awards

He regularly attends tastings in Gornja Radgona and Ljubljana, where he has already received a good number of bronze, silver and gold medals.

Culinary recommendations

He especially recommends Dolenjskan ham and salami with his wines, in particular with Modra Frankinja or Cviček.

2000 Modra Frankinja

12.2% vol., dry, ★★★

An intense ruby red colour with purple notes, still youthful in appearance. A fruitiness, openness and sense of the grape variety in the bouquet distinguish this wine, which delivers ripe grapes, jam made from dark berries and scents of baking or roasting (bread crusts, coffee) on the nose. The first impression on the palate is very pleasant, almost youthful, even though this wine is already four years old. The vibrant acidity contributes to this, arousing the tannins and enhancing its youthful personality. The wine has matured slowly and there are still some tannins developing, so it will maintain this fresh flavour for some time to come. This wine could be a model for Franconian wines from Dolenjska, classically produced in large barrels.

Recommended dishes: Dolenjskan ham, salami cold cuts, Carniolan sausage, fried liver, duck with flat cake and red cabbage, grilled meat.

DOLENJSKA WINE-GROWING DISTRICT

2000 Modra Frankinja

DOLENJSKA WINE-GROWING DISTRICT

Vinogradništvo Pekel

Anton Ajster, Krška vas 6, si-8262 Krška vas
Phone: +386 (0) 7 495 94 64, (0) 70 689 046, (0) 31 589 894

Wine selling ❧ Wine tasting
Wine cellar tours ❧ Wine route
❧ Production of wine and food for announced groups

The wine trade came to life at the Ajster's in 1971. They fill the vast majority of their bottles with Cviček produced from Žametna Črnina, Modra Frankinja, Laški Rizling, Kraljevina and Rumeni Plavec. They also produce predicates of Modra Frankinja, Laški Rizling and Renski Rizling, equal in importance and profile to Cviček.
The best specimens still available are 2000 Modra Frankinja, 2001 Renski Rizling and 2001 Laški Rizling.

Mix of wines on offer
40% Cviček PTP, 25% Modra Frankinja, 25% Renski Rizling *Pozna Trgatev* and 10% Laški Rizling *Pozna Trgatev*.

Awards
In seven years of participating at tastings in Gornja Radgona they have been awarded five gold, six silver and five bronze medals. They also received a silver medal at Ptuj in 1999.

Culinary recommendations
Homemade bread and delicacies made of leavened dough are the favoured companions to their wines.

2000 Modra Frankinja
12.4% vol., dry, ★★★

A very intense ruby red colour with beautiful, ripe brick tones that command respect. A complex, open bouquet emanates from the glass, which suggests a continuing improvement in quality and delivers very ripe fruits (blueberries, blackberries) on the nose. Fragrances of roasting coffee are clearly present, followed by chocholate and some more delicate animal scents (fur).
The first impression on the palate is very pleasant: all the senses are engaged, and the tannins are sweet and ripe, not allowing the proportionally higher level of acidity to throw them off balance. After swallowing the enjoyment continues, although not for long — about five to six seconds. Although the label states this is a quality wine, it could definitely rank as high-quality before a judging committee today.
Recommended dishes: Salami cold-cuts, Carniolan sauasage, grilled liver, duck with flat cake and red cabbage, grilled meat.

DOLENJSKA WINE-GROWING DISTRICT

2000 Modra Frankinja

DOLENJSKA WINE-GROWING DISTRICT

Martinčič

Vinarska zadruga Martinčič — Vina s petelinom
Franc, Jernej in Martin Martinčič, Šmalčja vas 16, si-8310 Šentjernej
Phone: +386 (0) 7 308 12 82, (0) 7 308 12 88, (0) 31 202 166, (0) 41 903 755
Fax: +386 (0) 7 308 12 82, Email: jernejmart@volja.net

Wine selling ❧ Wine tasting
Wine cellar tours for announced groups ❧ Wine route
❧ Tour of the vineyards, tastings with the sommelier

The tradition of viticulture and the wine trade dates back to the nineteenth century, but they have focused more specifically on the market for the wines they offer since 1962. Most of their output consists of Cviček. The rest is white wine: 'Šentjernejc' (a blend of Laški Rizling, Chardonnay and Silvanec), Modra Frankinja, Chardonnay and Sivi Pinot. They also tend a descendant of the Lent vine — the oldest vine in Europe — and produce the wine Lentar. They are proudest of their dry red wines, especially some of the bottles in storage: Beli Pinot (1990, 1991 and 1997), Chardonnay (1990, 1991, 1997 and 2003) and Modra Frankinja (1994 and 1999).

Mix of wines on offer

90% Cviček PTP, 2% Modra Frankinja, 2% Chardonnay, 2% Sivi Pinot in 4% 'Šentjernejc' blend.

Awards

They have successfully presented their wines at tastings in Gornja Radgona and Ljubljana, as witnessed by five silver medals, a gold and a grand gold, as well as four championship titles from Kostanjevica on Krka.

Culinary recommendations

Their vegetable and cheese *štruklji* are complemented by 'Šentjernejc', while pork, sausage and St Martin's goose with cabbage are to be savoured with a Cviček.

2003 Cviček PTP

9.9% vol., dry, ★

The vivacious ruby red colour promises a fresh and relaxing wine. The aroma of this Cviček bears a fruity stamp, delivered as red grapes, cherries, strawberries and redcurrants on the nose. A variety of flavours are pleasingly disclosed on the palate, but the wine still has plenty of backbone, resembling the character of richer red wines from the Posavje region. There is just enough acidity for a Cviček, balancing the freshness but without upsetting the tannins.
A good example of how to work with the grapes that make up this variety to create an interesting character combined with the traditional Cviček flavour.
Recommended dishes: Mushroom soup, lighter 'spoon' dishes, light meat dishes served with *matevž*, sausages, Carniolan sausages, lighter roasts.

DOLENJSKA WINE-GROWING DISTRICT

2003 Cviček PTP   2003 Chardonnay

2003 Chardonnay

11.3% vol., semi-sweet, ★

The pale yellow appearance with a hint of green and numerous tiny bubbles declares youth and a fresh character, and this freshness is immediately delivered on the nose. The bouquet is still shy, but is released nevertheless, yielding at first the characteristics of blossom (hawthorn, meadow flowers), then fruity aromas redolent of green apples and exotic fruit (mango). On tasting, sweetness immediately overwhelms the palate, soon followed by a mild acidity and complex fruit sensations (peach) that remain for us to enjoy after swallowing. It is too early to give the final word on this wine, which will have much more to show in a year's time.

Recommended dishes: Vegetable and cheese *štruklji*, *prosta potica*, pancakes with walnuts, fruit cakes.

DOLENJSKA WINE-GROWING DISTRICT

Janez Žaren

Nemška vas 1, si-8273 Leskovec
Phone: +386 (0) 7 492 22 92, Fax: +386 (0) 7 490 22 92
Email: vzzaren@butn.net

- Wine selling
- Wine tasting for announced groups
- Wine cellar tours
- Wine route
- Production of wine and food for announced groups

Mix of wines on offer

95% Cviček PTP, 2% Modra Frankinja and 3% white blend.

Bela krajina
Wine-Growing District
Posavje Wine-growing Region

BELA KRAJINA WINE-GROWING DISTRICT

Družina Absec

Mihelja vas 12a, si-8340 Črnomelj, Phone: +386 (0) 7 305 25 66, (0) 41 385 457, (0) 31 450 005
Email: francel@volja.net

Wine selling ❧ Wine tasting for announced groups
Wine cellar tours for announced groups ❧ Wine route
❧ Production of wine and food for announced groups

The tradition of wine growing and trading in the Absec family dates back to 1850. Their bottles first bore wine labels in 1987. Today their bottles are mainly filled with Belokranjec, Modra Frankinja, Chardonnay and Sauvignon, as well as Renski Rizling, Modri Pinot and various predicates. They have greatest expectations of the Modra Frankinja, Metliška Črnina and the Belokranjec. The following top specimens are still available: 2003 Sauvignon, 2003 Renski Rizling, 2002 Chardonnay and 1998 Laški Rizling *Ledeno Vino*.

Mix of wines on offer

20% 'Belokranjec' blend, 20% Modra Frankinja, 15% Sauvignon, 15% Chardonnay, 10% Renski Rizling, 8% Modri Pinot and 12% predicates.

Awards

They participate at tastings in Ljubljana and Gornja Radgona.

2003 Sauvignon

11.7% vol., semi-dry, ★

This pale yellow wine with occasional green notes suggests a fresh palate. The tender, floral-fruit nose, accompanied by the scents of garden plants such as tomato bushes, gives away what type of wine this is. Its fruity and herbaceous character continues on the tongue. The wine is youthful, vibrant and complex: characteristics that make an appealing palate. The body is medium-built, the Sauvignon character of the wine opens up and the wine is drinkable: all things that lend distinctions to this Sauvignon.
Recommended dishes: Bela Krajina flat cake, meat and vegetable ragout, tarragon *potica*, goat's cheese.

BELA KRAJINA WINE-GROWING DISTRICT

2003 Sauvignon

BELA KRAJINA WINE-GROWING DISTRICT

Ivan Bajuk

Radovica 54a, si-8330 Metlika
Phone: +386 (0) 7 363 57 00, (0) 41 365 054, Fax: +386 (0) 7 305 86 70
Email: vesna.bajuk@email.si

Wine selling ❧ Wine tasting for announced groups
Wine cellar tours for announced groups ❧ Wine route
❧ Production of wine and food for announced groups

He has been dedicated to the wine trade since 1987, and even more so since 1988 when he printed his first wine label. Metliška Črnina and the white Belokranjec are the pride of his cellar, and they also constitute the bulk of the wine on offer. The best vintage is 2002, with bottles of Chardonnay, Renski Rizling and Laški Rizling still available.

Mix of wines on offer

35% 'Belokranjec' white blend, 25% Metliška Črnina, 10% Chardonnay, 10% Renski Rizling, 10% Laški Rizling and 10% Modra Frankinja.

Awards

So far they have received two gold, four silver and two bronze medals at tastings in Gornja Radgona.

Culinary recommendations

Their wines are at their finest accompanied by Bela Krajina flat cake and ham.

2002 Chardonnay

12.1% vol., semi-sweet, ★★★

This pale yellow, clear and glowing wine effervesces with hundreds of tiny bubbles when poured. It immediately delivers a complex nose, blooming with scents of blossom (acacia, honeysuckle) and fruit (ripe apples, white peaches, pears); variety is the key note of this tender and lively wine.
The fruit fragrances are also delivered on the palate, and contribute to its interesting character whilst distinguishing the variety. The residual sugar is mild, refreshed by a vibrant acidity. The medium structure is very balanced and tasty. No effort is required to perceive and enjoy the quality of this wine; it is naturally open in character and gives itself up easily to all our senses.
Recommended dishes: Bela Krajina flat cake, prosta *potica*, pancakes with walnuts, fruit cake.

BELA KRAJINA WINE-GROWING DISTRICT

2002 Chardonnay

BELA KRAJINA WINE-GROWING DISTRICT

Ivan Bukovec — Janko
Roška 8, si-8333 Semič, Phone: +386 (0) 7 306 74 04, (0) 7 356 51 45, (0) 41 697 860

Wine selling ❦ Wine tasting
Wine cellar tours ❦ Wine route
❦ Production of wine and food for announced groups

Mix of wines on offer
25% Laški Rizling, 25% Modra Frankinja, 20% Žametna Črnina, 10% Kraljevina, 10% Chardonnay and 10% Muškat Ottonel.

Stanislav Kralj
Dobliče 4, si-8340 Črnomelj

❦ Wine selling

Mix of wines on offer
20% Renski Rizling, 15% Laški Rizling, 20% Modra Frankinja and 45% white blend.

Anton Malešič
Radoviči 24, si-8330 Metlika, Phone: +386 (0) 7 305 84 17

Wine tasting ❦ Production of wine and food
❦ Wine cellar tours

Mix of wines on offer
40% 'Belokranjec' white blend, 20% Rumeni Muškat, 20% Laški Rizling and 20% Modra Frankinja.

Jože Mavretič
Drašiči 2b, si-8330 Metlika
Phone: +386 (0) 7 305 86 44, (0) 41 372 885, (0) 41 779 273, Fax: +386 (0) 7 305 86 44

Wine selling ❦ Wine tasting for announced groups
Wine cellar tours for announced groups ❦ Wine route
❦ Production of wine and food for announced groups

Mix of wines on offer
40% 'Belokranjec' white blend, 15% Sauvignon, 10% Rumeni Muškat, 10% Chardonnay, 10% Modra Frankinja, 5% Metliška Črnina and 10% Zeleni Silvanec.

BELA KRAJINA WINE-GROWING DISTRICT

Silvester Murgelj

Prečna 9, SI-8000 Novo mesto
Phone: +386 (0) 7 334 85 16, Fax: +386 (0) 7 334 85 17
Email: murgelj@siol.net

Wine selling ❧ Wine tasting for announced groups

Mix of wines on offer

25% 'Belokranjec' white blend, 25% Modra Frankinja, 17% Laški Rizling, 17% Rumeni Muškat and 16% Šentlovrenka.

Anton Nemanič

Slamna vas 1a, SI-8330 Metlika, Phone: +386 (0) 7 305 81 50, (0) 7 305 93 83, (0) 41 385 877

❧ Wine selling

Mix of wines on offer

40% 'Belokranjec' white blend, 30% Metliška Črnina, 10% Laški Rizling, 7% Modra Frankinja, 5% Chardonnay, 4% Renski Rizling and 4% Rumeni Muškat.

Martin Nemanič

Drašiči 40, SI-8330 Metlika
Phone: +386 (0) 7 306 00 73, Email: dnemanic@msn.com

Wine selling ❧ Wine tasting for announced groups
Production of wine and food ❧ Wine cellar tours
❧ Wine route

Mix of wines on offer

33% 'Belokranjec' white blend, 33% Metliška Črnina, 17% Portugalka, 8,5% Rosé and 8,5% Sauvignon.

Martin Pečarič

Čurile 7, SI-8330 Metlika, Phone: +386 (0) 7 305 90 16, (0) 41 217 950
Email: vino.pecaric@email.si
Website: www.geocities.com/vinopecaric

Wine selling ❧ Wine tasting
Wine cellar tours ❧ Wine route
❧ Honey and brandy products

Mix of wines on offer

33% Metliška Črnina, 19% 'Belokranjec' white blend, 15% Rumeni Muškat, 10% Modra Frankinja, 5% Portugalka, 5% Laški Rizling, 5% Sauvignon, 4% Sivi Pinot and 4% Chardonnay.

BELA KRAJINA WINE-GROWING DISTRICT

Alojz Hoznar

Ručetna vas 8, si-8340 Črnomelj, Phone: +386 (0) 7 305 29 48, (0) 41 215 862

Wine selling ❧ Wine tasting
❧ Production of wine and food

At Hoznars' wine growing is a family tradition. They produce Belokranjsko white, blended varieties and predicates. Their highest hopes are for the Belokranjsko, Metliška Črnina and predicates. The finest examples of their predicates are 2001 *Ledeno Vino*, 2003 Sauvignon *Jagodni Izbor*, 2003 Sivi Pinot *Jagodni Izbor* and 2003 Sauvignon *Suhi Jagodni Izbor*.

Wines on offer

'Belokranjsko' white blend, Modra Frankinja, Sauvignon (also *Jagodni Izbor*, *Suhi Jagodni Izbor* and *Ledeno Vino*), Renski Rizling and Sivi Pinot *Jagodni Izbor*.

Awards

Their pride and inspiration is the gold medal they won at the international wine tasting in Ljubljana, as well as four grand gold, four gold and three silver medals at the Gornja Radgona tasting.

2001 Sauvignon *Ledeno Vino*
10.5% vol., sweet, ★★★

The golden, sunny colour glows in the glass like a precious stone, and the fresh nose is floral and fruity in character. It is redolent of dried flowers, and over-ripe and dried white fruit. The palate presents a wine of rich, dense content, which preoccupies the tongue for many seconds. It delivers a variety of fruit sensations, which return to the nose and combine to make a colourful, aromatic mosaic. The sugar tastes as if it has been roasted by the sun and marks the wine's predominant character. A wonderful wine: on the nose an *Ledeno Vino* in character, whereas on the palate it comes closest to a *Suhi Jagodni Izbor*.
Recommended dishes: *Prosta potica*, pancakes with walnuts, fruit cakes, fruit salads made with apple purée and lemon.

BELA KRAJINA WINE-GROWING DISTRICT

2001 SAUVIGNON *Ledeno Vino*

BELA KRAJINA WINE-GROWING DISTRICT

KZ Metlika

Kmetijska zadruga Metlika, Cesta 15. brigade 2, si-8330 Metlika
Phone: +386 (0) 7 363 70 00, (0) 7 363 70 50, Fax: +386 (0) 7 363 70 51
Email: m.kzmetlika@siol.net
Website: www.kz-metlika.si

- Wine tasting for announced groups
- Wine cellar tours for announced groups
- Wine selling
- Wine route
- Production of wine and food for announced groups

Photo: KZ Metlika

The Agricultural Cooperative obtained this wine cellar in 1966, and over time they redecorated it; built a grape processor, a bottling room and a warehouse; and increased the cellar's capacity. They grow fourteen grape varieties in their vineyards. Aside from Metliška Črnina — their mass product — their best wines are 'Belokranjec' white blend, Portugalka and the predicate wines of the 'Kolednik' brand. The best vintages still available are 1999 and 2000 Metliška Črnina, 2000 Modra Frankinja, predicates of the 1997—9 vintages and selected wines from 2003.

Mix of wines on offer

42% Metliška Črnina, 20% white blend, 15% 'Belokranjec' white blend, 8% Modra Frankinja, 7% red blend, 5% Laški Rizling, 0,7% predicates, 0,7% sparkling 'Metliška Penina', 0,5% Rumeni Muškat, 0,5% Sauvignon, 0,3% Chardonnay and 0,3% Rosé.

Awards

The wines of the Agricultural Cooperative have been awarded a grand gold medal, and gold and silver medals on numerous occasions in Gornja Radgona, Zagreb and Split.

Culinary recommendations

Metliška Črnina is a good wine to accompany roast lamb, grilled food, pork or Easter ham in dough. Belokranjec on the other hand goes well with pork and sausages or *matevž* with sour turnip, and Portugalka with roasted chestnuts.

BELA KRAJINA WINE-GROWING DISTRICT

2000 Metliška Črnina

12.0% vol., dry, ★★★

The medium-intense ruby red appearance of this wine with its purple notes suggests youth, while it is beginning to show nuances of fiery brick. The aroma of red berries and fruit (predominantly raspberries, black cherries, plums and mulberries) is reminiscent of over-ripe, even sun-dried, fruit, and complements the fragrances of roasting (coffee, carob) and a slight animal tinge (fresh leather). The tannin content is medium, having already toned down, and has a velvety flavour. The acidity is there only to preserve the juiciness of the wine, and does not disturb the tannin balance. It is a good blend of different varieties (Modra Frankinja, St Laurent's, Velvet, and Portuguese) formed by tradition, becoming a medium-full wine that by its character belongs to the family of red wines from Primorska and Posavje.

It has a unique character, is easily recognizable and very easy to drink.

Recommended dishes: Baked Easter ham in dough, grilled lamb and other grilled dishes, roast goose, duck, turkey.

BELA KRAJINA WINE-GROWING DISTRICT

2003 Rumeni Muškat

11.5% vol., dry, ★★★

Pale yellow and glowing in appearance. The delicate bouquet of the variety is pleasant and delivers Rumeni Muškat on the nose in colourful tones. There are floral-fruit scents of flowers and fruit (lemon, apricots, citrus fruit, tropical fruit), and a clear smell of spice (anise). A freshness prevails on the tongue and in the oral cavity, full of the relaxed scents of young flowers and fruit. The body is of medium structure, but seems slim and vibrant. There is just enough acidity to maintain the fruitiness and freshness. Finally, one detects a pleasant bitterness, the autograph of excellent Muscat wines, and confirmation of the bond between this variety and the soil where it feels at home.

Recommended dishes: Serve as an aperitif or with omelette, smoked salmon, asparagus with seafood and balsamic vinegar, fruit salads of peaches and pears.

BELA KRAJINA WINE-GROWING DISTRICT

2003 Izbrani Belokranjec

12.5% vol., dry, ★

This pale yellow wine with a green tinge looks crystal clear. The floral-fruit nose is pleasantly fresh and colourful, and offers a complex bouquet of nature's scents. The fragrances of white and yellow fruit prevail (green apples, peaches). The fresh, dry flavour is anticipated on the palate and complements the nose. The body has a solid foundation and exhibits a pleasing complexity, without a doubt attributable to the varieties the wine comprises, as well as to the ripeness of the grapes. One can pick out all the fundamental flavours that add to the well-designed character of this dry white wine. Liveliness is provided by the pleasant acidity. A lovely wine to accompany several tradtional Slovene dishes.
Recommended dishes: *Matevž* and sour turnip, *sauerkraut* dishes (*sarma, jota*), farm pork and sausage, casseroles, risottos, Carniolan sausage.

BELA KRAJINA WINE-GROWING DISTRICT

Anton Kostelec

Drašiči 13, si-8330 Metlika, Phone: +386 (0) 7 305 90 93, (0) 41 788 938

Wine selling ❧ Wine tasting
Wine cellar tours ❧ Wine route

After eight years of wine growing and trading Kostelec has decided it's time to take the plunge and go for his own wine labels. He grows numerous grape varieties in his vineyards and the most promising at the moment is the Laški Rizling. The best of the available wines are all predicates, and above all *Izbor* of a number of varieties.
Best vintages: 2000 Laški Rizling *Izbor*, 2000 Chardonnay *Izbor*, 1999 Sivi Pinot *Suhi Jagodni Izbor*, 1998 Laški Rizling *Ledeno Vino* and 1997 Laški Rizling *Suhi Jagodni Izbor*.

Wines on offer
50% Metliška Črnina, 15% 'Belokranjec' white blend, 5% Chardonnay, 5% Sivi Pinot, 5% Sauvignon, 5% Modra Frankinja and 10% predicates.

Awards
At the Gornja Radgona wine tasting they have been twice winners of variety champion, and in Ljubljana they won the grand gold medal.

Culinary recommendations
Their wines are best complemented by Bela Krajina flat cake.

2000 Laški Rizling *Izbor*
14.1% vol., semi-sweet, ★★★

The golden, sunny colour has a festive, persuasive appearance that attracts attention. The abundant nose opens up as soon as the glass is raised, with plentiful aromas of dried flowers, and dried and and baked white and yellow fruit. Gentle, delicate fragrances of dried figs, honey and caramel follow. On the palate it still seems youthful and fresh beyond all expectation. The liveliness is due to a rich acidity, which contributes to the impression of slenderness, though the wine is rich in fundamental flavours.
After swallowing, the pleasant impressions linger and seem hesitant to leave. A very suitable wine for cellarage, ensuring pleasant surprises for a decade to come.
Recommended dishes: Bela Krajina flat cake, prosta *potica*, pancakes with walnuts, fruit cake, blue cheese.

BELA KRAJINA WINE-GROWING DISTRICT

2000 Laški Rizling *Izbor*

BELA KRAJINA WINE-GROWING DISTRICT

Samuel Malnarič

Vavpča vas 40, si-8333 Semič, Phone: +386 (0) 7 306 72 06, (0) 41 799 037

Wine selling ❧ Wine tasting
Wine cellar tours ❧ Wine route
Sales material ❧ Guided tastings
❧ Production of wine and food for announced groups

Wine growing and trading has passed from generation to generation in the Malnarič family. They started in a big way in 1990, and produced their first label for their Laški Rizling in 1992. Their three most promising wines are the Modra Frankinja, Modri Pinot and the 'Belokranjsko' white blend; the latter is also produced in the largest quantities. Their best vintages still available are 1998 Chardonnay barrique, 1999 and 2002 Laški Rizling, 2001 and 2002 Chardonnay, 2000 and 2001 Modri Pinot barrique, 1998 Chardonnay *Ledeno Vino*, 1999 Chardonnay *Suhi Jagodni Izbor* and 1999 Laški Rizling *Ledeno Vino*.

Mix of wines on offer

35% 'Belokranjsko' white blend, 15% 'Belokranjec' red blend, 10% Laški Rizling, 18% Chardonnay (also barrique and predicates), 5% Modra Frankinja, 5% Kerner, 5% Sauvignon, 5% Modri Pinot barrique, and 2% Kraljevina.

Awards

Between 1994 and 1997 they have received several gold medals in Gornja Radgona, and their honorary commendations remind them of the Ljubljana fair and the Chivalric Tournament.

Culinary recommendations

To go with Bela Krajina flat cake they recommend dry wines with a higher level of acidity, for example the 'Belokranjsko' white blend or the Modra Frankinja.

1999 Laški Rizling

11.8% vol., dry, ★★

A pale yellow appearance with straw-like tones; its subtle nuances predict a mature wine. Even a still glass shows off the successful development of the bouquet. After the first gentle aromas, swilling the wine in the glass delivers the mature scents of dried fruit, hazelnuts and fresh butter: in other words, a wine at its highest point. The maturity is similarly well-expressed on the palate, with the agreeable structure of this dry wine subtly revealing itself. The balance of sweet and sour is in harmony, and the finish confirms a good vintage as well as a wine showing all the distinction of of its variety and the care with which it has been nurtured.
Recommended dishes: Risotto (especially poultry risotto), *štruklji*, sweet and sour cabbage with partly smoked meat, asparagus dishes, soured beef with onions, trout prepared Trieste-style.

BELA KRAJINA WINE-GROWING DISTRICT

1999 Laški Rizling

BELA KRAJINA WINE-GROWING DISTRICT

Anton Plut

Drašiči 48, si-8330 Metlika, Phone: +386 (0) 7 363 53 90, (0) 7 363 53 91
Email: antonp@siol.net

Wine selling 🌿 Wine tasting for announced groups

The year 1852, carved into the wine press at Pluts', attests to a lengthy wine-growing tradition. The bottles first received wine labels in 1993. Sivi Pinot, Rumeni Muškat and Modra Frankinja are grapes that simply thrive in the vineyards, and it is these varieties that produce the most promising wines. Some are still available: 1998 Rumeni Muškat *Ledeno Vino*, 2001 Sivi Pinot *Izbor* and 2001 Modra Frankinja.

Mix of wines on offer

25% Metliška %ornina, 20% 'Belokranjec' white blend, 15% Modra Frankinja, 15% Rumeni Muškat, 10% Sauvignon, 5% Sivi Pinot, 5% Portugalka, 4% Chardonnay and 1% Laški Rizling.

Awards

They have had success at the Gornja Radgona wine fair.

Culinary recommendations

With roasted smoked ham in dough or with grilled lamb they recommend Metlika Crnina; with walnut *potica* a Rumeni Muškat or Sauvignon.

2001 Modra Frankinja

12.2% vol., dry, ★★★

A medium-intense ruby red colour, still with some vibrant purple reflections. An open and candid fruit fragrance prevails and resembles very ripe grapes, purple berries and newish leather. The palate is tender and vibrant. The tannins are velvety, the acidities mild, creating a pleasant and juicy balance. The body is medium-built, the basic flavours are well-balanced. The variety is easily recognizable, both from the aroma and the taste. This wine has almost finished its development and is currently at its peak.
Recommended dishes: Baked Bela Krajina ham in dough, homemade salami, grilled lamb, roast turkey, goose.

BELA KRAJINA WINE-GROWING DISTRICT

2001 Modra Frankinja

BELA KRAJINA WINE-GROWING DISTRICT

Jožef Prus

Krmačina 6, si-8330 Metlika
Phone: +386 (0) 7 305 90 98, (0) 41 690 112, Fax: +386 (0) 7 305 90 98

Wine selling ❧ Wine tasting for announced groups
Wine cellar tours ❧ Accommodation
Honey on sale ❧ Wine and food for announced groups

Several generations of the Prus family have been in the wine trade, and since 1980 Jožef has actively participated. The areas of Repica and Vidošiči with the best wine-growing terrain are suited to varieties such as Rumeni Muškat, Sauvignon, Modra Frankinja and Gamay, and produces the most promising wines. The best vintages stored in the Prus cellar are: 1997 Laški Rizling, 1998 Renski Rizling, 2003 Sauvignon, 2001 Renski Rizling, 1998 Rumeni Muškat, 2001 Sauvignon, a special high-quality natural wine produced from dried grapes, 1999 Rumeni Muškat, 2001 Renski Rizling and 2001 Sauvignon.

Wines on offer

'Belokranjec' white blend, Metliška Črnina, 'Repičan' blend, Laški Rizling, Renski Rizling, Sauvignon, Rumeni Muškat, Sivi Pinot, Kerner, Portugalka, Modra Frankinja (also barrique), Gamay barrique, Traminec, Cabernet Sauvignon and predicates.

Awards

Prus has won over thirty medals at tastings in Gornja Radgona alone. In Ljubljana and Zagreb he has been honoured with twelve grand gold medals, and at all three locations his wines have four times won the championship title.

Culinary recommendations

Red wines are the best choice to accompany Bela Krajina flat cake and smoked meat.

2001 Sauvignon *Suhi Jagodni Izbor*

11.3% vol., sweet, ★★★

This golden-yellow wine, which has retained some green notes, glows proudly in the glass. Really dense floral and fruit bouquets of high maturity exhibit a complex mix of scents and remind us of camomile, raisins from ripe grapes, dried pears and apricots, tree roots, fresh almonds, roasted fruit, fresh bread, oranges and beeswax, with the noble scent of botrytis in close companionship with all these lovely fragrances. Sweetness with the character of honey prevails on the palate, still holding some freshness. One cannot sense the alcohol, but one can guess at the diplomatic role it plays in harmonizing the thousand wonderful nuances that this wine delivers. The harmony is unique and the wonderful length of the bouquet, fit for a king, stays with us long after swallowing. This is a wine with a bright future ahead, destined to be a top choice among the best wines of its kind.

Recommended dishes: Walnut and sweet tarragon *potica*, pancakes with walnuts, fruit desserts with ice-cream, rice puddings and stewed fruit.

BELA KRAJINA WINE-GROWING DISTRICT

2001 SAUVIGNON *Suhi Jagodni Izbor*   1998 RENSKI RIZLING *Ledeno Vino*

1998 RENSKI RIZLING *Ledeno Vino*
9.5 vol. % alk., sweet, ★★★★

This golden-yellow wine with its unique depth pours noiselessly and indicates its rich conent by the way it flows from the bottle. The nose seems mature, with toasty nuances. Caramel is in the foreground, with fragrances redolent of dried figs and peaches, roasted quince and spices. The palate is full and confirms straightaway what the eyes have already seen. The hints of honey are a sign of the high concentration of sugar in the grape. They are accompanied by a freshness, giving the wine complexity and appeal. The aroma of noble rot goes hand in hand with this variety, and the two seem to sing together in harmony; one can almost hear a tenor. Finally, there is an expressive balance between the acidity's liveliness and the sweetness of the wine. The over-ripe character does not prevail, as the backbone intervenes and adds a mineral tone, giving greater breadth and with that an excellence that this mature wine deserves.
Recommended dishes: Bela Krajina flat cake, walnut and sweet tarragon *potica*, pancakes with a mixed filling of chocolate, oranges, dried apricots and vanilla.

BELA KRAJINA WINE-GROWING DISTRICT

Jože Šuklje

Trnovec 22, si-8330 Metlika, Phone: +386 (0) 7 305 91 64, (0) 41 554 120

Wine selling ❧ Wine tasting
Wine cellar tours for announced groups ❧ Wine route
❧ Production of wine and food for announced groups

Jože Šuklje has been in the wine trade since the late 1980s. In his vineyards he grows all the grape varieties necessary for the creation of an excellent Metliška Črnina, and Metliška Črnina is the wine he produces most of, but he also grows white grapes for predicates and some for the production of good-quality wine blends. In his opinion the soil here is best suited to Modra Frankinja which, besides Metliska Crnina, is his top wine. There are still some wines available from the 2003 vintage: Modra Frankinja, Kerner *Izbor* and Sauvignon *Izbor*.

Wines on offer

50% Metliška Črnina, 10% Modra Frankinja, 10% Kerner, 20% white blend, 5% Sivi Pinot and 5% Sauvignon.

Awards

He has won several golds in Gornja Radgona and another at the Ljubljana wine tasting.

2003 Metliška Črnina

10.95% vol., dry, ★★

A beautiful ruby red wine, adorned by vivacious purple notes, giving the impression of youth and clarity. The fragrances are intense and open, and resemble very ripe grapes, boiled grape juice and burnt crusts of bread. On the palate it seems vibrant, youthful and quite fresh. The tannins are moderate, as is best for a Metliska Crnina; their presence is accentuated by a vibrant acidity, which maintains the youthful character and the fruity flavour in this pleasant and drinkable wine. It is likeable in all respects, and although it has not yet demonstrated all it can (it will continue to improve in quality for about a year) it is currently best suited to the local taste of Bela Krajina.
Recommended dishes: Carniolan sausage, roasted Easter ham in dough, grilled lamb, roast goose, turkey.

BELA KRAJINA WINE-GROWING DISTRICT

2003 Metliška Črnina

BELA KRAJINA WINE-GROWING DISTRICT

Otmar Šturm

Butična vinska klet, Mestni trg 25, si-8330 Metlika
Phone: +386 (0) 7 305 85 07, (0) 7 363 53 50, (0) 41 632 470

Wine selling ❧ Wine tasting
Wine cellar tours for announced groups ❧ Sales material
❧ Production of wine and food for announced groups

The beginnings of wine growing and trading in the Šturm family go back to the 1970s, their first wine labels dating from the middle of that decade. The grapes in the vineyards are grown in equal proportion to the wines they produce. Their biggest success is their Rumeni Muškat, which is in great demand and is the cause of much pride to the family. For some time to come their cellar will continue to hold the best vintages of Modri Pinot and the wine best suited to the European market - Modra Frankinja.

Mix of wines on offer

40% Rumeni Muškat, 20% Modra Frankinja, 10% Sauvignon, 10% Modri Pinot, 5% Traminec, 5% Chardonnay, 5% Laški Rizling and 5% Portugalka.

Awards

Between 1976 and 1992 they have successfully participated in the tastings at Ljubljana and Gornja Radgona.

Culinary recommendations

Their wines are best complemented by bread, the local dishes of Bela Krajina and lamb.

2002 Modra Frankinja

12.5% vol., dry, ★★★

A deep ruby red colour, almost opaque. The wine acquires a purple hue towards the edge of the glass and and takes on brick tones. The beautiful array of fragrances release themselves with intensity on the nose, resembling above all aromas of roasting and spices (vanilla, pepper, carob); further on one detects bread crusts, dark chocolate and leather. The rich body presents itself on the palate in complex form and exhibits a fruity character (purple berries), toned by the wonderful tannins, still youthful in temperament. The acidity enhances the freshness, expresses the distinctive characteristics of the variety and predicts that this wine is going to develop wonderfully. The cohabitation of wine and oak has produced a mediterranean character, which proves the potential of a Franconian grown on good terrain.
Recommended dishes: Bela Krajina ham, Karstic prosciutto, grilled lamb, roast turkey, goose, duck with flat cake and red cabbage.

BELA KRAJINA WINE-GROWING DISTRICT

2002 Modra Frankinja

2003 Rumeni Muškat

2003 Rumeni Muškat

11.5% vol., semi-sweet, ★★★

A pale yellow, almost colourless and crystal-clear wine. Some enticing bubbles adorn the rim of the glass where the wine meets it. The bouquet is medium-intense and floral above all with the scent of blossom in character. Aromas of fruit awaken in the glass, redolent of lemons, green apples and grapefruit. On the palate the wine is at first vibrant, pleasant, light and gentle, as if wanting to fly. As it develops it exhibits a good composition; its sweetness contributes to its overall mildness, but after a second or two there comes a fresh acidity, which livens up pleasantly on the tongue, and the flavour gains breadth. The grape variety is also confirmed by an attractive bitterness, appropriate for this wine, and its style is marked by a slim body. A wine currently at its best.
Recommended dishes: Asparagus in cream, smoked salmon, fruit salad with melon and peaches.

BELA KRAJINA WINE-GROWING DISTRICT

Jože Simčič

Železniki 4, si-8330 Metlika, Phone: +386 (0) 7 305 80 94, (0) 41 655 019

Wine selling ❧ Wine tasting
❧ Wine cellar tours for announced groups

Mix of wines on offer

Wine on tap: 40% 'Belokranjec' white blend, 30% Metliška Črnina, 10% Chardonnay, 10% Sauvignon, 5% Laški Rizling and 5% Rumeni Muškat.

Jože Stariha

Drašiči 46, si-8330 Metlika, Phone: +386 (0) 7 305 86 04, (0) 41 753 017

Wine selling ❧ Wine cellar tours for announced groups
Wine cellar tours for announced groups ❧ Production of wine and food for announced groups

Mix of wines on offer

35% Metliška Črnina, 30% 'Belokranjec' white blend, 15% Modra Frankinja, 15% Rumeni Muškat and 5% Portugalka.

Ivan Suhorepec

Ručetna vas 2, si-8340 Črnomelj
Phone: +386 (0) 7 305 29 54, (0) 41 542 599, Fax: +386 (0) 7 305 29 54

Wine selling ❧ Wine tasting

Mix of wines on offer

20% Renski Rizling, 20% Modra Frankinja and Žametna Črnina, 20% 'Belokranjec' white blend, 15% Chardonnay, 10% Laški Rizling, 10% Sauvignon and 5% Sivi Pinot.

Stanko Turk

Jelševnik 15, si-8340 Črnomelj, Phone: +386 (0) 7 354 00 96

Wine selling ❧ Wine tasting for announced groups
Wine cellar tours for announced groups ❧ Wine route

Mix of wines on offer

40% 'Belokranjec' white blend, 30% 'Belokranjec' red blend, 20% Laški Rizling and 10% Rumeni Muškat.

Goriška Brda Wine-Growing District

PRIMORSKA WINE-GROWING REGION

GORIŠKA BRDA WINE-GROWING DISTRICT

Belica

Zlatko Mavrič, Medana 32, si-5212 Dobrovo v Brdih
Phone: +386 (0)5 304 21 04, Fax: +386 (0)5 395 91 09

Wine selling ❧ Wine tasting
Production of wine and food ❧ Wine cellar tours
Wine route ❧ Accommodation
❧ Sales material

Wines on offer

Chardonnay, Rebula, Furlanski Tokaj, Sauvignon, Merlot, Sivi Pinot,
Cabernet Sauvignon, Rumeni Muškat and Modri Pinot.

Debenjak - D

Bruno & Edi Debenjak, Kozana 9, si-5212 Dobrovo v Brdih, Phone: +386 (0)5 304 12 64

Wine selling ❧ Wine tasting for announced groups
❧ Wine route

Wines on offer

Sivi Pinot, Chardonnay, Rebula, Malvazija,
Furlanski Tokaj, Merlot Cabernet.

Kmetija 'Pod - Dob' Ceglo

Žarko Cukjati, Ceglo 25A, si-5212 Dobrovo v Brdih
Phone: +386 (0)5 304 21 89, (0)41 775 060, Fax: +386 (0)5 304 21 89
Email: martina_cukjati@email.si

Wine selling ❧ Wine tasting for announced groups
Wine cellar tours for announced groups ❧ Wine route

Mix of wines on offer

60% white varieties (Rebula, Chardonnay, Beli Pinot, Sauvignon),
10% white blend, 30% Cabernet Sauvignon and Merlot.

Kmetija Prinčič

Tomaž Prinčič, Kozana 11, si-5212 Dobrovo v Brdih
Phone: +386 (0)5 304 12 72, (0)41 721 929, Fax: +386 (0)5 304 12 72
Email: tomaz.princic@siol.net, Website: www.geocities.com/princic

Wine selling ❧ Wine tasting for announced groups
Wine cellar tours for announced groups ❧ Wine route
❧ Sales material

Wines on offer

Sivi Pinot, Chardonnay, Sauvignon, Modri Pinot, Merlot; white 'Mihael' blend,
red 'Mihael' blend and 'Mulit' blend.

GORIŠKA BRDA WINE-GROWING DISTRICT

KLAVORA

Zdenko Kabaj, Šlovrenc 3a, si-5212 Dobrovo v Brdih
Phone: +386 (0)5 304 57 08, (0)41 953 282, Fax: +386 (0)5 304 57 08

Wine selling ❦ Wine tasting for announced groups
❦ Wine cellar tours for announced groups

MIX OF WINES ON OFFER

20% Refošk, 18% Cabernet Sauvignon, 13% Sivi Pinot, 10% Sauvignon, 8% Furlanski Tokaj, 7% Chardonnay, 15% white 'Briško' blend and 9% red 'Briško' blend.

KLINEC - MEDANA

Aleks Klinec, Medana 20, si-5212 Dobrovo v Brdih,
Phone: +386 (0)5 304 50 92, Fax: +386 (0)5 304 50 92
Email: klinec-medana@s5.net, Website: www.klinec-medana.com

Wine selling ❦ Wine tasting
Production of wine and food ❦ Wine cellar tours
Wine route ❦ Accommodation
Sales material ❦ Art gallery, conference room

MIX OF WINES ON OFFER

25% red 'Qula' blend (Merlot, Cabernet Sauvignon), 25% white 'Modana' blend, 15% Sivi Pinot, 12.5% Chardonnay, 10% Furlanski Tokaj, 7.5% Rebula and 5% Verduc.

IRENA IN ROBERT GAŠPARIN OBLJUBEK

Drnovk 11, si-5212 Dobrovo v Brdih
Phone: +386 (0)5 304 53 36, Fax: +386 (0)5 304 53 36

Wine selling ❦ Wine tasting
Wine cellar tours for announced groups ❦ Wine route

MIX OF WINES ON OFFER

30% white 'Hrast' blend, 30% red 'Hrast' blend, 15% Chardonnay, 15% Cabernet Sauvignon and 10% Rebula.

KMETIJA PRI ŠTAKLJEVIH

Roman in Anuška Štekar, Snežatno 26, si-5211 Kojsko, Phone: +386 (0)5 304 65 40

Wine selling ❦ Wine tasting
Production of wine and food ❦ Wine cellar tours for announced groups
Wine route ❦ Accommodation
Sales material ❦ Typical local cuisine

WINES ON OFFER

Wine on tap, Rebula, Chardonnay, Sivi Pinot, Sauvignon and Cabernet Sauvignon.

GORIŠKA BRDA WINE-GROWING DISTRICT

BJANA

Miran Sirk, Biljana 38. si-5212 Dobrovo v Brdih
Phone: +386 (0)5 304 50 76, (0)41 711 760. Fax: +386 (0)5 333 19 32
Email: miran.sirk@hit.si

Wine selling ❧ Wine tasting
Wine cellar tours ❧ Wine cellar tours for announced groups
❧ Wine route

The hundred-year-old family tradition of wine growing acquired its first wine label in 1985. Over half of the wine on offer is sparkling, the other half being divided between 'Cuvée Merlot'; Cabernet Sauvignon; Furanski Tokaj; and white cuvée, produced from Chardonnay and Rebula. The future promises sparkling wines and white non-sparkling wines, all made using traditional methods. Best available vintages: 1999 and 2000 sparkling 'Cuvée Prestige' produced in classical way, and 2001 red 'Cuvée Status'.

Mix of wines on offer
65% sparkling wine, 20% red wine and 15% white non-sparkling wine.

Awards
Bronze medals in Ljubljana and Verona, silver in Brussels.

2003 Furlanski Tokaj
13.5% vol., dry, ★

The pale yellow colour of the wine exhibits some green shades; a proof of its youth. Not fully open, the wine at first reveals a discreetly floral nose; in time its intensity is enhanced and develops herbaceous aromas. The youth of the wine and its potential is clearly evident on the palate. The flavours are pleasant, the freshness is ever-present and fundamental components complement each other well. On swallowing, the palate lingers, and the finish is pleasant, even suave, for such a young wine. This wine has entered the limelight too early, however, so we must wait and see!
Recommended dishes: frittata with seasonal herbs, turkey and veal pâtés, white meat with gravy.

GORIŠKA BRDA WINE-GROWING DISTRICT

2003 Furlanski Tokaj

1999 Cuvée Prestige Brut

1999 Cuvée Prestige Brut

13.5% vol., dry, ★★★

With its yellow straw colour and lots of tiny, long-lasting bubbles that fizz in the glass and seem to whisper their story, this sparkling wine delights us even before we use our other senses. The necklace of bubbles forming a circle on the wine's surface immediately commands attention. The bouquet, constantly freshened by the sparkling of the bubbles, encompasses a variety of fragrances beginning with flowers and fruit. The fragrances continue with rusk, beeswax and aromatic spices. The liveliness of the wine is apparent on the palate, but the full body and backbone are engaging and we enjoy the dichotomy between the freshness and the full body. There is a flavour of fresh bread crumbs, which gives this sparking wine an extra glow and prolongs the bouquet. In short, a sparkling wine for the general wine lover and the connoisseur alike.

Recommended dishes: With its richness and character this sparkling wine can be served not only as an aperitif, but also as an accompaniment to various dishes, above all fish, smoked salmon and shrimp cocktail.

GORIŠKA BRDA WINE-GROWING DISTRICT

Blažič

Borut Blažič, Plešivo 30, si-5212 Dobrovo v Brdih
Phone: +386 (0)5 304 54 45, (0)41 516 149, Fax: +386 (0)5 304 54 45
Email: blazic.borut@hotmail.com

Wine selling ❧ Wine tasting
Wine tasting for announced groups ❧ Wine cellar tours

Borut Blažič has been in the wine trade since 1990, and he has been labelling his bottles since 1993. The vineyards are predominantly planted with Rebula, Sauvignon and Sivi Pinot. Lately the sales of Furlanski Tokaj have increased, and this, alongside Rebula, is the most promising wine in the cellar. Best vintages: 1997 and 1999 red blend 'Blaž', 1999 white blend 'Blaž', 2000 Furlanski Tokaj.

Mix of wines on offer

25% Rebula, 10% Furlanski Tokaj, 20% Sauvignon, 10% Sivi Pinot, 7% Beli Pinot, 13% Chardonnay, white blend 'Blaž' (Chardonnay, Beli Pinot) and 15% red blend 'Blaž' (Cabernet Sauvignon, Merlot).

Awards

As proof of their success, they hold two gold medals and the title of variety champion from the Ljubljana fair. They also take pride in the title of chivalric champion of the dry wines.

Culinary recommendations

Red 'Blaž' accompanied well by fried prosciutto with polenta; Furlanski Tokaj by asparagus with eggs.

2001 Furlanski Tokaj

13.5% vol., dry, ★★★

The yellowy wine with golden reflections has a glowing, seductive appearance. On the nose it identifies itself as an aromatic wine with a number of primary aromas. Floral scents overshadow fruit, but in time the balance tends increasingly to fruitiness, just as if eating the grapes themselves. The tension builds, as does our curiosity. The palate delivers a complexity, which seems to resemble a peacock's tale: characteristics open up, disappear, appear again - a feast for all the senses. The lasting impression is a highly pleasing and unforgettable one.

Recommended dishes: Frittata with seasonal herbs, smoked trout with asparagus, and seafood such as scampi with grilled courgettes.

GORIŠKA BRDA WINE-GROWING DISTRICT

2001 Furlanski Tokaj

GORIŠKA BRDA WINE-GROWING DISTRICT

Brandulin

Boris Kristančič, Plešivo 4, si-5212 Dobrovo v Brdih
Phone: +386 (0)5 303 56 57, (0)5 304 21 39, (0)41 561 22
Email: brandulin@volja.net

Wine selling ❧ Wine tasting for announced groups
❧ Wine cellar tours for announced groups

They first went into viticulture and the wine trade in 1985, and their first labelled bottled vintage came in 1994. The vineyard is predominantly planted with varieties such as Chardonnay, Beli Pinot, Rebula and Furlanski Tokaj, the last two being the best. Most promising are the Rebula, Furlanski Tokaj, Beli Pinot and the two 'Brandulin' blends. With the exception of the last, the best vintages are still available.

Mix of wines on offer

10% Rebula, 10% Furlanski Tokaj, 15% Beli Pinot, 10% Sivi Pinot, 20% Chardonnay, 15% red 'Brandulin' and 20% white 'Brandulin'.

Awards

Their success at wine tastings in Ljubljana is shown by their five silver medals.

Culinary recommendations

The best accompaniment to their wines is local, homemade cuisine.

2001 Beli Pinot

13.5 vol.% alk., dry, ★

The golden-yellow appearance of this wine with its attractive glow promises something to be savoured. The ripe nose gives off a gentle fruitiness with hints of hazelnuts, spices, bread crusts and freshly churned butter. The wine is full-bodied and yields a complex palate, rounded and full of energy, taking its time to say farewell.

Recommended dishes: Grilled polenta with cheese and prosciutto, soup with truffles, frittata with prosciutto and fennel, grilled turkey steaks.

GORIŠKA BRDA WINE-GROWING DISTRICT

2001 Beli Pinot

GORIŠKA BRDA WINE-GROWING DISTRICT

Cjanova Kmetija

Zvonimir Prinčič, Gornje Cerovo 23, si-5211 Kojsko
Phone: +386 (0)5 304 40 20, (0)41 698 623, Fax: +386 (0)5 304 40 20

Wine selling ❧ Wine tasting
Production of wine and food ❧ Wine cellar tours
Sales material ❧ Dried grape pressing (7 February)

The wine-growing tradition has been in the Prinčič family since the eighteenth century, and they opted to start labelling their wines in 1988. Besides such promising wines as Merlot, Rebula and Furlanski Tokaj, the cellar speciality is 'Poezija' ('poetry'), a special natural wine from dried Rebula grapes that bears the highest alcohol content for wine in the world. All wines are still available.

Wines on offer

Merlot, Rebula, Furlanski Tokaj, Cabernet Sauvignon, Sivi Pinot; 'Veliko Belo', 'Veliko Rdeče' and 'Poezija'.

Awards

The Prinčičs are the proud recipients of a silver medal from Ljubljana and a bronze from the Gornja Radgona fair.

Culinary recommendations

The 'Veliko Rdeče' wine is served with venison goulash. Walnut cake is good with 'Poezija', and Soča trout with Rebula.

1999 Poezija

17.0% vol., semi-sweet, ★★★

The beautiful golden colour of this crystal-clear wine with its amber reflections gives the impression of thickness. The legs around the glass also appear thick in their own way, and follow their paths slowly down the glass. The rich nose opens up in complexity and resembles the noble bouquet of wine kept 'under the veil' (so called owing to the 'veil' of live yeast that accumulates on the wine's surface and prevents oxidation). Dried fruits such as pears, apricots and figs; citrus zest; some nuances of fried food, the scents of honey brandy - all these make up the abundant blend of fragrances. The palate is dry and lively in character, even more than you would anticipate. Warmth and a sweetish flavour of alcohol form the basis of the wine's character which, in spite of its rich content, remains fresh and gentle, and lingers on. It is an interesting wine for connoisseurs - 'listen' to it with all your senses and hear the its song.
Recommended dishes: Sweetened, mixed fruit salad; apricot cake; pancakes stuffed with walnuts.

GORIŠKA BRDA WINE-GROWING DISTRICT

1999 Poezija

GORIŠKA BRDA WINE-GROWING DISTRICT

Constantiní

Dušan Humar, Plešivo 32, si-5212 Dobrovo v Brdih
Phone: +386 (0)5 395 95 77, (0)41 771 449, Fax: +386 (0)5 395 95 76
Email: constantini@siol.net

Wine selling ❧ Wine tasting for announced groups
Accommodation ❧ Sales material
❧ Wine Route

For the Humars, wine growing and selling have been a traditional part of life for several generations. In 1993 they decided to label their wines. 'Vitis' is a blend of Chardonnay, Tokay and Sauvignon which, alongside Cabernet Sauvignon, Merlot and Sivi Pinot, thrives in the vineyards and promises good wine in the future.
Best vintages available: 1997, 1998 Cabernet Sauvignon and 2000 Cabernet Franc.

Mix of wines on offer

25% 'Vitis', 24% Sivi Pinot, 21% Merlot, 15% Cabernet Sauvignon,
10% Sauvignon and 5% Cabernet Franc.

Culinary recommendations

The Sivi Pinot and 'Vitis' make a good complement to noodles with prosciutto and onions, while grilled rabbit with dumplings made according to the house recipe goes well with Cabernet Sauvignon. Roast duck or venison are also good accompaniments to Cabernet Sauvignon; roast goose and apple stuffing with Merlot. Pork fillet and wheatmeal dumplings work well served with Sivi Pinot.

2000 Cabernet Franc

12.2% vol., dry, ★★

The intense ruby red colour with vibrant reflections makes this wine appealing to the eye, and the beautiful legs promise a firm backbone. Initially the nose is one of lovely herbaceous fragrances, soon joined by grapes fermenting in an open vat. The nose remains mild and pleasant with great nobility, and these characteristics continue on the palate, where a flavour of roasted coffee beans is released, although the fruit fragrances continue to prevail. There are more tannins than one would expect of a Cabernet Franc, but most of them have reached a sweet maturity and lend the wine a velvety quality. In a year or two more this wine will develop to the full, as promised by the still vocal tannins. An opportunity not to be missed.
Recommended dishes: Noodles with prosciutto and onions; ham; veal shoulder with boletus; grilled goose with apple stuffing; grilled dishes, especially barbecued meats.

GORIŠKA BRDA WINE-GROWING DISTRICT

2000 Cabernet Franc

GORIŠKA BRDA WINE-GROWING DISTRICT

ČARGA 1767

Dušan in Edbin Erzetič, Pristavo 2, si-5212 Dobrovo v Brdih
Phone: +386 (0)5 304 25 00, (0)5 395 94 96, (0)41 363 039, (0)41 692 292, Fax: +386 (0)5 395 94 97
Email: carga1767@siol.net, edbin.carga1767@volja.net, Website: www.carga1767.com

- Wine selling
- Production of wine and food
- Sales material
- Wine tasting for announced groups
- Wine cellar tours
- Praise of the parish's patron saint at a feast held in front of the church
- Tours of the vineyard and local sights

In the Erzetič family the winegrowing tradition goes back an impressively long way to 1767. The second turning point was 1985, when their first wine label was printed. The vineyard grows a lot of Merlot, which makes a fresh, young wine, Rosé, as well as aged wine in wooden barrels. Besides Merlot the top variety is Rebula, from which they make sparkling wine; 'Čarvina', a sweet wine made from dried grapes; and fresh dry wine. For the European market the most interesting Brda specialities are Rebula, Furlanski Tokaj, Pikolit, Verduc and Merlot. Best vintages: 1998-2000 sparkling 'Donna Regina', 2000 'Čarvina' (sweet), 2000 Merlot, 2001 Sauvignon *Pozna Trgatev*, 2001 Cabernet Sauvignon, 2002 Rebula, 2000 Beli Pinot.

Mix of wines on offer

18% Chardonnay, 14% Sivi Pinot, 10% Merlot, 10% Furlanski Tokaj, 6% Rebula, 6% 'Donna Regina', 6% Beli Pinot, 6% Cabernet Franc, 12% Cabernet Sauvignon, 8% Sauvignon, 6% young red wine 'Vinova', 4% Modri Pinot, 2% Rumeni Muškat, 1,8% Verduc, 1% Pikolit and 1% 'Čarvina' (produced from dried grapes).

Awards

Although they have not attended any tastings in the last couple of years, they nevertheless hold two gold medals from Gornja Radgona, a gold and two silvers from Zagreb, and four silvers from Ljubljana.

Culinary recommendations

Their wines make an excellent accompaniment to Primorskan cuisine (especially that of Brda and Furlanija). The local walnut cake is lovely accompanied by 'Čarvina', and prosciutto by Merlot, while St Martin's goose is best with the young, red 'Vinovo'.

GORIŠKA BRDA WINE-GROWING DISTRICT

1998 Donna Regina

12.4% vol., dry, ★★

The yellow straw colour of this sparkling wine with its golden notes and a vibrant sparkle augur well for the palate. The complete necklace of bubbles at the surface is proof of its quality. On the nose, the first impression is of dried fruit, and it has a serene quality. Later we encounter hazelnuts, freshly churned butter and hay. The maturity of the wine is further in evidence on the palate, with the bubbles producing a mild but fresh sensation. The final impression is pleasant and soothing.
Recommended dishes: This is a very appropriate wine to accompany simple conversation, a non-sweet dessert or rusk.

GORIŠKA BRDA WINE-GROWING DISTRICT

ČETRTIČ

Matjaž Četrtič, Kojsko 5c, si-5211 Kojsko
Phone: +386 (0)5 304 36 00, (0)41 621 494, Fax: +386 (0)5 304 36 01
Email: matjaz.cetrtic@email.si

Wine selling ❧ Wine tasting
Wine cellar tours ❧ Accommodation
Cold cuts for announced groups ❧ Sales material

They entered the wine trade in 1996 and labelled their first bottles a year later. Although 40% of the vineyard grows Merlot, they devote most attention to Rebula which, alongside red and white 'Ferdinand', is the cellar's greatest hope. Best vintages are the 1998 Sivi Pinot, the 1999 Sivi Pinot 'Magnum', the 2000 Chardonnay 'Magnum' and the 2000 Rebula.

Mix of wines on offer

40% white 'Ferdinand', 25% red 'Ferdinand', 15% Rebula, 10% Chardonnay and 10% Sivi Pinot.

Awards

A silver medal from Gornja Radgona and the title of Slovenian champion of its variety from Ljubljana testify to the quality of their produce.

Culinary recommendations

Homemade salami (*briški šalam*) is a fine complement to red 'Ferdinand'. Rebula is recommended with any kind of fish.

1999 Sivi Pinot

14.0% vol., dry, ★★

The lovely yellowy colour with a few golden notes causes the glass to shine. On the nose you immediately sense the breadth and openness of the bouquet, which rewards gentle swilling of the glass. The aroma of dried white fruit is complemented by a barely perceptible hint of frying, spices, crusts of bread and vanilla: the bouquet of a fine maturity. The body is full but mild on the palate. The grape variety comes through clearly and persuasively; the diversity of the palate is very much in evidence, and its components work well together, continuing to linger. The palate continues to develop and the wine is still growing in quality, although it is already very interesting and affords great pleasure.

Recommended dishes: Grilled polenta with cheese and prosciutto, frittata with prosciutto and fennel, grilled turkey and veal fillets, and even beef.

GORIŠKA BRDA WINE-GROWING DISTRICT

1999 Sivi Pinot

GORIŠKA BRDA WINE-GROWING DISTRICT

Dobuje

Roman and Robert Bučinel, Snežeče 16, SI-5212 Dobrovo v Brdih
Phone: +386 (0)5 395 92 20, (0)5 395 92 22, Fax: +386 (0)5 395 92 21
Email: dobuje@volja.net, Website: www.dobuje.com

Wine selling ❧ Sales material
Wine cellar tours for announced groups ❧ Wine tasting for announced groups

With wine growing already in the family, they began trading in 1985, and seven years later they produced their first labelled bottle. The Bucinel Chardonnay, Merlot and Rebula are their best and most dominant varieties, with Sivi Pinot, Cabernet Sauvignon, Sauvignon and Furlanski Tokaj also playing their part. Rebula, Tokaj, Merlot, and red and white blends are considered to have the most potential.
The best vintage from this cellar is 1999: Chardonnay, Merlot and Sauvignon.

Wines On Offer
Rebula, Chardonnay, Sivi Pinot, Sauvignon, Merlot.

Awards
Success at the Ljubljana fair is demonstrated by their silver medals, and also by a gold and a variety championship title.

1999 Chardonnay
14.5% vol., dry, ★★★

Yellow, straw-like reflections shine from the glass. Firm legs run elegantly down the sides, as if to make clear that this wine has a firm backbone. The nose anticipates a fresh, youthful character, even though it has been aged for five years. The fruit-floral scents are pure; to begin with one detects over-ripe melon, complemented by over-ripe grapes and pears. The full flavour of the wine is, as expected, fresh and fruity. Chardonnay is known for its adaptability: though happy enough in a small barrel, the same wine can be allowed to develop fully in a vat, acquiring a distinctive character that has many fans of its own. This great Chardonnay confirms this particular ability: it has a character that is more a reflection of the variety in general than of the way this particular wine was cultivated. The pleasing first impression develops into a pot-pourri of all the elemental components, which balance each other well, and ends with a warm, long finish. This is a wine that connoisseurs will want to acquire for their own cellars.
Recommended dishes: Grilled polenta with cheese and prosciutto, thick soup with truffles, frittata with prosciutto and fennel, grilled turkey fillets.

GORIŠKA BRDA WINE-GROWING DISTRICT

1999 Chardonnay

GORIŠKA BRDA WINE-GROWING DISTRICT

Dolfo

Rudolf in Marko Skočaj, Ceglo 3a, , si-5212 Dobrovo v Brdih,
Phone: +386 (0)5 304 53 91

Wine selling ❧ Wine tasting
❧ Wine cellar tours

The breakdown of the wines on offer is the same as the distribution of the vineyards. They grow mostly Sivi Pinot and Merlot, which in their most successful vintages can compete with the best.

Mix of wines on offer

30% Sivi Pinot, 20% Merlot, 20% Rebula, 10% Chardonnay, 10% Cabernet Sauvignon, 5% Beli Pinot and 5% Furlanski Tokaj.

2002 Sivi Pinot

12.5 vol.% alk., dry, ★

The wine's pale, yellowy appearance testifies to its youth, and one's first impression is of a radiant glow. The nose seems more mature: there is a note of dried flowers, the fruity scent of pears and quinces, and something of a herbaceous quality. The body is still forming, and it feels youthful and vibrant on the palate. It is fun to analyse the balance and harmony: the body has complexity, the acidity tastes well, and together they give the wine a freshness and all-round drinkability.
To experience it at its best you should wait at least a year before opening.
Recommended dishes: Seafood of all kinds, steamed dentex (a European marine fish) and chicory with nuts, turkey veal and pork fillets.

GORIŠKA BRDA WINE-GROWING DISTRICT

2002 SIVI PINOT

GORIŠKA BRDA WINE-GROWING DISTRICT

Jakončič

Igor and Aljoša Jakončič, Kozana 5, si-5212 Dobrovo v Brdih
Phone: +386 (0)5 304 12 15, (0)41 676 803. Fax: +386 (0)5 304 12 15
Email: aljosa_jakoncic@siol.net

Wine selling ❧ Wine tasting for announced groups
Wine cellar tours for announced groups ❧ Accommodation

Viticulture and wine trading have a tradition going back many years at the Jakončič farm, where the first labels were produced in 1990. Of the range they produce their greatest hopes are for the red and white 'Carolina' blends. The 2001 red 'Carolina' and the 1999 sparkling 'Carolina' are their best, and both are still available from the cellar.

Wines on offer

Cabernet Sauvignon, Modri Pinot, Merlot, Furlanski Tokaj, red 'Carolina', white 'Carolina', Rebula, Chardonnay, Sauvignon, Sivi Pinot and sparkling 'Carolina'.

Awards

Success at Ljubljana has brought the title of Champion of Slovenia, along with gold, silver and bronze medals.

Culinary recommendations

They recommend red wines as an accompaniment to prosciutto and black olives.

2000 Carolina, red

13% vol., dry, ★★★

The intense ruby red colour with its brick tones suggests a wine full of energy. The complex nose manifests itself as over-ripe red fruit verging towards caramel, enhanced with spices and scents from the animal world. The alcohol makes its presence felt as its warmth opens up the bouquet. This is a good example of a fine vintage, exhibiting a rich and mature tannin structure, a taste of chocolate and a juiciness on the palate with a good balance. After swallowing, only pleasant impressions remain and continue to linger. This wine is at its peak.

Recommended dishes: Prosciutto, *fuži* with truffles, roast lamb, pork chop.

GORIŠKA BRDA WINE-GROWING DISTRICT

2000 Carolina, red   2001 Modri Pinot

2001 Modri Pinot

12.9% vol., dry, ★★

    The typical bright red colour of this variety, with its cherry and brick tones, is vibrant in appearance. The attractive bouquet is inviting, and yields an array of fragrances from raisins to over-ripe redcurrants and cherries to sweet spices: very much an aromatic wine. The wine is soft on the palate, in spite of its higher-than-average alcohol content. The flavour and balance, which rest on the pleasing freshness, are good compensation for the more modest tannin level, so that they are not missed in this fine wine. After swallowing, the bouquet lingers for some time and this persistence is well in keeping with the wine's general character.
    Recommended dishes: Home-baked bread with olives, cold cuts of smoked meat, *fuži* with truffles, roast pork, kid in blueberry sauce.

GORIŠKA BRDA WINE-GROWING DISTRICT

Kabaj

Estera Kabaj and Jean Michel Morel, Šlovrenc 4, si-5212 Dobrovo v Brdih
Phone: +386 (0)5 395 95 60, (0)41 637 694, Fax: +386 (0)5 395 95 60
Email: kabaj.morel@email.si

Wine selling ❧ Wine tasting
Production of wine and food ❧ Wine cellar tours for announced groups
Accommodation ❧ The Festival of Cherries
❧ The celebration of the feast
of St Laurence

The beginnings of their involvement with wine growing and the trade go back to 1840, and they have been bottling their wines since 1993. As they do not produce blended varieties, the quantities of the wines produced mirror the distribution of grape varieties planted. The demand is greatest for their Furlanski Tokaj, Merlot and Beli Pinot. Their best vintages still available are their 1994 and 1999 Tokaj, their 1999 Rebula and their 1999 Sivi Pinot.

Mix of wines on offer

20% Merlot, 10% Furlanski Tokaj, 10% Beli Pinot, 10% Sivi Pinot, 10% Sauvignon, 10% Cabernet Sauvignon, 10% Rebula, 10% Chardonnay and 10% Cabernet Franc.

Awards

The wines of which they are most proud are Tokaj and Beli Pinot.

Culinary recommendations

Herb frittata goes well with Tokay; white polenta and prosciutto in gravy with Sivi Pinot. Venison is recommended, cooked in a wine sauce of Cabernet Franc or Merlot.

1999 Tokaj

13.2% vol., dry, ★★★

The yellow, straw-like colours have an interesting nuance: the wine just glows in the glass. Delightful scents are immediately released on the nose. Herbaceous fragrances are very much to the fore, with newly mown grass followed by fresh, dry odours of mint, smoke, and even nuances of tobacco. The palate continues in a similar vein as one would expect, building well on the impressions established by the bouquet. It is full and still fresh, the complexity a sign of the vine's favourable position, which befits the variety and brings out its characteristics, as well as those of the soil from which the grapes were grown. I estimate that this wine is just approaching its peak, a true delight for connoisseurs.
Recommended dishes: Herb frittata with herbs, thick soup with *trumes*, grilled turkey fillet on grill with hard cheeses as dessert

GORIŠKA BRDA WINE-GROWING DISTRICT

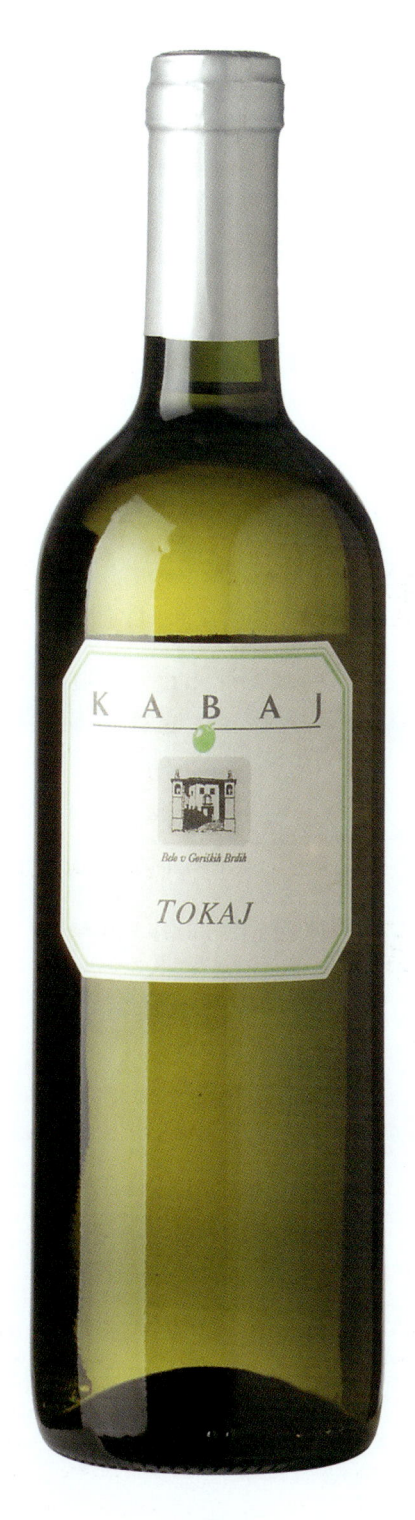

1999 Tokaj

GORIŠKA BRDA WINE-GROWING DISTRICT

Roman in Edvin Kocijančič

Neblo 4, si-5212 Dobrovo v Brdih, Phone: +386 (0)5 304 51 87, (0)40 898 401

Wine selling ❧ Wine tasting
Wine cellar tours for announced groups ❧ Wine route

Wines on offer

Sauvignon, Sivi Pinot, Cabernet Sauvignon, Chardonnay, Rebula, Tokaj and Merlot.

Iztok in Borut Mužič

Plešivo 5, si-5212 Dobrovo v Brdih, Phone: +386 (0)5 304 21 34
Email: batick@volja.net

Wine selling ❧ Wine tasting for announced groups
Wine cellar tours for announced groups ❧ Wine route

Mix of wines on offer

40% red blend, 20% Sivi Pinot, 20% Beli Pinot and 20% white blend.

Piro

Marjan Jakončič, Vipolže 16, si-5212 Dobrovo v Brdih
Phone: +386 (0)5 304 20 42

Wine selling ❧ Wine tasting for announced groups
Wine cellar tours for announced groups ❧ Wine route
❧ Sales material

Mix of wines on offer

20% Chardonnay, 30% Sivi Pinot, 20% Furlanski Tokaj,
20% Cabernet Sauvignon and 10% Sauvignon.

Oton Reya

Kozana 18a, si-5212 Dobrovo v Brdih
Phone: +386 (0)5 304 12 65, (0)31 352 200, Email: reya.oton@volja.net

Wine selling ❧ Wine tasting
Wine route ❧ Sales material
❧ Production of wine and food for announced groups

Mix of wines on offer

20% Beli Pinot, 30% Merlot, 20% red blend and 30% Chardonnay.

GORIŠKA BRDA WINE-GROWING DISTRICT

Maksimiljan de Reya

Kozana, si-5212 Dobrovo v Brdih, Phone: +386 (0)5 304 12 30

Wine selling ❧ Wine tasting

Mix of wines on offer

10-15% wine in bottles (Sivi Pinot, Chardonnay, Sauvignon, Beli Pinot, Rebula, Merlot, Cabernet Sauvignon), 85-90% wine on tap (white and red).

Ronk - Vina iz Goriških Brd

Stojko Kristančič, Vipolže 94, si-5212 Dobrovo v Brdih
Phone: +386 (0)5 304 51 76, (0)41 524 676, (0)41 846 470
Email: davor.kristancic@volja.net

Wine selling ❧ Wine tasting for announced groups
Sales material ❧ Wine cellar tours for announced groups

Mix of wines on offer

28% Merlot, 18% Sivi Pinot, 18% Chardonnay, 9% Beli Pinot, 9% Rebula, 9% Sauvignon and 9% Cabernet Sauvignon.

Marko Sirk

Biljana 21, si-5212 Dobrovo v Brdih, Phone: +386 (0)5 304 56 27, (0)41 520 892

Wine selling ❧ Wine tasting for announced groups
Wine route ❧ Cherries
❧ Wine cellar tours for announced groups

Mix of wines on offer

40% white blend 20% Sivi Pinot, 20% Merlot, 8% Cabernet Sauvignon and 12% red blend.

Valter Sirk

Višnjevik 38, si-5212 Dobrovo v Brdih, Phone: +386 (0)5 304 53 63, (0)41 752 582
Email: valter.sirk@siol.net

Wine tasting for announced groups ❧ Wine cellar tours for announced groups
Wine route ❧ Sales material

Mix of wines on offer

14% Rebula, 14% Tokaj, 8% Malvazija, 14% Sivi Pinot, 14% Chardonnay, 5% Sauvignon, 8% 'Bela Tereza' blend, 8% 'Rdeča Tereza' blend and 15% Cabernet Sauvignon.

GORIŠKA BRDA WINE-GROWING DISTRICT

Kristančič iz Medane

Dušan Kristančič, Medana 29, si-5212 Dobrovo v Brdih
Phone: +386 (0)5 395 95 3, Fax: +386 (0)5 395 95 34
Email: vinarstvo.kristancic@siol.net
Website: www.kristancic.si

Wine selling ❧ Wine tasting for announced groups
Wine cellar tours ❧ Sales material
Guided tasting ❧ Wine route

The Kristančič family began to produce and sell wine in 1970, and labelled their wines in 1989. The vineyards, spread over seventeen hectares of land, are composed of varieties such as Cabernet Sauvignon and Sivi Pinot, which give top results. Heading the diverse list of wines on offer are three of the most promising: Cabernet Sauvignon, Sivi Pinot and Chardonnay. The cellar still holds some of their best vintages, including 2000 red 'Pavo' and 2001 white 'Pavo'.

Mix of wines on offer

15% Sivi Pinot, 20% Cabernet Sauvignon, 7% Chardonnay, 5% Beli Pinot, 8% Merlot, 8% Modri Pinot, 6,5% Sauvignon, 10% white and red 'Pavo'; 20% white and red 'Medana'; 0.5% Pikolit.

Awards

Among the more important awards they have received we should mention the title of Champion Chardonnay 1992, as well as gold and silver medals, all obtained at Ljubljana.

Culinary recommendations

Their wines are best complemented by homemade prosciutto and salami or sausages, and *štokwiš* (cod).

2002 Cabernet Sauvignon

12.5% vol., dry, ★

The medium-intense ruby red colour is already acquiring brick tones. The straightforward bouquet is pleasant and dominated by a fruity character (over-ripe blueberries, black cherries). The flavour has a medium structure. The tannins are still noticeably restless, whilst the acidities are still seeking their balance and need more time, but the wine is already suitable for drinking and has little to be gained by longer storage.
Recommended dishes: Smoked cold cuts: homemade prosciutto, salami, sausages; roast pork; kid in blueberry sauce.

GORIŠKA BRDA WINE-GROWING DISTRICT

2002 Cabernet Sauvignon   2001 Pavo, white

2001 Pavo, white

13.0% vol., dry, ★★

The toned-down yellow of this wine implies that it was ripened in barrels, with a consequent richness. The bouquet confirms familiarity with the barrel; it shows a wonderful potential (dried white fruit, vanilla, coconut), but needs time to develop further and gain refinement. The pleasing structure is marked by tannin from the wood, which as yet seems restless, but promising. The acidity is well expressed and contributes further to the wine's character. This also makes for a very dry wine on the palate. In a year or two this wine should prove gentler and better harmonized.

Recommended dishes: Grilled polenta with cheese and prosciutto, frittata with prosciutto and fennel, grilled turkey fillets, *štokviš* with potatoes.

GORIŠKA BRDA WINE-GROWING DISTRICT

Mavrič

Avguštin in Danilo Mavrič, Plešivo 36a, si-5212 Dobrovo v Brdih
Phone: +386 (0)41 320 916
Email: vinarstvo.mavric@volja.net

Wine tasting ❦ Wine cellar tours

The beginnings of wine cultivation and trading here date back to 1907, and a decade has now passed since the filling of their first labelled bottle. Although a quarter of the vineyards are devoted to Chardonnay, their major ventures are Furlanski Tokaj and Sivi Pinot. Other varieties grown here are Cabernet Sauvignon, Merlot, Sauvignon and Rebula. Best vintages available: 1999 Sivi Pinot, 1999 Cabernet Sauvignon, 2000 Cabernet Sauvignon, 2001 Merlot.

Wines on offer

Chardonnay, Furlanski Tokaj, Sivi Pinot, Cabernet Sauvignon, Merlot, Sauvignon and Rebula.

Awards

Their wines have won silver medals at the Ljubljana wine fair.

Culinary recommendations

Frittata is the best dish to accompany Sauvignon or Furlanski Tokaj; aged Bovec cheese goes best with Cabernet Sauvignon barrique or Chardonnay barrique.

1999 Sivi Pinot

13.5% vol., dry, ★★★

A crystal-clear wine, yellow and straw-like in colour with golden notes, which simply glows in the glass. The bouquet is of moderate intensity, but one can sense its composition and the ripeness of the grapes. At first fragrances of yellow fruit come forward (especially peaches and apricots). Scents of boiled fruit, spices and honey follow, giving the impression of a rich wine. It shows itself to be pleasant and broad with a strong backbone (alcohol) on the palate as well, with a sense of balance and roundness. The persistence of the bouquet testifies to the high quality and it finishes with a pleasant whiff of smoke.
Recommended dishes: Various seafoods, pike Cerknica-style, smoked dentex and chicory with pine nuts, Carniolan sausage, grilled veal and beef.

GORIŠKA BRDA WINE-GROWING DISTRICT

1999 Sivi Pinot

GORIŠKA BRDA WINE-GROWING DISTRICT

Jožko Mavrič

Šlovrenc 9, si-5212 Dobrovo v Brdih
Phone: +386 (0)5 304 53 16, (0)41 537 949, Fax: +386 (0)5 304 52 07,
Email: jozko.mavric@volja.net

Wine selling ❧ Wine tasting for announced groups
Wine cellar tours for announced groups ❧ Wine route
❧ Sales material

The farm has been cultivating wine since 1828 and moved into the wine trade in 1987. By 1992 their bottled wine bore labels. The distribution of the grape varieties in the vineyards is the same as that of the cellar. Their top varieties are Rebula, Sauvignon, Sivi Pinot, Merlot and Cabernet Sauvignon. Best vintages available: 2002 in 2003 Sivi Pinot, 2002 Chardonnay.

Mix of wines on offer

20% Sivi Pinot, 20% Cabernet Sauvignon, 20% Merlot, 10% Chardonnay, 10% Beli Pinot, 10% Rebula, 5% Furlanski Tokaj and 5% Sauvignon.

Awards

Two gold medals at the Ljubljana wine fair, and the title of Variety Champion.

Culinary recommendations

They offer a piece of general culinary advice: serve white wine with fish and red with meat.

2002 Sivi Pinot

13.5% vol., dry, ★★

The yellow, straw-like appearance gives an air of serenity to the wine. The thick legs suggest a full-bodied wine; the nose is open, mature and developed. The character of the bouquet is redolent of very ripe grapes, hazelnuts and, even citrus marmalade. The palate is oily, smooth, poised and well-balanced. The wine is already fully developed and is now best suited for drinking.

Recommended dishes: Seafood of all kinds, smoked dentex and chicory with nuts, turkey, veal and pork fillets.

GORIŠKA BRDA WINE-GROWING DISTRICT

2002 SIVI PINOT

GORIŠKA BRDA WINE-GROWING DISTRICT

MEDOT

Zvonimir Simčič, Šolska ulica 17, si-5250 Solkan
Phone: +386 (0)5 300 55 28, Fax: +386 (0)5 300 55 29
Email: esimit@esimit.it

Wine cellar tours ❧ Sales material

After 180 years of wine growing and wine selling, they printed their first wine labels in 1991. A vast 70% of the vineyards is planted with selected Rumena Rebula, which represents their most important variety of sparkling 'Medot' alongside Chardonnay and Modri Pinot.
The best vintage is 1997.

Wine on offer
The unique sparkling wine 'Medot'.

Awards
They do not take part in tastings.

Culinary recommendations
Their wine goes excellently with cold and warm hors d'oeuvres, fish and white meat.

Medot
12.0% vol., dry, ★★★

Yellowy and straw-like with a few golden reflections this crystal-clear, slightly sparkling wine is inviting indeed. After the initial sense of lemons and freshly picked apples on the nose, maturer fragrances emerge: first dried white fruit, then flowers, rusk and fresh breadcrumbs, all of which are characteristics appreciated in fine wines. On the palate this wine has a mildness in spite of its freshness. The bubbles calm and soothe - in short, a sparkling wine to be drunk as an aperitif, good for inspiring conversation or to accompany fish dishes.
After swallowing we are left with the impression of a well-proportioned, high-quality wine, which preserves its freshness and balance from start to finish.
Recommended dishes: A very suitable wine to accompany conversation at meal times, when visiting good friends and with fish dishes.

GORIŠKA BRDA WINE-GROWING DISTRICT

Medot

GORIŠKA BRDA WINE-GROWING DISTRICT

Movia

Aleš in Mirko Kristančič, si-Ceglo 18, 5212 Dobrovo v Brdih
Phone: +386 (0)5 395 95 10, (0)41 735 777

- Wine selling
- Wine tasting for announced groups
- Wine cellar tours for announced groups
- Production of wine and food for announced groups

Viticulture and wine trading have been in this family since 1820, and in the 1980s their bottles were labelled for the first time. Of all the varieties grown in the vineyards - Chardonnay, Sivi Pinot, Furlanski Tokaj, Merlot, Cabernet Sauvignon and Modri Pinot - the most impressive is Rebula. They sell their wines under the trademarks 'Movia' and 'Vila Marija', and the most promising are the 'Veliko Belo', 'Veliko Rdeče' and Rebula.
Best vintages that are still available: 1993, 1998, 1999 'Veliko Belo' and 1992, 1995, 1996, 1997 'Veliko Rdeče'.

Wines on offer
'Veliko Belo', 'Veliko Rdeče', Rebula, Sivi Pinot, Chardonnay, Sauvignon, Merlot, Cabernet Sauvignon and Modri Pinot.

Awards
So far their wines have been awarded a championship title at the Ljubljana fair, six golds and over thirty other medals. They are also proud owners of great gold medal from Bruxelles.

Culinary recommendations
Brda prosciutto is well complemented by Furlanski Tokaj.

GORIŠKA BRDA WINE-GROWING DISTRICT

2001 Rebula
13.0% vol., dry, ★★★

The wine is a glowing, straw-like yellow in appearance, with some golden lights. The attentive eye will enjoy the numerous, tiny bubbles, indicative of the wine's freshness. Clearly visible legs trace beautiful images on the glass, enhancing the aesthetic pleasure to be derived from this wine. The fragrance of the wine promises a rich nose, achieved by maturing in small barrels. Aromas of vanilla and coconut are gently supported by over-ripe grapes, dried flowers and hazelnuts on the nose. The medium-rich flavour has a youthful character, which it owes to a vibrant, tasty acidity and to the tiny bubbles that are a trademark of Brda Rebulas. Exploring this variety and its balance will be much enjoyed by connoisseurs of the Rebulas of Brda and their varying characters. The wine is still developing and we predict less vivacity and increased smoothness over time.

Recommended dishes: Chicken medallions with figs and almonds, chicken or veal stew, seafood risotto, smoked trout.

GORIŠKA BRDA WINE-GROWING DISTRICT

1999 Veliko Belo
13.5 vol.% alk., dry, ★★★★

  The yellow, straw-like colour is accompanied by a smooth, oily and mature appearance. After some skilful swilling the legs on the glass seem slow and dignified. The nose preoccupies us again. As with the previous wine we pick up on Rebula's own distinctive style, which again shines through in the bouquet: maturation in oak barrels has refined the wine, which takes on the quality of the oak. After such generous fragrances our curiosity and engagement grow. The word *veliko* ('great') on the label commits the producer to something special and tempts the wine taster, but expectations are happily confirmed on the palate. This wine yields immense pleasure if we heed our tastebuds; the years have done their task, and the flavours can truly be described as 'great'. The wine is certainly mature, but the term seems inadequate here to convey the full perfection, beauty and harmony of the experience - a wine for the connoisseur indeed. Wines that create such an experience leave us speechless; words seem unimportant, so rather than desecrate the experience by trying to describe it further let us enjoy this wine in silence!
  Recommended dishes: The full-bodied wine is a good accompaniment to strongly flavoured dishes: thick soup with truffles, smoked trout with polenta or asparagus, frittata with prosciutto and fennel.

GORIŠKA BRDA WINE-GROWING DISTRICT

2000 Chardonnay
13.5% vol., dry, ★★★

The wine has a glowing yellow, straw-like appearance with some golden streaks. The legs on the glass contribute to the aesthetic effect and attest to a wine with backbone. The intensity of the bouquet, although this is a non-aromatic variety, confirms the visual impression of a rich wine. The preparation of the wine in oak barrels has contributed to the character of the bouquet, and the first aroma of over-baked breadcrust is complemented by the scent of vanilla. The palate proves this natural affinity of Chardonnay with oak. I imagine that the crop load of vine was small, and that the grapes come from old vines, as the ratio of wine to oak swings in the wine's favour. The palate's soft complexity is pleasing, releasing itself juicily in the finish: the role of the acidity. This wine needs more time to reach its full, glowing maturity.

Recommended dishes: Smoked trout with polenta, veal fillet with mushrooms, prosciutto, hard cheeses for dessert.

GORIŠKA BRDA WINE-GROWING DISTRICT

Nando

Andrej in Mirko Kristančič, Plešivo 20, si-5212 Dobrovo v Brdih
Phone: +386 (0)5 304 21 29, (0)40 799 471

Wine selling ❦ Wine tasting for announced groups
❦ Wine cellar tours

The tradition of wine growing and trading here goes back to the late nineteenth century, and they began to bottle their wines at the end of the twentieth, in 1994. The vineyards are spread over six hectares. Chardonnay and Sauvignon stand out as the varieties of highest quality. They set most store by the white varieties such as Furlanski Tokaj and Rebula.
Red '*Eugen*' (Cabernet Sauvignon) dating from 1999 is the best vintage, and is still available.

Mix of wines on offer
30% Chardonnay, 30% Sauvignon, 15% Sivi Pinot, 10% Rebula, 10% Cabernet Sauvignon and 5% Merlot.

Awards
They have stopped attending tastings in the last couple of years.

1999 Eugen, red
13.0% vol., dry, ★★

A deep, ruby red colour with fiery tones and thick legs around the glass promise a rich and fulfilling wine. The bouquet bursts from the glass, engaging senses and spirit. This wine is mature, open and relaxed in character.
First impressions of subtle odours from the animal world are soon pleasantly joined by sun-dried red grapes and fruit on the nose. The bouquet clearly indicates the presence of alcohol, which blends smoothly with other aromas and spices up the whole. The taste is juicer than we might expect from the wine's appearance. The lively acidity helps awaken the somewhat dreary tannins.
This wine has completed its development and is best suited for drinking immediately.
Recommended dishes: Cold cuts of smoked meat, roast pork, gnocchi with venison, roast duck with plum sauce, roast lamb.

GORIŠKA BRDA WINE-GROWING DISTRICT

1999 Eugen, red

GORIŠKA BRDA WINE-GROWING DISTRICT

Peršolja

Dejan Peršolja, Kozana 19, si-5212 Dobrovo v Brdih
Phone: +386 (0)5 304 37 26, Fax: +386 (0)5 304 37 27
Email: persolja.vina@siol.net

Wine selling ❧ Wine tasting for announced groups
Wine cellar tours ❧ Wine and food for announced groups
❧ Wine cellar tours for announced groups

The Peršoljas have been in viticulture and the wine trade since 1909, and in 1991 they printed their first wine labels. The varieties with the biggest potential are Chardonnay, Rebula, Cabernet Franc and Merlot. A rosy future is predicted for all the white wines, especially Rebula. The best vintages still available are the 2002 Chardonnay and the 2000 Cabernet Franc.

Mix of wines on offer

Rebula, Chardonnay, Sivi Pinot, Sauvignon, Furlanski Tokaj, 'Cvet' blend, Modri Pinot, Cabernet Franc barrique, Merlot and Merlot barrique.

Awards

In Gornja Radgona they have received six silver and seven gold medals, as well as two championship titles. In Ljubljana they have been awarded five silver and three gold medals.

Culinary recommendations

Chardonnay or Sivi Pinot are served with grilled white polenta together with cheese and prosciutto. Shoulder of venison goes well with Cabernet Franc or Merlot.

2000 Cabernet Franc

13.59% vol., dry, ★★★

The velvet, ruby colour lends this wine a festive appearance. Tinges of brick contribute to its handsome appearance and tell of the maturing process. The first aroma is an attractive one of oak. Further exploration will pick out smooth fragrances of ripe blackberries accompanied by roasting coffee and chocolate, beautifully rounding off the nose. The roasted-coffee aspect continues on the palate, where the tannins are sufficiently present, but not so much as to burden the wine. The harmony of the main ingredients is very good. Ripening in barriques has stamped it with a personality of its own, although the generic characteristics of this variety are preserved in its nobility. This is an exceptional Cabernet Franc, which will reward even further in a year or two.
Recommended dishes: Smoked meats, medallion of foal with marrow, shoulder of venison and game dishes.

GORIŠKA BRDA WINE-GROWING DISTRICT

2000 Cabernet Franc   2002 Chardonnay

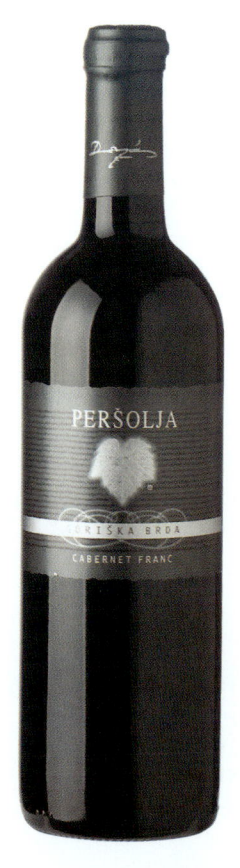

2002 Chardonnay

14.5% vol., dry, ★★★

The golden-yellow wine simply glows in the glass, and promises an interesting experience from a relatively young wine. Curiously shaped, good-sized legs on the walls of the glass predict a full flavour. The initial effect on the nose is promising. The bouquet is released on swilling the wine in the glass, and its pleasant flowery-fruity nature effortlessly yields a delight: an open, pleasant wine. Delight continues on the palate: the pleasant first impression is long-lasting, and the rich body masks the acidity, allowing it only enough freedom to liven up the palate's full complexity. The warming quality on the tongue puts us in mind of the wine's history, which began happily one spring in the vineyard and brought the joy of ripe grapes at harvest time. The wine flaunts its perfection, the stamp of this house's happy heritage: a champion wine.
Recommended dishes: Heartier pork and beef dishes. This Chardonnay would be sure to brighten the atmosphere served together with grilled white polenta with cheese and prosciutto.

GORIŠKA BRDA WINE-GROWING DISTRICT

Prinčič

Jožef in Damjan Prinčič, Kozana 118a, si-5212 Dobrovo v Brdih
Phone: +386 (0)5 304 36 46, (0)41 403 734

Wine selling ❦ Wine tasting
Wine cellar tours for announced groups ❦ Production of wine and food for announced groups

They have been devoted to wine growing and selling since 1979, and their bottles have borne labels for over a decade. Although all grape varieties grow on the best terrain here – which shows in some excellent results – two stand out: Sivi Pinot and Cabernet Franc.
Best vintages still available: 2001 Sivi Pinot and Sauvignon.

Mix of wines on offer
Chardonnay, Sivi Pinot, Cabernet Sauvignon, Cabernet Franc, Rebula and Sauvignon.

Awards
Their wines have been awarded gold and silver medals in Gornja Radgona and a silver in Ljubljana.

Culinary recommendations
Chardonnay goes best with fish and Cabernet Franc with venison.

2001 Sivi Pinot
13.0% vol., dry, ★

The yellow, straw-like appearance has that rosy tint characteristic of Sivi Pinot. The bouquet is quite reticent, and doesn't leap from the glass, but the floral and fruit fragrances – in particular of pears and peaches – yield a sweet, straightforward aroma of ripened grapes. The signs of a good wine continue on the palate and reveal the wine's originality: it seems full, juicy and tasty. The bouquet lingers and the finish remains firm but pleasant.
Recommended dishes: Grilled polenta with cheese and prosciutto, frittata with prosciutto and fennel, grilled food, fish, St Martin's goose.

GORIŠKA BRDA WINE-GROWING DISTRICT

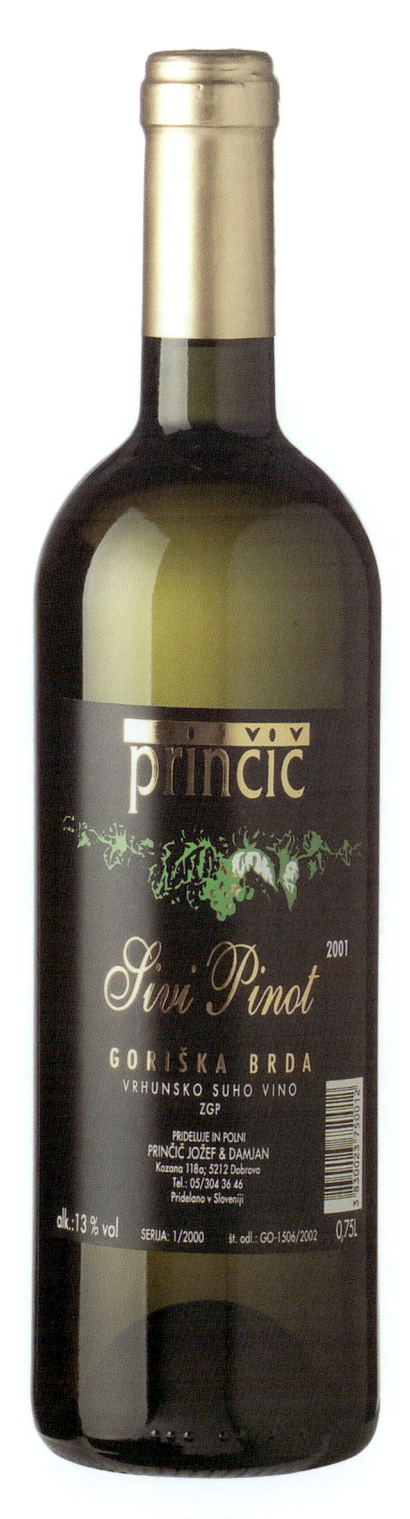

2001 Sivi Pinot

GORIŠKA BRDA WINE-GROWING DISTRICT

Simčič

Salko in Marjan Simčič, Ceglo 3b, si-5212 Dobrovo v Brdih
Phone: +386 (0)5 395 92 00, (0)41 614 768

- Wine selling
- Wine tasting for announced groups
- Wine cellar tours for announced groups

The beginnings of wine growing and trading date back to 1860; their first labels are dated 1988. They grow a variety of wines, among which Rebula, Furlanski Tokaj, Sivi Pinot, Sauvignon and Merlot achieve the highest level of quality. Their top show wines are Rebula Réserve, Sauvignon Réserve, Furlanski Tokaj, 'Teodor' Réserve white , Sivi Pinot and 'Teodor' Réserve red.
Best vintages still available: 1999, 2000 'Teodor' Réserve red,
1999-2001 'Teodor' Réserve white.

Mix of wines on offer
Chardonnay, Furlanski Tokaj, Sivi Pinot, Cabernet Sauvignon, Chardonnay Réserve, Sauvignon Réserve, 'Teodor' Réserve white, Rebula Réserve, Cabernet Sauvignon Réserve, Modri Pinot Réserve, 'Teodor' Réserve red
and 'Leonardo' (wine made from dried grapes).

Awards
They have achieved fifty gold and silver medals in Ljubljana and Gornja Radgona, a bronze in Canada and both a bronze and a silver in France.

Culinary recommendations
All Mediterreanen dishes go well with their wines.

GORIŠKA BRDA WINE-GROWING DISTRICT

2001 Chardonnay Réserve

14.0% vol., dry, ★★★

The golden-yellow appearance has an interesting and unique nuance to it. The label states that the wine has not been filtered, which suggests that the filter did not have the chance to dull the precious colouring. An initial, intense bouquet is released on swilling the wine in the glass. Besides the scent of coconut and vanilla, there is a hint of boiling-hot cooking fat, which lends the nose a wonderful aura. The wine's youth declares itself also on the palate. We detect some herbaceous oak characteristics, an indicator of the way this wine has developed and a guarantee for the attainment of even higher quality in time. A degree of acidity brightens the wine. The palate is multi-layered, vibrant and complex; it is an interesting experience and it takes some seconds for the wine to tell us its story, as yet unfinished. Take a moment to enjoy this: a guarantee of pleasure every six months if you allow the wine to continue maturing in your own cellar.

Recommended dishes: Mediterranean food such as scampi with grilled courgettes, seafood, roast beef with olives, lamb, mutton.

GORIŠKA BRDA WINE-GROWING DISTRICT

2001 Teodor Réserve, white
14.0% vol., dry, ★★★

The golden appearance of this unfiltered wine is interesting, glowing and serene. The eye can enjoy the legs, which resemble the windows of a small Gothic church. Straightaway this wine is a feast for the senses, which continues on the palate. We encounter the distinctive house style, which expresses the regional terroir, the attitude in the vineyard and the way the wines are nurtured in the cellar. The nose is vibrant, with aromas of herbs and frying a constant; fruit and floral scents are less in evidence. On the palate the aroma is completed, and the tastebuds enriched. The wine is still playful, indicating its continuing growth, but nevertheless makes an interesting companion and, in spite of its strong backbone, is very drinkable. The finish is very pleasant and it is easy to forget that this wine still has an impressive future ahead of it.

Recommended dishes: Mediterranean food such as scampi with grilled courgettes, seafood, roast beef with olives, lamb, mutton.

GORIŠKA BRDA WINE-GROWING DISTRICT

2000 Teodor Réserve, red
14.0% vol., dry, ★★★★

The deep ruby red colour with blue and purple undertones, together with some nuances of fire at the rim of the glass and larger-than-average legs, indicate a rich wine. The mixed aroma is candid and generous. The complex bouquet puts one in mind of several different groups of wine aromas: fruit fragrances (over-ripe purple berries), roasting (bread crusts, coffee, dark chocolate), spices (vanilla, coconut), vegetation (undergrowth) and animal scents (fresh leather). This wine has inexhaustible spirit, and constantly delivers new sensations, fine in quality and full of originality, like a calm pool of spring water. The palate offers yet more abundant pleasures, all beautifully balanced. The body is lively, but mild.

There are a lot of tannins, but they are velvety-sweet. The composition and the balance of the acidity with the tannins are perfect. Warm sensations contribute to the unique harmony of this wine. In a nutshell, this is a wine just approaching its peak. It is already showing its final character, which will last for several years. In addition to the rich body that all great wines should have, it has all the elements of quality, reflected in the balance of flavours, the appropriate bouquet and fitting appearance. Many fortuitous circumstances coincided for Teodor Red to be able to combine so many of the characteristics of success in a single wine.

Recommended dishes: Cold cuts of smoked meat, prosciutto, kid in blueberry sauce, *fuži* with truffles, roast lamb, wild boar chop.

GORIŠKA BRDA WINE-GROWING DISTRICT

Edi Simčič

Vipolže 39a, si-5212 Dobrovo v Brdih, Phone: +386 (0)5 395 91 74
Email: valter.simcic@amis.net

Wine selling ❦ Wine tasting
Wine cellar tours ❦ Wine tasting for announced groups
❦ Production of wine and food for
announced groups

Wine growing and selling captivated the Simčič family in 1950, and they started printing wine labels in 1989. Working in the vineyards, where they grow varieties such as Merlot, Sauvignon, Chardonnay, Rebula, Cabernet Sauvignon, Sivi Pinot, Cabernet Franc and Beli Pinot, they rely on quality and not quantity. They have highest hopes for their Rebula, 'Duet' and 'Duet' Riserva.

Mix of wines on offer

18% Sauvignon, 15% Chardonnay, 15% Rebula, 10% Sivi Pinot,
15% 'Duet' Riserva, 20% 'Duet' and 7% 'Trojka' blend.

Awards

They take part in tastings in Gornja Radgona and Ljubljana.

Culinary recommendations

Sauvignon is best accompanied by herb frittata,
'Duet' Riserva by prosciutto or game.

2001 Duet

12.5% vol., dry, ★★★

The wine has an intense ruby red colour with youthful tones. The legs trace interesting shapes and promise a satisfying wine. The bouquet is fairly intense and yields aromas of spices, very ripe red fruit, roasting and leather, and is mildly reminiscent of venison in character. The body is well shaped, and we pick up a good number of tannins. The wine's fruitiness asserts itself the whole time on the palate. After swallowing we sense burnt overtones, which prolong the aroma and the wine's overall length. This wine has a pleasing personality. Another year and this wine will reach its peak.
Recommended dishes: Prosciutto, roast lamb, medallion of foal with marrow, boar chop.

GORIŠKA BRDA WINE-GROWING DISTRICT

2001 DUET

GORIŠKA BRDA WINE-GROWING DISTRICT

Aljoša Sirk

Višnjevik 20, si-5212 Dobrovo v Brdih
Phone: +386 (0)5 395 92 03, (0)41 377 420, Fax: +386 (0)5 395 92 04
Email: sirk.a@siol.net

Wine selling ❦ Wine tasting for announced groups
Wine cellar tours for announced groups ❦ Production of wine and food for announced groups

In 1996 they labelled their first wine bottles. In the Sirks' vineyards the optimum varieties are Furlanski Tokaj and Cabernet Sauvignon, which also produce the best-quality wines. Merlot and Rebula also feature among the best on offer.

Mix of wines on offer

20% Cabernet Sauvignon, 20% Cabernet Franc, 15% Merlot, 12% Furlanski Tokaj, 10% Rebula, 10% Sivi Pinot, 10% Chardonnay and 3% Pikolit.

Awards

In Ljubljana the Cabernet Sauvignon was awarded the gold medal, while the Merlot and the Furlanski Tokaj won the silver medal.

2003 Pikolit

13.5% vol., semi-sweet, ★★★

A pale yellow colour with green hues predicts freshness and youth. The legs promise firmness. The nose, initially grassy, expands to include other herb and fruit fragrances: oranges and grapefruit are joined by the aromas of mint, absinthe and green tobacco on the nose. The palate continues in similar vein, with interesting hints of grapefruit, green walnuts and peach stones. The structure is medium; it is not bursting with energy in spite of the high alcohol content, and the wine seems light. It has a very interesting character, complex and, notwithstanding the sugar, very light to drink - in short, a speciality wine that deserves more attention in Slovene wine offers.
Recommended dishes: Fruit salad of citruses, kiwi fruit and pears; sweetened, stuffed pears; walnut croissant; assorted pastries with almonds.

GORIŠKA BRDA WINE-GROWING DISTRICT

2003 Pikolit

GORIŠKA BRDA WINE-GROWING DISTRICT

Stojan Ščurek

Ščurek vino - wine, Plešivo 44, si-5212 Dobrovo v Brdih
Phone: +386 (0)5 304 50 21, (0)41 625 842, Fax: +386 (0)5 304 50 21
Email: scurek.stojan@siol.net, Website: www.scurek.com

Wine selling ❧ Wine tasting
Wine cellar tours ❧ Accommodation
Sales materi ❧ Cold cuts along the tasting
Wine route ❧ Production of wine and food for announced groups

Mix of wines on offer

19% Sivi Pinot, 8% red 'Stara Brajda' barrique, 8% Cabernet Franc, 7% Chardonnay, 7% Sauvignon, 6% Merlot, 6% Cabernet Sauvignon, 5% Furlanski Tokaj, 5% Rumena Rebula, 4% Beli Pinot, 4% 'Dugo', 4% white 'Stara Brajda', 4% Modri Pinot, 4% 'Up' barrique, 3% 'Tokaj Jazbina', 3% Rosé, 1.5% Pikolit, 0.5% 'Story' (special wine made from dried grapes).

Culinary recommendations

The white 'Stara Brajda' goes well with frittata or white grilled polenta with prosciutto. Red wine should be served with cheeses, prosciutto, salami, pancetta or ham.

2001 Stara Brajda, red

13.0% vol., dry, ★★

A ruby red wine with cherry and brick tones. The bouquet exhibits a certain intensity, opening up with complexity to yield fragrances of jam made from forest berries, black olives, pepper, roasting and the constant energetic presence of alcohol. The palate, with its fresh quality and vivacious tannins presents a youth that still needs time to form. A herbaceous character of green paprika is prominent. A wine suitable for cellarage.
Recommended dishes: Prosciutto, salami, pancetta, ham, Carniolan sausage, gnocchi with venison, kid in blueberry sauce.

GORIŠKA BRDA WINE-GROWING DISTRICT

2001 Stara Brajda, red   2001 Stara Brajda, white

2001 Stara Brajda, white

13.5% vol., dry, ★★★★

A pale yellow wine, crystal-clear with golden reflections. On first acquaintance the bouquet is eloquent and promises an interesting sensory analysis. On the nose we pick up boiled fruit, vanilla, beeswax, warm bread and butter, and hazelnuts. The palate discovers fullness, fruitiness, caramel: a wonderful balance of roundness and freshness. The body is concentrated and gives off an energy, though subtly, and this characterizes the finish. An unusual character for a wine on the Slovene market, but worthy of attention and imitation.
Recommended dishes: Various frittatas, grilled white polenta with prosciutto. Make sure you get to try this wine with lobster.

GORIŠKA BRDA WINE-GROWING DISTRICT

ŠIBAU

Dušica, univ. dipl. inž., and Ljubko Šibav, Fojana 15, si-5212 Dobrovo v Brdih
Phone: +386 (0)5 304 50 62, (0)41 588 579, Fax: +386 (0)5 304 50 62

Wine selling ❧ Wine tasting for announced groups
Wine cellar tours for announced groups ❧ Wine route
Sales material ❧ Prosciutto, salamis, season fruit
(cherries, peaches, apricots, figs)

Wines on offer

Rebula, Furlanski Tokaj, Merlot, Chardonnay, Sivi Pinot, Sauvignon and Pikolit.

Miran in Alojz Šibav

Neblo 45, si-5212 Dobrovo v Brdih, Phone: +386 (0)5 304 25 87, (0)41 818 163
Fax: +386 (0)5 304 25 87, Email: sibav@siol.net

Wine selling ❧ Wine tasting
❧ Sales material

Mix of wines on offer

25% Rebula, 14% Furlanski Tokaj, 10% Beli Pinot, 10% Chardonnay, 10% Sauvignon, 30% Merlot, Cabernet Sauvignon and Cabernet Franc; 1% Rumeni Muškat.

Vina Franko

Franko Reja, Neblo 1a, si-5212 Dobrovo v Brdih, Phone: +386 (0)5 395 92 06, (0)31 632 230
Fax: +386 (0)5 395 92 07, Email: vina-franko@volja.net

Wine selling ❧ Wine tasting for announced groups
Wine cellar tours for announced groups ❧ Sales material

Mix of wines on offer

20% Chardonnay in bottles, 10% open Furlanski Tokaj, 10% open Rebula, 5% Sauvignon in bottles, 10% blend 'Kaberlot' (Cabernet Sauvignon + Merlot) in bottles, 10% open Merlot, 20% open white blend and 15% open Chardonnay.

Vina Kumar

Radovan Kumar, Snežatno 23a, si-5211 Kojsko
Phone: +386 (0)5 304 61 81, (0)41 737 233, Fax: +386 (0)5 304 61 81
Email: vina_kumar@siol.net

Wine selling ❧ Wine cellar tours
Wine route ❧ Accommodation
❧ Sales material

Wines on offer

Wine in bottles: Rebula, Beli Pinot, Sivi Pinot, Chardonnay, Cabernet Sauvignon, Merlot, Tokaj; wine on tap: Rebula, Beli Pinot, Cabernet, Merlot, Tokaj.

GORIŠKA BRDA WINE-GROWING DISTRICT

Vina Srebrnič

Vojko Srebrnič, Plešivo 46, si-5212 Dobrovo v Brdih
Phone: +386 (0)5 304 21 35, (0)41 671 898, Fax: +386 (0)5 304 50 54

Wine selling ❧ Wine tasting
Wine cellar tours ❧ Wine route
Accommodation ❧ Sales material

Mix of wines on offer

Chardonnay, Sivi Pinot, Furlanski Tokaj, Rebula, Cabernet Sauvignon; blends.

Valter Zalatel

Hruševlje 6, si-5212 Dobrovo v Brdih,
Phone: +386 (0)5 304 25 94, (0)31 629 328, Fax: +386 (0)5 304 25 94

Wine selling ❧ Wine route
❧ Sales material

Mix of wines on offer

35% quality white blend, 12% quality red blend, 10% quality Beli Pinot, 6% quality Sivi Pinot, 12% quality Merlot, 5% Sivi Pinot; wine in bottles: 5% Chardonnay, 5% Rebula, 5% Merlot and 5% Cabernet Sauvignon.

Vinarstvo Sosolič - Šturnšče

Izidor and Dominik Sosolič, Zali Breg 10A, si-5212 Dobrovo v Brdih,
Phone: +386 (0)5 304 51 31

Wine selling ❧ Wine cellar tours for announced groups
Sales material ❧ Production of wine and food for announced groups

Mix of wines on offer

High quality wine: 5% Rebula, 10% Chardonnay, 10% Sivi Pinot, 5% Sauvignon, 15% Cabernet Sauvignon, 5% Merlot, 5% Rumeni Muškat; 10% quality red and white 'Karolina'; and 40% wine on tap.

Vinarstvo Egon in Marko Zuljan

Vipolže 89A, si-5212 Dobrovo v Brdih, Phone: +386 (0)5 304 51 26, (0)41 521 428

Wine selling ❧ Wine tasting
Wine cellar tours for announced groups ❧ Wine route

Mix of wines on offer

17% Cabernet Sauvignon, 12% Sivi Pinot, 10,6% Chardonnay, 10% Sauvignon, 9% Tokaj, 8,5% Beli Pinot, 7.8% Rebula, 7.1% Merlot, 5.6% Modri Pinot, 5% Refošk, 3.9% Pikolit, 2.8% Rumeni Muškat and 1% Barbera.

GORIŠKA BRDA WINE-GROWING DISTRICT

Vinska Klet Goriška brda

Zadružna cesta 9, si-5212 Dobrovo v Brdih
Phone: +386 (0)5 331 01 00, (0)5 304 50 20, Fax: +386 (0)5 331 01 09
Email: info@klet-brda.com, Website: www.klet-brda.com

- Wine selling
- Wine tasting
- Sales material
- Wine cellar tours
- Wine route
- Multi-purpose hall

The tradition of viticulture and wine trading goes back to 1927; thirty years later a wine cellar was built and the first label printed. Their main product is Rebula, which along with Sivi Pinot, Merlot, Cabernet and Sauvignon represent the most promising varieties in their vineyards. The strongest links in their market chain are the brand names 'Quercus' and 'Bagueri'. They also produce Chardonnay, Furlanski Tokaj, sparkling Rebula and others.
All vintages from 1957 onwards are available; the best are 1964, 1968, 1974, 1975 and 1983.

Mix of wines on offer

25% Rebula, 18% Merlot, 16% Chardonnay, 15% Sivi Pinot, 8% Furlanski Tokaj, 4% sparkling Rebula, 4% Cabernet Sauvignon.

Awards

They have been awarded many medals and awards at all the important tastings. They are proudest of the Order of St Fortune, the Grand Prix de Vin and the Maison de Qualité.

Culinary recommendations

The three best combinations of Slovene cuisine are Soča trout with Rebula, non-smoked salami with Merlot, and *štruklji* with Pikolit.
The house dishes are the best accompaniment for their own wines: Mediterranean food, and fish and vegetable dishes.

GORIŠKA BRDA WINE-GROWING DISTRICT

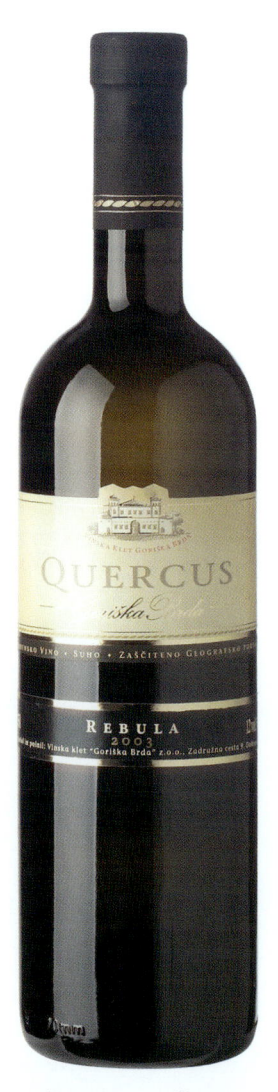

2003 Rebula Quercus
12.0% vol., dry, ★★

The promise of a fresh wine can be seen in its pale yellow colour with green notes and a number of tiny bubbles that disappear quickly. The floral-fruit scent is natural and sparkling in quality, reminding us of blossom, lemons, green apples and fresh hazelnuts: all light and pleasant fragrances. Youth and fruitiness are also the predominant characteristics on the palate. The body shows a moderate structure, composed but vibrant. There are only pleasant things to savour as the flavour develops on the palate. A very drinkable wine, which easily attracts customers, even at first tasting. In spite of its youth this wine is already at its best, and there is no need for waiting or cellarage.
Recommended dishes: *Jota*, frittata with seasonal herbs, grilled chicken, Soča trout with polenta.

GORIŠKA BRDA WINE-GROWING DISTRICT

2001 Merlot Bagueri

12.5% vol., dry, ★★

A wine of ruby red colour with brick notes. The intense aroma is complex and confirms the wine's maturity. It is reminiscent of very ripe grapes, scents of roasting, forest undergrowth and a dash of fresh leather. A good structure is delivered on the palate after a second, showing the wine's quality. The generic characteristics of the variety are there to be experienced on the palate, where we sense the softness of the tannins, ensured by the ripe Merlot grapes. The wine has kept their juiciness, thanks to these delicious tannins and a barely perceptible acidity, which together maintain a good balance. A delightful wine.

Recommended dishes: Cold cuts of smoked meat, Carniolan sausage, gnocchi with venison, kid in blueberry sauce.

GORIŠKA BRDA WINE-GROWING DISTRICT

2002 Chardonnay Bagueri

13.5% vol., dry, ★★★

A pale yellow colour with golden reflections and a vibrant glow appealing to the eye. It has a moderate aroma of fruitiness accompanied by spices, redolent of pears, melons, rusk and white tobacco. The bouquet is complex, he grape variety purely expressed with plenty of finesse. The palate is initially mild and develops on the tongue to become full and sturdy, fully engaging the taste buds. The sturdy structure has a great deal to offer; the complex flavours open up and it is difficult to decide when it is time to take the next mouthful. After swallowing the fragrances linger and their farewell is juicy and pleasing. A wine of high quality that has successfully preserved the character of the grapes.

Recommended dishes: Mediterranean dishes, truffles with pasta (*fuži*), wild asparagus with *fuži*, fish carpaccio, bržola with olives, heartier pork dishes, hard cheeses.

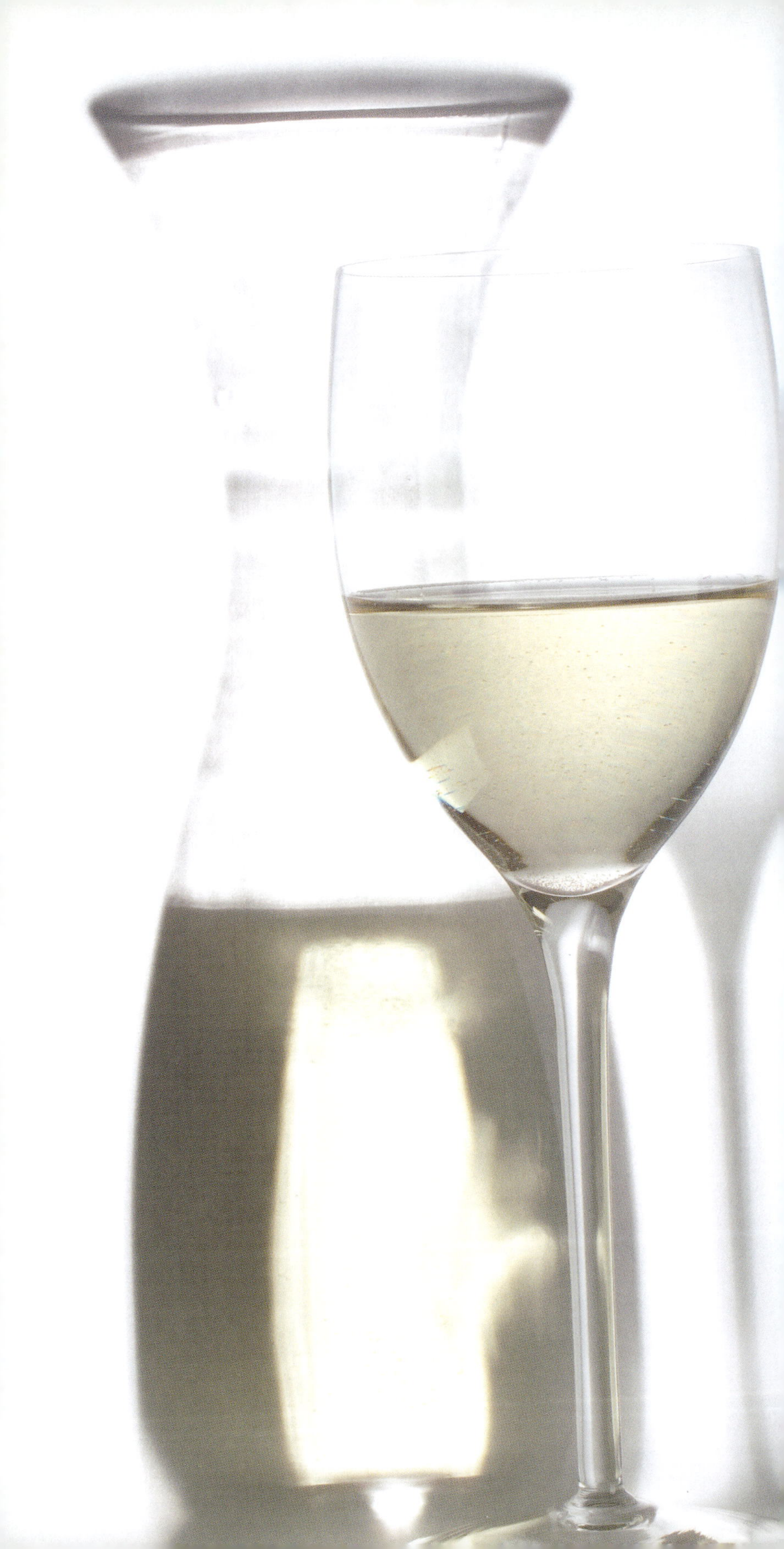

Vipavska dolina Wine-Growing District

PRIMORSKA WINE-GROWING REGION

VIPAVSKA DOLINA WINE-GROWING DISTRICT

Andlovic

Rajko Andlovic, Gradišče pri Vipavi 18, si-5271 Vipava
Phone: +386 (0)5 366 51 49, (0)41 678 634

Wine selling ❧ Wine tasting
Production of wine and food ❧ Wine cellar tours
Wine route ❧ Sales material

In 1990, the family tradition of wine growing and selling became a business venture. The grapes that predominate in their vineyards are Cabernet Sauvignon, Merlot, Rebula, Barbera and Sauvignon. The Sauvignon and Pinela vines, typical of the Vipava region, bear the grapes of the highest quality. The most promising wines in the cellar are said to be Cabernet Sauvignon, Pinela and Sauvignon.

Mix of wines on offer
25% white blend, 15% red blend, 10% Sauvignon, 15% Pinela, 10% Rumeni Muškat, 25% Cabernet Sauvignon.

Awards
For nine years now the family has successfully participated at the wine tastings held in Gornja Radgona.

Culinary recommendations
With venison you will be served Cabernet, while apple strudel and other desserts go nicely with Rumeni Muškat.

2002 Pinela
11.45% vol., semi-dry, ★

A pale yellow appearance of low intensity, with a fresh, candid, fruity aroma accompanied by the fragrance of blossom in the background. This is a pleasant wine, mild in taste but with some vitality. The aroma on the palate completes the fruitiness, with characteristics of lemon, ripening apples and gooseberries. The structure is simple and undemanding. This wine will suit a range of tastes: pleasant, drinkable and well suited to light conversation.
Recommended dishes: Serve as an aperitif, or with dishes of polenta and white meat, seafood risotto, pizza (without added oil), or spaghetti with melted cheese.

VIPAVSKA DOLINA WINE-GROWING DISTRICT

2002 Pinela

VIPAVSKA DOLINA WINE-GROWING DISTRICT

Batič

Ivan Batič, Šempas 130, si-5261 Šempas
Phone: +386 (0)5 308 86 76, Fax: +386 (0)5 307 85 29
Email: mihabatic@hotmail.com

Wine selling ❧ Wine tasting
Wine cellar tours ❧ Wine route
Accommodation ❧ Sales material
❧ Wine and food for announced groups

The history of the tradition of wine growing and trading here is formidable, dating back as it does to 1592. The very first bottle of Batič wasn't filled until 1987, however. The top-quality wines produced in the Batič vineyards are Cabernet Franc, Merlot, Chardonnay, Rebula and Pinela. The most promising wines in the cellar are said to be Rebula and Pinela. Best vintages: 1997 Sivi Pinot, 1999 Chardonnay, 1999 Rosé Batič, 2001 Sauvignon.

Wines on offer

Young Rosé and Rebula; barrique (Pinela, Sivi Pinot, Chardonnay, Sauvignon, Merlot, Cabernet Franc), 'Valentino' (dried Rebula).

Awards

Two championship titles from Gornja Radgona, five gold medals from Ljubljana and also a gold medal from France.

Culinary recommendations

Their wines are very rich in flavour, creating a perfect match for fish and meat dishes.

2002 Pinela

12.5% vol., dry, ★★★

The wine lover is drawn to this wine for its serenity and quite intense yellow hue, with an oily consistency that can be seen when the wine is poured. The nose confirms what the eye has seen: the bouquet is mild, offering an openness of sensory experience. The fragrance of ripe fresh fruit (peaches, apricots) and a mild proportion of vanilla remind us of the grapes, generously filled with sunshine. The exquisite bouquet attests to a development far beyond what one might expect in a two-year-old wine, and the ageing process has been faster than is usual in the standard maturing methods, with fortuitous results, however. The palate only confirms the wine's harmony in both appearance and smell. There is a lingering soft note experienced immediately after tasting it. All the components of the wine work in harmony and balance from the first to the last drop. The character is unique, reflecting the wine's *terroir*, as the French would say. It has a lasting soothing effect, which is why it is so rich and distinctive. This wine is proof enough that Pinela can produce some interesting results.

Recommended dishes: Dishes with polenta and white meat, veal steak with mushrooms. This wine can also be enjoyed on its own, however, or accompanied by homemade bread; in this way one can experience its richness and flavour to the full.

VIPAVSKA DOLINA WINE-GROWING DISTRICT

2002 PINELA

VIPAVSKA DOLINA WINE-GROWING DISTRICT

Jordan Cigoj

Turistična kmetija Arkade, Črniče 91, si-5262 Črniče
Phone: +386 (0)5 366 60 09, (0)5 364 47 70, (0)5 364 47 71, Fax: +386 (0)5 364 47 80
Email: maja_cigoj@siol.net
Website: www.arkade.lajf.net

Wine selling ❧ Wine tasting
Production of wine and food ❧ Wine cellar tours for announced groups
Accommodation ❧ Sales material

For the Cigoj family wine growing and selling have always been a part of family tradition. Only since 1989, however, have their bottled wines had their own label. They grow traditional grapes, such as Cabernet Sauvignon, Merlot, Chardonnay and Furlanski Tokaj. In particular they are famous for some indigenous top-quality grape varieties, such as Zelen, Klarnica, Malvazija and Rebula. Best vintages: 1999-2003 Cabernet Sauvignon, 2002-3 Zelen.

Mix of wines on offer

30% Cabernet Sauvignon; 15% 'Cigoj' red blend; 10% 'Cigoj' white; 10% Chardonnay; 10% Malvazija; 5% Zelen; 5% Merlot; 5% Klarnica; 4% Rebula; riserva from 2% each of Klarnica, Malvazija and Chardonnay.

Awards

Their wines have won gold and silver medals at tastings in Ljubljana and Gornja Radgona.

Culinary recommendations

They serve delicacies and specialities of the Vipava valley and accompany them with a full and carefully chosen assortment of wines.

2002 Zelen

12.6% vol., dry, ★★★

The shining yellow straw-like colour, shot through with an occasional glint of gold, makes this wine highly attractive and seductive, and promises an interesting tasting experience. One immediately notices the freshness of the bouquet, even if this has already matured. On the nose it is rich, full, wide open and pleasant - a feast for the senses. Harmony and complexity also continue on the palate: a whole tasting adventure lies ahead. The first impression is pleasantly sweet, with no explicit sign of sugar. This is soon to be succeeded by freshness, with a tinge of acid, which creates a nice balance with the sweet body. To enhance the wine's complexity and quality even more, one experiences in the finish a distinct bitterness, which spices up and rounds off the tasting experience with a delicious final note. The taste lingers nicely on the palate. This wine is a fine example of Zelen and of the whole vintage, and as such it is a pride and joy for the vintner.
Recommended dishes: Vegetable platter, dishes with polenta and white meat, asparagus dishes, seafood risotto, smoked trout.

VIPAVSKA DOLINA WINE-GROWING DISTRICT

2002 Zelen

VIPAVSKA DOLINA WINE-GROWING DISTRICT

Božičev hram

Marjan Božič, Planina 66, si-5270 Ajdovščina
Phone: +386 (0)5 364 25 92, (0)41 857 235, (0)41 554 379, (0)41 238 551

Wine selling ❧ Wine tasting
Production of wine and food ❧ Wine cellar tours
❧ Sales material

Mix of wines on offer

'Božičevo vino' blend; 40% Rebula, 15% Pinela, 15% Sauvignon, 10% Barbera, 10% Chardonnay, 5% Merlot and 5% Rumeni Muškat.

Peter Curk

Vrhpolje 31, si-5271 Vipava, Phone: +386 (0)41 311 049

Wine selling ❧ Wine tasting
Wine cellar tours for announced groups ❧ Wine route

Mix of wines on offer

25% Merlot, 20% Laški Rizling, 5% Zelen, 5% Rumeni Muškat and 45% blend.

Aleš Čehovin

Brje 76b, si-5263 Dobravlje, Phone: +386 (0)5 368 81 11, (0)41 507 675, (0)41 953 448
Email: kmetija_cehovin@volja.net,
Website: www.kmetija-cehovin.cjb.net

Wine selling ❧ Wine tasting for announced groups
Wine cellar tours ❧ Wine route
Sales material ❧ Production of wine and food for announced groups

Mix of wines on offer

50% white blend, 20% red blend, 15% Sauvignon, 5% Chardonnay and 10% Cabernet Sauvignon.

Fajdigov hram

Božo Fajdiga, Goče 4a, si-5271 Vipava, Phone: +386 (0)5 364 55 13, (0)31 299 093

Wine selling ❧ Wine tasting
Wine cellar tours for announced groups ❧ Wine route
Sales material ❧ Ogled kulturnih znamenitosti kraja

Mix of wines on offer

40% Chardonnay, 15% Sauvignon, 25% Laški Rizling, 20% Merlot.

VIPAVSKA DOLINA WINE-GROWING DISTRICT

Boris Ferjančič

Gradišče pri Vipavi 11a, si-5271 Vipava
Phone: +386 (0)5 368 52 83, (0)31 892 585

Wine selling ❧ Wine tasting for announced groups
Wine route ❧ Production of wine and food for announced groups

Mix of wines on offer

35% Cabernet Sauvignon, 20% Pinela, 20% Rebula, 25% Sauvignon.

Jožef in Ivan Fornazarič

Vogrsko 167, si-5293 Volčja Draga
Phone: +386 (0)5 301 23 06, (0)41 383 879, Fax: +386 (0)5 301 23 07
Email: ivan.fornazaric@siol.net

Wine selling ❧ Wine tasting
Wine cellar tours ❧ Wine route

Mix of wines on offer

30% Chardonnay, 10% Furlanski Tokaj and white blend.

Fortunatov hram

Družina Marc, Planina 96, si-5270 Ajdovščina
Phone: +386 (0)5 368 04 00, (0)41 595 128, Fax: +386 (0)5 368 04 01
Email: fortunatov.hram@email.si

Wine selling ❧ Wine tasting
Wine cellar tours ❧ Wine route
Sales material ❧ Scenic route
❧ Production of wine and food for announced groups

Mix of wines on offer

30% Sauvignon, 30% Merlot, 20% Pinela, 10% Barbera,
5% Chardonnay and 5% Rumeni Muškat.

Frlanova kmetija

Ivan Bric, Vogrsko 126, si-5293 Volčja Draga, Phone: +386 (0)5 301 20 25, (0)41 341 126

Wine selling ❧ Wine tasting
Wine cellar tours ❧ Wine route

Mix of wines on offer

30% white wine, 12% Beli Pinot, 12% Sauvignon, 17% Cabernet Sauvignon,
10% Chardonnay, 13% Merlot, 3% Barbera, 3% Rumeni Muškat.

VIPAVSKA DOLINA WINE-GROWING DISTRICT

Kmetija Furlan

Branko Furlan, Zavino 33, si-5295 Branik
Phone: +386 (0)5 305 71 01, (0)41 728 587, Fax: +386 (0)5 305 71 01
Email: branko@furlan.org

Wine selling ❧ Wine tasting for announced groups
Wine cellar tours for announced groups ❧ Wine route
❧ Sales material

In 1970, Branko Furlan took over his father's wine business, which acquired a label of is own in 1993. Among the dozen grape varieties grown in his vineyards the biggest share is represented by Sauvignon, Cabernet Sauvignon, Malvazija and Rebula. However, in terms of quality Furlan prides himself on his Pinela, Zelen, Chardonnay and Rumeni Muškat. It is Pinela and Zelen that are felt to be showing the most interest and potential for the European market.

Wines on offer

They bottle up to 10% of their entire output: Pinela, Zelen, Vitovska Grganja, Chardonnay, Cabernet Sauvignon and Modri Pinot.

Awards

They have not taken part at international tastings, but they have a good record at the appraisals in Gornja Radgona, where they have won several gold and silver medals.

2001 Pinela
12.94% vol., semi-dry, ★★

A bright yellow colour, typical of this variety, is perked up further by tiny bubbles that promise a fresh aroma and an invigorating taste. Pleasant and distinctly fruity fragrances emanate from the wine, the most pronounced being that of almonds and hazelnuts. Gradually one senses a hint of freshly mown grass - the closing chapter to the olfactory part of the tasting experience. The palate is initially mild, owing to a tinge of sugar that has not changed into alcohol. Eventually, the wine develops a lively and fresh taste with a vivacious but rapid finish - a tendency with dry wines.
Recommended dishes: Dishes with polenta and white meat, kidneys, veal sweetbread, skinned-fruit desserts.

VIPAVSKA DOLINA WINE-GROWING DISTRICT

2001 Pinela

VIPAVSKA DOLINA WINE-GROWING DISTRICT

Lisjak

Radivoj Lisjak, Zalošče 62, si-5294 Dornberk
Phone: +386 (0)5 301 84 87

Wine selling ❧ Wine tasting for announced groups
Wine cellar tours for announced groups ❧ Wine route

This vintner's first wine labels date back to 1977. Both white and red grapes are grown in the vineyards, which provide the most favourable soil for the Beli Pinot grape. They only produce varieties such as Beli Pinot, Chardonnay and Merlot, which have proved to be of most interest for the Slovene and European markets.

Wines on offer
Beli Pinot, Sivi Pinot, Chardonnay, Sauvignon, Pinela, Zelen, Rumeni Muškat, Merlot, Cabernet Sauvignon, Barbera, Modri Pinot.

Awards
So far they have won over sixty medals at various international tastings.

Culinary recommendations
To accompany Sauvignon, Vipava frittata is recommended.

2002 Zelen
12.0% vol., dry, ★

This bright yellow wine shines beautifully in the glass and confirms its youth and fresh character. After a rather sealed initial bouquet one soon senses its fruity (almond) and herbal (peppermint) scents. The palate is vivaciously youthful. Its medium-structured body is colourful and lively, and yet a shade unbalanced. It is grouped among light wines that have no particularly long-term prospects and are at their best up to three years after production.
Recommended dishes: Vegetable platter, Vipava frittata, polenta with white meat, seafood risotto, pasta Bolognese.

VIPAVSKA DOLINA WINE-GROWING DISTRICT

2002 ZELEN

VIPAVSKA DOLINA WINE-GROWING DISTRICT

Kraljič

Ivo Čotar, Tabor 1a, si-5294 Dornberk
Phone: +386 (0)5 301 80 32, (0)41 622 726

Wine selling ❦ Wine tasting
Production of wine and food ❦ Wine cellar tours
Wine route ❦ Accommodation

Wines on offer

White blend, Laški Rizling, Chardonnay, Sauvignon, Rumeni Muškat, Barbera, Merlot, Cabernet Sauvignon and red blend.

Jože Ličen

Brje 104, si-5263 Dobravlje, Phone: +386 (0)5 364 75 23

Wine selling ❦ Wine route
❦ Sales material

Wines on offer

Furlanski Tokaj, Sauvignon, Laški rizling, Barbera and Cabernet Sauvignon.

Rajko Lisjak

Saksid 26, si-5294 Dornberk, Phone: +386 (0)5 301 80 85, (0)31 264 398
Email: ana.lisjak@volja.net

Wine selling ❦ Wine tasting
❦ Production of wine and food for announced groups

Mix of wines on offer

20% Barbera, 20% Merlot, 20% Sauvignon, 30% white 'Vipavsko' blend, 10% Cabernet Franc.

Bernarda Lozej

Podraga 58, si-5272 Podnanos, Phone: +386 (0)5 366 90 58

Wine selling ❦ Wine tasting
Production of wine and food ❦ Wine route

Wines on offer

Rebula, Sauvignon, Pinela, Zelen, Rumeni Muškat.

VIPAVSKA DOLINA WINE-GROWING DISTRICT

Martin Marc

Planina 82, si-5270 Ajdovščina, Phone: +386 (0)5 364 25 85, (0)41 520 923

Wine selling ❧ Wine tasting
Production of wine and food ❧ Wine cellar tours
❧ Wine route

Mix of wines on offer

50% Rebula, 20% Sauvignon, 20% Barbera, 10% Zelen.

Miran Marc

Slap 83a, si-5271 Vipava, Phone: +386 (0)5 368 71 26, (0)41 362 825

Wine selling ❧ Wine tasting
❧ Wine route

Mix of wines on offer

25% Sauvignon, 20% Zelen (dry and semi-dry), 20% Merlot, 11% Barbera, 9% Pinela, 8% Laški Rizling and 7% Chardonnay.

Srečko Marc

Slap 24, si-5271 Vipava, Phone: +386 (0)5 364 57 32, (0)41 698 566

Wine selling ❧ Wine tasting
Wine cellar tours ❧ Wine route
❧ Production of wine and food for announced groups

Mix of wines on offer

30% Sauvignon, 20% Zelen, 17% Cabernet Sauvignon, 13% Merlot, 10% Laški Rizling and 10% Rebula.

Boleslav Mervič

Šempas 57c, si-5261 Šempas
Phone: +386 (0)5 308 8693, (0)41 363 160, (0)41 506 689, Fax: +386 (0)5 307 85 15
Email: kristina.mervic@email.si

Wine selling ❧ Wine tasting

Mix of wines on offer

35% Chardonnay, 30% Furlanski Tokaj, 20% Merlot, 10% Cabernet Sauvignon, 5% Rebula.

VIPAVSKA DOLINA WINE-GROWING DISTRICT

Mansus

Bogdan Makovec, Brje 79, si-5263 Dobravlje
Phone: +386 (0)5 364 75 60, (0)41 648 524, Fax: +386 (0)5 368 80 38
Email: mansus-makovec@volja.net

Wine selling • Wine tasting for announced groups
Wine cellar tours for announced groups • Wine route
Sales material • Production of wine and food for announced groups

Bogdan Makovec took over this farm in 1986 and in 1990 finally decided to produce his own labels. Eleven types of grape grow in his vineyards, which are especially renowned for the vintage Klarnica grape. They produce dry, sweet and semi-sweet wines, marketed under the 'Mansus' brand-name. Rebula, Klarnica and Barbera are felt to be the most promising of the varieties they offer.
Best vintages: 1999 Klarnica (made from dried grapes), 2001 Merlot.

Mix of wines on offer

15% Merlot, 15% Cabernet Sauvignon, 10% Beli Pinot, 10% Chardonnay, 10% Klarnica, 10% Sivi Pinot, 7% Laški Rizling, 7% Rebula, 6% Rumeni Muškat, 7% Barbera and 8% Furlanski Tokaj.

Awards

They have won a gold medal in Gornja Radgona, a silver medal in Ljubljana and a silver medal in the Muscatel World Cup.

Culinary recommendations

Bread dumplings and pork rolls in carrot sauce are served with dry Furlanski Tokaj.

2001 Merlot

12.02% vol., dry, ★

An intense ruby red colour, with a vivacious necklace of bubbles and sheen. The legs are nicely shaped. Herbaceous (wild asparagus) and fruity (red and blue berries) characteristics merge on the nose into a pleasant and simple whole; pleasure continues on the palate. The body is medium in structure. This wine is vivacious, brisk, very agreeable and the best they have produced so far.
Recommended dishes: Smoked meat platter, roast pork, gnocchi with venison, kid in blueberry sauce.

VIPAVSKA DOLINA WINE-GROWING DISTRICT

2001 Merlot   1999 Klarnica

1999 Klarnica

15.0% vol., sweet, ★★★

The colour of wine made from dried grapes is denser and more concentrated in appearance than that of dry wines - the only logical explanation for the unique appearance of Klarnica, which gradually develops its 'golden' hue during the period when the grapes are dried. On pouring the wine you will notice its viscosity and noiseless flow, features typical of the dried-grape varieties. The pleasant nose of white fruit jam (white plum, quince), oranges, beeswax and sweet spices rises luxuriously out of the glass; there is no need to swill the wine at all. This wine is full and rich in every way; all the senses are needed in order to experience the richness and sweet harmony it delivers on the palate. Despite its rich concentration of alcohol, sugar and other elemental components, the wine contains enough acid to make it vivacious, perky and perfect for slow, unhurried enjoyment.

It will leave you impressed by its excellent blend of flavour and aroma.

Recommended dishes: Sweet fruit salad of white fruits and kiwi fruit, fruit cake, walnut *potica*.

VIPAVSKA DOLINA WINE-GROWING DISTRICT

Mlečnik

Valter in Ines Mlečnik, Bukovica 31, si-5293 Volčja Draga
Phone: +386 (0)5 395 53 23, Fax: +386 (0)5 395 53 23, Email: mlecnik@email.si

Wine selling ❧ Wine tasting for announced groups
❧ Wine cellar and vineyard tours
for announced groups

Here, the tradition of wine growing dates back to 1820. Today, Valter and Ines Mlečnik, who were the first to label their wines, successfully continue the tradition. They are mostly known for the indigenous Furlanski Tokaj and Rebula, which are in great demand and show much promise on both the Slovenian and European markets.
White wines can be purchased two-and-a-half years, and red wines four years, after the date of production, and sell within the year.

Mix of wines on offer
53% Chardonnay, 25% Rebula, 15% Merlot,
6% Furlanski Tokaj and 1% Sauvignon.

Culinary recommendations
Their wines can be served with any Slovenian dish except for beef soup.

2001 Rebula
12.5% vol., dry, ★★★

The wine's intense yellow colour, like antique gold, captures our attention straightaway. The nose immediately tells us that the wine has been produced from very ripe grapes that have been processed using carefully chosen methods. The ripeness of the fragrances now oozing from the glass is a direct consequence of these very ripe grapes, which have freely developed to this stage under the watchful eye of the vintner. It is a classic bouquet consisting of fruit (lychees), flowers (camomile, dried roses, violets, lime blossom), a hint of spice (vanilla) and honey. A decent mouthful of Rebula will invigorate and activate all the senses of the mouth and tongue, its aromas spreading and returning to the nasal cavity, where they work in harmony with the interesting and slightly unusual character typical of this particular type of Slovenian white wine. It contains mild tannins, more typical of red wines, which enrich its character yet further tannin, and they are a logical continuation of its appearance and personality. The whole is wittily shaped into harmony, making it a highly interesting creation. Rebula stimulates the imagination, making us ask ourselves 'Where is the vineyard, what are its soil and climate like, what is the philosophy of the vintner who produced such a wine?' An efficient marketing strategy!
Recommended dishes: Frittata with seasonal herbs; hard, mature cheeses (*zbrinc* and parmesan). With its exceptional richness this wine can be combined with dishes usually accompanied by red wines, such as chicken fillet with mushrooms, roast pork and even beef steak.

VIPAVSKA DOLINA WINE-GROWING DISTRICT

2001 Rebula   2000 Rebula

2000 Rebula
12.6% vol., dry, ★★★

The wine has an intense yellow colour like amber. Nowhere else on the market will you find a wine of Slovene origin that matches this one in terms of its youth and appearance. The previous Rebula is similar to this vintage, but by no means is it equal. This difference proves the great potential of these wines; two vintages, even if grown and produced in the same location, can never be the same. I shall compare them nonetheless, because they do have some characteristics in common.

The 2000 Rebula has gained much in the exquisiteness of aroma and flavour. A distinguished vintage of ripe grapes is delivered brilliantly on the nose. The fruit and flower aromas that characterize the 2001 Rebula differ slightly from those of the 2000, as if all the flower and fruit essences were striving towards the same goal: a vintage full of mutual harmony. A mouthful of the 2001 Rebula is mild on the palate, but develops into a definite and decisive flavour. Tannins are present, but in tiny proportions, and have a sweetening effect. The acid is hardly noticeable either, but contributes to the fine quality of the content and to the balance of the wine. The wine has already reached its peak, but it is not certain how long this stage will last. I would advise drinking the two Rebulas in the order shown here.

Recommended dishes: I recommend this wine with the same dishes as the previous Rebula, but one needs to be even more careful and sensitive during their preparation. Good company with good taste and plenty of time are required.

VIPAVSKA DOLINA WINE-GROWING DISTRICT

Pasji Rep

Franc Premrn, Orehovica 11a, si-5272 Podnanos, Phone: +386 (0)5 366 91 19

Wine selling ❧ Wine tasting
Wine cellar tours ❧ Wine route

Wines on offer
Zelen and Sivi Pinot.

Petrov Pil

Jožef Tomažič, Vrhpolje 77, si-5271 Vipava, Phone: +386 (0)5 366 53 18

Wine selling ❧ Wine tasting
Wine cellar tours ❧ Wine route
❧ Sales material

Mix of wines on offer
50% white 'Petrov Pil' blend, 30% red 'Petrov Pil' blend,
10% Chardonnay and 10% Cabernet Sauvignon.

Franc Potočnik

Orehovica 24, si-5272 Podnanos, Phone: +386 (0)5 366 91 02

Wine selling ❧ Wine tasting
❧ Wine route

Mix of wines on offer
39% Zelen, 33% Laški Rizling, 21% Malvazija, 7% Merlot.

Peter in Rajko Rondič

Slap 48, si-5271 Vipava, Phone: +386 (0)5 364 57 51

Wine selling ❧ Wine tasting
Wine cellar tours ❧ Wine route
❧ Sales material

Mix of wines on offer
30% Sauvignon, 30% Cabernet Sauvignon, 20% Rebula,
10% Beli Pinot; Malvazija, Merlot, Rumeni Muškat, Zelen.

VIPAVSKA DOLINA WINE-GROWING DISTRICT

Jožef Simončič

Šmarje 57, si-5295 Branik, Phone: +386 (0)5 364 86 66

Wine selling ❧ Wine tasting
Wine cellar tours ❧ Wine route
❧ Sales material

Mix of wines on offer

80% Refošk and 20% blend.

Marko Stibilj

Ustje 37b, si-5270 Ajdovščina, Phone: +386 (0)5 366 24 59, (0)41 432 521

Wine selling ❧ Wine cellar tours
❧ Wine route

Mix of wines on offer

50% red 'Vipavsko' blend and 50% white 'Vipavsko' blend.

Jožko Tratnik

Vodnikova 33, si-5294 Dornberk, Phone: +386 (0)41 742 174, Fax: +386 (0)5 301 84 10

Wine selling ❧ Wine tasting
Wine cellar tours for announced groups ❧ Wine route
❧ Production of wine and food for announced groups

Mix of wines on offer

30% white blend, 30% red blend, 20% Cabernet Sauvignon, 5% Merlot, 5% Barbera, 5% Chardonnay, 5% Sauvignon.

Stojan Trošt

Slap 72, si-5271 Vipava, Phone: +386 (0)5 364 57 22, (0)41 594 285

Wine selling ❧ Wine tasting for announced groups
Wine cellar tours for announced groups ❧ Wine route

Mix of wines on offer

18% Zelena, 6% Pinela, 6% Rebula, 31% Laški Rizling, 5% Chardonnay, 15% red wine (Merlot, Barbera), 9% white blend, 8% Cabernet Sauvignon.

VIPAVSKA DOLINA WINE-GROWING DISTRICT

Rikot

Rafael in Majda Baša, Zalošče 15a, si-5294 Dornberk, Phone: +386 (0)5 301 85 40

Wine selling ❧ Wine tasting
Wine cellar tours ❧ Wine route
Sales material ❧ Vineyard route
❧ Production of wine and food for announced groups

Wine growing and selling have always been a family tradition on this farm, and they first labelled their wines in 1990. The wines they offer encompass a broad, rich and colourful selection of over fourteen different varieties. Their leading labels are Merlot, Zelen, Rebula and Barbera.
Best vintages: 1995 and 2000 Merlot, 1998 Sauvignon PVVC, 2000 Zelen.

Mix of wines on offer

11% white blend, 10% red blend, 15% Merlot, 10% Cabernet Sauvignon, 8% Sauvignon, 9.4% Sivi Pinot, 5% Rebula, 5% Barbera, 4.2% Laški Rizling, 4.5% Chardonnay, 3% Beli Pinot, 3.1% Rumeni Muškat, 2.7% Zelen, 2.8% Refošk, 0.5% Malvazija and special wine made from dried grapes.

Awards

They have won two gold medals and a championship title at the Gornja Radgona wine tasting, three silvers and a gold in Ljubljana, and a grand gold medal at the Novi Sad tasting.

Culinary recommendations

Sauvignon is best served with prosciutto or frittata, Barbera with *kruhna* (barley soup), Rebula with *jota*, and Rumeni Muškat with *štruklji* or *potica*.

2000 Zelen

11.0% vol., semi-dry, ★

This wine has yellowish and straw-like tones; it is clear but with no particular shine or sparkle. Initially it has a pleasant, simple and uncomplicated aroma which, with a bit of patience, eventually develops into a mature character of medium breadth. To start with the palate is mild, as is typical of semi-dry wines. Later a vivacious acidity is activated adding a good sense of youth to its initially mild serenity. This wine is the perfect example of a drinking wine, with the distinct characteristics of its kind. It is recommended to wine-lovers who do not look for a rich body with a prolonged finish.
Recommended dishes: Dishes with polenta and white meat, seafood risotto, chicken or veal ragout.

VIPAVSKA DOLINA WINE-GROWING DISTRICT

2000 ZELEN

VIPAVSKA DOLINA WINE-GROWING DISTRICT

Slavček

Franc Vodopivec, Potok pri Dornberku 29, si-5294 Dornberk
Phone: +386 (0)5 301 87 45, (0)41 742 182, Fax: +386 (0)5 301 87 45

- Wine selling
- Wine tasting for announced groups
- Wine cellar tours for announced groups
- Wine route
- Accommodation
- Sales material
- Vineyard tour and visit to historical Tabor nad Dornberkom village
- Production of wine and food for announced groups

The first written documents to mention the Slavček ('Nightingale') farm date back to 1769, whilst the beginnings of their viticultural and wine-trading ventures are not recorded until 1970. In the late nineties they decided to label and launch their own wines. They produce only vintage wines, among which Rebula and Merlot form the vast majority both in the vineyards and in the cellars.
The best vintages they have produced and still available are from 2001-2003.

Mix of wines on offer
30% Rebula, 10% Chardonnay, 10% Sauvignon, 10% Malvazija, 10% Merlot, 10% Cabernet Sauvignon, 10% Barbera, 10% Teran.

Awards
Evidence of a wine-growing tradition of the highest quality can be seen in the form of several gold medals from the Ljubljana wine fair and a championship title from Gornja Radgona.

Culinary recommendations
Their broad selection of wines can be accompanied by Karstic prosciutto, homemade and home-smoked salami or homemade bread. They also serve a typical Primorskan dish - *jota*.

2001 Rebula
13.0% vol., dry, ★★

The wine is yellowish and straw-coloured, promising the imminent development of subtle golden nuances. The exquisitely shaped legs drizzling quietly down the wall of the glass are the prologue to a powerful tasting experience. The aroma is only moderately strong at first, but gains in intensity after a longer period in the open air. This intensity is next confirmed on the palate, where all the experiences of the senses harmonize gently with the warm body, charged with energy. The finish delivers long-lasting mildness and softness, perfectly rounding up the tasting experience.
Recommended dishes: Home-baked bread, *jota*, white meat in sauce, seafood risotto.

VIPAVSKA DOLINA WINE-GROWING DISTRICT

2001 Rebula

VIPAVSKA DOLINA WINE-GROWING DISTRICT

Sutor

Edvard Lavrenčič, Podraga 30,31, si-5272 Podnanos
Phone: +386 (0)5 366 93 67, (0)41 363 272, Fax: +386 (0)5 366 90 68
Email: sutor@siol.net, Website: www.sutorvino.com

Wine selling ❧ Wine tasting
Wine cellar tours ❧ Wine route
Sales material ❧ Production of wine and food for announced groups

The Lavrenčič family have been active in viticulture and the wine trade since 1884, but decided to market their own labels just thirteen years ago. Chardonnay delivers a high return of quality crops as the variety that predominates in their vineyards and consequently in the wines they offer, but Rebula is also very promising and has a bright future ahead of it. Best vintages: 2000 and 2002 Chardonnay, 2000 Sauvignon 'Primus Magnum', 1999 Chardonnay 'Magnum' and 2003 Merlot 'Primus'.

Mix of wines on offer
25% Chardonnay, 22% Sauvignon, 19% Rebula, 15% Merlot,
15% Modri Pinot and 4% Malvazija.

Culinary recommendations
Vegetables with oats make a perfect dish served with Chardonnay; Sauvignon goes well with *loška smojka* (turnip stuffed with millet accompanied by traditional side dishes).

2000 Sauvignon
14.0% vol., dry, ★★★

The slightly yellow, straw-like appearance tells of a wine that has already reached a settled maturity. Its compound aroma simultaneously expresses characteristics of the variety as a whole, and of the methods used to produce this particular wine. It delivers a mixture of generic fragrances (plants, pine resin) and tertiary ones (minerals, smoke and burning, spices). On the palate one senses its vivacity, well in tune with the rich fundamental flavours and aromatic power of this wine. Tasting it one feels its long-lasting effect, and the spice aromas typical of the variety are well expressed at this stage. The maturing process is still under way, and details that will accentuate the wine's finesse still further are yet to come. Sauvignon grapes must reach full maturity for the wine to be at its best.
Recommended dishes: Thick soup with truffles, fennel frittata, grilled Soča trout, tarragon *potica*.

VIPAVSKA DOLINA WINE-GROWING DISTRICT

2000 SAUVIGNON

VIPAVSKA DOLINA WINE-GROWING DISTRICT

Sveti Martin

Boža Stegovec, Brje 121, si-5263 Dobravlje
Phone: +386 (0)5 305 77 00, (0)41 369 633, (0)31 200 111
Elektronskinaslov: p_stegovec@hotmail.com
Website: www.slovino.com/stegovec

Wine selling ⚜ Wine tasting
Production of wine and food ⚜ Wine cellar tours
Wine route ⚜ Sales material
⚜ Scenic route and visit
to St Martin's church

In 1988, after ten years of actively growing and selling wine, the Stegovec family decided to begin marketing their own labels. Barbera is a speciality of the hilly vine country located at higher altitudes than usual; it is a grape of top quality, perfect for production of a pure wine or as a part ingredient in various blended reds. Zelen, Pinela and Klarnica also feature on the A-list among the wines they offer.
Best vintages: 1999 Rebula, 2001 Merlot, 2002 red and white blends.

Mix of wines on offer

15% white blend, 15% Barbera, 12% Zelen, 12% Pinela, 12% Rebula, 12% Rosé, 7% Merlot, 5% Klarnica and 10% red blend.

Awards

They have won several gold and silver medals at the international wine tasting in Ljubljana.

1999 Merlot

13.0% vol., dry, ★

It is a crystal-clear wine of intense ruby red colour, mixed with brick-like hues. One perceives clearly the aromas of over-ripe black berries, plums and toasting. This soft, open wine-blend has developed a palate that tends towards fruitiness, and thereby it has effectively reached its full range. It leaves a strong, long-lasting impression on the palate, even after swallowing.
Recommended dishes: Smoked meat platter, roast pork, gnocchi with venison, *fuži* with truffles, roast lamb.

VIPAVSKA DOLINA WINE-GROWING DISTRICT

1999 Merlot

VIPAVSKA DOLINA WINE-GROWING DISTRICT

Tilia

Melita in Matjaž Lemut, Potoče 41, si-5263 Dobravlje, Phone: +386 (0)5 364 66 84

Wine selling ❧ Wine tasting
Sales material ❧ Wine debates

In 1994, three years after purchasing the farm, they planted their first vineyards. Three years later, in 1997, they launched their first wine label (the 1996 vintage) on to the market. Sivi Pinot and Modri Pinot are the most fully represented varieties, both in their vineyards and in the cellars. They sell their wines under the 'Sončna Tilia' and 'Zlata Tilia' brand-names. Their Sivi Pinot, Rumeni Muškat, Merlot and Modri Pinot make up the core of the selection they have on offer.
Best vintages: 1997 and 2000 Merlot, 2001 Cabernet Sauvignon, 2001 Chardonnay and 1997 Cabernet Sauvignon 'Unique'.

Wines on offer
Sivi Pinot, Sauvignon, Rumeni Muškat, Cabernet Sauvignon, Chardonnay, Modri Pinot, 'Rubido' blend and 'Adelaida' (dried Rumeni Muškat).

Awards
They have won five gold medals in Gornja Radgona, while in Ljubljana they have gained two gold and three silver medals.

Culinary recommendations
Most seafood dishes go well with Sivi Pinot. Rubido is perfect with *Idrijski žlikrofi* - a traditional dish of ravioli stuffed with potato and chives, originally eaten by miners in the town of Idrija; frittata with Chardonnay.

2001 Cabernet Sauvignon
12.9% vol., dry, ★★★

The deep ruby red colour with its violet and brick tones is the sign of a full body. The candid and intense nose, with a character very typical of the variety, comprises fruit fragrances (forest berries), roasting smells (smoke), and aromas of the pine forest. The bouquet opens up like a peacock's tail. The solid structure contains solid tannins, still in good shape, combined with the ingredients provided by well-ripened grapes. The rich palate completely engages the taste buds and we experience the release of vibrant sensations. Harmony is maintained on the palate between the mature fruitiness, the fresh acidity and the power of the tannins, promising an interesting development to come. The bouquet lingers on, with the suggestion of an animal quality, and promises an exceptionally mature wine.
Recommended dishes: Prosciutto, smoked pork shoulder with beans, shoulder of venison in prosciutto gravy, venison thigh in blackcurrant sauce.

VIPAVSKA DOLINA WINE-GROWING DISTRICT

2001 CABERNET SAUVIGNON

VIPAVSKA DOLINA WINE-GROWING DISTRICT

Erik Uršič

Slap 76, si-5271 Vipava, Phone: +386 (0)5 364 56 40, Fax: +386 (0)5 364 57 16

Wine selling ❧ Wine tasting
Wine cellar tours ❧ Wine route
❧ Sales material

Wines on offer

Barbera, Sauvignon, Merlot, Laški Rizling, Cabernet Sauvignon, Rebula, white blend, red blend, Pinela, Zelen and Rumeni Muškat.

Marjan Vidmar

Ustje 42, si-5270 Ajdovščina, Phone: +386 (0)5 368 16 06, (0)41 323 860, Email: eljo@volja.net

Wine selling ❧ Wine tasting
Wine cellar tours ❧ Wine route
❧ Sales material

Mix of wines on offer

25% Sauvignon, 20% Laški Rizling, 10% Rumeni Muškat, 15% Merlot, 10% Rebula, 20% white blend.

Vina Kavčič

Andrej in Miran Kavčič, Brje 84, si-5263 Dobravlje
Phone: +386 (0)5 364 76 75, +386 (0)40 287 882

Wine selling ❧ Wine tasting
Wine cellar tours ❧ Wine route
❧ Sales material

Mix of wines on offer

10% Malvazija, 10% Rebula, 30% red blend, 30% white blend, 5% Sauvignon, 5% Beli Pinot, 4% Rumeni Muškat, 3% Modri Pinot, 3% Klarnica.

Vina Orse

Bruno Gregorič, Prvačina 59, si-5297 Prvačina, Phone: +386 (0)51 343 183

Wine selling ❧ Wine tasting
Production of wine and food ❧ Wine route

Wines on offer

Sauvignon, Zelen, Pinela, Beli Pinot, Cabernet Sauvignon, Laški Rizling.

VIPAVSKA DOLINA WINE-GROWING DISTRICT

Vina Poljšak

Samuel Poljšak, Gradišče pri Vipavi 39a, si-5271 Vipava
Phone: +386 (0)5 366 53 59, (0)41 441 001, Fax: +386 (0)5 366 53 59
Email: samo.poljsak@volja.net, Website: www.users.volja.net/spoljs

Wine selling ⁂ Wine tasting
Wine cellar tours ⁂ Wine route
⁂ Sales material

Mix of wines on offer

30% Cabernet Sauvignon, 16% Zelen, 8% Rumeni Muškat,
8% Sauvignon, 20% white blend, 18% red blend.

Vina Ušaj

Stojan Ušaj, Črniče 56, si-5262 Črniče, Phone: +386 (0)5 366 60 75, (0)41 518 171
Email: davorin.usaj@amis.net

Wine selling ⁂ Wine tasting
Wine cellar tours for announced groups ⁂ Wine route

Mix of wines on offer

50% Merlot, 20% white '+Vipavec' blend, 10% Sauvignon,
10% Rebula, 10% Cabernet Sauvignon.

Vindor

Matjaž Berce, Draga 20a, si-5294 Dornberk, Phone: +386 (0)5 301 76 56, (0)31 886 277
Email: vindor@siol.net, Website: www.vindor.com

Wine selling ⁂ Wine tasting
Production of wine and food ⁂ Wine cellar tours
Wine route ⁂ Sales material
⁂ Liqueur and home-made juice tasting

Mix of wines on offer

40% white 'Dornbersko' blend, 20% red 'Dornbersko', 10% Cabernet
Sauvignon, 5% Barbera, 5% Sauvignon, 5% Chardonnay, 5% Rumeni Muškat,
5% white sparkling, 5% sparkling Rosé.

Vinogradništvo in Vinarstvo Pipan

Jože Pipan, Planina 62, si-5270 Ajdovščina, Phone: +386 (0)5 364 25 84

Wine selling ⁂ Wine tasting
Wine cellar tours ⁂ Wine route
⁂ Production of wine and food for
announced groups

Mix of wines on offer

40% Rebula, 20% Beli Pinot, 20% Sauvignon, 10% Laški Rizling, 10% Barbera.

VIPAVSKA DOLINA WINE-GROWING DISTRICT

Vipava 1894

Vinarska cesta 5, si-5271 Vipava,
Phone: +386 (0)5 367 12 40, Fax: +386 (0)5 367 12 44
Email: info@vipava1894.si, Website: www.vipava1894.si

- Wine selling
- Wine tasting for announced groups
- Production of wine and food
- Wine cellar tours for announced groups
- Wine route
- Sales material

This company has been in viticulture and the wine trade since 1894, and their cellar is the biggest both in terms of capacity and the number of wines acquired each year. They labelled their own wines as early as 1951. They produce high-quality red and white wines, sold under three brand-names: 'Vipava 1894', 'Kindermacher' and 'Lanthieri'. Currently the Sauvignon and Merlot grapes are their most rewarding varieties, but they have high hopes for Pinela and Zelen as well.
Best vintages still available: 1992 Barbera, 1994 Merlot, 1994 Cabernet Sauvignon, 1997 Chardonnay, 1998 Merlot and 2000 Sauvignon.

Mix of wines on offer
21% Merlot, 18% Malvazija, 8% Laški Rizling, 7% Rebula, 5% Sauvignon, 6% Cabernet Sauvignon, 5% Barbera, 5% 'Vrtovčan' blend, 5% Beli Pinot and 5% Chardonnay.

Awards
They are the proud winners of two gold medals and a silver from Paris, and have been awarded the title of overall champion as well as variety championship titles in Gornja Radgona, but most of all they pride themselves on their two championship titles from the Ljubljana wine fair.

Culinary recommendations
They will offer you Pinela with prosciutto and Beli Pinot with cheese-and-walnut dumplings.

VIPAVSKA DOLINA WINE-GROWING DISTRICT

2001 Sauvignon Zemono Lanthieri

11.5% vol., dry, ★★★★

This pale yellow wine with its golden reflections is crystal-clear. The aroma is typically Sauvignon, but at the same time unique and interesting. It reminds us of the best-known European Sauvignons from the Loire Valley in France, the birthplace of Sauvignon wine. It is the famous terrain of Pouilly Fumé that produces Sauvignons with a 'scent of smoke'. The term refers to the typical scent of grass and vegetation, without the wine being kept in charred barriques. The flavour resembles redcurrants: fresh, colourful, complex and, above all, fruity. Taking these characteristics together we have a wine that is intriguing, different. It has Sauvignon character but also an attractive one of its own, which widens the Sauvignon range. This must be the product of a clutch of fortunate natural coincidences between the soil and the terrain. The finish is fruity and pleasant.

Recommended dishes: Asparagus dishes, frittata with seasonal herbs, hard goat's cheeses, pies, seafood.

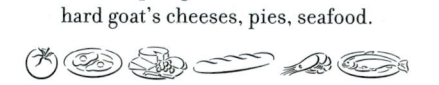

VIPAVSKA DOLINA WINE-GROWING DISTRICT

1997 Cabernet Sauvignon Lanthieri

12.0% vol., dry, ★★★

This wine, ruby red with some brick tones, looks promising and appealing to the eye. The candid bouquet is typical of this variety. It resembles the ripe scents of dark berries (blackcurrants, blackberries, mulberries), and this pleasing aroma is followed by scents of roasting, dark chocolate, coffee, spices and fresh leather. The palate is surprisingly fresh for a six-year-old wine; the tannins have reached tasty maturity. With the softness of the tannins, the current acidity is welcome, and seems agreeable in the context of the composition as a whole. This wine has not fully completed its development, but suits Slovene tastes in its current form.

Recommended dishes: Cold cuts of smoked meat, homemade prosciutto, roast veal or pork, kid in blueberry sauce.

VIPAVSKA DOLINA WINE-GROWING DISTRICT

2002 Zelen Lanthieri

11,5% vol., semi-dry, ★★

This pale yellow wine with its hidden green rainbow is beautiful and glowing. It has a candid aroma of floral and fruit fragrances, such as dried flowers, mint tea, white peaches, fresh almonds, hazelnuts and sweet spices: a complex bouquet, all beautifully in harmony. The wine remains pleasantly fresh and candid throughout, in spite of its mild sugar, and finishes with a fruity bouquet on the palate, reminiscent of green apples and lemon.
Recommended dishes: Dishes with polenta and white meat, *jota*, seafood risotto, chicken or veal ragout.

VIPAVSKA DOLINA WINE-GROWING DISTRICT

Vi-Vin Saksida

Ingrid in Jožko Saksida, Zalošče 12a, si-5294 Dornberk
Phone: +386 (0)5 301 78 53, (0)41 208 345, Fax: +386 (0)5 301 78 54
Email: vi-vin@volja.net

Wine tasting ❦ Wine cellar tours for announced groups

The Saksida family have been dedicated wine growers and traders since 1970, and decided to label their own wines in the late eighties. Their vineyards are mainly planted with Merlot, Rebula and Beli Pinot. The most promising wines in their cellar are red and white 'Carisma Cuvée', Zelen and Merlot.

Mix of wines on offer

15% Merlot, 5% Modri Pinot, 5% Cabernet Sauvignon, 25% red 'Carisma Cuvée', 25% white 'Carisma Cuvée', 5% Zelen, 10% Beli Pinot and 10% Chardonnay.

Awards

They have won ten gold medals and one championship title in Gornja Radgona, and seven gold medals and one variety championship title in Ljubljana.

Culinary recommendations

Grilled polenta and sausage will taste even better with Merlot; prosciutto makes a good accompaniment to Beli Pinot.

1999 Beli Pinot

13.0% vol., dry, ★★★

Its beautifully intense colour with its noticeable sheen implies a mature wine rich in content. The aroma is fairly pronounced and redolent of dried pears and honey, while in the background one detects the fragrances of dried flowers. It is strong in flavour, but very pleasant. It is an open wine and so offers a wide variety of well-tuned and lasting flavours on the palate: proof of a good vintage. Tasting requires the employment of the whole oral cavity, the palate delivering a series of colourful flavours that make up for what may be missing from the nose. The acidity is noticeable only insofar as it accentuates the basic juiciness of the wine and tells us of its possible long-term career. This wine is appropriate for tasting and cellarage.
Recommended dishes: With its rich structure Beli Pinot is perfect for serving with heavier meals (roast pork, roast veal), quite fatty dishes, and smoked meats, as well as with freshwater and marine fish.

VIPAVSKA DOLINA WINE-GROWING DISTRICT

1999 Beli Pinot

VIPAVSKA DOLINA WINE-GROWING DISTRICT

Zaloščan

De Adami, Zalošče 12b, si-5294 Dornberk
Phone: +386 (0)5 301 78 56, (0)41 352 045, (0)41 411 835, Fax: +386 (0)5 301 78 58
Website: www.slovino.com/zaloscan

Wine selling ❧ Wine tasting
Wine cellar tours ❧ Wine route
Sales material ❧ Medieval grape harvest
❧ Production of wine and food for announced groups

The agricultural cooperative has been in the wine industry since 1989, and they launched their own label in 1990 under the brand-name 'De Adami'. They produce the best high-quality wines, the core of their output being represented by Merlot, Cabernet, Sivi Pinot and Zelen. Best vintages: 1996 and 1999 Merlot, 2001 Cabernet Sauvignon.

Mix of wines on offer

30% white blend, 30% red blend, 5% Sivi Pinot, 6% Beli Pinot, 5% Chardonnay, 2% Zelen, 2% Rumeni Muškat, 8% Merlot, 7% Cabernet Sauvignon and 5% Modri Pinot.

Awards

Their veritable treasury of accolades comprises one hundred medals and three championship titles from the Gornja Radgona fair, thirty medals from the Ljubljana fair, and eight medals plus another championship title from Novi Sad.

2002 Zelen
11.86% vol., dry, ★★★

This pale yellow wine with wheat-like reflections has an exceptional glow. The thick legs trace interesting windows on the wall of the glass, confirming the wine's richness. The pleasant, fresh, fruit-floral aroma is a distinctive feature of this variety, and again shows a rich composition. It resembles ripe peaches, grapefruit, fresh hazelnuts, dried flowers, tea and the smell of mild cigarettes. The first impression on the palate is very complex and confirms the wine as a Zelen; the way the flavours develop on the tongue is interesting, and they remain in harmony throughout the tasting. There is much sweetness here - even though this wine is dry - but there is just enough acidity to maintain a sense of freshness. During the tasting diverse fragrances are released, once again identifying the variety, and they linger after swallowing. A lovely example of Zelen.

Recommended dishes: Vegetable platter, frittata with seasonal herbs, dishes with polenta and white meat, seafood risotto, smoked trout.

VIPAVSKA DOLINA WINE-GROWING DISTRICT

2002 ZELEN

VIPAVSKA DOLINA WINE-GROWING DISTRICT

Vinska klet Žorž

Jurij Žorž, Slap 13, si-5271 Vipava
Phone: +386 (0)5 364 57 35, (0)41 698 556, Fax: +386 (0)5 364 57 35
Email: vino.zorz.slap.13@siol.net

Wine selling ❦ Wine tasting
Wine cellar tours ❦ Wine route
❦ Sales material

The Žorž family have a long tradition of wine-growing, which has been managed successfully by Jurij since 1980. Their vineyards are renowned for excellent Merlot and Cabernet Sauvignon. They are also convinced that there is great potential in the indigenous Zelen and Pinela varieties, as well as in Sauvignon and Sivi Pinot, already known worldwide and which have been planted anew. Best vintages: 1998 Pinela, 2000 Sauvignon, 2000 Rumeni Muškat, 2003 Merlot barrique, 2002 Zelen.

Mix of wines on offer

30% Cabernet Sauvignon, 20% white wine blends, 15% Merlot, 10% Sauvignon, 10% Laški Rizling, 15% others.

Awards

They have won several gold and silver medals in Ljubljana and Gornja Radgona.

Culinary recommendations

Cabernet Sauvignon or Merlot go very well with prosciutto, while Merlot barrique is perfectly accompanied by polenta with venison.

1998 Pinela

11.24% vol., semi-dry, ★★

The bright yellow colour and sparkling appearance belie the true nature of this wine, which is now entering its sixth year. The maturity of the aromas reminds us that the vintage is no mistake. The initially herbaceous character of the nose is reminiscent of dried grass cuttings and essences of tobacco, while in the background moderate quantities of fruit aromas emerge, mainly ripe pears and peaches. On the palate the aroma expresses its predominantly herbaceous quality. The youthful and fresh flavour is mainly due to an emphatic acidity, almost as strong as in dry wines, despite some residual traces of sugar. The slender body is very agreeable when tasted, but very short in duration. Pinela has reached its peak of maturity, and we therefore strongly recommend consumption while this level of quality remains.
Recommended dishes: Dishes with polenta and white meat, offal of pork and veal (kidneys, sweetbread), cheeses (goat's cheese, blue cheese), skinned-fruit desserts.

VIPAVSKA DOLINA WINE-GROWING DISTRICT

1998 Pinela

VIPAVSKA DOLINA WINE-GROWING DISTRICT

Milan Živec

Osek 48, si-5261 Šempas, Phone: +386 (0)5 308 88 28

Wine selling ❧ Wine tasting for announced groups

Mix of wines on offer

70% Beli Pinot and 30% Merlot.

Vinogradništvo Štrukelj

Selo 2a, si-5262 Črniče, Phone: +386 (0)41 790 741, Fax: +386 (0)5 368 47 74

Wine selling ❧ Wine tasting for announced groups
Production of wine and food ❧ Wine cellar tours for announced groups
❧ Wine route

Wines on offer

Cabernet Sauvignon, Furlanski Tokaj, Sauvignon, Laški Rizling, white blend, red blend, Rumeni Muškat.

Vinska Klet Jejčič

Robert Jejčič, Spodnja Branica 12, si-5295 Branik
Phone: +386 (0)5 305 79 11, Fax: +386 (0)5 305 79 10
Email: vino.jejcic@siol.net

Wine selling ❧ Wine tasting
Wine cellar tours ❧ Wine route

Mix of wines on offer

25% Cabernet Sauvignon, 15% Chardonnay, 10% Sauvignon, 10% Rebula, 10% Laški Rizling, 10% Malvazija, Rumeni Muškat; 8% Merlot, 7% Barbera, 5% Beli Pinot; special wine produced from the dried grapes.

Vinska Klet Plahuta

Katarina and Drago Plahuta, IV. prekomorske brigade 74, si-5270 Ajdovščina,
Phone: +386 (0)5 366 17 90, (0)41 822 971

Wine selling ❧ Wine tasting for announced groups
Wine cellar tours for announced groups ❧ Wine route
❧ Production of wine and food for announced groups

Mix of wines on offer

20% Rebula, 12% Furlanski Tokaj, 22% blend, 34% Merlot, °12% Cabernet Sauvignon.

VIPAVSKA DOLINA WINE-GROWING DISTRICT

Vinski hram Štokelj

Damjan Štokelj, Planina 9, si-5270 Ajdovščina
Phone: +386 (0)5 368 02 03, (0)41 483 777 , Email: damjan.stokelj@volja.net

Wine selling ❧ Wine tasting for announced groups
Wine cellar tours ❧ Wine route
❧ Sales material

Mix of wines on offer

40% Rebula, 30% Pinela, 30% red 'Planta' blend (Merlot in Barbera); 'Ambrosia' (sweet wine from dried Rebula grapes).

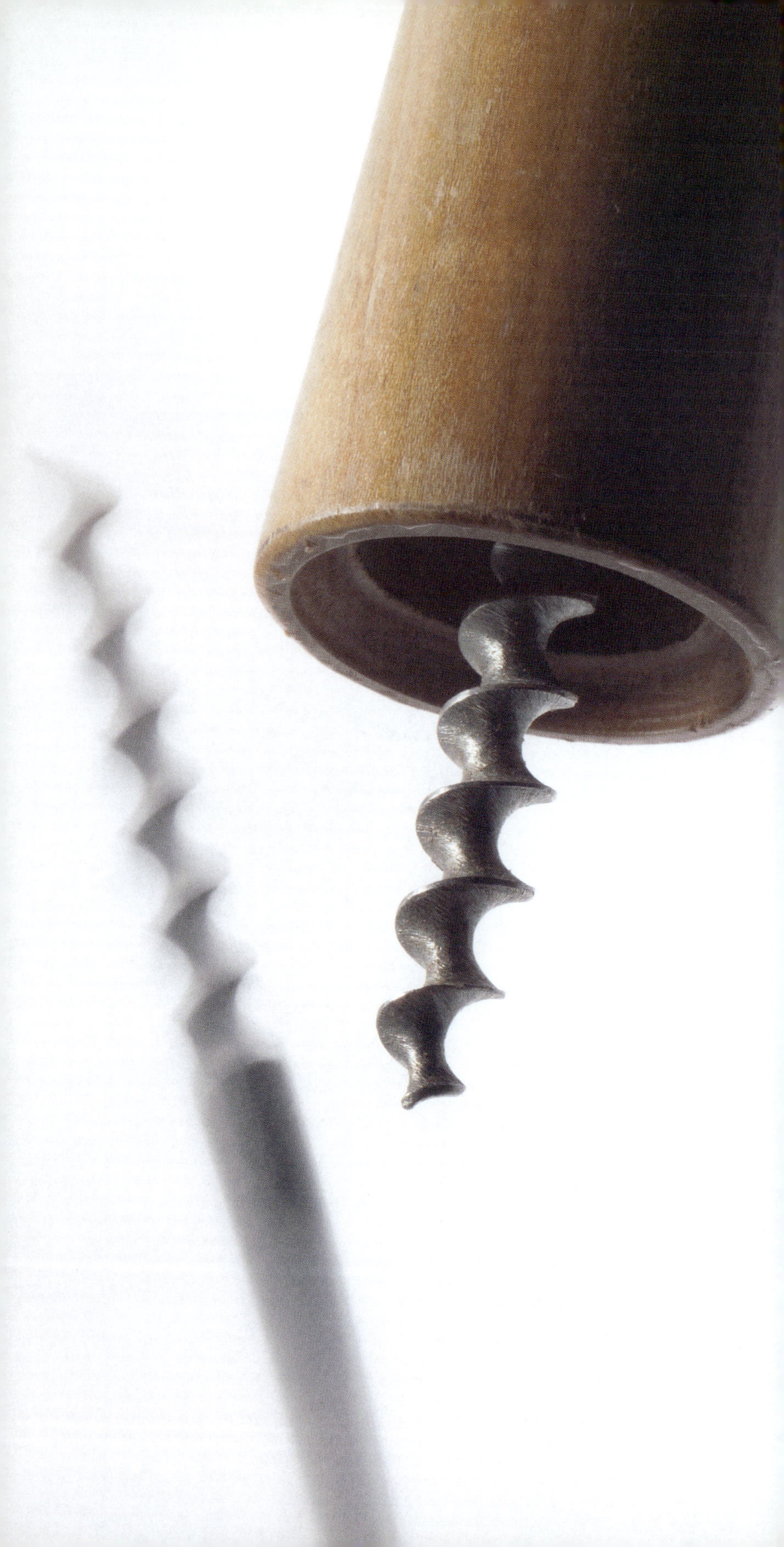

Kras
Wine-Growing District
Primorska Wine-Growing Region

KRAS WINE-GROWING DISTRICT

BORIS

Boris Masten, Preserje pri Komnu 2a, si-6223 Komen
Phone: +386 (0)5 766 82 01, (0)41 361 739, Fax: +386 (0)5 731 02 05
Email: boris.masten@bonus.si

❧ Wine tasting for announced groups

MIX OF WINES ON OFFER
40% Teran PTP, 25% Chardonnay, 20% Malvazija,
10% Vitovska Grganja, 5% Pinot.

MARJAN COLJA

Coljava 10, si-6223 Komen, Phone: +386 (0)5 766 80 95, (0)41 403 512
Email: vina.colja@email.si

Wine selling ❧ Wine tasting for announced groups
Production of wine and food ❧ Wine cellar tours for announced groups
❧ Sales material

MIX OF WINES ON OFFER
80% Teran PTP, 10% Teran liqueur, 8% sparkling Teran
and 2% white predicate wine from dried grapes.

ANDREJ GRMEK

Kobjeglava 78, si-6222 Štanjel, Phone: +386 (0)31 330 813

Wine selling ❧ Wine tasting
Wine cellar tours ❧ Wine route

MIX OF WINES ON OFFER
90% Teran PTP, 5% Chardonnay, 3% Malvazija, 2% Rumeni Muškat.

EDVARD JERMAN

Šepulje 1d, si-6210 Sežana, Phone: +386 (0)5 764 06 86
Email: leon.jerman@guest.arnes.si
Website: http://www2.arnes.si/~ngiae27/

❧ Wine selling

WINE ON OFFER
Teran PTP.

KRAS WINE-GROWING DISTRICT

Kmetija Petelin - Durcik

Franko Durcik, Pliskovica 93, si-6221 Dutovlje
Phone: +386 (0)5 764 00 28, (0)5 764 05 51, (0)31 654 171, (0)41 519 253

Wine selling ❧ Wine tasting
Wine cellar tours ❧ Wine route
Accomodation ❧ Sales material
Tour of the farm ❧ Production of wine and food
and local educational walks   for announced groups

Mix of wines on offer
95% Teran PTP and 5% white 'Kamarela' blend.

Viljem in Jadran Petelin

Pliskovica 52, si-6221 Dutovlje
Phone: +386 (0)5 764 05 39, (0)31 829 909, (0)41 573 177
Email: jadranp@volja.net

Wine selling ❧ Wine tasting
Wine cellar tours ❧ Wine route
❧ Sales material

Mix of wines on offer
83% Teran PTP, 10% white blend; the rest Cabernet Sauvignon, Beli Pinot, Rebula, Sauvignon and Malvazija.

Dušan Rebula

Brestovica pri Komnu 32, si-6223 Komen, Phone: +386 (0)5 766 43 39, (0)41 238 569

Wine selling ❧ Wine tasting
Production of wine and food ❧ Wine cellar tours
❧ Wine route

Mix of wines on offer
70% Teran PTP, 15% Malvazija and 15% blend for sparkling wines.

Šempolajc

Rado Macarol, Križ 191, si-6210 Sežana, Phone: +386 (0)41 448 349

Wine selling ❧ Wine tasting
❧ Wine cellar tours

Wine on offer
Teran PTP.

KRAS WINE-GROWING DISTRICT

Branko in Vasja Čotar

Gorjansko 18, si-6223 Komen
Phone: +386 (0)5 766 82 28, (0)5 766 81 94, (0)5 766 80 23, Fax: +386 (0)5 766 82 28
Email: vasjacotar@volja.net
Website: www.cotar.vinarstvo.info

Wine selling ❧ Wine tasting for announced groups
Wine cellar tours for announced groups ❧ Wine route
Sales material ❧ Production of wine and food for announced groups

The Čotars first went into wine growing and the wine trade in 1975; thirteen years later they labelled their first bottles. Besides Refošk, their largest crop, the Malvazija, Vitovska Grganja and Merlot varieties also do well. From Teran, Merlot and Cabernet Sauvignon they produce a blend called 'Terra Rossa'. In their view it is the indigenous varieties that show the most promise. Best vintages available: 1999 (Teran, Merlot, Cabernet Sauvignon, 'Terra Rossa').

Wines on offer

Teran PTP, Cabernet Sauvignon, 'Terra Rossa', Malvazija, Vitovska Grganja, Merlot, Sauvignon and Chardonnay.

Awards

They believe it is important for buyers to taste their wines in their own wine cellar.

Culinary recommendations

They guarantee that their wines make a great accompaniment to all Mediterranean cuisine. They also organize food and wine tastings.

1999 Terra Rossa

13.0% vol., dry, ★★★

The wine is a lovely ruby red colour with fiery tints and notes of violet. Beautifully formed legs further enhance the aesthetic pleasure afforded by this wine, and attest to its structure. Nobility and maturity emanate from the glass, the nose bringing reminiscences of cooked and stewed fruits, freshly roasted coffee beans, spices and nuances of the animal world such as fresh leather, as well as the smell of the Karstic region in autumn following the grape harvest. On the palate the wine reveals a freshness in spite of its rich body. The juicy flavour is probably thanks to the Refosco grape, which most strongly retains its own characteristics in the company of other grape varieties. The wine's coexistence with oak can be discerned, although this is merely present as an undertone; far more, we can enjoy the characters of fruit of spice, both on the nose and on the palate.
Recommended dishes: Aged prosciutto, pheasant breast with figs, shoulder of venison with prosciutto gravy, grilled boar thigh.

KRAS WINE-GROWING DISTRICT

1999 Terra Rossa

KRAS WINE-GROWING DISTRICT

Boris Lisjak

Dutovlje 31, si-6221 Dutovlje, Phone: +386 (0)5 764 00 63, (0)41 652 039

Wine selling ❧ Wine tasting
Production of wine and food ❧ Wine cellar tours
❧ Wine route

Boris Lisjak started to grow and sell wine in 1968, first labelling his bottles six years later. The main variety grown here is Refošk, which gives excellent results. He grows only high-quality vines, and the cellar's show wines are Teran PTP and Cabernet Sauvignon.
Best vintages available: 2002 Teran PTP, 1998 Cabernet Sauvignon, 1997 red 'Sara' blend, 1997 Vitovska Grganja - wine produced from dried grapes.

Mix of wines on offer

80% Teran PTP, 10% Cabernet Sauvignon; 10% Merlot, Vitovska Grganja, Cabernet Franc, Chardonnay, Beli Pinot and Furlanski Tokaj.

Awards

Their wines were awarded with five grand gold medals in Ljubljana, and in Gornja Radgona they have won the championship three times and been awarded champion within variety seventeen times.

Culinary recommendations

Teran is a good accompaniment to prosciutto or cheeses.
With Cabernet Sauvignon you should have venison or grilled meat.

2002 Izbrani Teran PTP

11.5% vol., dry, ★★★

The wine at first is an opaque, dark red cherry colour, which becomes transparent and glows in the glass. This Teran gives off a distinctive scent of Karstic vegetation, and has a fresh, juniper-like quality on the nose. A fruity fragrance with an undertone of smoke augments this and builds a unique character in combination with it. The wine is highly drinkable, thanks to its slim structure and gentle acidity. After swallowing, the lingering impression is wholly pleasant, and soon fades, leaving one wanting more.
Recommended dishes: Karstic prosciutto, Primorskan tripe soup, veal chop with apple sauce, pheasant breast with figs.

KRAS WINE-GROWING DISTRICT

2002 Izbrani Teran PTP

KRAS WINE-GROWING DISTRICT

Joško Renčel

Dutovlje 24, si-6221 Dutovlje, Phone: +386 (0)5 764 00 12

Wine selling ❧ Wine tasting for announced groups
Wine cellar tours for announced groups ❧ Wine route
Sales material ❧ Production of wine and food for announced groups

Like many other inhabitants of Kras, the Renčels have produced Teran and other wines for some time, and Joško Renčel took over the business in 1980. Refošk accounts for half the crops in the vineyard, the rest being divided up between Malvazija, Chardonnay, Sauvignon, Cabernet Sauvignon, Merlot and Modri Pinot. He attributes his success on the world market - and of course at home - to a limited offer of special wines, and this is what he focuses on with dedication.
His best vintages still available are the cellared vintages from 1994, 1997, 1999 and 2002, and all 2003 wines.

Wines on offer

Teran PTP, Malvazija, Chardonnay, Sauvignon, Cabernet Sauvignon, Merlot, Modri Pinot, different blends and 'Zlate Solzice' a special wine made from dried grapes.

Awards

He has not attended wine tastings or competitions since 1996; prior to that he regularly attended tastings at Ljubljana, where he won a good number of gold and silver medals.

Culinary recommendations

Karstic prosciutto should be accompanied by Teran or Malvazija, and sweet desserts by 'Zlate Solzice'. Another wonderful combination is a red cuvée and smoked shoulder of venison with goat's-milk butter and thyme, or a red cuvée with duck breasts in orange sauce.

2002 Zlate Solzice

11.0% vol., sweet, ★★★

An intense, deep amber colour with golden tones ranging from pale yellow to dark, lends this wine an intriguing character. The fragrances of very ripe grapes, boiled fruit (quince cheese, peaches, citrus fruits) and mango are delivered very candidly and are enhanced by the aromas of various spices - all indicate a wine rich in composition. The full and vivacious palate with its plentiful freshness supplied by a good portion of acidity, is well balanced. The sweetness that we expect in abundance from such a wine is not there at first, but makes its mark in the background. A wide array of aromas is also delivered on the palate, and the finish lasts long after swallowing.
Recommended dishes: Pancakes with walnuts, walnut *štruklji*, fried *fritole* and *kroštole* (*miške* and *flancati*).

KRAS WINE-GROWING DISTRICT

2002 Zlate Solzice

2001 Malvazija

2001 Malvazija

14.0% vol., dry, ★★★

The almost yellow colour with its golden tones shows this to be a classical Malvasia, as we expect much grapeskin extract in the wine. The mature fruit aroma gives us sun-scorched grapes, dried pears, spices, vanilla and rosemary; this is a variety that rewards patience as we discover more and more of nature in the nose. The sweetness gently warms us up, seems to encase the palate, and tones down the variety of sensations yielded by this relatively young wine of exceptional character. I would propose this wine as an examplar for Primorskan dry wines; it is suitable for cellarage, lacks residual sugar but nonetheless has an element of sweetness, and remains rich but offers freshness. A very interesting wine for tasting, with a great deal of promise; it still needs some time to develop, and it will be interesting to encounter it again when it has taken the last step towards quality.

Recommended dishes: Prosciutto, frittata with seasonal herbs, sausages and prosciutto, seafood, pizza, turkey steaks.

KRAS WINE-GROWING DISTRICT

Milivoj Širca

Dutovlje 66, si-6221 Dutovlje
Phone: +386 (0)5 764 04 53, (0)41 745 250, Fax: +386 (0)5 764 21 39

Wine selling ❧ Wine tasting for announced groups
❧ Wine cellar tours for announced groups

Wine on offer
Teran PTP.

Izidor Škerlj

Tomaj 53, si-6221 Dutovlje, Phone: +386 (0)5 764 06 73, (0)31 306 919, Fax: +386 (0)5 764 06 67
Email: skerlj.tomaj@siol.net

Wine selling ❧ Wine tasting
Production of wine and food ❧ Wine cellar tours
Wine route ❧ Accomodation

Mix of wines on offer
80% Teran PTP, 10% Sauvignon, 10% Cabernet Sauvignon.

Jožef Škerlj

Tomaj 46, si-6221 Dutovlje, Phone: +386 (0)5 764 06 67

Wine selling ❧ Wine cellar tours
❧ Wine route

Wine on offer
Teran PTP.

Milivoj Tavčar

Kreplje 2a, si-6221 Dutovlje, Phone: +386 (0)5 764 12 92, (0)31 645 808

Wine selling ❧ Wine tasting for announced groups
Wine route ❧ Production of wine and food for announced groups

Mix of wines on offer
85% Teran PTP and 15% Vitovska Grganja

KRAS WINE-GROWING DISTRICT

Vina Urdih

Dragotin Urdih, Škrbina 38, si-6223 Komen, Phone: +386 (0)5 766 81 58, (0)40 216 200

Wine selling ❦ Wine tasting
Wine cellar tours ❦ Wine route

Mix of wines on offer

40% Teran PTP, 35% sparkling Chardonnay and 25% sparkling wine white blend (produced using traditional methods).

Vinarstvo Šuc

Milko and Peter Šuc, Dutovlje 92, si-6221 Dutovlje
Phone: +386 (0)5 764 20 66, (0)41 417 098
Email: suc@siol.net, Website: www.sucteran.com

Wine selling ❦ Wine tasting
Wine cellar tours ❦ Wine route

Mix of wines on offer

85% Teran PTP, 10% Malvazija, 3% Rizvanec, 2% Cabernet Sauvignon.

Vinogradništvo in Kletarstvo Buntovi

Bogdan Cotič, Škrbina 62, si-6223 Komen, Phone: +386 (0)5 766 70 25, (0)31 867 632

Wine selling ❦ Wine tasting
Wine cellar tours ❦ Wine route

Mix of wines on offer

90% Teran PTP, 10% white blend and Teran liqueur.

Vinska Klet Orel

Avber 10, si-6210 Sežana, Phone: +386 (0)5 768 50 03, (0)41 361 822

Wine selling ❦ Wine tasting for announced groups
Wine route ❦ Wine cellar tours for announced groups

Mix of wines on offer

90% Teran PTP and 10% Malvazija.

KRAS WINE-GROWING DISTRICT

Širca — Kodrič

Edvin Širca and Stane Kodrič, Godnje 19, si-6221 Dutovlje, Phone: +386 (0)5 764 06 32

Wine selling ❧ Wine tasting
Wine cellar tours ❧ Wine route

Širca and Kodrič have grown and sold wine since 1973, filling their first labelled bottle in 1990. In the vineyards it is the Refošk grape that dominates: a typical Karstic grape and as such a Slovene speciality. Other varieties grown here are Sauvignon, Cabernet Sauvignon, Merlot and Malvazija. The main products of the cellar, by which they also set the greatest store, are Teran and Malvazija. Best vintages available: 2003 Teran PTP and 1999 blend 'Jerina'.

Mix of wines on offer

40% Izbrani Teran PTP, 35% Teran PTP, 7% Cabernet Sauvignon, 3% Malvazija, 3% Merlot and blend 'Jerina'.

Awards

Participation in the Ljubljana and Gornja Radgona fairs has earnt them several gold and silver medals.

Culinary recommendations

Together with their wines they recommend spiced, grilled food, smoked meats and vintage cheeses.

2003 Izbrani Teran PTP

11.8% vol., dry, ★★★

This is an exceptionally dark-hued wine, the colour of black cherries, opaque and mysterious. Youthful fragrances of red berries (raspberry, blueberry, blackberry) prevail on the nose at first, and give off a special and primal character, resembling the smell of Karstic vegetation. The wine's untamed youth and the immediate complexity on the palate show this wine to have an uncommon and intriguing character. The structure is firm, hale and fresh, though the basic flavours are relatively well in harmony in spite of the wine's youth. In the finish it has a touch of youthful ruggedness, but not disturbingly so. Looking to the bottom of the glass our eyes stop at that unique, purple coloration - pure pleasure.

Recommended dishes: Aged prosciutto, Primorskan tripe soup, veal chop with apple sauce, shoulder of venison with prosciutto gravy.

… KRAS WINE-GROWING DISTRICT

2003 Izbrani Teran PTP

KRAS WINE-GROWING DISTRICT

David Štok

Dutovlje 40c, si-6221 Dutovlje
Phone: +386 (0)5 764 04 75, (0)41 349 198, Fax: +386 (0)5 764 05 02

Wine selling ❧ Wine tasting
Wine cellar tours ❧ Wine route

At Štoks', viticulture and the wine trade have a hundred-year-old tradition. Bottled wines have borne labels since 1980. The vineyards are 95% planted with Refošk, the remainder being devoted to white varieties: Malvazija, Vitovska Grganja and Furlanski Tokaj. The cellar's reputation is built on the Teran grape, and they are especially proud of their Izbrani (selected) Teran.
Best vintage available: 2003 Teran PTP.

Mix of wines on offer
30% Izbrani Teran PTP, 65% Teran PTP and 5% white blend.

Awards
They have had success at tastings, winning five silver medals at the Ljubljana fair, and six silver and eleven gold medals in Gornja Radgona.

2002 Izbrani Teran PTP
11.8% vol., dry, ★★★

This intensely coloured wine has the hue of black cherries and is almost opaque. Delectable fragrances of very ripe berries (rasperry, blueberry, blackcurrant) surround us as soon as we raise the glass. The unique smells of Karstic vegetation can be detected on the nose, which has its own individual character and pleasing overtones. On the palate the wine is noble and purebred. The tannins are expressive and vocal, but still positive and gentle. The taste is full and fruity, with a steely structure. At the finish the wine has a certain individual rugged quality; the tannins and the acidity compete for dominance, but therein lies the future of the wine, and it holds interesting potential for maturing.
Recommended dishes: Karstic prosciutto, Primorskan tripe soup, pork chop and apple sauce, pheasant breast with figs.

KRAS WINE-GROWING DISTRICT

2002 Izbrani Teran PTP

KRAS WINE-GROWING DISTRICT

Primož in Tadej Štoka

Krajna vas 32, si-6221 Dutovlje, Phone: +386 (0)5 764 03 27, (0)41 667 125

Wine selling ❧ Wine tasting
Wine cellar tours ❧ Wine route
❧ Production of wine and food for announced groups

The Štokas have been growing and selling wine since 1975 and opted for their own labels after fifteen years. Most of the vines are Refošk, the remainder being Cabernet Sauvignon, Merlot and the white varieties. Their main product, and the best wine in their cellar, is Teran PTP.
Best vintages available: 2003 Teran PTP, 2001 Cabernet Sauvignon and 2003 Chardonnay.

Mix of wines on offer

70% Teran PTP, 10% Cabernet Sauvignon, 10% Merlot, 5% Chardonnay and 5% Vitovska Grganja.

Awards

Besides many other awards and honorary commendations, the Štokas are the winners of twelve gold and fifteen silver medals at Ljubljana, and twenty gold medals at Gornja Radgona.

Culinary recommendations

Prosciutto and venison complement their wines best.

2003 Izbrani Teran PTP

11.5% vol., dry, ★★

The wine is bright cherry red in colour, almost opaque. The fruity nose is like a basket of ripe red berries, which are soon joined by the smells of Karstic vegetation. The initial mildness on the tongue is pleasing. The development of the palate yields up a complex experience of Teran's characteristics lasting several moments, though this medium-structured wine is better balanced than one might expect of a typical Teran. The bouquet is consistently maintained on the palate and lingers on after swallowing.
Recommended dishes: Karstic prosciutto, Primorskan tripe soup, veal chop with apple sauce, shoulder of venison with prosciutto gravy.

KRAS WINE-GROWING DISTRICT

2003 Izbrani Teran PTP

KRAS WINE-GROWING DISTRICT

Vinakras Sežana

Sejmiška pot 1a, si-6210 Sežana
Phone: +386 (0)5 734 15 11, Fax: +386 (0)5 730 06 55
Email: vinakras@siol.net, Website: www.vinakras.com

Wine selling ❧ Wine tasting
Wine cellar tours for announced groups ❧ Wine route
Sales material ❧ Production of wine and food for announced groups

In 1861 their first wine cellar was built. In the vineyard cooperative, founded in 1955, over 90% the vines planted are Refošk. The cooperative takes 50%-60% the total Refošk produced from the Karstic farmers, and 40%-50% the white grapes. Their main product is Teran PTP which, together with their cellared wines such as Teranton, is their cellar's prize possession. Best vintages available: 1988 and 1997 Teranton.

Mix of wines on offer

22% Izbrani Teran PTP, 36% Teran PTP, Kraška Penina (Teranova Penina) and Teran liqueur, 15% Chardonnay, 3% Sauvignon, 2% Sivi Pinot and Beli Pinot, 12% Malvazija and 10% blends and Marmorna Penina (white).

Awards

They have received many awards in Ljubljana, Gornja Radgona and Verona, with a high proportion of gold medals and championship titles.

Culinary recommendations

Prosciutto or cold cuts are a good accompaniment to their Teran, and venison to the Teranton.

2002 Izbrani Teran PTP

11.0% vol., dry, ★★★

It is a dark, opaque cherry red, which slowly becomes transparent. The distinctive aroma of Teran has kept some of its youthful freshness. The nose is still surprisingly sharp and fruity, as if besides the ripe fruit we were encountering a pine forest. On the palate the wine has a typical Teran flavour, which beautifully accompanies its complex ticklishness overall, with that individuality that only a Karstic Teran can achieve. At the finish it bids a lively farewell as it should, but the vivid purple colour at the bottom of the glass begins to take on a crimson hue.

Recommended dishes: Aged prosciutto, Primorskan tripe soup, pork chop with apple sauce, shoulder of venison with prosciutto gravy.

KRAS WINE-GROWING DISTRICT

2002 Izbrani Teran PTP   2001 Kraška Penina

2001 Kraška Penina

11.5% vol., semi-dry, ★

The intense carmine-red colour actually hinders the eye's ability to enjoy the aesthetic pleasures this wine has to offer. Once the wine is poured we can finally spot the circled necklace of tiny bubbles, which break on surface of the wine and cling to the walls of the glass. The fragrance of raspberries is well developed, typically for Refosco and Karstic sparkling wine, and is strengthened by the bubbles, which carry up the fruit bouquet encased within the wine and burst under the nostrils. This Karstic sparkling wine also yields a pleasant freshness on the palate. We feel the carbon dioxide gently melt on the tongue emphasizing the fruitiness of the wine, especially juicy in the red wine of the Kras region.
Recommended dishes: Karstic prosciutto, bread with smoked salmon, caviar.

KRAS WINE-GROWING DISTRICT

Vinska Klet Škerlj - Ščuka

Darja Škerlj and Marjan Ščuka, Godnje 21, si-6221 Dutovlje
Phone: +386 (0)5 764 05 27, (0)31 235 293, (0)41 528 573
Email: darja.skerlj@siol.net

Wine selling ❧ Wine tasting
Wine cellar tours ❧ Wine route

Mix of wines on offer
85% Teran PTP and 15% Malvazija.

Bojan Vovk

Dutovlje 46a, si-6221 Dutovlje, Phone: +386 (0)5 764 00 54
Email: bojan.vovk@limona.si

Wine selling ❧ Wine tasting
Wine cellar tours ❧ Production of wine and food for announced groups

Wine on offer
Teran PTP.

Živcova Vina

Bojan Radišič, Skopo 24, si-6221 Dutovlje
Phone: +386 (0)5 764 10 66, (0)31 385 511, (0)31 317 559

Wine selling ❧ Wine tasting for announced groups
Wine cellar tours ❧ Wine route
❧ Tour of the farm,
Karstic architectural style

Mix of wines on offer
70% Teran PTP, 15% blend with Chardonnay 'Šartok', 10% Vitovska Grganja and 5% Rumeni Muškat (the latter is not officially classified as a Kras wine but unofficially it is considered so and gives good results).

Koper Wine-Growing District
Primorska Wine-Growing Region

KOPER WINE-GROWING DISTRICT

Brič

Brič Ltd., Boštjan Zidar, Dekani 3a, si-6271 Dekani
Phone: +386 (0)5 669 91 03, (0)5 669 91 05, (0)41 770 147, Fax: +386 (0)5 658 04 65
Email: natalija@kemiplas.si
Website: www.freetime-slovenija.tv/05/vino/6271_dekani/bric/bric.htm

- Wine selling
- Wine tasting
- Production of wine and food
- Wine cellar tours
- Wine route
- Sales material
- Day of Muscat and strawberries

The Brič company has been in the wine-growing business since 1997 and began to trade in 2001. Their first bottles were fillled in 2002 with that year's vintage. They produce high-quality and quality wines, and among the most promising are the Rumeni Muškat, Malvazija, Merlot, Sivi Pinot and Refošk, all adapted to foreign markets.
Best vintage available: 2001

Mix of wines on offer

12.5% Malvazija, 12.4% Chardonnay, 6% Sivi Pinot, 17.5% Rumeni Muškat, 2% Sauvignon, 14.5% Refošk, 12.2% Merlot, 19.1% Cabernet Sauvignon and 2% Sladki Muškat.

Awards

In recent years they have won several awards: eight silver medals in Gornja Radgona, a silver in Ljubljana, five silver and two gold medals in Zagreb and a silver medal in France.

Culinary recommendations

Malvazija is well complemented by wild asparagus with eggs, and Chardonnay by wild asparagus with *fuži*. Refošk is a good accompaniment for salty fish with polenta, while Merlot or Sladki Muškat complement polenta with truffles.

KOPER WINE-GROWING DISTRICT

2001 Chardonnay
13.0% vol., dry, ★★★

The golden-yellow appearance of the wine resembles the glowing gold of the sun's rays. The legs are beautiful and promise real pleasure. The wine's appearance alone is an aesthetic pleasure that excites anticipation for sensations to come. There is a sweet, mild nose of vanilla; mild, freshly churned butter; and even muscat. After a few minutes the fragrances multiply, with definite aromas of nuts such as almonds and hazelnuts. On the palate the pleasing sensations just seem to swing between these elements. The wine has a full body, but is nevertheless fresh, soft, almost light. All the fundamental flavours are there to enjoy, well-balanced and in harmony with one another. Special marks go to the pleasant acidity, which soothes the palate and makes for drinkability. The final impression is wholly pleasant and leaves one ready for more.

Recommended dishes: Truffles with pasta (*fuži*), wild asparagus, sea bass carpaccio, roast beef with olives, strongly flavoured pork dishes, hard cheeses.

KOPER WINE-GROWING DISTRICT

2001 Rumeni Muškat
11.5% vol., dry, ★★

The pale yellow colour with some golden reflections sparkles crystal-clear in the glass. Muscat has most to offer in terms of its bouquet, and immediately yields much. This variety is distinguished by a pure, simple bouquet that has not been robbed of Muscat's unique character in the fermenting process. We get flowers (withered roses), grapes, melon, orange zest and nectarines on the nose, but the Muscat bouquet is ever present, both on the nose and, later, on the palate. As you might expect, the sensations are not enhanced on the palate with particular rapidity, but an acidity arises after a moment and yields other nuances. The body is pleasant, but does not have lasting presence and quickly ceases in short bursts of attractive bitterness, just as a Muscat should. In this wine we have experienced a great Muscat, which has preserved all that the vintage and the grape have to offer.

Recommended dishes: Goose pâté, omelette, scampi with grilled courgettes, mussels in vinegar with asparagus, fruit salads of peaches and pears.

KOPER WINE-GROWING DISTRICT

2001 Cabernet Sauvignon
12.5% vol., dry, ★★★

The deep ruby colour with vibrant purple tones is reminiscent of warm places where the vines soak up the sun. The purity and firmness communicated at first on the nose speak of a wine produced from beautifully ripe and healthy grapes. The fruity bouquet competes with a spiciness introduced by the oak barrels, and the marriage of these two is very enticing. The fragrance of purple grapes is only further enhanced by undertones of coffee, dark chocolate and spices. At first it seems that the firm tannins are the main backbone of the wine, but on the palate we discover that this backbone is fortified by all kinds of delicious ingredients that testify to ripe grapes and a young wine. After this you will want to encounter it again in, say, two years' time, to experience the full nobility that it already predicts today.
Recommended dishes: Prosciutto, smoked pork shoulder with beans, shoulder of venison with prosciutto gravy, venison thigh in blackcurrant sauce, Karstic *mulce*.

KOPER WINE-GROWING DISTRICT

Klet Rodica

Marinko Rodica, Truške 1c, si-6273 Marezige
Phone: +386 (0)5 655 00 70, (0)41 695 019

Wine selling ❧ Wine tasting for announced groups
Wine cellar tours for announced groups ❧ Wine route

Marinko Rodica has been in the wine trade for only six years, but already he is achieving visible results. He says that demand outstrips supply, so he intends to bottle his wines in larger quantities in the future. He is most pleased with his Refošk, Malvazija, Merlot and Rumeni Muškat, and intends to focus even more attention on these varieties.

Mix of wines on offer
60% Refošk, 30% Malvazija, 3% Merlot, 3% Sivi Pinot and 3% Rumeni Muškat.

Awards
He has been awarded a silver medal for Refošk in Gornja Radgona, and a gold in Poreč.

Culinary recommendations
Refošk goes best with Istrian prosciutto.

2003 Refošk
11.5% vol., dry, ★★

The walls of the glass seem painted with the lovely deep, carmine red colour of the wine, which exudes youthful glow and potential. On the nose we first encounter fruitiness, followed by aromas of ripe grapes and purple berries. They are accompanied by the ethereal fragrances of juniper, pinewood, resin and spices - in short, much of the generic character of Refošk - and the scents of the Istrian landscape on an autumn evening. The structure is moderately rich and already seems quite calm on the palate, having had a beautiful and successful development. The tannins still have more to offer in future, and the acidity, fairly mild for a Refosco, contributes to a wine that is already light and drinkable. The eye cannot help but be caught again, admiring that gorgeous purple hue: a beautiful sight.
Recommended dishes: Mature prosciutto, grilled meat sausages, roast pork with prunes, shoulder of venison in prosciutto gravy or blackcurrant sauce, Karstic *mulce*.

KOPER WINE-GROWING DISTRICT

2003 Refošk

KOPER WINE-GROWING DISTRICT

Korenika & Moškon

Matej Korenika, Korte 115c, si-6310 Izola, Phone: +386 (0)5 642 00 30
Email: korenika_moskon@volja.net

Wine selling ❧ Wine tasting for announced groups
Wine cellar tours for announced groups ❧ Wine route
❧ Sales material

They began growing and trading in wine in 1984 and six years later they labelled their first bottle. If Malvazija and Refošk are the show wines of the house, Cabernet Sauvignon and Merlot are the elite among the red wines of the world. Rumeni Muškat is commonly referred to as the dessert of Slovene Istria, but here they see potential in the region's indigenous varieties.
Best vintages available: 2002 Malvazija barrique, 2002 Cabernet barrique, 2003 Merlot barrique, 2003 Refošk barrique and 2003 barrique white blend.

Mix of wines on offer
40% Malvazija (also barrique), 38% Refošk (also barrique), 3.5% Rumeni Muškat, 3.5% Merlot barrique, 3.5% Cabernet Sauvignon barrique, 3.5% Sivi pinot, 3.5% blend and 3.5% Chardonnay.

Awards
So far they have received two gold medals, one silver, and variety championship in Gornja Radgona. They have taken silver in Ljubljana, and have been awarded two golds and a silver in Bratislava.

Culinary recommendations
Malvazija goes well with fish dishes, Cabernet Sauvignon or Merlot with venison, and white barrique wines with grilled food.
Potica is lovely with Rumeni Muškat.

2002 Malvazija
14.0% vol., dry, ★★★

The wine has light, yellow colours, straw-like notes and substantial, well-formed legs. The nose is fresh, distinctive of this variety, with floral-fruit characteristics and, finally, a suggestion of mint tea. On the palate these fragrances are accompanied by stronger herbaceous scents (mint, pine resin and even tobacco). The herbaceous character manifests itself in the interesting complexity of the flavour, probably a reflection of the soil that produced the vines and the grape variety. The wine is quite light, in spite of a high alcohol content. The acidity is just right, and the final impression is one of juiciness.
Recommended dishes: Noodles with courgettes, mushrooms and mint, seafood, polenta, pizza, turkey steaks.

KOPER WINE-GROWING DISTRICT

2002 MALVAZIJA

KOPER WINE-GROWING DISTRICT

Santomas

Ludvik Nazarij Glavina, Šmarje pri Kopru 10, si-6274 Šmarje pri Kopru
Phone: +386 (0)5 639 26 51, (0)5 656 03 24, (0)41 728 724, Fax: +386 (0)5 639 26 53
Email: santomas@monteko.si
Website: www.monteko.si/santomas

Wine selling ❧ Wine tasting
Wine cellar tours for announced groups ❧ Wine route
Sales material ❧ Production of wine and food for announced groups

The tradition of wine growing and selling goes back to before 1800. The first wine labels were added to bottles in 1997. Most of the vineyards are planted with Refošk grapes, from which they produce 'Grand Cuvée' and 'Antonius'. Besides Refošk, the two most promising wines in their cellar are Malvazija and 'Santomas'.
Best vintages available: 1999 and 2000 Refošk 'Antonius' and 1999 and 2000 'Grand Cuvée'.

Mix of wines on offer

55% Refošk, 20% Refošk 'Antonius', 15% Malvazija and 10% 'Grand Cuvée'.

Awards

They derive pride and inspiration from the gold medals they have won at the Gornja Radgona fair along with two silvers, one from Croatia and the other from America.

Culinary recommendations

Refošk is best complemented by prosciutto in homemade olive oil. With Refošk 'Antonius' and Grand Cuvée they recommend smoked boar thigh with polenta.

2000 Refošk

13.5% vol., dry, ★★★

The deep crimson colour resembles that of black cherries, is almost opaque and has an air of mystery. The ripe bouquet, which we do not often encounter with a Refošk, suggests cooked red fruit and herbs (undergrowth, roasted coffee beans, spices) with scents of the animal world (leather, fur). The fine palate is enhanced by the powerful structure of the wine, which warms in the mouth. The sweet tannins set the tone of the wine's character; they are well blended into the whole and barely noticeable. The acidity, a usual Refošk trait, is toned down and has only a mild presence. After swallowing, the bouquet lingers and subsides with pleasant, fragrant flavours. A very interesting wine, and proof that Refošk can surprise.
Recommended dishes: Aged prosciutto, roast pork with prunes, shoulder of venison in prosciutto gravy, roast boar thigh in blackcurrant sauce, Karstic *mulce*.

KOPER WINE-GROWING DISTRICT

2000 Refošk   2000 Grand Cuvée

2000 Grand Cuvée

13.5 vol.%, dry, ★★★

This rich ruby red colour could only have been achieved in a good vintage, produced from vines grown on good terrain with plenty of sun. The thick, colourless legs create patterns on the side of the glass and promise great things. Pleasing and very pronounced fragrances result from the rich potential of the grape and are further enhanced by maturing in barrels. They resemble the aromas of cooked purple fruit, roasted coffee beans, pine forests and spices. The palate is both solid and delicious: open, complex and clear. The tannins abound, but are toned down and predict further development to come. Last impressions are still strong and the finish has notes of roasting and vanilla.

Recommended dishes: Aged prosciutto, roast pork with prunes, shoulder of venison in prosciutto gravy, roast boar thigh.

KOPER WINE-GROWING DISTRICT

Dorjano in Andrej Šuber

Osp 18, si-6275 Črni Kal
Phone: +386 (0)5 659 21 21, (0)41 607 529, (0)41 607 541
Email: andrej.suber@email.si

Wine selling ❧ Wine tasting
Wine cellar tours ❧ Wine route

Mix of wines on offer
70% Malvazija and 30% Refošk.

Vina Bordon

Boris Bordon, Dekani 63, si-6271 Dekani
Phone: +386 (0)5 658 22 60, (0)41 721 228, Email: kmetija.bordon@email.si

Wine selling ❧ Wine tasting
Wine cellar tours ❧ Wine route
Accomodation ❧ Sales material
❧ Production of wine and food for announced groups

Wines on offer
Refošk, Chardonnay, Malvazija, Merlot and red 'Bordon' blend.

Vina Simeon

Silvan and Edmond Glavina, Šmarje pri Kopru 32a, si-6274 Šmarje pri Kopru
Phone: +386 (0)5 565 04 19, (0)41 451 633, Fax: +386 (0)5 656 04 19
Email: simeon.glavina@telemach.net

Wine selling ❧ Wine tasting for announced groups
Wine cellar tours for announced groups ❧ Wine route

Mix of wines on offer
80% Malvazija and 20% Refošk.

Vinogradništvo Ferran in Rupnik

David Rupnik, Sv. Peter 26, si-6333 Sečovlje
Phone: +386 (0)5 672 60 63, (0)5 672 51 90, Email: david.rupnik@siol.net

Wine selling ❧ Wine tasting for announced groups
Wine cellar tours for announced groups ❧ Wine route
❧ Sales material

Wines on offer
Malvazija and Refošk.

KOPER WINE-GROWING DISTRICT

Vinska Klet 'D in V'

Viljem Turk, Klanec 3, Sveti Anton, si-6276 Pobegi, Phone: +386 (0)5 653 31 59

Wine selling ❧ Wine tasting for announced groups
Wine cellar tours for announced groups ❧ Wine route

Mix of wines on offer
50% Refošk and 50% Malvazija.

Vinska Klet Markočič

Milan Markočič, Spodnje Škofije 68b, si-6281 Škofije
Phone: +386 (0)5 654 92 69, (0)41 828 574

Wine selling ❧ Wine tasting
Wine cellar tours for announced groups ❧ Wine route

Wine on offer
Refošk.

KOPER WINE-GROWING DISTRICT

Vinakoper

Vinakoper Ltd., Šmarska cesta 1, si-6000 Koper
Phone: +386 (0)5 663 01 36 (Sales Koper), (0)1 242 02 32 (Sales Ljubljana),
Fax: +386 (0)5 663 01 06
Email: vinakoper@vinakoper.si
Website: www.vinakoper.si

- Wine selling
- Wine tasting
- Wine cellar tours
- Sales material

The company was founded in 1947 and three years later they labelled their first bottled wines. In vineyards spread over some 500 hectares of selected terrain, Refošk is the predominant variety, and likewise is their most prominent wine, alongside Chardonnay, Rumeni Muškat, Cabernet Sauvignon, Syrah and Malvazija. They produce prestigious wines such as 'Capo d'Istria', sparkling wines, high-quality, quality and table wines. Their most promising wine is 'Capris'.
Best vintages available: 2002 Merlot 'Capris', 2000 'Plemenito Belo', 2001 Cabernet Sauvignon 'Capo d'Istria', 1999 Malvazija 'Capo d'Istria', 2000 Cabernet Sauvignon - Syrah 'Capris' and 2000 'Plemenito Rdeče Capris'.

Wines on offer
Sparkling wine 'Capris', Sivi Pinot, Rumeni Muškat, Sladki Muškat, Rosé, Merlot, Malvazija, Chardonnay, 'Capris' red, 'Capris' white, Cabernet Sauvignon, Chardonnay *Izbor* and Malvazija *Pozna Trgatev*.

Awards
They hold numerous awards and medals from the wine fairs in Ljubljana and Gornja Radgona, as well as from locations abroad including Split, Verona, Brussels, London and Paris.

Culinary recommendations
Malvazija 'Capris' is best accompanied by seafood or marinated anchovies. Cabernet Sauvignon 'Capris' is complemented by *fuži* in blueberry sauce, or kid, also in blueberry sauce. Merlot goes well with gnocchi and venison, and Chardonnay 'Ricorvo' with wild asparagus.

KOPER WINE-GROWING DISTRICT

1998 Malvazija Capo d' Istria

12.5 vol.%, dry, ★★★

The wine's yellow hue, already tinged with golden nuances, simply glows in the glass. The well-formed legs add to the pleasure of tasting this wine. It has a mature fragrance of fruit and and a somewhat herbaceous character. The delightful, complex spirit of the wine comes through clearly, comprising almonds, mint and mild vanilla. The medium structure is pleasing on the palate and, in spite of a solidity in the fundamental flavours, light. The noble, bitter taste of almond husk and the pleasant, sweet vanilla aftertaste subtly suggest maturing in a barrique. The wine's herbaceous character prevails and gives it its style. It has been well nurtured and has reached its peak, so it is one to look out for soon.

Recommended dishes: Noodles with courgettes, mushrooms and mint, seafood, noodles with truffles, fish, frittata with asparagus.

KOPER WINE-GROWING DISTRICT

2000 CHARDONNAY *Izbor*

13.0% vol., semi-sweet, ★★★

The golden appearance of the wine resembles the over-ripe, transparent, sun-scorched grapes of a mature Chardonnay. The fruit-and-flowers aroma is pleasant and mild, resembling flowers, ripe pears, orange marmalade and honey on the nose. The first impression on the palate is one of sweetness, like eating grapes. The bouquet develops wonderfully on the palate and the pleasure of the wine's delicious, complex juiciness is further enhanced. The wine is rounded, full, still light and very drinkable. It is perfect for epicures, and a pleasing experience for the connoisseur, as wines of this character are rare in the Koper region. A new manifestation of Slovenia's winemaking possibilities and another addition to the diversity Slovenia has to offer.

Recommended dishes: Primorskan desserts, walnut *potica*. It is also suitable for drinking outside mealtimes, as an accompaniment to conversation.

KOPER WINE-GROWING DISTRICT

2001 Capris Plemenito Rdeče
12.5% vol., dry, ★★★

A beautiful ruby red wine with brick tones reminds us of ripe cherries and suggests a certain maturity. The fragrances resemble forest berries, and have a distinctive spiced quality with scents of roasting and a hint in the background of mint and truffles. The pleasant fruitiness of the wine continues on the palate, where the tannins have already achieved some softness, confirming the wine's successful ongoing development. In sum, this wine represents a successful coexistence of the three red wine varieties of Primorska, with a noble character due to Refošk. This wine is in top form and in this phase of its development it is ready to be enjoyed.

Recommended dishes: Cold cuts of smoked meats, red meat, lamb, kid in blueberry sauce, hare, *fuži* with truffles.

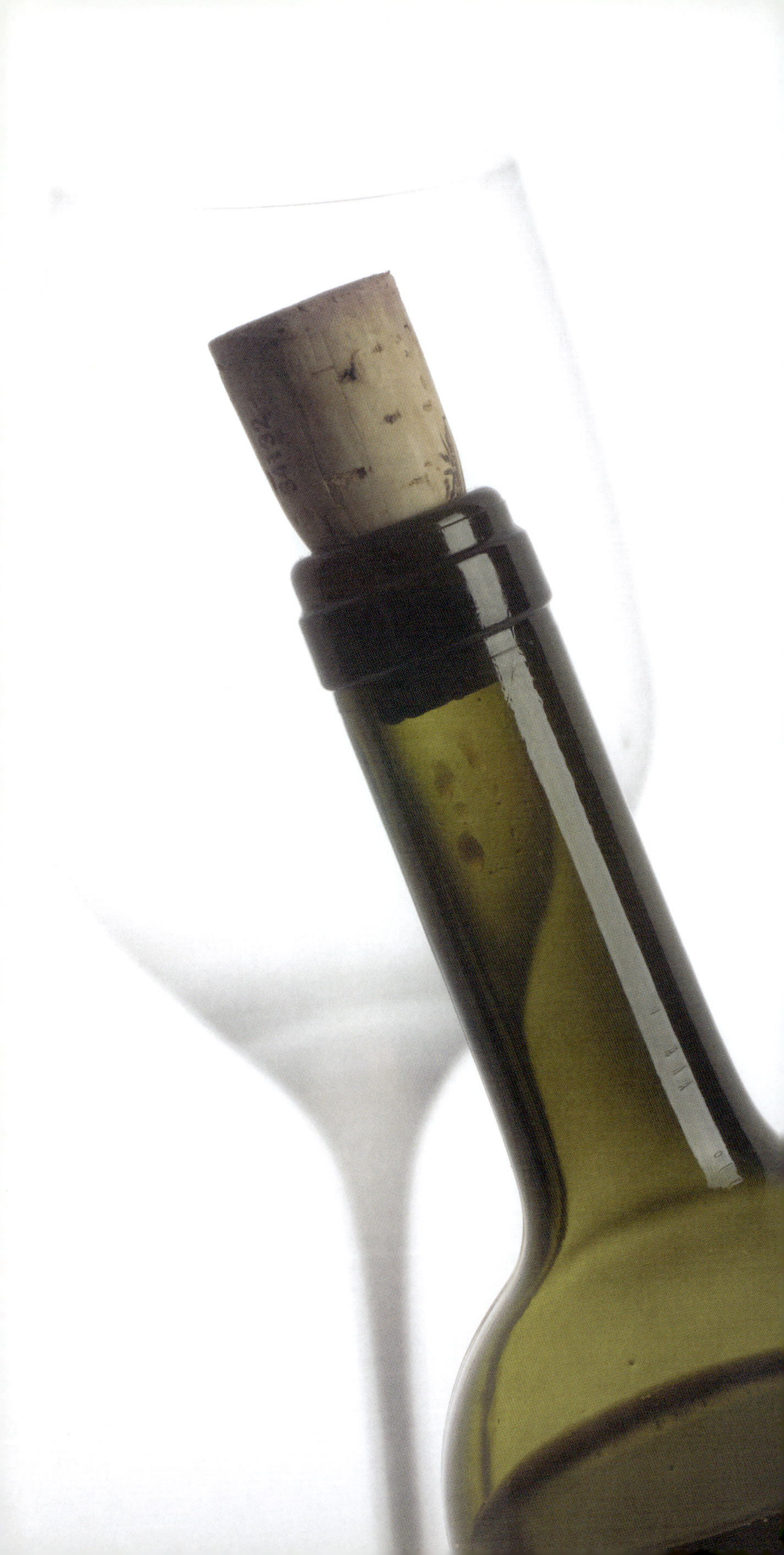

Slovenian Wines from Italy

SLOVENIAN WINES FROM ITALY

La Castellada

Niko Bensa, Oslavje/Oslavia 1, I-34070 Gorica/Piuma Gorizia, Italy

Wine selling Wine tasting for announced groups
 Wine cellar tours for announced groups

They have been in viticulture and the wine trade since 1975. Five years later the first bottles were labelled and after another five years they founded the farm 'La Castellada'. The vineyards predominantly grow Sauvignon, Sivi Pinot and Chardonnay. They see most potential in white wines, especially in Rumena Rebula, their 'Bianco della Castellada' blend and Furlanski Tokaj. They don't have any storage cellar because all the wines are sold in little more than two years.

Mix of wines on offer

39% 'Bianco della Castellada' white blend (50% Sivi Pinot, 25% Chardonnay, 15% Sauvignon, 10% Furlanski Tokaj), 23% Ribolla Gialla (Rumena Rebula), 15% Chardonnay, 13% Sauvignon and 10% 'Rosso della Castellada' red blend (85% Merlot and 15% Cabernet Sauvignon).

AWARDS

In recent years they haven't attended any appraisals.

CULINARY RECOMMENDATIONS

They stress the importance of eating good food with good wine.

2000 Ribolla Gialla

12.5% vol., dry, ★★★

The glowing golden-yellow appearance of the wine and the walls of the glass adorned by abundant legs hold much promise. The powerful bouquet of dried flowers and over-ripe fruit presents itself in fine form and ends with herb-like notes together with vanilla and spices. The very first moment we taste we can sense a full palate to match the nose; the wine has a persuasive sincerity and complexity, developing good balance and length. Wonderfully integrated elements of oak in the character of the wine testify to successful and professional nurturing: further proof of the great potential of Rebula, which is capable of competing with the most popular white wines.
Recommended dishes: *Jota*; frittata with seasonal herbs; grilled chicken; smoked trout with polenta; prosciutto; hard, mature cheeses (*zbrinc*, parmesan).

SLOVENIAN WINES FROM ITALY

2000 RIBOLLA GIALLA   2001 SAUVIGNON

2001 SAUVIGNON

14.5% vol., dry, ★★★

This wine has a glowing, pale yellow and golden appearance, unusually intense for a Sauvignon. The splendid legs add to its fine appearance - they promise much and engender great expectations. The characteristic Sauvignon nose is hardly noticeable at first, but later weaves its way free of the scents of spices (vanilla) and the fine, barely detectable scent of smoke, giving the wine an unforgettable signature. We experience the release of fine, interesting fragances more intensely on the palate, but the full body comes through, demonstrating beauty and quality: a wine that fully engages the senses, offering an interesting sensory analysis and above all a delight for all wine lovers.

The experiences of all the senses are persuasive, and the harmony of appearance, bouquet and flavour is exceptional: top marks to this great wine.

Recommended dishes: Thick soup with truffles, frittata with fennel, baked Soča trout, tarragon *potica*.

SLOVENIAN WINES FROM ITALY

Gravner

Joško Gravner
Via Lenzuolo Bianco 9, Oslavia, I-34070 Piuma Gorizia, Italy

Wine selling

Photo: Dean Dubokovič for Zlati Kapital magazine

Joško Gravner is Slovenian, but his is a well-known name in the Italian wine trade. His estate in Oslavje has densely planted vineyards with low vines - the first requirement for a good wine. The climate is said to be very favourable, but a lot is also achieved through Gravner's hard work. As a point of interest, his wines do not rest in barrels, but in amphoras (from Georgia) kept underground.

Wines on offer
'Bianco Breg' white blend, Ribolla Gialla (Rumena Rebula), Chardonnay, Sauvignon, 'Rosso' red blend and 'Rujno' blend.

2000 Bianco Breg
13.5% vol., dry, ★★★★

This wine has an intense golden-yellow appearance with notes of fire and amber. Generous, thick legs on the wall of the glass predict a rich wine. The aroma is fresh, rich and fine in composition, with overwhelming fruit (melon, dried peaches and apricots, lychees, orange zest) and spices on the nose. The palate delivers plenty in the first moment; it has an exceptionally full body giving the wine a definite attraction. The complexity is enhanced by fragrances of dried flowers and spices, with a sense of fruitiness. The agreeably rich foundation of the wine, very candid and well-balanced, contains tasty tannins, hardly present at all, but a pleasant contribution to the character and identity of the wine. The finish gives us roasted almonds, spices and a sense of juiciness. Every mouthful of this wine gives us new sensations as, little by little, it warms in the glass.

Recommended dishes: Smoked salmon, all seafood, pike served Cerknica-style, Carniolan sausauge, grilled veal and beef steaks, goat's cheese marinated in olive oil.

SLOVENIAN WINES FROM ITALY

2000 Bianco Breg

SLOVENIAN WINES FROM ITALY

1999 Rosso
13.0% vol., dry, ★★★

This purple wine, very intense with purple and chestnut-brown notes, has an air of mystery. Aromas of black cherries and blueberries release themselves assertively, and fragrances of roasting, spices, liquorice root, hints of animal (fresh leather) and tobacco follow with intensity. The bouquet is well-expressed, alcoholic and attractive. The palate is well-rounded, containing tasty, silky tannins that do not conceal their potential, in spite of a sense of lightness. Notwithstanding the wine's richness, it is freshness, derived from the excellent grapes and preserved in the wine, that is its trademark. This wine still needs a year to develop and the result will undoubtedly be of interest to discerning wine lovers: an interest that can probably be attributed to the soil, terrain and the innovation of the wine grower.

Recommended dishes: Prosciutto, harrow in dough with fennel, roast pork with prunes, veal chop with apple sauce, medallion of foal with marrow.

SLOVENIAN WINES FROM ITALY

2000 RIBOLLA
12.0% vol., dry, ★★★

The intense golden-yellow appearance with its amber reflections predicts a wine of unique character. The bouquet immediately opens up wide with fruit-floral scents, soon joined by sweet spices. The attractiveness of the bouquet fills one with the desire to explore further and discover yet more; it has a continuous candour, confirming the individual character of the wine. The complexity of the bouquet continues logically on the palate, as a colourful mosaic of arresting flavours; the first mild impressions are like honey, soon refreshed by a tender acidity, in keeping with the fine quality of the wine. The tongue constantly feels the breadth of the wine, all the taste buds are engaged, all the fundamental flavours are there to enjoy, complementing each other, covering each other, creating harmony, and offering a great deal of pleasure.

The finish promises a beautiful development yet to come. As yet, the wine still has some youthful temperament in its character, which should be subdued over time to be replaced by the suave finesse of maturity.

Recommended dishes: Frittata with seasonal herbs, hard mature cheeses (*zbrinc*, parmesan), stuffed chicken thigh, seafood and Soča trout.

SLOVENIAN WINES FROM ITALY

Kante

Edi Kante, Prepotto 1a, I-34011 Duino Aurissina, Italy

Wine tasting for announced groups ❧ Wine route
❧ Wine cellar tours for announced groups

In 1980 they began to grow and sell wine, and bottled their own label. Most of the vineyard is devoted to Sauvignon and Malvazija, with some to Chardonnay and Vitovska Grganja, and a very small portion to Refošk. Among all the varieties produced the most promising are Vitovska Grganja and Teran PTP.
The best vintage is 1999.

Mix of wines on offer
30% Sauvignon, 25% Malvazija, 20% Vitovska Grganja, 20% Chardonnay and 5% Teran PTP.

2001 Malvasia
12.5% vol., dry, ★★★

The yellow appearance with some green tints promises freshness and youth. The nose at first has a certain reticence, but the wine soon takes its first breath, and we are overwhelmed by scents of the garden: fresh leaves, elder flowers and meadow flowers, as well as nuances of unripe lemons and green apples. On the palate we instantly sense the fresh, unspoilt nature of the wine, which we readily expect on reading the label, stating as it does that this is an 'unfiltered wine'. There is a pervasive mineral quality. All the basic flavours from sweet to salty, sour to bitter are there, blending with and complementing each other, lending the wine an impressive style that reflects its complexity. The length of the bouquet is good and shows the wine's mineral character to best effect. This is a unique wine with interesting style, but it is too soon for its final appraisal. Let's wait and see!
Recommended dishes: Noodles with courgettes, mushrooms with mint, seafood, polenta, pizza, turkey steaks.

SLOVENIAN WINES FROM ITALY

2001 Malvasia   1999 Vitovska Grganja

1999 Vitovska Grganja

13.0% vol., dry, ★★★

This wine's pale yellow colour, with its straw-like ripe wheat tones and above-average thick legs stimulates the imagination. The nose offers maturity and breadth: dried leaves, hay, dried orange zest, almonds, smoke and even some nuances of a packet of cigarettes. The abundant nose is followed by a suitably grounded flavour; the wine seems full, strong and settled. The fruity, herb and mineral characteristics are the trademarks of a well-structured wine with good length, and for many years to come it should tell the attentive connoisseur an interesting story of the soil, the grapes and the care that produced it.
Recommended dishes: This rich wine has most impact with heavier dishes such as thick soup with truffles, smoked trout with polenta or asparagus, and frittata with prosciutto and fennel.

SLOVENIAN WINES FROM ITALY

Radikon

Stanislao (Stanko) Radikon, Az. agr. Radikon,
Tre Buchi 4, Oslavia, I-34070 Piuma Gorizia, Italy

Wine tasting for announced groups ❦ Wine cellar tours for announced groups

The beginnings of wine growing and trading here go back to 1946, and since 1979 they have been producing wine labels. The 'Oslavje' blend, made from a blend of Chardonnay, Sivi Pinot and Sauvignon is, besides the indigenous Rebula, the most promising wine.
The best vintages of both wines are still available in their cellars: 1999 and 2000.

Mix of wines on offer

50% 'Oslavje' white blend, 30% Rumena Rebula (Ribolla Gialla), 10% Furlanski Tokaj and 10% Merlot.

CULINARY RECOMMENDATIONS
They recommend their wines as a good accompaniment to hors d'oeuvres as well as meat dishes.

2000 Ribolla Gialla

12.5% vol., dry, ★★★

The golden-yellow colour of this three-year-old wine glows seductively from the glass like the sun just before it sets, arousing curiosity. The primary bouquet suggests a wine made in the traditional way. A vast array of impressions follows, afforded by the complex, seemingly endless bouquet of aromas: dried flowers, hay just barely dried, grapes dried by the air, pears, nuances of honey and toast. The first mouthful seems mild and smooth yet full, and soon a rainbow palate opens up. Tannins - which could be from the grapes or acquired in the barrel - come to the surface tastily in keeping with the wine's appearance and bouquet. The acidity makes a vibrant contribution, and one must remember that this relatively young wine will improve further in quality. But this wine hasn't yet divulged all, and it lingers on the palate after swallowing. The good structure needs a year or two more fully to shape its final character. Such a wine as this invites the oft-made comparison with a work of art. Every artist expresses his views on the object of his work through the artwork produced, whether it is a painting, a musical composition or a work of poetry. A vintner who takes this approach to his wine not only wishes to express the generic characteristics of the variety, but also its individual heritage and vintage, in his own unique way. Such an approach brings about greater diversity in wine characteristics and without a doubt enhances the possibilities for exploring and discovering wine as a reflection of its region's cultural heritage.

Recommended dishes: *Jota*, frittata with seasonal herbs, stewed beef, grilled chicken, grilled Soča trout, prosciutto, hard mature cheeses (*zbrinc*, parmesan).

SLOVENIAN WINES FROM ITALY

2000 Ribolla Gialla   2000 Oslavje

2000 Oslavje

13.5% vol., dry, ★★★

The similiarity in appearance with Rebula is obvious, but perhaps the intensity of the colour is a shade greater, with more golden nuances and even more radiance. The bouquet is complex: there is a similarity in spirit to Rebula, but this bouquet offers more. The differences are in the fine nuances, which have a softer quality. The generic traits of the variety take second or even third place to the influences of the soil, the vintage, the methods of cultivating the vines and the nurturing of the wine. Its character reveals the vintner and the place where the wine was produced. The flavour of this wine fills the oral cavity and fully engages the tastebuds. A higher-than-average alcohol content has a soothing effect and disguises the tannin, but a vibrant acidity also plays an important role, ensuring that the tannins are still voiced and further moulding the wine's personality. The finish is glorious, continues to linger and finally leaves pleasant impressions. You might think this wine has already attained its goal, but its best is yet to come. Yearly observations of its progress should prove interesting.

Recommended dishes: *Jota*, stewed beef, grilled chicken, grilled Soča trout, prosciutto, hard mature cheeses (*zbrinc*, parmesan).

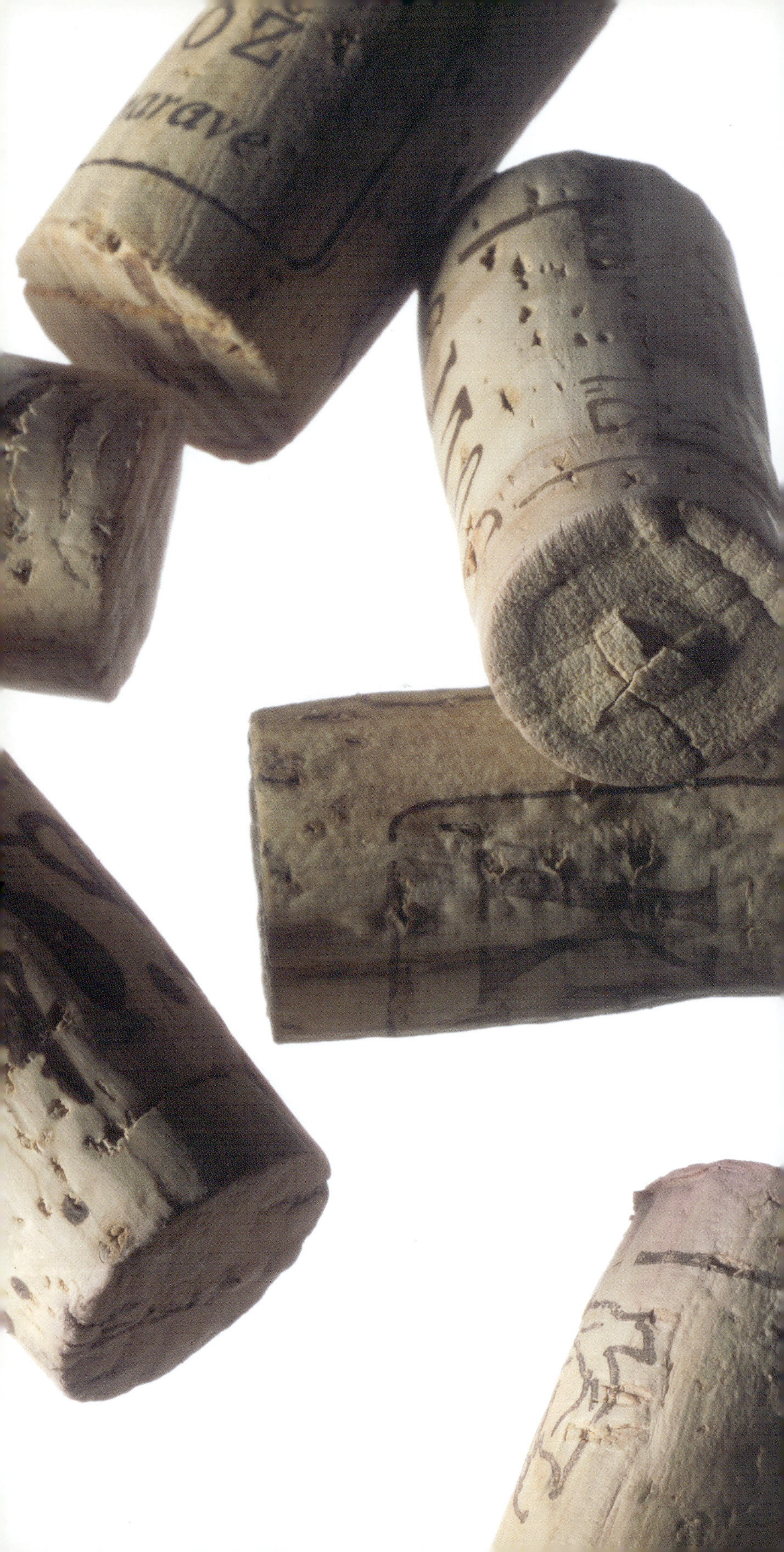

Map and Indexes

MAP OF WINE-GROWING DISTRICTS IN SLOVENIA

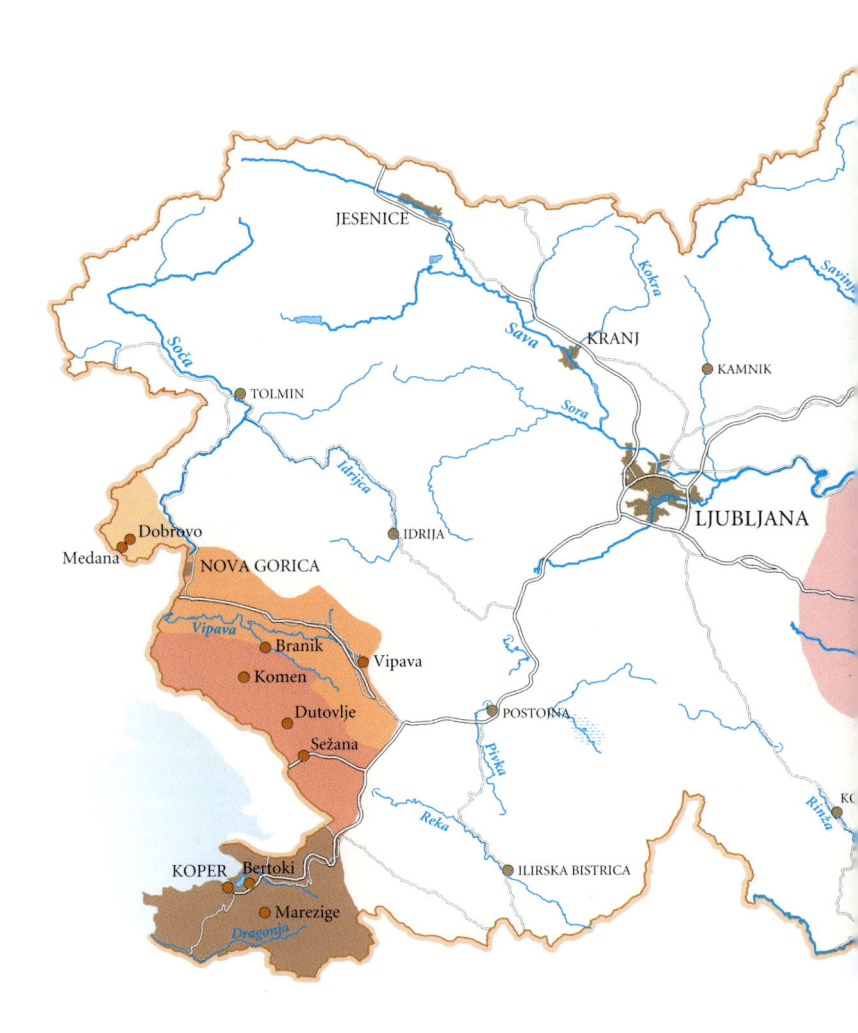

MAP OF WINE-GROWING DISTRICTS IN SLOVENIA

Podravje Wine-Growing Region
- Prekmurje
- Radgona – Kapela
- Ljutomer – Ormož
- Srednje Slovenske Gorice
- Maribor
- Haloze
- Šmarje – Virštanj

Posavje Wine-Growing Region
- Bizeljsko – Sremič
- Dolenjska
- Bela Krajina

Primorska Wine-Growing Region
- Goriška Brda
- Vipavska Dolina
- Kras
- Koper

AUTHOR'S TOP RECOMMENDATIONS

★★★★

2001 Sauvignon Zemono Lanthieri	Vipava 1894	335
2000 Bianco Breg	Gravner	390
2000 Teodor Réserve, red	Simčič	285
2001 Stara Brajda, white	Stojan Ščurek	291
1999 Veliko Belo	Movia	274
1983 Renski Rizling Izbor	Ptujska Klet	95
1998 Renski Rizling Ledeno Vino	Jožef Prus	231
1997 Sauvignon Pozna Trgatev	Meranovo	48
2000 Sauvignon Suhi Jagodni Izbor	Čurin	101

★★★

WHITE WINE

1999 Beli Pinot	Vi-Vin Saksida	338
1999 Chardonnay	Dobuje	254
2000 Chardonnay	Movia	275
2001 Chardonnay	Brič	369
2001 Chardonnay Réserve	Simčič	283
2001 Chardonnay	Marjan Zupan	72
2002 Chardonnay	Ivan Bajuk	214
2002 Chardonnay	Peršolja	279
2002 Chardonnay Holermuos	Jeruzalem Ormož	108
2002 Chardonnay Bagueri	Vinska Klet Goriška Brda	297
1999 Tokaj	Kabaj	260
2001 Furlanski Tokaj	Blažič	242
2003 Kerner Pletér	Kartuzija Pleterje	199
1999 Klarnica	Mansus	317
2001 Laški Rizling	Vinag	65
1998 Malvazija Capo d' Istria	Vinakoper	383
2001 Malvasia	Kante	394
2001 Malvazija	Joško Renčel	355
2002 Malvazija	Korenika & Moškon	376
2003 Pikolit	Aljoša Sirk	288
2002 Pinela	Batič	302
2000 Ribolla	Gravner	393
2000 Ribolla Gialla	La Castellada	388
2000 Rebula	Mlečnik	319
2000 Ribolla Gialla	Radikon	396
2001 Rebula	Movia	273
2001 Rebula	Mlečnik	318

AUTHOR'S TOP RECOMMENDATIONS

2001 Renski Rizling	Anton Skaza	138
2002 Renski Rizling	Milan Krajnc	112
2003 Rumeni Muškat 'Mašno Vino'	Klet Bistrica	47
2003 Rumeni Muškat	KZ Metlika	222
2003 Rumeni Muškat	Otmar Šturm	235
2000 Sauvignon	Sutor	326
2001 Sauvignon	La Castellada	389
2002 Sauvignon Réserve	MiroVino	120
2002 Sauvignon	Valdhuber	60
1999 Sivi Pinot	Mavrič	266
2001 Sivi Pinot	Joannes	54
2003 Sivi Pinot	Ptujska Klet	94
2000 Šipon	Čurin	99
2002 Šipon	Stanovščak	126
1993 Traminec	Kapela	78
1999 Traminec	Čurin	100
1999 Vitovska Grganja	Kante	395
2002 Zelen	Jordan Cigoj	304
2002 Zelen	Zaloščan	340

RED WINE

2000 Cabernet Franc	Peršolja	278
1997 Cabernet Sauvignon Lanthieri	Vipava 1894	336
2001 Cabernet Sauvignon	Brič	371
2001 Cabernet Sauvignon	Tilia	330
2002 Izbrani Teran PTP	Boris Lisjak	352
2002 Izbrani Teran PTP	David Štok	360
2002 Izbrani Teran PTP	Vinakras Sežana	364
2003 Izbrani Teran PTP	Širca-Kodrič	358
1999 Modra Frankinja Barrique	Jože Frelih	195
2000 Modra Frankinja	Vinko Štemberger	204
2000 Modra Frankinja	Vinogradništvo Pekel	206
2001 Modra Frankinja	Anton Plut	228
2002 Modra Frankinja	KZ Krško	203
2002 Modra Frankinja	Otmar Šturm	234
2001 Modri Pinot (Modri Burgundec)	Vino Kupljen	133
2002 Modri Pinot Barrique	Istenič	177
2003 Modri Pinot	Blažova Gorca	172
2000 Refošk	Santomas	378

AUTHOR'S TOP RECOMMENDATIONS

BLEND

2001 Teodor Réserve, white	Simčič	284
2001 Duet	Edi Simčič	286
2000 Grand Cuvée	Santomas	379
2000 Metliška Črnina	KZ Metlika	221
2000 Oslavje	Radikon	397
2001 Capris Plemenito Rdeče	Vinakoper	385
2000 Carolina, red	Jakončič	258
1999 Rosso	Gravner	392
2001 Steyer Mark Cuvée	Steyer	85
1999 Terra Rossa	Branko in Vasja Čotar	350
2002 Zlate Solzice	Joško Renčel	354

SPARKLING WINE

1999 Cuvée Prestige Brut	Bjana	241
1999 Penina Od Fare	Jože Frelih	194
Medot	Medot	270
2000 Prestige Barrique	Istenič	176
Zlata Radgonska Penina	Radgonske Gorice	83

PREDICATE AND SPECIAL WINE

2000 Chardonnay *Izbor*	Vinakoper	384
2000 Kerner *Pozna Trgatev*	Urbajs	163
1990 Kerner Suhi *Jagodni Izbor*	Matjaž Jenšterle	178
2000 Laški Rizling *Pozna Trgatev*	Jože Šnajder	128
2000 Laški Rizling *Izbor*	Anton Kostelec	224
2002 Laški Rizling *Suhi Jagodni Izbor*	Bojan Lubaj	116
1999 Laški Rizling *Ledeno Vino*	Ernest Novak	154
2001 Laški Rizling *Ledeno Vino*	Vino Brežice	184
2001 Laški Rizling *Ledeno Vino*	Vinar Kupljen	86
1999 Poezija	Cjanova Kmetija	246
2003 Renski Rizling *Pozna Trgatev*	Franc Planinc	196
1999 Rumeni Plavec *Pozna Trgatev*	Vino Graben	187
2001 Sauvignon *Suhi Jagodni Izbor*	Jožef Prus	230
2001 Sauvignon *Ledeno Vino*	Alojz Hoznar	218
2000 Sauvignon with Predicate	Keltis	180
2000 Šipon *Suhi Jagodni Izbor*	Saško Štampar	130
1998 Šipon *Ledeno Vino*	Očkerl	52

LIST OF WINE GROWERS

A
Absec, see Družina Absec
Ajster, Anton, see Vinogradništvo Pekel
Amon, Olimje, 160
Anderlič, Franc in Borut, Maribor, 32
Andlovic, Gradišče pri Vipavi, 300
Apatič, Drago, Beltinci, 148
Arkade, see Cigoj
Ave, see Kmetija Fajdiga 'Ave'

B
Babič, Silvano, Dejan in Matjaž, see Kmetija Babič - Šalara
Bajnof, Novo mesto, 190
Bajuk, Ivan, Metlika, 214
Balažek, Jožef, Velika Polana, 148
Balon, Aleš, Drenovec, 170
Balon, Družina, see Bela Gorca
Barbarič, Štefan, Turnišče, 148
Baša, Rafael in Majda, see Rikot
Batič, Šempas, 302
Bela Gorca, Bizeljsko, 174
Belica, Medana, 238
Bensa, Niko, see La Castellada
Berce, Matjaž, see Vindor
Bezjak, Dušan, see Vinoreja Bezjak Haloze
Biološko Dinamično Vinogradništvo Urbajs, see Urbajs
Bistrica, see Klet Bistrica
Bizjak, Radivoj in Tomaž, see Kmetija Bizjak - Branik
Bjana, Biljana, 240
Blažič, Plešivo, 242
Blažova gorca, Bizeljsko, 172
Bobnjar, Albina in Avgust, Veržej, 102
Bonin, Rudolf, Koper, 374
Bordon, Boris, see Vina Bordon
Boris, Preserje pri Komnu, 348
Borko, Danijela, Gornja Radgona, 76
Bostele, Janko, Oklukova Gora, 174
Božič, Marjan, see Božičev hram
Božičev hram, Planina, 306
Bračko, Boštjan in Franc, Spodnje Hlapje, 32
Brandulin, Plešivo, 244
Brcar, Bojan, Hom, 192
Brežice, see Vino Brežice
Brglez-Šparovec, Brezje pri Oplotnici, 32

Bric, Ivan, see Frlanova kmetija
Brič, Dekani, 368
Brus, Branislav in Terezija, Gornja Radgona, 76
Bučinel, Roman in Robert, see Dobuje
Bukovec, Ivan - Janko, Semič, 216
Buntovi, see Vinogradništvo in Kletarstvo Buntovi

C
Castellada,La, see La Castellada
Celcer, Milan, Slovenske Konjice, 32
Cigoj, Črniče, 304
Cjanova Kmetija, Gornje Cerovo, 246
Colja, Marjan, Coljava, 348
Constantini, Plešivo, 248
Cotič, Bogdan, see Vinogradništvo in Kletarstvo Buntovi
Cuk, Ludvik, Lendavske Gorice, 148
Cukjati, Žarko, see Kmetija 'Pod - Dob' Ceglo
Curk, Vrhpolje, 306
Cvelbar, Marko, see Bajnof
Cvetko, Dušan, Mihovci, 76
Cvetko, Zlatka in Franci, see Kogl
Cvitanič, Jurij, Gorišnica, 144

Č
Čarga 1767, Pristavo, 250
Čebular, Jožef, Sladka Gora, 164
Čehovin, Aleš, Brje, 306
Čerič, see Vinogradništvo Čerič
Černe, Igor, Ankaran, 374
Četrtič, Kojsko, 252
Čotar, Branko in Vasja, Gorjansko, 350
Čotar, Ivo, see Kraljič
Črni kos, Maribor, 33
Črnko, Jareninski Vrh, 34
Čurin, Kog, 98
Čurin, Stanko, Vuzmetinci, 102

D
D in V, see Vinska klet 'D in V'
De Adami, see Zaloščan
Debenjak-D, Kozana, 238
Diona, Dolnja Počehova, 36
Dobaj, Ivan in Tomaž, Jurski Vrh, 33
Dobuje, Snežeče, 254
Dolfo, Ceglo, 256

LIST OF WINE GROWERS

Domiana, Nova Vas nad Dragonjo, 374
Dopler - Krsnik, see Diona
Dreisiebner, Ivan, Špičnik, 33
Druzovič, Mojca in Marjan, see Hiša Hrane in Vina 'Pri Kapeli'
Družina Absec, Mihelja Vas, 212
Družina Balon, see Bela Gorca
Družina Dopler - Krsnik, see Diona
Družina Marc, see Fortunatov Hram
Družina Sumrak, Mali Vrh, 175
Durcik, Franko, see Kmetija Petelin - Durcik
Dvorsko Vino, Pesnica pri Mariboru, 33

E

Engel, Matjaž, Vavta Vas, 200
Erniša, Janez, Suhi Vrh, 149
Erniša, Miran, Suhi Vrh, 149
Erzetič, Dušan in Edbin, see Čarga 1767

F

Fabijan, Karl, Zgornje Hlapje, 38
Fabjančič, Andrej, Brestanica, 174
Fajdiga, Božo, see Fajdigov hram
Fajdiga, Marjan, see Kmetija Fajdiga 'Ave'
Fajdigov Hram, Goče, 306
Fakulteta za Kmetijstvo, see Meranovo
Faust, Maribor, 40
Ferenc, Vlado, Veržej, 102
Ferjančič, Boris, Gradišče pri Vipavi, 307
Ferjančič, see Kmetija Ferjančič
Ferran, see Vinogradništvo Ferran in Rupnik
Flegar, Franc, Gerlinci, 149
Fleisinger, Zvonko, Spodnji Ivanjci, 76
Fornazarič, Jožef in Ivan, Vogrsko, 307
Fortunatov hram, Planina, 307
Frangež, Štefan in Jernej, Gornja Radgona, 77
Franko, see Vina Franko
Frelih, Jože, Šentrupert, 194
Frlanova kmetija, Vogrsko, 307
Furlan, Bojan, see Furlanov Hram
Furlan, Branko, see Kmetija Furlan
Furlanov hram, Zavino, 310

G

Gadova Peč, see Vinotrs - Klet Gadova Peč

Gašparin Obljubek, Irena in Robert, Drnovk, 239
Gaube, Alojzij, Špičnik, 42
Gjerkeš, Matija, Fikšinci, 146
Gjuran, Jožef, Lendava, 149
Glas, Milan, Sremič, 174
Glavina, Ludvik Nazarij, see Santomas
Glavina, Silvan in Edmond, see Vina Simeon
Goriška Brda, see Vinska Klet Goriška Brda
Grabar, Janez in Nada, Prosenjakovci, 152
Graben, see Vino Graben
Grajska Klet Lendava, Lendava, 150
Gravner, Joško, Oslavje, 390
Gregorič, Bruno, see Vina Orse
Grmek, Andrej, Kobjeglava, 348
Gruškovnjak, Peter, Beltinci, 152

H

Hafner, Robert, Krivi Vrh, 96
Hajšek, Viktor, Maribor, 38
Hančik, Jožef, see Hani
Hani, Dobrovnik, 152
Herga, Franc, Ormož, 102
Heric, Bogomir, Križevci pri Ljutomeru, 103
Hiša Hrane in Vina 'Pri Kapeli', Drbetinci, 103
Hiša Kakovosti Čurin - Praprotnik, see Čurin
Hiša Vin, see Cuk
Hlade, Dušan, Kamnica, 38
Hlebec, Milan, Kog, 104
Hlupič, Jurij, Maribor, 38
Hojnik, Alojz, Zgornja Polskava, 39
Horvat, Jakob, Maribor, 39
Hoznar, Alojz, Ručetna Vas, 218
Humar, Dušan, see Constantini

I

Imeno, see Klet Imeno
Ipavec, Roman, Osek, 311
Istenič, Ljubljana, 176

J

Jakončič, Igor in Aljoša, Kozana, 258
Jakončič, Marjan, see Piro
Jamnik, Ignac, Svečina, 39
Janežič, Gustek, see Vinogradništvo Janežič

LIST OF WINE GROWERS

Jankovič, Franc, Rogaška Slatina, 164
Janžekovič, Konrad, see Turčan
Jarc, Maksimilijan (Milan), Zgornja Kungota, 39
Jarkovič, Robert, see Vinotrs - Klet Gadova Peč
Jejčič, see Vinska Klet Jejčič
Jenšterle, Matjaž, Sremič, 178
Jerič, Martin, Rakičan, 152
Jerman, Edvard, Šepulje, 348
Jeruzalem Ormož, Ormož, 106
Joannes, Vodole, 54
Jošar, Franc, Prosenjakovci, 153
Jureš, Dušan in Dejan, Ljutomer, 103

K

Kabaj, Estera in Morel, Jean Michel, Šlovrenc, 260
Kabaj, Zdenko, see Klavora
Kaloh, Anton, see Košaki
Kante, Edi, Praprot, 394
Kapela, Radenci, 78
Kartuzija Pleterje, Šentjernej, 198
Kaučič, Branko in Zdenka, Ivanjševski Vrh, 77
Kauran, Zlatko, Sladki Vrh, 44
Kavčič, Andrej in Miran, see Vina Kavčič
Kebrič, Gregor, Spodnji Jakobski Dol, 45
Kelenc, Vladimir, Lendavske Gorice, 153
Kelhar, Marjan, see Keltis
Keltis, Vrhovnica, 180
Kepe, Štefan, Gaberje, 153
Kisilak, see Vinarstvo Kisilak
Klabjan - Vina Izpod Stene, Osp, 374
Klavora, Šlovrenc, 239
Klet Bistrica, Slovenska Bistrica, 46
Klet Gadova Peč, see Vinotrs - Klet Gadova Peč
Klet Imeno, Šmarje pri Jelšah, 165
Klet Kregar, Cerovec pod Bočem, Rogaška Slatina, 165
Klet Kropec - Sonce ` spod Pohorja, Kovača Vas, 44
Klet Lendava, see Grajska Klet Lendava
Klet Rodica, Truške, 372
Klinec - Medana, Medana, 239
Kmečka Zadruga Krško, see KZ Krško
Kmetija Babič - Šalara, Koper, 375
Kmetija Bizjak - Branik, Branik, 310
Kmetija Fajdiga 'Ave', Lože, 310
Kmetija Ferjančič, Planina, 311
Kmetija Furlan, Zavino, 308
Kmetija Petelin - Durcik, Pliskovica, 349
Kmetija 'Pod - Dob' Ceglo, Ceglo, 238
Kmetija pri Štakljevih, Snežatno, 239
Kmetija Prinčič, Kozana, 238
Kmetija Rojc & Polanec, Zalošče, 311
Kmetija Šfiligoj - Kočevar, see Šfiligoj
Kmetija z Nastanitvijo 'Hiša Vin', see Cuk
Kmetija Žvokelj, Ustje, 311
Kmetijska in Gospodinjska Šola Šentjur, see Šolski Center Šentjur
Kmetijska Zadruga Metlika, see KZ Metlika
Kmetijska Zadruga Šmarje, see Klet Imeno
Kmetijsko Gospodarstvo Lendava, see Grajska Klet Lendava
Kobal, Ivan, Budanje, 310
Kocijančič, Roman in Edvin, Neblo, 262
Kociper, Milan, Ivanjkovci, 103
Kocuvan, Jakob, Sv. Jurij ob Ščavnici, 77
Kočevar, see Šfiligoj
Kodrič, Stane, see Širca - Kodrič
Kogl, Velika Nedelja, 80
Kolarič, Milan in Margita, Norički Vrh, 88
Kolbl, Franc, Ljutomer, 110
Kolbl, Slavko, Okoslavci, 88
Kolmanič, Slavko, see Vino Kolmanič
Korenika & Moškon, Korte, 376
Korpar, Tanja in Zlatko, Osluševci, 111
Kos, Andrej, see Črni Kos
Kos, Mitja, Ključarovci, 110
Kosi, Edi in Anica, Radomerščak, 110
Kostelec, Anton, Drašiči, 224
Košaki, Stolni Vrh, 45
Kovačič, Martin, see Blaževa Gorca
Krajnc, Milan, Lahonci, 112
Krajnc, Mirko, Veliki Brebrovnik, 110
Kralj, Stanislav, Črnomelj, 216
Kralj, Vjekoslav, Črešnjevec ob Bistrici, 164
Kraljič, Tabor, 314
Krampač, Štefan, Ljutomer, 111
Kraner - Plateis, Zgornje Hlapje, 44
Kren, Ivan in Tomaž, Zgornja Kungota, 44
Kristančič iz Medane, Medana, 264
Kristančič, Aleš in Mirko, see Movia

LIST OF WINE GROWERS

Kristančič, Andrej in Mirko, see Nando
Kristančič, Boris, see Brandulin
Kristančič, Dušan, see Kristančič iz Medane
Kristančič, Stojko, see Ronk - Vina iz Goriških Brd
Kropec, Vinko, see Klet Kropec
Krsnik, see Diona
Krško, see KZ Krško
Kržič, Franc, see Vovk
Kulčar, Štefan, Lendava, 153
Kumar, Radovan, see Vina Kumar
Kunej, Lojze, Brestanica, 182
Kupljen, Franc in Vlado, see Vinar Kupljen
Kupljen, Jože, see Vino Kupljen
Küzmič, Bela, Murska Sobota, 156
Kvartuh, Mihael, Koritno, 200
KZ Krško, Krško, 202
KZ Metlika, Metlika, 220

L

La Castellada, Oslavje, 388
Lah, Frančišek Alojzij, see Stanovščak
Lah, Marjan, Ptuj, 96
Lavrenčič, Edvard, see Sutor
Leber, Jakob-Igor, Zgornja Kungota, 45
Lemut, Melita in Matjaž, see Tilia
Lendava, see Grajska klet Lendava
Lesjak, Rado, Vuzmetinci, 111
Levačič, Marijan, Lendava, 156
Ličen, Jože, Brje, 314
Lipič, see Vinotoč Lipič - Passero
Lisjak, Boris, Dutovlje, 352
Lisjak, Radivoj, Zalošče, 312
Lisjak, Rajko, Saksid, 314
Ljutomerčan, Ljutomer, 114
Lozej, Bernarda, Podraga, 314
Lubaj, Bojan, Kidričevo, 116
Lunežnik, Ivan, Murska Sobota, 156

M

Macarol, Rado, see Šempolajc
Magdič, Janko, Ljutomer, 118
Mak, Vlado, Maribor, 45
Makovec, Bogdan, see Mansus
Malešič, Anton, Metlika, 216
Malnarič, Samuel, Vavpča Vas, 226
Mansus, Brje, 316
Marc, družina, see Fortunatov hram
Marc, Martin, Planina, 315

Marc, Miran, Slap, 315
Marc, Srečko, Slap, 315
Markočič, Milan, see Vinska Klet Markočič
Martinčič, Šmalčja Vas, 208
Maslo, Pavel, Koper, 375
Masten, Boris, see Boris
Mastnak, Zdravko, Sevnica, 175
Mavretič, Jože, Drašiči, 216
Mavrič, Avguštin in Danilo, Plešivo, 266
Mavrič, Jožko, Šlovrenc, 268
Mavrič, Zlatko, see Belica
Medot, Solkan, 270
Meranovo, Limbuš, 48
Mervič, Boleslav, Šempas, 315
Metlika, see KZ Metlika
Mijošek, Ivan, Zgornje Negonje, 165
MiroVino, Jastrebci, 120
Missia, Edvard, Kocjan, 88
Mlaker, Franc, see Vino Vrhovšek
Mlaker, see Vinogradništvo Mlaker
Mlaker, Ivan, Bodrišna vas, 165
Mlečnik, Bukovica, 318
Morel, Jean Michel, see Kabaj
Movia, Ceglo, 272
Mulec, Roman, Ročica, 50
Munda Miro, see MiroVino
Munda, Angela in Viktor, Prerad, 111
Munih, Miloš, Trška gora, 200
Murgelj, Silvester, Novo Mesto, 217
Mužič, Iztok in Borut, Plešivo, 262

N

Nando, Plešivo, 276
Nemanič, Anton, Slamna Vas, 217
Nemanič, Martin, Drašiči, 217
Nerad, Stanko, Črenšovci, 156
Novak, Ernest, Puconci, 154

O

Obljubek, see Gašparin Obljubek, Irena in Robert
Očkerl, Mirko in Boris, Šentilj, 52
Orešič, Tine, see Vina Orešič
Orse, see Vina Orse

P

Panker, Ivan, Beltinci, 157
Papež, Janko, Fram, 50
Pasji rep, Orehovica, 320

LIST OF WINE GROWERS

Passero, Nada, see Vinotoč Lipič - Passero
Pečarič, Martin, Metlika, 217
Pečnik, Mira in Franc, Grušce, 50
Pečnik, Rajko, Buče, 166
Pekel, see Vinogradništvo Pekel
Perko, Anton in Marjeta, Sp. Velka, 50
Peršolja, Kozana, 278
Petelin, see Kmetija Petelin - Durcik
Petelin, Viljem in Jadran, Pliskovica, 349
Petkoski, Zoran, Ptuj, 96
Petrov Pil, Vrhpolje, 320
Pipan, Jože, see Vinogradništvo in Vinarstvo Pipan
Pirc, Alojz, Krško, 200
Piro, Vipolže, 262
Plahuta, Katarina in Drago, see Vinska Klet Plahuta
Plajnšek, Franci, Potni Vrh, 122
Planinc, Franc, Dolenje Grčevje, 196
Plateis, see Kraner - Plateis
Plečko, Alojzij, Radizel, 51
Plemenič, Miran, see Vino Plemenič
Pleterje, see Kartuzija Pleterje
Plut, Anton, Drašiči, 228
Pod - Dob, see Kmetija 'Pod - Dob' Ceglo
Polanec, Andrej in Anka, see Kmetija Rojc & Polanec
Poljšak, Samuel, see Vina Poljšak
Polovič, Franc, Dobova, 175
Potočnik, Franc, Orehovica, 320
Prah, Jože, Velike Malence, 201
Praprotnik, see Čurin
Premrn, Franc, see Pasji Rep
Pri Kapeli, see Hiša Hrane in Vina 'Pri Kapeli'
Prinčič, Jožef in Damjan, Kozana, 280
Prinčič, Tomaž, see Kmetija Prinčič
Prinčič, Zvonimir, see Cjanova Kmetija
Prosenc, Daniel, Jakobski Dol, 51
Protner, Bojan, see Protner
Protner, Boštjan, see Joannes
Protner, Pernica, 51
Protnerjeva Hiša Joannes, see Joannes
Prus, Jožef, Krmačina, 230
Ptujska klet, Ptuj, 92
Pucer, Franc, see Domiana
Püklavec, Franček, see Vinska Klet Püklavec

R

Radgonske Gorice, Gornja Radgona, 82
Radikon, Stanislao (Stanko), Oslavje, 396
Radišič, Bojan, see Živcova Vina
Ramšak, Matjaž, Maribor, 51
Ratek, Vinko, Mali Brebrovnik, 122
Rebernik, Zdenko, Dragonja, 375
Rebula, Dušan, Brestovica pri Komnu, 349
Reja, Franko, see Vina Franko
Renčel, Joško, Dutovlje, 354
Reya, Maksimiljan de, Kozana, 263
Reya, Oton, Kozana, 262
Režonja, Alojz, Murska Sobota, 157
Rikot, Zalošče, 322
Rodica, Marinko, see Klet Rodica
Rojc, see Kmetija Rojc & Polanec
Rondič, Peter in Rajko, Slap, 320
Ronk - Vina iz Goriških Brd, Vipolže, 263
Roškar, Anton, Lastomerci, 88
Rožman, Štefan, Dolgovaške Gorice, 157
Rupnik, David, see Vinogradništvo Ferran in Rupnik

S

Saksida, Ingrid in Jožko, see Vi-Vin Saksida
Santomas, Šmarje pri Kopru, 378
Savič, Dušan, Maribor, 56
Sekirnikova Gorca, Kamence, 168
Senekovič, Ivo, Spodnji Jakobski Dol, 56
Senekovič, Milan, Lomanoše, 89
Sever, Jana, see Dvorsko Vino
Sežana, see Vinakras Sežana
Simčič, Ceglo, 282
Simčič, Edi, Vipolže, 286
Simčič, Jože, Železniki, 236
Simčič, Salko in Marjan, see Simčič
Simčič, Zvonimir, see Medot
Simončič, Jožef, Šmarje, 321
Sirk, Aljoša, Višnjevik, 288
Sirk, Marko, Biljana, 263
Sirk, Miran, see Bjana
Sirk, Valter, Višnjevik, 263
Skaza, Anton, Ptuj, 138
Skočaj, Rudolf in Marko, see Dolfo
Slavček, Potok pri Dornberku, 324
Slavinec, Jože, Mihalovci, 124
Sonce 'spod Pohorja, see Klet Kropec
Sosolič, Izidor in Dominik, see

LIST OF WINE GROWERS

Vinarstvo Sosolič
Srebrnič, Vojko, see Vina Srebrnič
Stanovščak, Podgorci, 126
Stariha, Jože, Drašiči, 236
Stegovec, Boža, see Sveti Martin
Stepančič, Nevijo, Pregara, 375
Steyer, Plitvica, 84
Stibilj, Marko, Ustje, 321
Suhorepec, Ivan, Ručetna Vas, 236
Sumrak, see Družina Sumrak
Sutor, Podraga, 326
Svenšek, Jakob, Lovrenc na Dravskem Polju, 122
Sveti Martin, Brje, 328

Š

Šadl, Avgust, Ljutomer, 123
Šalara, see Kmetija Babič - Šalara
Ščuka, Marjan, see Vinska Klet Škerlj - Ščuka
Ščurek, Stojan, Plešivo, 290
Šebart, Marko, Lenart v Slovenskih Goricah, 56
Šekoranja, Janez in Mihela, see Vino Graben
Šempolajc, Križ, 349
Šfiligoj, Dušan, Limbuš, 56
Šibau, Fojana, 292
Šibav, Dušica in Ljubko, see Šibau
Šibav, Miran in Alojz, Neblo, 292
Šiker, Milan, Pernica, 58
Širca - Kodrič, Godnje, 358
Širca, Edvin, see Širca - Kodrič
Širca, Milivoj, Dutovlje, 356
Škerlj, Darja, see Vinska Klet Škerlj Ščuka
Škerlj, Izidor, Tomaj, 356
Škerlj, Jožef, Tomaj, 356
Škofija Maribor, see Klet Bistrica
Šmarje, see Klet Imeno
Šmigoc, Jožef, Repišče, 140
Šnajder, Jože, Ormož, 128
Šolski center Šentjur, Šentjur, 164
Šparovec, see Brglez - Šparovec
Špiler, Peter, Krško, 175
Šprajc, Viktor, see Viktorin
Štakljevi, see Kmetija pri Štakljevih
Štampar, Saško, Kajžar, 130
Štekar, Roman in Anuška, see Kmetija pri Štakljevih
Štemberger, Vinko, Šentjernej, 204

Štok, David, Dutovlje, 360
Štoka, Primož in Tadej, Krajna Vas, 362
Štokelj, Damjan, see Vinski Hram Štokelj
Štrukelj, see Vinogradništvo Štrukelj
Šturm, Otmar, Metlika, 234
Šturnšče, see Vinarstvo Sosolič
Šuber, Dorjano in Andrej, Osp, 380
Šuc, Milko in Peter, see Vinarstvo Šuc
Šuklje, Jože, Metlika, 232
Šumak, Jože, Vaneča, 157
Šumenjak, Srečko, Spodnje Hlapje, 57

T

Tavčar, Milivoj, Kreplje, 356
Tilia, Potoče, 330
Tomažič, Jožef, see Petrov Pil
Tratnik, Jožko, Dornberk, 321
Tremel, Mihael, Bokrači, 158
Trojner, Miroslav, Jakobski Dol, 57
Trop, Emil, Lahonci, 122
Trop, Miran - Ferdo, Runeč, 123
Trošt, Stojan, Slap, 321
Trstenjak, Ivo-Janez, Stročja Vas, 123
Turčan, Turški Vrh, 142
Turistična kmetija Arkade, see Cigoj
Turk, Stanko, Jelševnik, 236
Turk, Viljem, see Vinska Klet 'D in V'

U

Univerza v Mariboru, Fakulteta za Kmetijstvo, see Meranovo
Urbajs, Rifnik, 162
Urdih, Dragotin, see Vina Urdih
Urisk, Sigfrid - Zmago, Dobrovnik, 158
Uršič, Erik, Slap, 332
Ušaj, Stojan, see Vina Ušaj

V

Valcl, Uroš, Zgornja Kungota, 57
Valdhuber, Svečina, 60
Valek, Milan, Koritno, 201
Valentan, Alojz, Malečnik, 57
Vesenjak, Vilko, Pesnica pri Mariboru, 62
Vidmar, Marjan, Ustje, 332
Viktorin, Zamušani, 144
Vina Bordon, Dekani, 380
Vina Franko, Neblo, 292
Vina Kavčič, Brje, 332
Vina Kumar, Snežatno, 292

LIST OF WINE GROWERS

Vina Orešič, Malečnik, 74
Vina Orse, Prvačina, 332
Vina Poljšak, Gradišče pri Vipavi, 333
Vina Simeon, Šmarje pri Kopru, 380
Vina Srebrnič, Plešivo, 293
Vina Urdih, Škrbina, 357
Vina Ušaj, Črniče, 333
Vinag, Maribor, 64
Vinakoper, Koper, 382
Vinakras Sežana, Sežana, 364
Vinar Kupljen, Okoslavci, 86
Vinar Okoslavci, see Vinar Kupljen
Vinarska zadruga Martinčič, see Martinčič
Vinarstvo Egon in Marko Zuljan, Vipolže, 293
Vinarstvo Kisilak, Černelavci, 158
Vinarstvo Sosolič-Šturnšče, Zali Breg, 293
Vinarstvo Šuc, Dutovlje, 357
Vincetič, Vid, Ormož, 123
Vindor, Draga, 333
Vino Brežice, Brežice, 184
Vino Graben, Bizeljsko, 186
Vino Kolmanič, Rožički Vrh, 89
Vino Kupljen, Ivanjkovci, 132
Vino Plemenič, Kog, 136
Vino Vrhovšek, Rogaška Slatina, 168
Vinogradniško-izletniška Kmetija 'Vitovc', see Prah
Vinogradništvo - Vinarstvo Trojner M&M, see Trojner
Vinogradništvo Čerič, Malečnik, 74
Vinogradništvo Ferran in Rupnik, Sv. Peter, 380
Vinogradništvo in Kletarstvo Buntovi, Škrbina, 357
Vinogradništvo in Vinarstvo Pipan, Planina, 333
Vinogradništvo Janežič Vinski vrh, Veliki Brebrovnik, 136
Vinogradništvo Mlaker, Pesnica pri Mariboru, 74
Vinogradništvo Pekel, Krška vas, 206
Vinogradništvo Štrukelj, Selo, 344
Vinoreja Bezjak Haloze, Gorišnica, 144
Vinotoč Lipič - Passero, Tešanovci, 158
Vinotrs - Klet Gadova peč, Brod v Podbočju, 201
Vinska Klet 'D in V', Sveti Anton, 381
Vinska Klet Goriška Brda, Dobrovo v Brdih, 294
Vinska Klet Jejčič, Spodnja Branica, 344
Vinska Klet Markočič, Spodnje Škofije, 381
Vinska Klet Orel, Avber, 357
Vinska Klet Plahuta, Ajdovščina, 344
Vinska Klet Püklavec, Zasavci, 134
Vinska Klet Škerlj -Sčuka, Godnje, 366
Vinska Klet Žorž, Slap, 342
Vinski Hram Štokelj, Planina, 345
Vinski Vrh, see Vinogradništvo Janežič
Vipava 1894, Vipava, 334
Vitovc, see Prah
Vi-Vin Saksida, Zalošče, 338
Vodopivec, Franc, see Slavček
Vovk, Bojan, Dutovlje, 366
Vovk, Ivan in Kržič, Franc, Mokronog, 201
Vrezner, Franc, Zgornja Kungota, 68
Vrhovšek, see Vino Vrhovšek

Z

Zabavnik, Jožefa, Jastrebci, 136
Zadruga Krško, see KZ Krško
Zadruga Metlika, see KZ Metlika
Zalatel, Valter, Hruševlje, 293
Zaloščan, Zalošče, 340
Zidar, Boštjan, see Brič
Zlati Grič, Slovenske Konjice, 70
Zuljan, Egon in Marko, see Vinarstvo Egon and Marko Zuljan
Zupan, Marjan, Celestrina, 72

Ž

Žaren, Janez, Nemška Vas, 210
Železnik, Blaž, see Faust
Živcova Vina, Skopo, 366
Živec, Milan, Osek, 344
Žličar, Franc, Ljutomer, 136
Žorž, see Vinska Klet Žorž
Žvokelj, Feliks, see Kmetija Žvokelj

WINE INDEX

WHITE WINE

Beli Pinot/Pinot Blanc

Brglez - Šparovec, 32 • Ivan Dreisiebner, 33 • Karl Fabijan, 38 • Alojz Hojnik, 39 • Jakob-Igor Leber, 45 • Vlado Mak, 45 • Klet Bistrica, 46 • Joannes, 54 • Dušan Savič, 56 • Ivo Senekovič, 56 • Milan Šiker, 58 • Vinag, 64 • Franc Vrezner, 68 • Marjan Zupan, 72 • Vina Orešič, 74 • Danijela Borko, 76 • Vinar Kupljen, 86 • Slavko Kolbl, 88 • Ptujska Klet, 92 • Stanko Čurin, 102 • Jeruzalem Ormož, 106 • Štefan Krampač, 111 • MiroVino, 120 • Vino Plemenič, 136 • Turčan, 142 • Ludvik Cuk, 148 • Hani, 152 • Martin Jerič, 152 • Štefan Kepe, 153 • Marijan Levačič, 156 • Amon, 160 • Vjekoslav Kralj, 164 • Blažova Gorca, 172 • Milan Glas, 174 • Franc Polovič, 175 • Jože Prah, 201 • Ivan Vovk in Franc Kržič, 201 • KZ Krško, 202 • Kmetija 'Pod - Dob' Ceglo, 238 • Blažič, 242 • Brandulin, 244 • Čarga 1767, 250 • Dolfo, 256 • Kabaj, 260 • Iztok in Borut Mužič, 262 • Oton Reya, 262 • Maksimiljan de Reya, 263 • Ronk - Vina iz Goriških Brd, 263 • Kristančič iz Medane, 264 • Jožko Mavrič, 268 • Stojan Ščurek, 290 • Miran in Alojz Šibav, 292 • Vina Kumar, 292 • Valter Zalatel, 293 • Vinarstvo Egon in Marko Zuljan, 293 • Frlanova Kmetija, 307 • Kmetija Fajdiga 'Ave', 310 • Roman Ipavec, 311 • Lisjak, 312 • Mansus, 316 • Peter in Rajko Rondič, 320 • Rikot, 322 • Vina Kavčič, 332 Vina Orse, 332 • Vinogradništvo in Vinarstvo Pipan, 333 • Vipava 1894, 334 • Vi-Vin Saksida, 338 • Zaloščan, 340 • Milan Živec, 344 • Vinska Klet Jejčič, 344 • Boris, 348 Viljem in Jadran Petelin, 349 • Boris Lisjak, 352 • Vinakras Sežana, 364

Chardonnay

Franc in Borut Anderlič, 32 • Boštjan in Franc Bračko, 32 • Milan Celcer, 32 • Dobaj, 33 • Ivan Dreisiebner, 33 • Črnko, 34 • Diona, 36 • Karl Fabijan, 38 • Dušan Hlade, 38 • Jurij Hlupič, 38 • Alojz Hojnik, 39 • Jakob Horvat, 39 • Ignac Jamnik, 39 • Maksimilijan (Milan) Jarc, 39 • Faust, 40 • Gaube, 42 • Ivan in Tomaž Kren, 44 • Kraner - Plateis, 44 • Jakob-Igor Leber, 45 • Klet Bistrica, 46 • Meranovo, 48 • Roman Mulec, 50 • Mira in Franc Pečnik, 50 • Anton in Marjeta Perko, 50 • Alojzij Plečko, 51 • Daniel Prosenc, 51 • Protner, 51 • Matjaž Ramšak, 51 • Očkerl, 52 • Joannes, 54 • Dušan Savič, 56 • Ivo Senekovič, 56 • Srečko Šumenjak, 57 • Uroš Valcl, 57 • Milan Šiker, 58 • Valdhuber, 60 • Vinag, 64 • Zlati Grič, 70 • Marjan Zupan, 72 • Vina Orešič, 74 • Vinogradništvo Mlaker, 74 • Danijela Borko, 76 • Branislav in Terezija Brus, 76 • Štefan in Jernej Frangež, 77 • Branko in Zdenka Kaučič, 77 • Kapela, 78 • Kogl, 80 • Radgonske Gorice, 82 • Steyer, 84 • Vinar Kupljen, 86 • Edvard Missia, 88 • Milan Senekovič, 89 • Vino Kolmanič, 89 • Ptujska Klet, 92 • Robert Hafner, 96 • Čurin, 98 • Albina in Avgust Bobnjar, 102 • Milan Kociper, 103 • Milan Hlebec, 104 • Jeruzalem Ormož, 106 • Mitja Kos, 110 • Edi in Anica Kosi, 110 • Štefan Krampač, 111 • Milan Krajnc, 112 • Ljutomerčan, 114 • Magdič, 118 • MiroVino, 120 • Franci Plajnšek, 122 • Emil Trop, 122 • Avgust Šadl, 123 • Miran-Ferdo Trop, 123 • Vid Vincetič, 123 • Jože Slavinec, 124 • Vino Kupljen, 132 • Vino Plemenič, 136 • Vinogradništvo Janežič Vinski Vrh, 136 • Jožefa Zabavnik, 136 • Anton Skaza, 138 • Turčan, 142 • Matija Gjerkeš, 146 • Štefan Barbarič, 148 • Janez Erniša, 149 • Franc Flegar, 149 • Grajska Klet Lendava, 150 • Janez in Nada Grabar, 152 • Peter Gruškovnjak, 152 • Martin Jerič, 152 • Franc Jošar, 153 • Štefan Kulčar, 153 • Ernest Novak, 154 •

WINE INDEX

Bela Küzmič, 156 • Ivan Lunežnik, 156 • Stanko Nerad, 156 • Ivan Panker, 157 • Štefan Rožman, 157 • Jože Šumak, 157 • Vinarstvo Kisilak, 158 • Vinotoč Lipič - Passero, 158 • Amon, 160 • Urbajs, 162 • Jožef Čebular, 164 • Franc Jankovič, 164 • Vjekoslav Kralj, 164 • Klet Imeno, 165 • Klet Kregar, 165 • Ivan Mijošek, 165 • Sekirnikova Gorca, 168 • Blažova Gorca, 172 • Bela Gorca, 174 • Janko Bostele, 174 • Andrej Fabjančič, 174 • Peter Špiler, 175 • Matjaž Jenšterle, 178 • Keltis, 180 • Vino Graben, 186 • Bajnof, 190 • Franc Planinc, 196 • Kartuzija Pleterje, 198 • Martinčič, 208 • Družina Absec, 212 • Ivan Bajuk, 214 • Ivan Bukovec - Janko, 216 • Jože Mavretič, 216 • Anton Nemanič, 217 • Martin Pečarič, 217 • KZ Metlika, 220 • Anton Kostelec, 224 • Samuel Malnarič, 226 • Anton Plut, 228 • Otmar Šturm, 234 • Jože Simčič, 236 • Ivan Suhorepec, 236 • Belica, 238 • Debenjak-D, 238 • Kmetija 'Pod - Dob' Ceglo, 238 • Kmetija Prinčič, 238 • Klavora, 239 • Klinec - Medana, 239 • Irena in Robert Gašparin Obljubek, 239 • Kmetija pri Štakljevih, 239 • Blažič, 242 • Brandulin, 244 • Čarga 1767, 250 • Četrtič, 252 • Dobuje, 254 • Dolfo, 256 • Jakončič, 258 • Kabaj, 260 • Roman in Edvin Kocijančič, 262 • Piro, 262 • Oton Reya, 262 • Maksimiljan de Reya, 263 • Ronk - Vina iz Goriških Brd, 263 • Valter Sirk, 263 • Kristančič iz Medane, 264 • Mavrič, 266 • Jožko Mavrič, 268 • Movia, 272 • Nando, 276 • Peršolja, 278 • Prinčič, 280 • Simčič, 282 • Edi Simčič, 286 • Aljoša Sirk, 288 • Stojan Ščurek, 290 • Šibau, 292 • Miran in Alojz Šibav, 292 • Vina Franko, 292 • Vina Kumar, 292 • Vina Srebrnič, 293 • Valter Zalatel, 293 • Vinarstvo Sosolič - Šturnšče, 293 • Vinarstvo Egon in Marko Zuljan, 293 • Vinska Klet Goriška Brda, 294 • Batič, 302 • Jordan Cigoj, 304 • Božičev Hram, 306 • Aleš Čehovin, 306 • Fajdigov Hram, 306 • Jožef in Ivan Fornazarič, 307 • Fortunatov Hram, 307 • Frlanova Kmetija, 307 • Kmetija Furlan, 308 • Furlanov Hram, 310 • Kmetija Bizjak - Branik, 310 • Kmetija Ferjančič, 311 • Kmetija Rojc & Polanec, 311 • Roman Ipavec, 311 • Lisjak, 312 • Kraljič, 314 • Miran Marc, 315 • Boleslav Mervič, 315 • Mansus, 316 • Mlečnik, 318 • Petrov Pil, 320 • Jožko Tratnik, 321 • Stojan Trošt, 321 • Rikot, 322 • Slavček, 324 • Sutor, 326 • Tilia, 330 • Vindor, 333 • Vipava 1894, 334 • Vi-Vin Saksida, 338 • Zaloščan, 340 • Vinska Klet Jejčič, 344 • Boris, 348 • Andrej Grmek, 348 • Branko in Vasja Čotar, 350 • Boris Lisjak, 352 • Joško Renčel, 354 • Primož in Tadej Štoka, 362 • Vinakras Sežana, 364 • Živcova Vina, 366 • Brič, 368 • Kmetija Babič - Šalara, 375 • Korenika & Moškon, 376 • Vina Bordon, 380 • Vinakoper, 382 • La Castellada, 388 • Gravner, 390 • Kante, 394

Dišeči Traminec/Fragrant Traminer
Dvorsko Vino, 33 • Vlado Mak, 45 • Steyer, 84 • Rado Lesjak, 111

Furlanski Tokaj/Tokay Friulano
Belica, 238 • Debenjak-D, 238 • Klavora, 239 • Klinec - Medana, 239 • Blažič, 242 • Brandulin, 244 • Cjanova Kmetija, 246 • Čarga 1767, 250 • Dolfo, 256 Jakončič, 258 • Kabaj, 260 • Roman in Edvin Kocijančič, 262 • Piro, 262 • Aljoša Sirk, 288 • Valter Sirk, 263 • Mavrič, 266 • Jožko Mavrič, 268 • Peršolja, 278 • Simčič, 282 • Stojan Ščurek, 290 • Šibau, 292 • Miran in Alojz Šibav, 292 • Vina Franko, 292 • Vina Kumar, 292 • Vina Srebrnič, 293 • Vinarstvo Egon in Marko Zuljan, 293 • Vinska Klet Goriška Brda, 294 • Jožef in Ivan Fornazarič, 307 • Jože Ličen, 314 • Boleslav Mervič, 315 • Mansus, 316 • Mlečnik, 318 • Vinogradništvo Štrukelj, 344 • Vinska Klet Plahuta, 344 • Boris Lisjak, 352 • La Castellada, 388 Radikon, 396

WINE INDEX

Kerner
Brglez - Šparovec, 32 • Milan Celcer, 32 • Ivan Dreisiebner, 33 • Dušan Hlade, 38 • Ignac Jamnik, 39 • Faust, 40 • Gaube, 42 • Ivan in Tomaž Kren, 44 • Kraner - Plateis, 44 • Jakob-Igor Leber, 45 • Klet Bistrica, 46 • Daniel Prosenc, 51 • Protner, 51 • Očkerl, 52 • Srečko Šumenjak, 57 • Alojz Valentan, 57 • Vinag, 64 • Marjan Zupan, 72 • Dušan Cvetko, 76 • Štefan in Jernej Frangež, 77 • Kogl, 80 • Mitja Kos, 110 • Ivo-Janez Trstenjak, 123 • Jože Šnajder, 128 • Saško Štampar, 130 • Janez Erniša, 149 • Stanko Nerad, 156 • Urbajs, 162 • Jožef Čebular, 164 • Matjaž Enšterle, 178 • Bajnof, 190 • Kartuzija Pleterje, 198 • Jože Prah, 201 • Ivan Vovk in Franc Kržič, 201 • Vinko Štemberger, 204 • Samuel Malnarič, 226 • Jožef Prus, 230 • Jože Šuklje, 232

Klarnica
Jordan Cigoj, 304 • Mansus, 316 • Sveti Martin, 328 • Vina Kavčič, 332

Kraljevina
Jožef Čebular, 164 • Ivan Bukovec - Janko, 216 • Samuel Malnarič, 226

Laški Rizling/Italian Riesling
Boštjan in Franc Bračko, 32 • Brglez - Šparovec, 32 • Dobaj, 33 • Ivan Dreisiebner, 33 • Jurij Hlupič, 38 • Alojz Hojnik, 39 • Jakob Horvat, 39 • Faust, 40 • Gaube, 42 • Zlatko Kauran, 44 • Ivan in Tomaž Kren, 44 • Klet Kropec - Sonce `spod Pohorja, 44 • Jakob-Igor Leber, 45 • Vlado Mak, 45 • Klet Bistrica, 46 • Mira in Franc Pečnik, 50 • Alojzij Plečko, 51 • Daniel Prosenc, 51 • Protner, 51 • Očkerl, 52 • Dušan Savič, 56 • Srečko Šumenjak, 57 • Milan Šiker, 58 • Valdhuber, 60 • Vilko Vesenjak, 62 • Vinag, 64 • Zlati Grič, 70 • Vina Orešič, 74 • Vinogradništvo Čerič, 74 • Danijela Borko, 76 • Jakob Kocuvan, 77 • Kapela, 78 • Kogl, 80 • Radgonske Gorice, 82 • Vinar Kupljen, 86 • Slavko Kolbl, 88 • Milan Senekovič, 89 • Ptujska Klet, 92 • Čurin, 98 • Albina in Avgust Bobnjar, 102 • Vlado Ferenc, 102 • Franc Herga, 102 • Bogomir Heric, 103 • Hiša Hrane in Vina 'Pri Kapeli`, 103 • Dušan in Dejan Jureš, 103 • Jeruzalem Ormož, 106 • Franc Kolbl, 110 • Mitja Kos, 110 • Edi in Anica Kosi, 110 • Mirko Krajnc, 110 • Štefan Krampač, 111 • Rado Lesjak, 111 • Angela in Viktor Munda, 111 • Ljutomerčan, 114 • Bojan Lubaj, 116 • Magdič, 118 • MiroVino, 120 • Jakob Svenšek, 122 • Emil Trop, 122 • Miran-Ferdo Trop, 123 • Ivo-Janez Trstenjak, 123 • Jože Slavinec, 124 • Stanovščak, 126 • Jože Šnajder, 128 • Saško Štampar, 130 • Vino Plemenič, 136 • Vinogradništvo Janežič Vinski Vrh, 136 • Jožefa Zabavnik, 136 • Franc Žličar, 136 • Turčan, 142 • Vinoreja Bezjak Haloze, 144 • Matija Gjerkeš, 146 • Drago Apatič, 148 • Jožef Balažek, 148 • Štefan Barbarič, 148 • Ludvik Cuk, 148 • Franc Flegar, 149 • Jožef Gjuran, 149 • Grajska Klet Lendava, 150 • Janez in Nada Grabar, 152 • Hani, 152 • Martin Jerič, 152 • Franc Jošar, 153 • Vladimir Kelenc, 153 • Štefan Kepe, 153 • Štefan Kulčar, 153 • Ernest Novak, 154 • Bela Küzmič, 156 • Ivan Panker, 157 • Alojz Režonja, 157 • Sigfrid-Zmago Urisk, 158 • Vinarstvo Kisilak, 158 • Vinotoč Lipič - Passero, 158 • Amon, 160 • Urbajs, 162 • Jožef Čebular, 164 • Vjekoslav Kralj, 164 • Klet Imeno, 165 • Ivan Mlaker, 165 • Rajko Pečnik, 166 • Andrej Fabjančič, 174 • Franc Polovič, 175 • Družina Sumrak, 175 • Matjaž Enšterle, 178 • Keltis, 180 • Lojze Kunej, 182 • Vino Graben, 186 • Bajnof, 190 • Bojan Brcar, 192 • Franc Planinc, 196 • Matjaž Engel, 200 •

WINE INDEX

Mihael Kvartuh, 200 • Jože Prah, 201 • Milan Valek, 201 • KZ Krško, 202 • Vinko Štemberger, 204 • Ivan Bajuk, 214 • Ivan Bukovec - Janko, 216 • Stanislav Kralj, 216 • Anton Malešič, 216 • Silvester Murgelj, 217 • Anton Nemanič, 217 • Martin Pečarič, 217 • KZ Metlika, 220 • Samuel Malnarič, 226 • Anton Plut, 228 • Jožef Prus, 230 • Otmar Šturm, 234 • Jože Simčič, 236 Ivan Suhorepec, 236 • Stanko Turk, 236 • Peter Curk, 306 • Fajdigov Hram, 306 • Ivan Kobal, 310 • Kmetija Fajdiga 'Ave', 310 • Kmetija Žvokelj, 311 • Kraljič, 314 • Jože Ličen, 314 • Miran Marc, 315 • Srečko Marc, 315 • Mansus, 316 • Franc Potočnik, 320 • Stojan Trošt, 321 • Rikot, 322 • Erik Uršič, 332 • Marjan Vidmar, 332 • Vina Orse, 332 • Vinogradništvo in Vinarstvo Pipan, 333 • Vipava 1894, 334 • Vinska Klet Žorž, 342 • Vinogradništvo Štrukelj, 344 • Vinska Klet Jejčič, 344

Malvazija/Malvasia
Debenjak-D, 238 • Valter Sirk, 263 • Jordan Cigoj, 304 • Furlanov Hram, 3104 • Kmetija Bizjak - Branik, 310 • Roman Ipavec, 311 • Franc Potočnik, 320 • Peter in Rajko Rondič, 320 • Rikot, 322 • Slavček, 324 • Sutor, 326 • Vina Kavčič, 332 • Vipava 1894, 334 • Vinska Klet Jejčič, 344 • Boris, 348 • Andrej Grmek, 348 • Viljem in Jadran Petelin, 349 • Dušan Rebula, 349 • Branko in Vasja Čotar, 350 • Joško Renčel, 354 • Vinarstvo Šuc, 357 • Vinska Klet Orel, 357 • Širca - Kodrič, 358 • Vinakras Sežana, 364 • Vinska Klet Škerlj - Ščuka, 366 • Brič, 368 • Klet Rodica, 372 • Rudolf Bonin, 374 • Igor Černe, 374 • Domiana, 374 • Klabjan - Vina izpod stene, 374 • Kmetija Babič - Šalara, 375 • Nevijo Stepančič, 375 • Korenika & Moškon, 376 • Santomas, 378 • Dorjano in Andrej Šuber, 380 • Vina Bordon, 380 • Vina Simeon, 380 • Vinogradništvo Ferran in Rupnik, 380 • Vinska Klet 'D in V', 381 • Vinakoper, 382 • Kante, 394

Muškat Ottonel/Muscat Ottonel
Franc in Borut Anderlič, 32 • Črnko, 34 • Diona, 36 • Karl Fabijan, 38 • Gaube, 42 • Protner, 51 • Milan Šiker, 58 • Vilko Vesenjak, 62 • Vina Orešič, 74 • Jakob Kocuvan, 77 • Kogl, 80 • Vinar Kupljen, 86 • Milan Senekovič, 89 • Ptujska Klet, 92 • Čurin, 98 • Milan Hlebec, 104 • Jeruzalem Ormož, 106 • Štefan Krampač, 111 • Rado Lesjak, 111 • Ljutomerčan, 114 • Avgust Šadl, 123 • Ivo-Janez Trstenjak, 123 • Jože Slavinec, 124 • Vid Vincetič, 123 • Vinska Klet Püklavec, 134 • Vino Plemenič, 136 • Turčan, 142 • Jurij Cvitanič, 144 • Stanko Nerad, 156 • Jože Šumak, 157 • Vinarstvo Kisilak, 158 • Rajko Pečnik, 166 Ivan Bukovec - Janko, 216

Neuburger
Vino Graben, 186

Pikolit/Picolit
Čarga 1767, 250 • Kristančič iz Medane, 264 • Aljoša Sirk, 288 • Stojan Sčurek, 290 • Šibau, 292 • Vinarstvo Egon in Marko Zuljan, 293

Pinela
Andlovic, 300 • Batič, 302 • Božičev Hram, 306 • Boris Ferjančič, 307 • Fortunatov Hram, 307 • Kmetija Furlan, 308 • Kmetija Fajdiga 'Ave', 310 • Kmetija Ferjančič, 311 • Lisjak, 312 • Bernarda Lozej, 314 • Miran Marc, 315 • Stojan Trošt, 321 • Sveti Martin, 328 • Erik Uršič, 332 • Vina Orse, 332 • Vinski Hram Štokelj, 345

WINE INDEX

Ranina
Karl Fabijan, 38 • Kogl, 80 • Radgonske Gorice, 82 • Vinar Kupljen, 86 • Milan in Margita Kolarič, 88 • Milan Senekovič, 89 • Robert Hafner, 96 • Ljutomerčan, 114

Renski Rizling/White Riesling
Franc in Borut Anderlič, 32 • Boštjan in Franc Bračko, 32 • Dobaj, 33 • Ivan Dreisiebner, 33 • Dvorsko Vino, 33 • Črnko, 34 • Diona, 36 • Karl Fabijan, 38 • Viktor Hajšek, 38 • Dušan Hlade, 38 • Jurij Hlupič, 38 • Alojz Hojnik, 39 • Jakob Horvat, 39 • Ignac Jamnik, 39 • Maksimilijan (Milan) Jarc, 39 • Faust, 40 • Gaube, 42 • Zlatko Kauran, 44 • Ivan in Tomaž Kren, 44 • Klet Kropec - Sonce ` spod Pohorja, 44 • Kraner - Plateis, 44 • Košaki, 45 • Jakob-Igor Leber, 45 • Vlado Mak, 45 • Klet Bistrica, 46 • Meranovo, 48 • Roman Mulec, 50 • Alojzij Plečko, 51 • Daniel Prosenc, 51 • Protner, 51 • Joannes, 54 • Dušan Savič, 56 • Ivo Senekovič, 56 • Dušan Šfiligoj, 56 • Srečko Šumenjak, 57 • Miroslav Trojner, 57 • Uroš Valcl, 57 • Alojz Valentan, 57 • Milan Šiker, 58 • Valdhuber, 60 • Vinag, 64 • Franc Vrezner, 68 • Zlati Grič, 70 • Marjan Zupan, 72 • Vina Orešič, 74 • Vinogradništvo Čerič, 74 • Danijela Borko, 76 • Dušan Cvetko, 76 • Zvonko Fleisinger, 76 • Branko in Zdenka Kaučič, 77 • Jakob Kocuvan, 77 • Kapela, 78 • Kogl, 80 • Radgonske Gorice, 82 • Steyer, 84 • Vinar Kupljen, 86 • Slavko Kolbl, 88 • Edvard Missia, 88 • Milan Senekovič, 89 • Vino Kolmanič, 89 • Ptujska Klet, 92 • Robert Hafner, 96 • Marjan Lah, 96 • Zoran Petkoski, 96 • Čurin, 98 • Hiša Hrane in Vina 'Pri Kapeli', 103 • Dušan in Dejan Jureš, 103 • Milan Kociper, 103 • Milan Hlebec, 104 • Jeruzalem Ormož, 106 • Franc Kolbl, 110 • Edi in Anica Kosi, 110 • Tanja in Zlatko Korpar, 111 • Štefan Krampač, 111 • Milan Krajnc, 112 • Ljutomerčan, 114 • Bojan Lubaj, 116 • Magdič, 118 • Franci Plajnšek, 122 • Vinko Ratek, 122 • Emil Trop, 122 • Avgust Šadl, 123 • Miran-Ferdo Trop, 123 • Jože Slavinec, 124 • Stanovšcak, 126 • Jože Šnajder, 128 • Saško Štampar, 130 • Vino Kupljen, 132 • Vinska Klet Püklavec, 134 • Vid Vincetič, 123 • Vino Plemenič, 136 • Franc Žličar, 136 • Anton Skaza, 138 • Turčan, 142 • Viktorin, 144 • Vinoreja Bezjak Haloze, 144, 96 • Matija Gjerkeš, 146 • Drago Apatič, 148 • Jožef Balažek, 148 • Ludvik Cuk, 148 • Janez Erniša, 149 • Grajska Klet Lendava, 150 • Peter Gruškovnjak, 152 • Hani, 152 • Martin Jerič, 152 • Vladimir Kelenc, 153 • Štefan Kepe, 153 • Štefan Kulčar, 153 • Ernest Novak, 154 • Alojz Režonja, 157 • Jože Šumak, 157 • Vinarstvo Kisilak, 158 • Vinotoč Lipič - Passero, 158 • Amon, 160 • Jožef Čebular, 164 • Franc Jankovič, 164 • Vjekoslav Kralj, 164 • Klet Imeno, 165 • Klet Kregar, 165 • Ivan Mijošek, 165 • Rajko Pečnik, 166 • Sekirnikova Gorca, 168 • Andrej Fabjančič, 174 • Franc Polovič, 175 • Družina Sumrak, 175 • Vino Graben, 186 • Franc Planinc, 196 • Družina Absec, 212 • Ivan Bajuk, 214 • Stanislav Kralj, 216 • Anton Nemanič, 217 • Alojz Hoznar, 218 • Jožef Prus, 230 • Ivan Suhorepec, 236

Rizvanec
Milan Šiker, 58 • Vilko Vesenjak, 62 • Kapela, 78 • Vinar Kupljen, 86 • Milan Senekovič, 89 • Milan Hlebec, 104 • Jeruzalem Ormož, 106 • Mitja Kos, 110 • Vinska Klet Püklavec, 134 • Turčan, 142 • Franc Flegar, 149 • Janez in Nada Grabar, 152 • Franc Jošar, 153 • Vinarstvo Šuc, 357

WINE INDEX

Rumena Rebula/Ribolla
Belica, 238 • Debenjak-D, 238 • Kmetija 'Pod - Dob' Ceglo, 238 • Klinec - Medana, 239 • Irena in Robert Gašparin Obljubek, 239 • Kmetija pri Štakljevih, 239 • Blažič, 242 • Brandulin, 244 • Cjanova Kmetija, 246 • Čarga 1767, 250 • Četrtič, 252 • Dobuje, 254 • Dolfo, 256 • Jakončič, 258 • Kabaj, 260 • Roman in Edvin Kocijančič, 262 • Maksimiljan de Reya, 263 • Ronk - Vina iz Goriških Brd, 263 • Valter Sirk, 263 • Mavrič, 266 • Jožko Mavrič, 268 • Movia, 272 • Nando, 276 • Peršolja, 278 • Prinčič, 280 • Simčič, 282 • Edi Simčič, 286 • Aljoša Sirk, 288 • Stojan Ščurek, 290 • Šibau, 292 • Miran in Alojz Šibav, 292 • Vina Franko, 292 • Vina Kumar, 292 • Vina Srebrnič, 293 • Valter Zalatel, 293 • Vinarstvo Sosolič - Šturnšče, 293 • Vinarstvo Egon in Marko Zuljan, 293 • Vinska Klet Goriška Brda, 294 • Batič, 302 • Jordan Cigoj, 304 • Božičev Hram, 306 • Boris Ferjančič, 307 • Kmetija Bizjak - Branik, 310 • Kmetija Žvokelj, 311 • Roman Ipavec, 311 • Bernarda Lozej, 314 • Martin Marc, 315 • Srečko Marc, 315 • Boleslav Mervič, 315 • Mansus, 316 • Mlečnik, 318 • Peter in Rajko Rondič, 320 • Stojan Trošt, 321 • Rikot, 322 • Slavček, 324 • Sutor, 326 • Sveti Martin, 328 • Erik Uršič, 332 • Marjan Vidmar, 332 • Vina Kavčič, 332 • Vina Ušaj, 333 • Vinogradništvo in Vinarstvo Pipan, 333 • Vipava 1894, 334 • Vinska Klet Jejčič, 344 • Vinska Klet Plahuta, 344 • Vinski Hram Štokelj, 345 • Viljem in Jadran Petelin, 349 • La Castellada, 388 • Gravner, 390 • Radikon, 396

Rumeni Muškat/Muscatel
Franc in Borut Anderlič, 32 • Boštjan in Franc Bračko, 32 • Milan Celcer, 32 • Črni Kos, 33 • Dobaj, 33 • Ivan Dreisiebner, 33 • Dvorsko Vino, 33 • Črnko, 34 • Karl Fabijan, 38 • Viktor Hajšek, 38 • Dušan Hlade, 38 • Jurij Hlupič, 38 • Jakob Horvat, 39 • Ignac Jamnik, 39 • Maksimilijan (Milan) Jarc, 39 • Faust, 40 • Gaube, 42 • Zlatko Kauran, 44 • Ivan in Tomaž Kren, 44 • Kraner - Plateis, 44 • Gregor Kebrič, 45 • Jakob-Igor Leber, 45 • Vlado Mak, 45 • Klet Bistrica, 46 • Roman Mulec, 50 • Mira in Franc Pečnik, 50 • Anton in Marjeta Perko, 50 • Matjaž Ramšak, 51 • Očkerl, 52 • Joannes, 54 • Ivo Senekovič, 56 • Srečko Šumenjak, 57 • Miroslav Trojner, 57 • Milan Šiker, 58 • Valdhuber, 60 • Vinag, 64 • Franc Vrezner, 68 • Vinogradništvo Čerič, 74 • Dušan Cvetko, 76 • Zvonko Fleisinger, 76 • Kogl, 80 • Vinar Kupljen, 86 • Milan in Margita Kolarič, 88 • Slavko Kolbl, 88 • Ptujska Klet, 92 • Robert Hafner, 96 • Zoran Petkoski, 96 • Čurin, 98 • Hiša Hrane in Vina 'Pri Kapeli', 103 • Milan Hlebec, 104 • Jeruzalem Ormož, 106 • Franc Kolbl, 110 • Mitja Kos, 110 • Rado Lesjak, 111 • Ljutomerčan, 114 • Franci Plajnšek, 122 • Vinko Ratek, 122 • Jakob Svenšek, 122 • Avgust Šadl, 123 • Miran-Ferdo Trop, 123 • Vid Vincetič, 123 • Jože Slavinec, 124 • Stanovščak, 126 • Vino Kupljen, 132 • Anton Skaza, 138 • Turčan, 142 • Viktorin, 144 • Matija Gjerkeš, 146 • Ludvik Cuk, 148 • Hani, 152 • Ivan Panker, 157 • Jožef Čebular, 164 • Šolski Center Šentjur, 164 • Rajko Pečnik, 166 • Sekirnikova Gorca, 168 • Bela Gorca, 174 • Janko Bostele, 174 • Milan Glas, 174 • Franc Polovič, 175 • Družina Sumrak, 175 • Matjaž Jenšterle, 178 • Keltis, 180 • Vino Graben, 186 • Jože Prah, 201 • Anton Malešič, 216 • Jože Mavretič, 216 • Silvester Murgelj, 217 • Anton Nemanič, 217 • Martin Pečarič, 217 • KZ Metlika, 220 • Anton Plut, 228 • Jožef Prus, 230 • Otmar Šturm, 234 • Jože Simčič, 236 • Jože Stariha, 236 • Stanko Turk, 236 • Belica, 238 • Čarga 1767, 250 • Miran in Alojz Šibav, 292 • Vinarstvo Sosolič-Šturnšče,

WINE INDEX

293 Vinarstvo Egon in Marko Zuljan, 293 • Andlovic, 300 • Božičev Hram, 306 • Peter Curk, 306 • Fortunatov Hram, 307 • Frlanova Kmetija, 307 • Kmetija Furlan, 308 • Furlanov Hram, 310 • Kmetija Bizjak - Branik, 310 • Kmetija Fajdiga 'Ave', 310 • Kmetija Rojc & Polanec, 311 • Lisjak, 312 • Kraljič, 314 • Bernarda Lozej, 314 • Mansus, 316 • Peter in Rajko Rondič, 320 • Rikot, 322 • Tilia, 330 • Erik Uršič, 332 • Marjan Vidmar, 332 • Vina Kavčič, 332 • Vina Poljšak, 333 • Vindor, 333 • Zaloščan, 340 • Vinogradništvo Štrukelj, 344 • Vinska Klet Jejčič, 344 • Andrej Grmek, 348 • Živcova Vina, 366 • Brič, 368 • Brič, 368 • Klet Rodica, 372 • Rudolf Bonin, 374 • Domiana, 374 • Klabjan - Vina izpod stene, 374 • Kmetija Babič - Šalara, 375 • Korenika & Moškon, 376 • Vinakoper, 382

Rumeni Plavec
Milan Hlebec, 104 • Bela Gorca, 174 • Peter Špiler, 175 • Vino Graben, 186

Sauvignon/Sauvignon Blanc
Franc in Borut Anderlič, 32 • Brglez - Šparovec, 32 • Črni Kos, 33 • Dobaj, 33 • Ivan Dreisiebner, 33 • Črnko, 34 • Diona, 36 • Karl Fabijan, 38 • Viktor Hajšek, 38 • Dušan Hlade, 38 • Jurij Hlupič, 38 • Jakob Horvat, 39 • Maksimilijan (Milan) Jarc, 39 • Ivan in Tomaž Kren, 44 • Klet Kropec - Sonce ` spod Pohorja, 44 • Kraner - Plateis, 44 • Gregor Kebrič, 45 • Jakob-Igor Leber, 45 • Klet Bistrica, 46 • Meranovo, 48 • Roman Mulec, 50 • Mira in Franc Pečnik, 50 • Alojzij Plečko, 51 • Daniel Prosenc, 51 • Protner, 51 • Očkerl, 52 • Joannes, 54 • Dušan Savič, 56 • Ivo Senekovič, 56 • Dušan Šfiligoj, 56 • Srečko Šumenjak, 57 • Miroslav Trojner, 57 • Alojz Valentan, 57 • Valdhuber, 60 • Vilko Vesenjak, 62 • Vinag, 64 • Franc Vrezner, 68 • Zlati Grič, 70 • Vina Orešič, 74 • Vinogradništvo Čerič, 74 • Danijela Borko, 76 • Branislav in Terezija Brus, 76 • Zvonko Fleisinger, 76 • Jakob Kocuvan, 77 • Kapela, 78 • Kogl, 80 • Steyer, 84 • Vinar Kupljen, 86 • Milan in Margita Kolarič, 88 • Edvard Missia, 88 • Milan Senekovič, 89 • Vino Kolmanič, 89 • Ptujska Klet, 92 • Robert Hafner, 96 • Čurin, 98 • Albina in Avgust Bobnjar, 102 • Stanko Čurin, 102 • Franc Herga, 102 • Bogomir Heric, 103 • Milan Hlebec, 104 • Jeruzalem Ormož, 106 • Mitja Kos, 110 • Mirko Krajnc, 110 • Štefan Krampač, 111 • Rado Lesjak, 111 • Angela in Viktor Munda, 111 • Milan Krajnc, 112 • Ljutomerčan, 114 • Bojan Lubaj, 116 • Magdič, 118 • MiroVino, 120 • Franci Plajnšek, 122 • Vinko Ratek, 122 • Emil Trop, 122 • Avgust Šadl, 123 • Miran-Ferdo Trop, 123 • Vid Vincetič, 123 • Stanovščak, 126 • Vino Kupljen, 132 • Vinska Klet Püklavec, 134 • Vinogradništvo Janežič Vinski Vrh, 136 • Anton Skaza, 138 • Turčan, 142 • Viktorin, 144 • Vinoreja Bezjak Haloze, 144 • Ludvik Cuk, 148 • Jožef Gjuran, 149 • Vladimir Kelenc, 153 • Štefan Kulčar, 153 • Ernest Novak, 154 • Bela Küzmič, 156 • Marijan Levačič, 156 • Ivan Panker, 157 • Alojz Režonja, 157 • Jože Šumak, 157 • Vinarstvo Kisilak, 158 • Vinotoč Lipič - Passero, 158 • Amon, 160 • Jožef Čebular, 164 • Šolski Center Šentjur, 164 • Vjekoslav Kralj, 164 • Klet Imeno, 165 • Klet Kregar, 165 • Rajko Pečnik, 166 • Vino Vrhovšek, 168 • Aleš Balon, 170 • Blažova Gorca, 172 • Janko Bostele, 174 • Andrej Fabjančič, 174 • Franc Polovič, 175 • Peter Špiler, 175 • Istenič, 176 • Matjaž Jenšterle, 178 • Keltis, 180 • Lojze Kunej, 182 • Vino Graben, 186 • Jože Prah, 201 • KZ Krško, 202 • Družina Absec, 212 • Jože Mavretič, 216 • Martin Nemanič, 217 • Martin Pečarič, 217 • Alojz Hoznar, 218 • KZ Metlika, 220 • Anton Kostelec, 224 •

WINE INDEX

Samuel Malnarič, 226 • Anton Plut, 228 • Jožef Prus, 230 • Jože Šuklje, 232 • Otmar Šturm, 234 • Jože Simčič, 236 • Ivan Suhorepec, 236 • Belica, 238 • Kmetija 'Pod - Dob' Ceglo, 238 • Kmetija Prinčič, 238 • Klavora, 239 • Kmetija pri Štakljevih, 239 • Blažič, 242 • Constantini, 248 • Čarga 1767, 250 • Dobuje, 254 • Jakončič, 258 • Kabaj, 260 • Roman in Edvin Kocijančič, 262 • Piro, 262 • Maksimiljan de Reya, 263 • Ronk - Vina iz Goriških Brd, 263 • Valter Sirk, 263 • Kristančič iz Medane, 264 • Mavrič, 266 • Jožko Mavrič, 268 • Movia, 272 • Nando, 276 • Peršolja, 278 • Prinčič, 280 • Simčič, 282 • Edi Simčič, 286 • Stojan Sčurek, 290 • Šibau, 292 • Miran in Alojz Šibav, 292 • Vina Franko, 292 • Vinarstvo Sosolič - Šturnšče, 293 • Vinarstvo Egon in Marko Zuljan, 293 • Andlovic, 300 • Batič, 302 • Božičev Hram, 306 • Aleš Čehovin, 306 • Fajdigov Hram, 306 • Boris Ferjančič, 307 • Fortunatov Hram, 307 • Frlanova Kmetija, 307 • Kmetija Furlan, 308 • Furlanov Hram, 310 • Ivan Kobal, 310 • Kmetija Bizjak - Branik, 310 • Kmetija Ferjančič, 311 • Kmetija Rojc & Polanec, 311 • Kmetija Žvokelj, 311 • Roman Ipavec, 311 • Lisjak, 312 • Kraljič, 314 • Jože Ličen, 314 • Rajko Lisjak, 314 • Bernarda Lozej, 314 • Martin Marc, 315 • Miran Marc, 315 • Srečko Marc, 315 • Mlečnik, 318 • Peter in Rajko Rondič, 320 • Jožko Tratnik, 321 • Rikot, 322 • Slavček, 324 • Sutor, 326 • Tilia, 330 • Erik Uršič, 332 • Marjan Vidmar, 332 • Vina Kavčič, 332 • Vina Orse, 332 • Vina Poljšak, 333 • Vina Ušaj, 333 • Vindor, 333 • Vinogradništvo in Vinarstvo Pipan, 333 • Vipava 1894, 334 • Vinska Klet Žorž, 342 • Vinogradništvo Štrukelj, 344 • Vinska Klet Jejčič, 344 • Viljem in Jadran Petelin, 349 • Branko in Vasja Čotar, 350 • Joško Renčel, 354 • Izidor Škerlj, 356 • Vinakras Sežana, 364 • Brič, 368 • Domiana, 374 • La Castellada, 388 • Gravner, 390 • Kante, 394

Sivi Pinot/Pinot Gris

Franc in Borut Anderlič, 32 • Boštjan in Franc Bračko, 32 • Brglez - Šparovec, 32 • Dobaj, 33 • Ivan Dreisiebner, 33 • Črnko, 34 • Karl Fabijan, 38 • Viktor Hajšek, 38 • Jakob Horvat, 39 • Gaube, 42 • Ivan in Tomaž Kren, 44 • Klet Kropec - Sonce ̀spod Pohorja, 44 • Kraner - Plateis, 44 • Jakob-Igor Leber, 45 • Vlado Mak, 45 • Klet Bistrica, 46 • Roman Mulec, 50 • Anton in Marjeta Perko, 50 • Protner, 51 • Matjaž Ramšak, 51 • Očkerl, 52 • Joannes, 54 • Dušan Savič, 56 • Ivo Senekovič, 56 • Srečko Šumenjak, 57 • Miroslav Trojner, 57 • Uroš Valcl, 57 • Valdhuber, 60 • Vinag, 64 • Danijela Borko, 76 • Zvonko Fleisinger, 76 • Jakob Kocuvan, 77 • Kogl, 80 • Radgonske Gorice, 82 • Steyer, 84 • Vinar Kupljen, 86 • Milan in Margita Kolarič, 88 • Milan Senekovič, 89 • Ptujska Klet, 92 • Robert Hafner, 96 • Čurin, 98 • Stanko Čurin, 102 • Hiša Hrane in Vina 'Pri Kapeli', 103 • Milan Kociper, 103 • Jeruzalem Ormož, 106 • Mitja Kos, 110 • Rado Lesjak, 111 • Milan Krajnc, 112 • Ljutomerčan, 114 • Magdič, 118 • Franci Plajnšek, 122 • Jakob Svenšek, 122 • Avgust Šadl, 123 • Jože Slavinec, 124 • Vinska Klet Püklavec, 134 • Franc Žličar, 136 • Anton Skaza, 138 • Turčan, 142 • Matija Gjerkeš, 146 • Grajska Klet Lendava, 150 • Hani, 152 • Martin Jerič, 152 • Ernest Novak, 154 • Marijan Levačič, 156 • Štefan Rožman, 157 • Vinarstvo Kisilak, 158 • Vinotoč Lipič - Passero, 158 • Amon, 160 • Urbajs, 162 • Jožef Čebular, 164 • Šolski Center Šentjur, 164 • Vjekoslav Kralj, 164 • Ivan Mijošek, 165 • Vino Vrhovšek, 168 • Janko Bostele, 174 • Keltis, 180 • Vino Graben, 186 • Vinko Štemberger, 204 • Martinčič, 208 • Martin Pečarič, 217 • Anton Kostelec, 224 • Anton Plut, 228 • Jožef Prus, 230 • Jože Šuklje, 232

WINE INDEX

Ivan Suhorepec, 236 • Belica, 238 • Debenjak-D, 238 • Kmetija Prinčič, 238 • Klavora, 239 • Klinec - Medana, 239 • Kmetija pri Štakljevih, 239 • Blažič, 242 • Brandulin, 244 • Cjanova Kmetija, 246 • Constantini, 248 • Čarga 1767, 250 • Četrtič, 252 • Dobuje, 254 • Dolfo, 256 • Jakončič, 258 • Kabaj, 260 • Roman in Edvin Kocijančič, 262 • Iztok in Borut Mužič, 262 • Piro, 262 • Maksimiljan de Reya, 263 • Ronk - Vina iz Goriških Brd, 263 • Marko Sirk, 263 • Valter Sirk, 263 • Kristančič iz Medane, 264 • Mavrič, 266 • Jožko Mavrič, 268 • Movia, 272 • Nando, 276 • Peršolja, 278 • Prinčič, 280 • Simčič, 282 • Edi Simčič, 286 • Aljoša Sirk, 288 • Stojan Ščurek, 290 • Šibau, 292 • Vina Kumar, 292 • Vina Srebrnič, 293 • Valter Zalatel, 293 • Vinarstvo Sosolič - Šturnšče, 293 • Vinarstvo Egon in Marko Zuljan, 293 • Vinska Klet Goriška Brda, 294 • Batič, 302 • Roman Ipavec, 311 • Lisjak, 312 • Mansus, 316 • Pasji Rep, 320 • Rikot, 322 • Tilia, 330 • Zaloščan, 340 • Vinakras Sežana, 364 • Brič, 368 • Klet Rodica, 372 • Domiana, 374 • Korenika & Moškon, 376 • Vinakoper, 382 • La Castellada, 388

Šipon
Milan Šiker, 58 • Danijela Borko, 76 • Jakob Kocuvan, 77 • Kogl, 80 • Vinar Kupljen, 86 • Ptujska Klet, 92 • Marjan Lah, 96 • Čurin, 98 • Vlado Ferenc, 102 • Bogomir Heric, 103 • Milan Hlebec, 104 • Jeruzalem Ormož, 106 • Franc Kolbl, 110 • Mitja Kos, 110 • Edi in Anica Kosi, 110 • Štefan Krampač, 111 • Rado Lesjak, 111 • Ljutomerčan, 114 • Bojan Lubaj, 116 • Magdič, 118 • MiroVino, 120 • Vid Vincetič, 123 • Jože Slavinec, 124 • Stanovščak, 126 • Jože Šnajder, 128 • Saško Štampar, 130 • Vino Kupljen, 132 • Vinska Klet Püklavec, 134 • Vino Plemenič, 136 • Vinogradništvo Janežič Vinski Vrh, 136 • Jožefa Zabavnik, 136 • Franc Žličar, 136 • Jurij Cvitanič, 144 • Drago Apatič, 148 • Štefan Kulčar, 153 • Ivan Panker, 157 • Sigfrid-Zmago Urisk, 158 • Vinarstvo Kisilak, 158 • Jožef Čebular, 164

Traminec/Traminer
Franc in Borut Anderlič, 32 • Ivan Dreisiebner, 33 • Črnko, 34 • Diona, 36 • Karl Fabijan, 38 • Viktor Hajšek, 38 • Jakob Horvat, 39 • Ignac Jamnik, 39 • Klet Kropec - Sonce `spod Pohorja, 44 • Kraner - Plateis, 44 • Jakob-Igor Leber, 45 • Roman Mulec, 50 • Očkerl, 52 • Dušan Savič, 56 • Ivo Senekovič, 56 • Miroslav Trojner, 57 • Valdhuber, 60 • Vinag, 64 • Zlati Grič, 70 • Vina Orešič, 74 • Vinogradništvo Čerič, 74 • Danijela Borko, 76 • Zvonko Fleisinger, 76 • Jakob Kocuvan, 77 • Kapela, 78 • Kogl, 80 • Radgonske Gorice, 82 • Vinar Kupljen, 86 • Milan Senekovič, 89 • Vino Kolmanič, 89 • Robert Hafner, 96 • Zoran Petkoski, 96 • Čurin, 98 • Stanko Čurin, 102 • Hiša Hrane in Vina 'Pri Kapeli', 103 • Milan Hlebec, 104 • Jeruzalem Ormož, 106 • Štefan Krampač, 111 • Milan Krajnc, 112 • Ljutomerčan, 114 • Avgust Šadl, 123 • Vino Kupljen, 132 • Vinska Klet Püklavec, 134 • Anton Skaza, 138 • Turčan, 142 • Jurij Cvitanič, 144 • Viktorin, 144 • Štefan Barbarič, 148 • Ludvik Cuk, 148 • Janez Erniša, 149 • Jožef Gjuran, 149 • Martin Jerič, 152 • Jožef Čebular, 164 • Rajko Pečnik, 166 • Janko Bostele, 174 • Keltis, 180 • Vino Graben, 186 • Jožef Prus, 230 • Otmar Šturm, 234

Verduc
Klinec - Medana, 239 • Čarga 1767, 250

WINE INDEX

VITOVSKA GRGANJA
Kmetija Furlan, 308 • Boris, 348 • Branko in Vasja Čotar, 350 • Boris Lisjak, 352 • Milivoj Tavčar, 356 • Primož in Tadej Štoka, 362 • Živcova Vina, 366 • Kante, 394

ZELEN
Jordan Cigoj, 304 • Peter Curk, 306 • Kmetija Furlan, 308 • Ivan Kobal, 310 • Kmetija Ferjančič, 311 • Kmetija Žvokelj, 311 • Lisjak, 312 • Bernarda Lozej, 314 • Martin Marc, 315 • Miran Marc, 315 • Srečko Marc, 315 • Pasji Rep, 320 • Franc Potočnik, 320 • Peter in Rajko Rondič, 320 • Stojan Trošt, 321 • Rikot, 322 • Sveti Martin, 328 • Erik Uršič, 332 • Vina Orse, 332 • Vina Poljšak, 333 • Vi-Vin Saksida, 338 • Zaloščan, 340

ZELENI SILVANEC/SYLVANER
Dušan Hlade, 38 • Alojz Hojnik, 39 • Gaube, 42 • Zlatko Kauran, 44 • Kraner - Plateis, 44 • Matjaž Ramšak, 51 • Joannes, 54 • Vinag, 64 • Vinar Kupljen, 86 • Ptujska Klet, 92 • Milan Hlebec, 104 • Franc Kolbl, 110 • Angela in Viktor Munda, 111 • Vino Plemenič, 136 • Janez Erniša, 149 • Jožef Čebular, 164 • Vjekoslav Kralj, 164 • Bela Gorca, 174 • Družina Sumrak, 175 • Peter Špiler, 175 • Vino Graben, 186 • Jože Frelih, 194 • KZ Krško, 202 • Jože Mavretič, 216

RDEČE VINO/RED WINE

BARBERA
Vinarstvo Egon in Marko Zuljan, 293 • Božičev Hram, 306 • Fortunatov Hram, 307 • Frlanova Kmetija, 307, 4 • Furlanov Hram, 310 • Ivan Kobal, 310 • Kmetija Žvokelj, 311 • Roman Ipavec, 311 • Lisjak, 312 • Kraljič, 314 • Jože Ličen, 314 • Rajko Lisjak, 314 • Martin Marc, 315 • Miran Marc, 315 • Mansus, 316 • Jožko Tratnik, 321 • Stojan Trošt, 321 • Rikot, 322 • Slavček, 324 • Sveti Martin, 328 • Erik Uršič, 332 • Vindor, 333 • Vinogradništvo in Vinarstvo Pipan, 333 • Vipava 1894, 334 • Vinska Klet Jejčič, 344

CABERNET FRANC
Constantiní, 248 • Čarga 1767, 250 • Kabaj, 260 • Peršolja, 278 • Prinčič, 280 • Aljoša Sirk, 288 • Stojan Sčurek, 290 • Miran in Alojz Šibav, 292 • Batič, 302 • Rajko Lisjak, 314 • Boris Lisjak, 352

CABERNET SAUVIGNON
Belica, 238 • Debenjak-D, 238 • Kmetija 'Pod - Dob' Ceglo, 238 • Klavora, 239 • Irena in Robert Gašparin Obljubek, 239 • Kmetija pri Stakljivih, 239 • Cjanova Kmetija, 246 • Constantiní, 248 • Čarga 1767, 250 • Dolfo, 256 • Jakončič, 258 • Kabaj, 260 • Roman in Edvin Kocijančič, 262 • Piro, 262 • Maksimiljan de Reya, 263 • Ronk - Vina iz Goriških Brd, 263 • Marko Sirk, 263 • Valter Sirk, 263 • Kristančič iz Medane, 264 • Mavrič, 266 • Jožko Mavrič, 268 • Movia, 272 • Nando, 276 • Prinčič, 280 • Simčič, 282 • Aljoša Sirk, 288 • Stojan Sčurek, 290 • Miran in Alojz Šibav, 292 • Vina Kumar, 292 • Vina Srebrnič, 293 • Valter Zalatel, 293 • Vinarstvo Sosolič - Šturnšče, 293 • Vinarstvo Egon in Marko Zuljan, 293 • Andlovic, 300 • Jordan Cigoj, 304 • Aleš Čehovin, 306 •

WINE INDEX

Boris Ferjančič, 307 • Frlanova Kmetija, 307 • Kmetija Furlan, 308 • Furlanov Hram, 310 • Ivan Kobal, 310 • Kmetija Bizjak - Branik, 310 • Kmetija Fajdiga 'Ave', 310 • Kmetija Ferjančič, 311 • Lisjak, 312 • Kraljič, 314 • Jože Ličen, 314 • Srečko Marc, 315 • Boleslav Mervič, 315 • Mansus, 316 • Petrov Pil, 320 • Peter in Rajko Rondič, 320 • Jožko Tratnik, 321 • Stojan Trošt, 321 • Rikot, 322 • Slavček, 324 • Tilia, 330 • Erik Uršič, 332 • Vina Orse, 332 • Vina Poljšak, 333 • Vina Ušaj, 333 • Vindor, 333 • Vipava 1894, 334 • Vi-Vin Saksida, 338 • Zaloščan, 340 • Vinska Klet Žorž, 342 • Vinogradništvo Štrukelj, 344 • Vinska Klet Jejčič, 344 • Vinska Klet Plahuta, 344 • Viljem in Jadran Petelin, 349 • Branko in Vasja Čotar, 350 • Boris Lisjak, 352 Joško Renčel, 354 • Izidor Škerlj, 356 • Vinarstvo Šuc, 357 • Širca - Kodrič, 358 • Primož in Tadej Štoka, 362 • Brič, 368 • Igor Černe, 374 • Klabjan - Vina izpod stene, 374 • Kmetija Babič - Šalara, 375 • Korenika & Moškon, 376 • Vinakoper, 382 • La Castellada, 388

Gamay
Amon, 160 • Vino Graben, 186 • Jožef Prus, 230

Merlot
Belica, 238 • Debenjak-D, 238 • Kmetija 'Pod - Dob' Ceglo, 238 • Kmetija Prinčič, 238 • Cjanova Kmetija, 246 • Constantini, 248 • Čarga 1767, 250 • Dobuje, 254 • Dolfo, 256 • Jakončič, 258 • Kabaj, 260 • Roman in Edvin Kocijančič, 262 • Oton Reya, 262 • Maksimiljan de Reya, 263 • Ronk - Vina iz Goriških Brd, 263 • Marko Sirk, 263 • Kristančič iz Medane, 264 • Mavrič, 266 • Jožko Mavrič, 268 • Movia, 272 • Nando, 276 • Peršolja, 278 • Aljoša Sirk, 288 • Stojan Sčurek, 290 • Šibau, 292 • Miran in Alojz Šibav, 292 • Vina Franko, 292 • Vina Kumar, 292 • Valter Zalatel, 293 • Vinarstvo Sosolič - Šturnšče, 293 • Vinarstvo Egon in Marko Zuljan, 293 • Vinska Klet Goriška Brda, 294 • Batič, 302 • Jordan Cigoj, 304 • Božičev Hram, 306 • Peter Curk, 306 • Fajdigov Hram, 306 • Fortunatov Hram, 307 • Frlanova Kmetija, 307 • Furlanov Hram, 310 • Ivan Kobal, 310 • Kmetija Bizjak - Branik, 310 • Kmetija Fajdiga 'Ave', 310 • Kmetija Ferjančič, 311 • Kmetija Rojc & Polanec, 311 • Kmetija Žvokelj, 311 • Roman Ipavec, 311 • Lisjak, 312 • Kraljič, 314 • Rajko Lisjak, 314 • Miran Marc, 315 • Srečko Marc, 315 • Boleslav Mervič, 315 • Mansus, 316 • Mlečnik, 318 • Franc Potočnik, 320 • Peter in Rajko Rondič, 320 • Jožko Tratnik, 321 • Stojan Trošt, 321 • Rikot, 322 • Slavček, 324 • Sutor, 326 • Sveti Martin, 328 • Erik Uršič, 332 • Marjan Vidmar, 332 • Vina Ušaj, 333 • Vipava 1894, 334 • Vi-Vin Saksida, 338 • Zaloščan, 340 • Vinska Klet Žorž, 342 • Milan Živec, 344 • Vinska Klet Jejčič, 344 • Vinska Klet Plahuta, 344 • Branko in Vasja Čotar, 350 • Boris Lisjak, 352 • Joško Renčel, 354 • Širca - Kodrič, 358 • Primož in Tadej Štoka, 362 • Brič, 368 • Klet Rodica, 372 • Klabjan - Vina izpod stene, 374 • Kmetija Babič - Šalara, 375 • Korenika & Moškon, 376 • Vina Bordon, 380 • Vinakoper, 382 • La Castellada, 388 Radikon, 396

Modra Frankinja/Blue Franconian
Brglez - Šparovec, 32 • Milan Celcer, 32 • Klet Bistrica, 46 • Mira in Franc Pečnik, 50 • Očkerl, 52 • Milan Šiker, 58 • Zvonko Fleisinger, 76 • Ptujska Klet, 92 • Janez Erniša, 149 • Janez in Nada Grabar, 152 • Martin Jerič, 152 • Ivan Lunežnik, 156 • Mihael Tremel, 158 • Vinarstvo Kisilak, 158 • Amon, 160 •

WINE INDEX

Franc Jankovič, 164 • Vjekoslav Kralj, 164 • Klet Imeno, 165 • Aleš Balon, 170 • Blažova Gorca, 172 • Andrej Fabjančič, 174 • Milan Glas, 174 • Franc Polovič, 175 • Družina Sumrak, 175 • Matjaž Jeršterle, 178 • Lojze Kunej, 182 • Vino Graben, 186 • Bajnof, 190 • Bojan Brcar, 192 • Jože Frelih, 194 • Matjaž Engel, 200 • Mihael Kvartuh, 200 • Miloš Munih, 200 • Jože Prah, 201 • Milan Valek, 201 • Vinotrs - Klet gadova peč, 201 • KZ Krško, 202 • Vinko Štemberger, 204 • Vinogradništvo Pekel, 206 • Martinčič, 208 • Janez Žaren, 210 • Družina Absec, 212 • Ivan Bajuk, 214 • Ivan Bukovec - Janko, 216 • Stanislav Kralj, 216 • Anton Malešič, 216 • Jože Mavretič, 216 • Silvester Murgelj, 217 • Anton Nemanič, 217 • Martin Pečarič, 217 • Alojz Hoznar, 218 • KZ Metlika, 220 • Anton Kostelec, 224 • Samuel Malnarič, 226 • Anton Plut, 228 • Jožef Prus, 230 • Jože Šuklje, 232 • Otmar Šturm, 234 • Jože Stariha, 236 • Ivan Suhorepec, 236

Modri Pinot/Pinot Noir

Franc in Borut Anderlič, 32 • Viktor Hajšek, 38 • Jurij Hlupič, 38 • Gaube, 42 • Ivan in Tomaž Kren, 44 • Klet Kropec - Sonce `spod Pohorja, 44 • Vlado Mak, 45 • Klet Bistrica, 46 • Roman Mulec, 50 • Očkerl, 52 • Joannes, 54 • Srečko Šumenjak, 57 • Vinag, 64 • Štefan in Jernej Frangež, 77 • Branko in Zdenka Kaučič, 77 • Kogl, 80 • Vinar Kupljen, 86 • Milan Senekovič, 89 • Ptujska Klet, 92 • Robert Hafner, 96 • Hiša Hrane in Vina 'Pri Kapeli', 103 • Milan Krajnc, 112 • Magdič, 118 • Vinko Ratek, 122 • Vino Kupljen, 132 • Vinska Klet Püklavec, 134 • Turčan, 142 • Janez Erniša, 149 • Franc Jošar, 153 • Vinarstvo Kisilak, 158 • Franc Jankovič, 164 • Vjekoslav Kralj, 164 • Rajko Pečnik, 166 • Sekirnikova Gorca, 168 • Blažova Gorca, 172 • Andrej Fabjančič, 174 • Peter Špiler, 175 • Istenič, 176 • Matjaž Jeršterle, 178 • Vino Graben, 186 • Miloš Munih, 200 • KZ Krško, 202 • Družina Absec, 212 • Stanislav Kralj, 216 • Samuel Malnarič, 226 • Otmar Šturm, 234 • Belica, 238 • Kmetija Prinčič, 238 • Čarga 1767, 250 • Jakončič, 258 • Kristančič iz Medane, 264 • Movia, 272 • Peršolja, 278 • Simčič, 282 • Stojan Ščurek, 290 • Vinarstvo Egon in Marko Zuljan, 293 • Kmetija Furlan, 308 • Lisjak, 312 • Sutor, 326 • Tilia, 330 • Vina Kavčič, 332 • Vi-Vin Saksida, 338 • Zaloščan, 340 • Joško Renčel, 354

Portugalka/Blue Portuguese

Matjaž Jeršterle, 178 • Martin Nemanič, 217 • Martin Pečarič, 217 • Anton Plut, 228 • Jožef Prus, 230 • Otmar Šturm, 234 • Jože Stariha, 236

Refošk/Refosco

Klavora, 239 • Vinarstvo Egon in Marko Zuljan, 293 • Furlanov Hram, 310 • Jožef Simončič, 321 • Rikot, 322 • Brič, 368 • Klet Rodica, 372 • Rudolf Bonin, 374 • Igor Černe, 374 • Domiana, 374 • Klabjan - Vina izpod stene, 374 • Kmetija Babič - Šalara, 375 • Pavel Maslo, 375 • Zdenko Rebernik, 375 • Nevijo Stepančič, 375 • Korenika & Moškon, 376 • Santomas, 378 • Dorjano in Andrej Šuber, 380 • Vina Bordon, 380 • Vina Simeon, 380 • Vinogradništvo Ferran in Rupnik, 380 • Vinska Klet 'D in V', 381 • Vinska Klet Markočič, 381

Syrah

Kogl, 80 • Vinakoper, 382

WINE INDEX

ŠENTLOVRENKA/ST LAURENT
Silvester Murgelj, 217

TERAN PTP
Slavček, 324 • Boris, 348 • Marjan Colja, 348 • Andrej Grmek, 348 • Edvard Jerman, 348 • Kmetija Petelin - Durcik, 349 • Viljem in Jadran Petelin, 349 • Dušan Rebula, 349 • Šempolajc, 349 • Branko in Vasja Čotar, 350 • Boris Lisjak, 352 • Joško Renčel, 354 • Milivoj Širca, 356 • Izidor Škerlj, 356 • Jožef Škerlj, 356 • Milivoj Tavčar, 356 • Vina Urdih, 357 • Vinarstvo Šuc, 357 • Vinogradništvo in Kletarstvo Buntovi, 357 • Vinska Klet Orel, 357 • Širca - Kodrič, 358 • David Štok, 360 • Primož in Tadej Štoka, 362 • Vinakras Sežana, 364 • Vinska Klet Škerlj - Sčuka, 366 • Bojan Vovk, 366 • Živcova Vina, 366 • Kante, 394

ZWEIGELT
Milan Hlebec, 104 • Janez Erniša, 149

ŽAMETNA ČRNINA
Klet Imeno, 165 • Vinag 64 • Ljutomerčan, 114 • Vino Graben, 186 • Ivan Bukovec - Janko, 216 • Anton Nemanič, 217 • Ivan Suhorepec, 236

ZVRST/BLEND

BELOKRANJEC
Družina Absec, 212 • Ivan Bajuk, 214 • Anton Malešič, 216 • Jože Mavretič, 216 • Silvester Murgelj, 217 • Anton Nemanič, 217 • Martin Nemanič, 217 • Martin Pečarič, 217 • Alojz Hoznar, 218 • KZ Metlika, 220 • Anton Kostelec, 224 • Samuel Malnarič, 226 • Anton Plut, 228 • Jožef Prus, 230 • Jože Šuklje, 232 • Jože Simčič, 236 • Jože Stariha, 236 • Ivan Suhorepec, 236 • Stanko Turk, 236

BIZELJČAN BELI/WHITE
Aleš Balon, 170 • Bela Gorca, 174 • Franc Polovič, 175 • Družina Sumrk, 175 • Vino brežice, 184 • Vino Graben, 186

BIZELJČAN RDEČI/RED
Aleš Balon, 170 • Bela Gorca, 174 • Franc Polovič, 175 • Družina Sumrak, 175 • Istenič, 176 • Vino Brežice, 184 • Vino Graben, 186

CVIČEK PTP
Bajnof, 190 • Bojan Brcar, 192 • Jože Frelih, 194 • Franc Planinc, 196 • Kartuzija Pleterje, 198 • Matjaž Engel, 200 • Mihael Kvartuh, 200 • Miloš Munih, 200 • Alojz Pirc, 200 • Jože Prah, 201 • Milan Valek, 201 • Vinotrs - Klet gadova peč, 201 • Ivan Vovk in Franc Kržič, 201 • KZ Krško, 202 • Vinko Štemberger, 204 • Vinogradništvo Pekel, 206 • Martinčič, 208 • Janez Žaren, 210

METLIŠKA ČRNINA
Ivan Bajuk, 214 • Jože Mavretič, 216 • Anton Nemanič, 217 • Martin Nemanič,

WINE INDEX

217 • Martin Pečarič, 217 • KZ Metlika, 220 • Anton Kostelec, 224 • Anton Plut, 228 • Jožef Prus, 230 • Jože Šuklje, 232 • Jože Simčič, 236 • Jože Stariha, 236

ROSÉ
Vina Orešič, 74 • Martin Nemanič, 217 • KZ Metlika, 220 • Batič, 302 • Kmetija Fajdiga 'Ave', 310 • Roman Ipavec, 311 • Sveti Martin, 328 • Vinakoper, 382

PENINA/SPARKLING WINE
Črnko, 34 • Diona, 36 • Karl Fabijan, 38 • Jurij Hlupič, 38 • Klet Bistrica, 46 • Protner, 51 • Joannes, 54 • Vinag, 64 • Zlati Grič, 70 • Štefan in Jernej Frangež, 77 • Kogl, 80 • Radgonske Gorice, 82 • Ptujska Klet, 92 • Jeruzalem Ormož, 106 • Ljutomerčan, 114 • Viktorin, 144 • Ivan Mijošek, 165 • Andrej Fabjančič, 174 • Zdravko Mastnak, 175 • Istenič, 176 • Vino Brežice, 184 • Bajnof, 190 • Jože Frelih, 194 • Kartuzija Pleterje, 198 • Vinko Štemberger, 204 • KZ Metlika, 220 • Bjana, 240 • Čarga 1767, 250 • Jakončič, 258 • Medot, 270 • Vinska Klet Goriška Brda, 294 • Vindor, 333 • Marjan Colja, 348 • Vina Urdih, 357 • Vinakras Sežana, 364 • Vinakoper, 382

PREDIKATNO VINO/PREDICATE WINE
Franc in Borut Anderlič, 32 • Boštjan in Franc Bračko, 32 • Milan Celcer, 32 • Črnko, 34 • Diona, 36 • Ignac Jamnik, 39 • Faust, 40 • Zlatko Kauran, 44 • Košaki, 45 • Gregor Kebrič, 45 • Klet Bistrica, 46 • Meranovo, 48 • Janko Papež, 50 • Očkerl, 52 • Marko Šebart, 56 • Uroš Valcl, 57 • Milan Šiker, 58 • Vesenjak, 62 • Franc Vrezner, 68 • Zlati Grič, 70 • Marjan Zupan, 72 • Branislav in Terezija Brus, 76 • Dušan Cvetko, 76 • Kapela, 78 • Kogl, 80 • Steyer, 84 • Anton Roškar, 88 • Zoran Petkoski, 96 • Dušan in Dejan Jureš, 103 • Milan Hlebec, 104 • Jeruzalem Ormož, 106 • Mitja Kos, 110 • Milan Krajnc, 112 • Ljutomerčan, 114 • Bojan Lubaj, 116 • Franci Plajnšek, 122 • Ivo-Janez Trstenjak, 123 • Vid Vincetič, 123 • Jože Slavinec, 124 • Vino Kupljen, 132 • Vinska Klet Püklavec, 134 • Vinogradništvo Janežič Vinski Vrh, 136 • Franc Žličar, 136 • Jožef Šmigoc, 140 • Turčan, 142 • Jurij Cvitanič, 144 • Miran Erniša, 149 • Hani, 152 • Vladimir Kelenc, 153 • Ernest Novak, 154 • Marijan Levačič, 156 • Štefan Rožman, 157 • Jože Šumak, 157 • Sigfrid-Zmago Urisk, 158 • Urbajs, 162 • Jožef Čebular, 164 • Ivan Mijošek, 165 • Aleš Balon, 170 • Blažova Gorca, 172 • Janko Bostele, 174 • Lojze Kunej, 182 • Vino Brežice, 184 • Bajnof, 190 • Bojan Brcar, 192 • Kartuzija Pleterje, 198 • Mihael Kvartuh, 200 • Vinko Štemberger, 204 • Vinogradništvo Pekel, 206 • Družina Absec, 212 • Alojz Hoznar, 218 • KZ Metlika, 220 • Anton Kostelec, 224 • Samuel Malnarič, 226 • Jožef Prus, 230 • Čarga 1767, 250 • Domiana, 374 • Vinakoper, 382

POSEBNO VINO/SPECIAL WINE
Cjanova Kmetija, 246 • Simčič, 282 • Stojan Sčurek, 290 • Batič, 302 • Kmetija Fajdiga 'Ave', 310 • Rikot, 322 • Tilia, 330 • Vinska Klet Jejčič, 344 • Vinski Hram Štokelj, 345 • Marjan Colja, 348 • Joško Renčel, 354

FOOD INDEX

Aperitif

2003 Renski Rizling, Črnko, 34 • 2003 Mariborčan, Lisičkino Vino, Vinag, 66 • 2000 Royal, Vinag, 67 • Zlata Radgonska Penina, Radgonske Gorice, 83 • 1999 Traminec, Čurin, 100 • 2002 Philippus Primus, Ljutomerčan, 114 • 2002 Renski Rizling, Jože Slavinec, 124 • 2002 Renski Rizling, Matija Gjerkeš, 146 • 2003 Sauvignon, Amon, 160 • 2000 Prestige Barrique, Istenič, 176 • 2003 Rumeni Muškat, KZ Metlika, 222 • 1999 Cuvée Prestige Brut, Bjana, 241 • 2002 Pinela, Andlovic, 300

Bread

2003 Rumeni Muškat, Mašno Vino, Klet Bistrica, 47 • 1998 Šipon Ledeno Vino, Očkerl, 52 • 2002 Renski Rizling, Franc Vrezner, 68 • 2001 Steyer Mark Cuvée, Steyer, 85 • 2000 Šipon, Čurin, 99 • 2003 Šipon, Jeruzalem Ormož, 107 • 2003 Muškat Ottonel, Vinska Klet Püklavec, 134 • 2000 Laški Rizling Izbor, Jožef Šmigoc, 140 • 2003 Sauvignon, Družina Absec, 212 • 2002 Chardonnay, Ivan Bajuk, 214 • 2000 Laški Rizling Izbor, Anton Kostelec, 224 • 1998 Renski Rizling Ledeno Vino, Jožef Prus, 231 • 1998 Donna Regina, Čarga 1767, 251 • 2001 Modri Pinot, Jakončič, 259 • 2002 Pinela, Batič, 302 • 2001 Rebula, Slavček, 324 • 2001 Sauvignon Zemono Lanthieri, Vipava 1894, 335

Cheese

1997 Sauvignon Pozna Trgatev, Meranovo, 48 • 2000 Sauvignon Suhi Jagodni Izbor, Čurin, 101 • 2002 Chardonnay Holermuos, Jeruzalem Ormož, 108 • 2003 Renski Rizling, Jeruzalem Ormož, 109 • 2000 Šipon Suhi Jagodni Izbor, Saško Štampar, 130 • 2000 Prestige Barrique, Istenič, 176 • 1990 Kerner Suhi Jagodni Izbor, Matjaž Jenšterle, 178 • 1999 Rumeni Plavec Pozna Trgatev, Vino Graben, 187 • 2003 Sauvignon, Družina Absec, 212 • 2000 Laški Rizling Izbor, Anton Kostelec, 224 • 2001 Beli Pinot, Brandulin, 244 • 1999 Sivi Pinot, Četrtič, 252 • 1999 Chardonnay, Dobuje, 254 • 1999 Tokaj, Kabaj, 260 • 2001 Pavo, white, Kristančič Iz Medane, 265 • 2000 Chardonnay, Movia, 275 • 2002 Chardonnay, Peršolja, 279 • 2001 Sivi Pinot, Prinčič, 280 • 2002 Chardonnay Bagueri, Vinska Klet Goriška Brda, 297 • 2001 Pinela, Kmetija Furlan, 308 • 2001 Rebula, Mlečnik, 318 • 2000 Rebula, Mlečnik, 319 • 2001 Sauvignon Zemono Lanthieri, Vipava 1894, 335 • 1998 Pinela, Vinska Klet Žorž, 342 • 2001 Chardonnay, Brič, 369 • 2000 Ribolla Gialla, La Castellada, 388 • 2000 Bianco Breg, Gravner, 390 • 2000 Ribolla, Gravner, 393 • 2000 Ribolla Gialla, Radikon, 396 • 2000 Oslavje, Radikon, 397

Dishes with Mushrooms

2003 Šipon, Jeruzalem Ormož, 107 • 2002 Chardonnay Holermuos, Jeruzalem Ormož, 108 • 2003 Muškat Ottonel, Vinska Klet Püklavec, 134 • 2000 Kerner Pozna Trgatev, Urbajs, 163 • 2002 Cviček PTP, Bojan Brcar, 192 • 2003 Cviček PTP Pletér, Kartuzija Pleterje, 198 • 2003 Cviček PTP, KZ Krško, 202 • 2003 Cviček PTP, Martinčič, 208 • 2001 Beli Pinot, Brandulin, 244 • 1999 Chardonnay, Dobuje, 254 • 2000 Carolina, red, Jakončič, 258 • 2001 Modri Pinot, Jakončič, 259 • 1999 Tokaj, Kabaj, 260 • 1999 Veliko Belo, Movia, 274 • 2000 Teodor Réserve, red, Simčič, 285 • 2002 Chardonnay Bagueri, Vinska Klet Goriška Brda, 297 • 2001 Rebula, Mlečnik, 318 • 2000 Rebula, Mlečnik, 319 • 2000 Sauvignon, Sutor, 326 • 1999 Merlot, Sveti Martin, 328 • 2001

FOOD INDEX

Chardonnay, Brič, 369 • 2001 Capris Plemenito Rdeče, Vinakoper, 385 • 2001 Sauvignon, La Castellada, 389 • 1999 Vitovska Grganja, Kante, 395

Egg Dishes
2003 Rumeni Muškat, Kz Metlika, 222 • 2003 Furlanski Tokaj, Bjana, 240 • 2001 Furlanski Tokaj, Blažič, 242 • 2001 Beli Pinot, Brandulin, 244 • 1999 Sivi Pinot, Četrtič, 252 • 1999 Chardonnay, Dobuje, 254 • 1999 Tokaj, Kabaj, 260 • 2001 Pavo, white, Kristančič Iz Medane, 265 • 1999 Veliko Belo, Movia, 274 • 2001 Sivi Pinot, Prinčič, 280 • 2001 Stara Brajda, white, Stojan Ščurek, 291 • 2003 Rebula Quercus, Vinska Klet Goriška Brda, 294 • 2002 Zelen, Lisjak, 312 • 2001 Rebula, Mlečnik, 318 • 2000 Rebula, Mlečnik, 319 • 2000 Sauvignon, Sutor, 326 • 2001 Sauvignon Zemono Lanthieri, Vipava 1894, 335 • 2002 Zelen, Zaloščan, 340 • 2001 Malvazija, Joško Renčel, 355 • 2001 Rumeni Muškat, Brič, 370 • 1998 Malvazija Capo d' Istria, Vinakoper, 383 • 2000 Ribolla Gialla, La Castellada, 388 • 2001 Sauvignon, La Castellada, 389 • 2000 Ribolla, Gravner, 393 • 1999 Vitovska Grganja, Kante, 395 • 2000 Ribolla Gialla, Radikon, 396

Pasta
2000 Cabernet Franc, Constantiní, 248 • 2000 Carolina, red, Jakončič, 258 • 2001 Modri Pinot, Jakončič, 259 • 1999 Eugen, red, Nando, 276 • 2000 Teodor Réserve, red, Simčič, 285 • 2001 Stara Brajda, red, Stojan Ščurek, 290 • 2001 Merlot Bagueri, Vinska Klet Goriška Brda, 296 • 2002 Chardonnay Bagueri, Vinska Klet Goriška Brda, 297 • 2002 Pinela, Andlovic, 300 • 2002 Zelen, Lisjak, 312 • 2001 Merlot, Mansus, 316 • 1999 Merlot, Sveti Martin, 328 • 2002 Zelen, Zaloščan, 340 • 2001 Chardonnay, Brič, 369 • 2002 Malvazija, Korenika & Moškon, 376 • 1998 Malvazija Capo d' Istria, Vinakoper, 383 • 2001 Capris Plemenito Rdeče, Vinakoper, 385 • 2001 Malvasia, Kante, 394

Vegetable Dishes
2003 Sivi Pinot, Gaube, 42 • 2003 Chardonnay, Klet Bistrica, 46 • 2002 Sauvignon, Valdhuber, 60 • 2003 Renski Rizling, Radgonske Gorice, 82 • 2000 Šipon, Čurin, 99 • 2002 Chardonnay Holermuos, Jeruzalem Ormož, 108 • 2002 Renski Rizling, Milan Krajnc, 112 • 2003 Laški Rizling, Ljutomerčan, 115 • 2002 Renski Rizling, Vino Kupljen, 132 • 2002 Sauvignon, Turčan, 142 • 2003 Sauvignon, Amon, 160 • 2000 Kerner Pozna Trgatev, Urbajs, 163 • 2001 Traminec, Rajko Pečnik, 166 • 2003 Bizeljčan, white, Aleš Balon, 170 • 1999 Penina Od Fare, Jože Frelih, 194 • 2003 Renski Rizling Pozna Trgatev, Franc Planinc, 196 • 2003 Cviček PTP Pletér, Kartuzija Pleterje, 198 • 2003 Cviček PTP, KZ Krško, 202 • 2003 Cviček PTP, Martinčič, 208 • 2003 Sauvignon, Družina Absec, 212 • 2003 Rumeni Muškat, KZ Metlika, 222 • 2003 Izbrani Belokranjec, KZ Metlika, 223 • 1999 Laški Rizling, Samuel Malnarič, 226 • 2003 Rumeni Muškat, Otmar Šturm, 235 • 2001 Rebula, Movia, 273 • 2003 Rebula Quercus, Vinska Klet Goriška Brda, 294 • 2002 Chardonnay Bagueri, Vinska Klet Goriška Brda, 297 • 2002 Zelen, Jordan Cigoj, 304 • 2002 Zelen, Lisjak, 312 • 2001 Rebula, Slavček, 324 • 2001 Sauvignon Zemono Lanthieri, Vipava 1894, 335 • 2002 Zelen Lanthieri, Vipava 1894, 337 • 2002 Zelen, Zaloščan, 340 • 2000 Ribolla Gialla, La Castellada, 388 • 2000 Bianco, Stanislao (Stanko) Radikon, 397

FOOD INDEX

Meat Dishes

2000 Traminec, Diona, 36 • 2000 Laški Rizling, Faust, 40 • 2003 Sivi Pinot, Gaube, 42 • 2003 Chardonnay, Klet Bistrica, 46 • 2003 Rumeni Muškat, Mašno Vino, Klet Bistrica, 47 • 2001 Sivi Pinot, Joannes, 54 • 2002 Sauvignon, Valdhuber, 60 • 2001 Laški Rizling, Vinag, 65 • 2003 Mariborčan, Lisičkino Vino, Vinag, 66 • 2002 Renski Rizling, Franc Vrezner, 68 • 2003 Renski Rizling, Zlati Grič, 70 • 2001 Chardonnay, Marjan Zupan, 72 • 2003 Auxerrois, Kogl, 80 • 2002 Magna Dominica Ruber, red, Kogl, 81 • 2003 Renski Rizling, Radgonske Gorice, 82 • 2003 Haložan, Ptujska Klet, 93 • 2003 Sivi Pinot, Ptujska Klet, 94 • 1999 Traminec, Čurin, 100 • 2003 Šipon, Milan Hlebec, 104 • 2003 Šipon, Jeruzalem Ormož, 107 • 2002 Chardonnay Holermuos, Jeruzalem Ormož, 108 • 2003 Renski Rizling, Jeruzalem Ormož, 109 • 2002 Renski Rizling, Milan Krajnc, 112 • 2003 Laški Rizling, Ljutomerčan, 115 • 2003 Modri Pinot, Magdič, 118 • 2002 Sauvignon Réserve, MiroVino, 120 • 2002 Šipon, Stanovščak, 126 • 2002 Renski Rizling, Vino Kupljen, 132 • 2001 Modri Burgundec (Modri Pinot), Vino Kupljen, 133 • 1997 Laški Rizling, Grajska Klet Lendava, 150 • 1999 Laški Rizling Ledeno Vino, Ernest Novak, 154 • 2003 Modri Pinot, Blažova Gorca, 172 • 2000 Prestige Barrique, Istenič, 176 • 2002 Modri Pinot Barrique, Istenič, 177 • 2003 Bizeljsko-Sremiško Vino, red, Lojze Kunej, 182 • 1999 Rumeni Plavec Pozna Trgatev, Vino Graben, 187 • 2003 Cviček PTP, Bajnof, 190 • 2002 Cviček PTP, Bojan Brcar, 192 • Modra Frankinja Barrique, 1999 Jože Frelih, 195 • 2003 Cviček PTP Pletér, Kartuzija Pleterje, 198 • 2003 Kerner Pletér, Kartuzija Pleterje, 199 • 2003 Cviček PTP, KZ Krško, 202 • 2002 Modra Frankinja, KZ Krško, 203 • 2000 Modra Frankinja, Vinko Štemberger, 204 • 2000 Modra Frankinja, Vinogradništvo Pekel, 206 • 2003 Cviček PTP, Martinčič, 208 • 2000 Metliška Črnina, KZ Metlika, 221 • 2003 Izbrani Belokranjec, KZ Metlika, 223 • 1999 Laški Rizling, Samuel Malnarič, 226 • 2001 Modra Frankinja, Anton Plut, 228 • 2003 Metliška Črnina, Jože Šuklje, 232 • 2002 Modra Frankinja, Otmar Šturm, 234 • 2000 Cabernet Franc, Constantini, 248 • 1999 Sivi Pinot, Četrtič, 252 • 2002 Sivi Pinot, Dolfo • 256 • 2000 Carolina, red, Jakončič, 258 • 2001 Modri Pinot, Jakončič, 259 • 2002 Cabernet Sauvignon, Kristančič Iz Medane, 264 • 1999 Sivi Pinot, Mavrič, 266 • 2002 Sivi Pinot, Jožko Mavrič, 268 • 2001 Rebula, Movia, 272 • 2000 Chardonnay, Movia, 275 • 1999 Eugen, red, Nando, 276 • 2000 Cabernet Franc, Peršolja, 278 • 2002 Chardonnay, Peršolja, 279 • 2001 Chardonnay Réserve, Simčič, 283 • 2001 Teodor, white, Simčič, 284 • 2000 Teodor Réserve, red, Simčič, 285 • 2001 Duet, Edi Simčič, 286 • 2001 Stara Brajda, red, Stojan Ščurek, 290 • 2001 Merlot, Vinska Klet Goriška Brda, 296 • 2002 Chardonnay Bagueri, Vinska Klet Goriška Brda, 297 • 2002 Pinela, Batič, 302 • 2001 Pinela, Kmetija Furlan, 308 • 2001 Merlot, Mansus, 316 • 2001 Rebula, Mlečnik, 318 • 2000 Rebula, Mlečnik, 319 • 2000 Zelen, Rikot, 322 • 1999 Merlot, Sveti Martin, 328 • 1997 Cabernet Sauvignon Lanthieri, Vipava 1894, 336 • 2002 Zelen Lanthieri, Vipava 1894, 337 • 1999 Beli Pinot, Vi-Vin Saksida, 338 • 1998 Pinela, Vinska Klet Žorž, 342 • 2002 Izbrani Teran PTP, Boris Lisjak, 352 • 2003 Izbrani Teran PTP, Širca—Kodrič, 358 • 2003 Izbrani Teran PTP, Primož In Tadej Štoka, 362 • 2002 Izbrani Teran PTP, Vinakras Sežana, 364 • 2001 Chardonnay, Brič, 369 • 2001 Cabernet Sauvignon, Brič, 371 • 2003 Refošk, Klet Rodica, 372 • 2000 Refošk, Santomas, 378 • 2000 Grand Cuvée, Santomas, 379 • 2001 Capris Plemenito Rdeče, Vinakoper, 385 •

FOOD INDEX

2000 Bianco Breg, Gravner, 390 • 1999 Rosso, Gravner, 392 • 2000 Ribolla Gialla, Radikon, 396 • 2000 Oslavje, Radikon, 397

Poultry Dishes

1998 Šipon Ledeno Vino, Očkerl, 52 • 2002 Renski Rizling, Franc Vrezner, 68 • 2003 Renski Rizling, Zlati Grič, 70 • 1993 Traminec, Kapela, 78 • 2003 Sivi Pinot, Ptujska Klet, 94 • 2000 Sauvignon Suhi Jagodni Izbor, Čurin, 101 • 2003 Šipon, Milan Hlebec, 104 • 2003 Šipon, Jeruzalem Ormož, 107 • 2003 Renski Rizling, Jeruzalem Ormož, 109 • 2002 Renski Rizling, Milan Krajnc, 112 • 2002 Laški Rizling Suhi Jagodni Izbor, Bojan Lubaj, 116 • 2003 Modri Pinot, Magdič, 118 • 2002 Šipon, Stanovščak, 126 • 2001 Renski Rizling, Anton Skaza, 138 • 2002 Renski Rizling, Matija Gjerkeš, 146 • 1997 Laški Rizling, Grajska Klet Lendava, 150 • 2001 Traminec, Rajko Pečnik, 166 • 2003 Bizeljčan, white, Aleš Balon, 170 • 2003 Modri Pinot, Blažova Gorca, 172 • 2000 Prestige Barrique, Istenič, 176 • 2002 Modri Pinot Barrique, Istenič, 177 • 1999 Rumeni Plavec Pozna Trgatev, Vino Graben, 187 • 1999 Modra Frankinja Barrique, Jože Frelih, 195 • 2003 Renski Rizling Pozna Trgatev, Franc Planinc, 196 • 2003 Kerner Pletér, Kartuzija Pleterje, 199 • 2002 Modra Frankinja, KZ Krško, 203 • 2000 Modra Frankinja, Vinko Štemberger, 204 • 2000 Modra Frankinja, Vinogradništvo Pekel, 206 • 2003 Sauvignon, Družina Absec, 212 • 2000 Metliška Črnina, KZ Metlika, 221 • 2003 Izbrani Belokranjec, KZ Metlika, 223 • 1999 Laški Rizling, Samuel Malnarič, 226 • 2001 Modra Frankinja, Anton Plut, 228 • 2003 Metliška Črnina, Jože Šuklje, 232 • 2002 Modra Frankinja, Otmar Šturm, 234 • 2003 Furlanski Tokaj, Bjana, 240 • 2001 Beli Pinot, Brandulin, 244 • 2000 Cabernet Franc, Constantini, 248 • 1999 Sivi Pinot, Četrtič, 252 • 1999 Chardonnay, Dobuje, 254 • 2002 Sivi Pinot, Dolfo • 256 • 1999 Tokaj, Kabaj, 260 • 2001 Pavo, white, Kristančič Iz Medane, 265 • 2002 Sivi Pinot, Jožko Mavrič, 268 • 2001 Rebula, Movia, 273 • 1999 Eugen, red, Nando, 276 • 2001 Sivi Pinot, Prinčič, 280 • 2003 Rebula Quercus, Vinska Klet Goriška Brda, 294 • 2002 Pinela, Andlovic, 300 • 2002 Pinela, Batič, 302 • 2002 Zelen, Jordan Cigoj, 304 • 2001 Pinela, Kmetija Furlan, 308 • 2002 Zelen, Lisjak, 312 • 2001 Rebula, Mlečnik, 318 • 2000 Rebula, Mlečnik, 319 • 2000 Zelen, Rikot, 322 • 2001 Rebula, Slavček, 324 • 2002 Zelen Lanthieri, Vipava 1894, 337 • 2002 Zelen, Zaloščan, 340 • 1998 Pinela, Vinska Klet Žorž, 342 • 2001 Malvazija, Joško Renčel, 355 • 2001 Rumeni Muškat, Brič, 370 • 2002 Malvazija, Korenika & Moškon, 376 • 2000 Ribolla Gialla, La Castellada, 388 • 2000 Ribolla, Gravner, 393 • 2001 Malvasia, Kante, 394 • 2000 Ribolla Gialla), Radikon, 396 • 2000 Oslavje, Radikon, 397

Game Dishes

2001 Chardonnay, Marjan Zupan, 72 • 2000 Laški Rizling Pozna Trgatev, Jože Šnajder, 128 • 2001 Modri Burgundec (Modri Pinot), Vino Kupljen, 133 • 2000 Carolina, red, Jakončič, 258 • 1999 Eugen, red, Nando, 276 • 2000 Cabernet Franc, Peršolja, 278 • 2000 Teodor Réserve, red, Simčič, 285 • 2001 Duet, Edi Simčič, 286 • 2001 Stara Brajda, red, Stojan Ščurek, 290 • 2001 Merlot Bagueri, Vinska Klet Goriška Brda, 296 • 2001 Merlot, Mansus, 316 • 1999 Merlot, Sveti Martin, 328 • 2001 Cabernet Sauvignon, Tilia, 330 • 1997 Cabernet Sauvignon Lanthieri, Vipava 1894, 336 • 1999 Terra Rossa, Branko in Vasja Čotar, 350 • 2002 Izbrani Teran PTP, Boris Lisjak, 352 • 2003 Izbrani

FOOD INDEX

Teran PTP, Širca—Kodrič, 358 • 2002 Izbrani Teran PTP, David Štok, 360 • 2003 Izbrani Teran PTP, Primož In Tadej Štoka, 362 • 2002 Izbrani Teran PTP, Vinakras Sežana, 364 • 2001 Cabernet Sauvignon, Brič, 371 • 2003 Refošk, Klet Rodica, 372 • 2000 Refošk, Santomas, 378 • 2000 Grand Cuvée, Santomas, 379 • 2001 Capris Plemenito Rdeče, Vinakoper, 385

Salamis and Sausages

2001 Sivi Pinot, Joannes, 54 • 2001 Laški Rizling, Vinag, 65 • 2001 Chardonnay, Marjan Zupan, 72 • 2002 Magna Dominica Ruber, red, Kogl, 81 • 2003 Sivi Pinot, Ptujska Klet, 94 • 2003 Šipon, Jeruzalem Ormož, 107 • 2003 Laški Rizling, Ljutomerčan, 115 • 2002 Šipon, Stanovščak, 126 • 2001 Modri Burgundec (Modri Pinot), Vino Kupljen, 133 • 2003 Bizeljčan, white, Aleš Balon, 170 • 2003 Modri Pinot, Blažova Gorca, 172 • 2002 Modri Pinot Barrique, Istenič, 177 • 2003 Bizeljsko-Sremiško Vino, red, Lojze Kunej, 182 • 2003 Cviček PTP, Bajnof, 190 • 2002 Cviček PTP, Bojan Brcar, 192 • 1999 Penina Od Fare, Jože Frelih, 194 • 1999 Modra Frankinja Barrique, Jože Frelih, 195 • 2003 Renski Rizling Pozna Trgatev, Franc Planinc, 196 • 2003 Cviček PTP Pletér, Kartuzija Pleterje, 198 • 2003 Cviček PTP, KZ Krško, 202 • 2002 Modra Frankinja, KZ Krško, 203 • 2000 Modra Frankinja, Vinko Štemberger, 204 • 2000 Modra Frankinja, Vinogradništvo Pekel, 206 • 2003 Cviček PTP, Martinčič, 208 • 2003 Izbrani Belokranjec, KZ Metlika, 223 • 1999 Laški Rizling, Samuel Malnarič, 226 • 2001 Modra Frankinja, Anton Plut, 228 • 2003 Metliška Črnina, Jože Šuklje, 232 • 2002 Modra Frankinja, Otmar Šturm, 234 • 2001 Beli Pinot, Brandulin, 244 • 2000 Cabernet Franc, Constantini, 248 • 1999 Sivi Pinot, Četrtič, 252 • 1999 Chardonnay, Dobuje, 254 • 2001 Modri Pinot, Jakončič, 259 • 2000 Carolina, red, Jakončič, 258 • 2002 Cabernet Sauvignon, Kristančič Iz Medane, 264 • 2001 Pavo, white, Kristančič Iz Medane, 265 • 1999 Sivi Pinot, Mavrič, 266 • 1999 Veliko Belo, Movia, 274 • 2000 Chardonnay, Movia, 275 • 1999 Eugen, red, Nando, 276 • 2002 Chardonnay, Peršolja, 279 • 2000 Cabernet Franc, Peršolja, 278 • 2001 Sivi Pinot, Prinčič, 280 • 2001 Chardonnay Réserve, Simčič, 283 • 2001 Teodor, white, Simčič, 284 • 2000 Teodor Réserve, red, Simčič, 285 • 2001 Duet, Edi Simčič, 286 • 2001 Stara Brajda, red, Stojan Ščurek, 290 • 2001 Stara Brajda, white, Stojan Ščurek, 291 • 2001 Merlot Bagueri, Vinska Klet Goriška Brda, 296 • 2001 Merlot, Mansus, 316 • 1999 Merlot, Sveti Martin, 328 • 2001 Cabernet Sauvignon, Tilia, 330 • 1997 Cabernet Sauvignon Lanthieri, Vipava 1894, 336 • 1999 Beli Pinot, Vi-Vin Saksida, 338 • 1999 Terra Rossa, Branko In Vasja Čotar, 350 • 2002 Izbrani Teran PTP, Boris Lisjak, 352 • 2001 Malvazija, Joško Renčel, 355 • 2003 Izbrani Teran PTP, Širca—Kodrič, 358 • 2002 Izbrani Teran PTP, David Štok, 360 • 2003 Izbrani Teran PTP, Primož In Tadej Štoka, 362 • 2002 Izbrani Teran PTP, Vinakras Sežana, 364 • 2001 Kraška Penina, Vinakras Sežana, 365 • 2001 Chardonnay, Brič, 369 • 2001 Cabernet Sauvignon, Brič, 371 • 2003 Refošk, Klet Rodica, 372 • 2000 Refošk, Santomas, 378 • 2000 Grand Cuvée, Santomas, 379 • 2001 Capris Plemenito Rdeče, Vinakoper, 385 • 2000 Ribolla Gialla, La Castellada, 388 • 2000 Bianco Breg, Gravner, 390 • 1999 Rosso, Gravner, 392 • 1999 Vitovska Grganja, Kante, 395 • 2000 Ribolla Gialla, Radikon, 396 • 2000 Oslavje, Radikon, 397 •

FOOD INDEX

Fish Dishes
2003 Chardonnay, Klet Bistrica, 46 • 2002 Sauvignon, Valdhuber, 60 • 2001 Laški Rizling, Vinag, 65 • 1993 Traminec, Kapela, 78 • 2003 Auxerrois, Kogl, 80 • Zlata Radgonska Penina, Radgonske Gorice, 83 • 2001 Steyer Mark Cuvée, Steyer, 85 • 1983 Renski Rizling Izbor, Ptujska Klet, 95 • 2002 Philippus Primus, Ljutomerčan, 114 • 2002 Sauvignon Réserve, MiroVino, 120 • 2002 Sauvignon, Turčan, 142 • 2003 Sauvignon, Amon, 160 • 2000 Prestige Barrique, Istenič, 176 • 1999 Rumeni Plavec Pozna Trgatev, Vino Graben, 187 • 2003 Renski Rizling Pozna Trgatev, Franc Planinc, 196 • 2003 Rumeni Muškat, Kz Metlika, 222 • 1999 Laški Rizling, Samuel Malnarič, 226 • 2003 Rumeni Muškat, Otmar Šturm, 235 • 1999 Cuvée Prestige Brut, Bjana, 241 • 2001 Furlanski Tokaj, Blažič, 242 • 2002 Sivi Pinot, Dolfo, 256 • 2001 Pavo, white, Kristančič Iz Medane, 265 • 1999 Sivi Pinot, Mavrič, 266 • 2002 Sivi Pinot, Jožko Mavrič, 268 • Medot, Medot, 270 • 2001 Rebula, Movia, 273 • 1999 Veliko Belo, Movia, 274 • 2000 Chardonnay, Movia, 275 • 2001 Sivi Pinot, Prinčič, 280 • 2001 Teodor, white, Simčič, 284 • 2003 Rebula Quercus, Vinska Klet Goriška Brda, 294 • 2002 Chardonnay Bagueri, Vinska Klet Goriška Brda, 297 • 2002 Pinela, Batič, 302 • 2002 Zelen, Jordan Cigoj, 304 • 2000 Sauvignon, Sutor, 326 • 2001 Sauvignon Zemono Lanthieri, Vipava 1894, 335 • 1999 Beli Pinot, Vi-Vin Saksida, 338 • 2002 Zelen, Zaloščan, 340 • 2001 Malvazija, Joško Renčel, 355 • 2001 Kraška Penina, Vinakras Sežana, 365 • 2001 Chardonnay, Brič, 369 • 1998 Malvazija Capo d' Istria, Vinakoper, 383 • 2000 Ribolla Gialla, La Castellada, 388 • 2001 Sauvignon, La Castellada, 389 • 2000 Bianco Breg, Gravner, 390 • 1999 Rosso, Gravner, 392 • 2000 Ribolla, Gravner, 393 • 1999 Vitovska Grganja, Kante, 395 • 2000 Ribolla Gialla, Radikon, 396 • 2000 Oslavje, Radikon, 397

Seafood Dishes
2003 Chardonnay, Klet Bistrica, 46 • 1997 Sauvignon Pozna Trgatev, Meranovo, 48 • 2003 Rumeni Muškat Pozna Trgatev, Milan Šiker, 58 • 2002 Sauvignon, Lvaldhuber, 60 • 2003 Mariborčan, Lisičkino Vino, Vinag, 66 • 2003 Renski Rizling, Zlati Grič, 70 • 2003 Renski Rizling, Radgonske Gorice, 82 • 2000 Sauvignon Suhi Jagodni Izbor, Čurin, 101 • 1999 Penina Od Fare, Jože Frelih, 194 • 2003 Rumeni Muškat, KZ Metlika, 222 • 1999 Cuvée Prestige Brut, Bjana, 241 • 2001 Furlanski Tokaj, Blažič, 242 • 2002 Sivi Pinot, Dolfo, 256 • 1999 Sivi Pinot, Mavrič, 266 • 2002 Sivi Pinot, Jožko Mavrič, 268 • 2001 Rebula, Movia, 273 • 2001 Chardonnay Réserve, Simčič, 283 • 2001 Teodor, white, Simčič, 284 • 2001 Stara Brajda, white, Stojan Ščurek, 291 • 2002 Pinela, Andlovic, 300 • 2002 Zelen, Jordan Cigoj, 304 • 2002 Zelen, Lisjak, 312 • 2000 Zelen, Rikot, 322 • 2001 Rebula, Slavček, 324 • 2001 Sauvignon Zemono Lanthieri, Vipava 1894, 335 • 2002 Zelen Lanthieri, Vipava 1894, 337 • 2002 Zelen, Zaloščan, 340 • 2001 Malvazija, Joško Renčel, 355 • 2001 Rumeni Muškat, Brič, 370 • 2002 Malvazija, Korenika & Moškon, 376 • 1998 Malvazija Capo d' Istria, Vinakoper, 383 • 2000 Bianco Breg, Gravner, 390 • 2000 Ribolla Gialla, Gravner, 393 • 2001 Malvasia, Kante, 394

FOOD INDEX

Sweet Dishes

2003 Renski Rizling, Črnko, 34 • 2000 Traminec, Diona, 36 • 2000 Laški Rizling, Faust, 40 • 2003 Chardonnay, Klet Bistrica, 46 • 2003 Rumeni Muškat, Mašno Vino, Klet Bistrica, 47 • 1997 Sauvignon Pozna Trgatev, Meranovo, 48 • 1998 Šipon Ledeno Vino, Očkerl, 52 • 2003 Rumeni Muškat Pozna Trgatev, Milan Šiker, 58 • 2003 Laški Rizling, Vilko Vesenjak, 62 • 2003 Mariborčan, Lisičkino Vino, Vinag, 66 • 2000 Royal, Vinag, 67 • 1993 Traminec, Kapela, 78 • 2001 Steyer Mark Cuvée, Steyer, 85 • 2001 Laški Rizling Ledeno Vino, Vinar Kupljen, 86 • 2000 Laški Rizling Pozna Trgatev, Wine Queen's' Wine, Vinar Kupljen, 87 • 1983 Renski Rizling Izbor, Ptujska Klet, 95 • 2000 Šipon, Čurin, 99 • 1999 Traminec, Čurin, 100 • 2002 Laški Rizling Suhi Jagodni Izbor, Bojan Lubaj, 116 • 2002 Sauvignon Réserve, MiroVino, 120 • 2002 Renski Rizling, Jože Slavinec, 124 • 2000 Laški Rizling Pozna Trgatev, Jože Šnajder, 128 • 2000 Šipon Suhi Jagodni Izbor, Saško Štampar, 130 • 2003 Muškat Ottonel, Vinska Klet Püklavec, 134 • 2001 Renski Rizling, Anton Skaza, 138 • 2000 Laški Rizling Izbor, Jožef Šmigoc, 140 • 2002 Sauvignon, Turčan, 142 • 2002 Renski Rizling, Matija Gjerkeš, 146 • 1999 Laški Rizling Ledeno Vino, Ernest Novak, 154 • 2003 Sauvignon, Amon, 160 • 2000 Kerner Pozna Trgatev, Urbajs, 163 • 2001 Traminec, Rajko Pečnik, 166 • 1990 Kerner Suhi Jagodni Izbor, Matjaž Jenšterle, 178 • 2000 Sauvignon with Predicate, Keltis, 180 • 2001 Laški Rizling Ledeno Vino, Vino Brežice, 184 • 2003 Chardonnay, Martinčič, 209 • 2003 Sauvignon, Družina Absec, 212 • 2002 Chardonnay, Ivan Bajuk, 214 • 2001 Sauvignon Ledeno Vino, Alojz Hoznar, 218 • 2000 Laški Rizling Izbor, Anton Kostelec, 224 • 2001 Sauvignon Suhi Jagodni Izbor, Jožef Prus, 230 • 1998 Renski Rizling Ledeno Vino, Jožef Prus, 231 • 1999 Poezija, Cjanova Kmetija, 246 • 2003 Pikolit, Aljoša Sirk, 288 • 1999 Klarnica, Mansus, 317 • 2000 Sauvignon, Sutor, 326 • 2002 Zlate Solzice, Joško Renčel, 354 • 2000 Chardonnay Izbor, Vinakoper 384 • 2001 Sauvignon, La Castellada, 389

Fruit Dishes and Compôtes

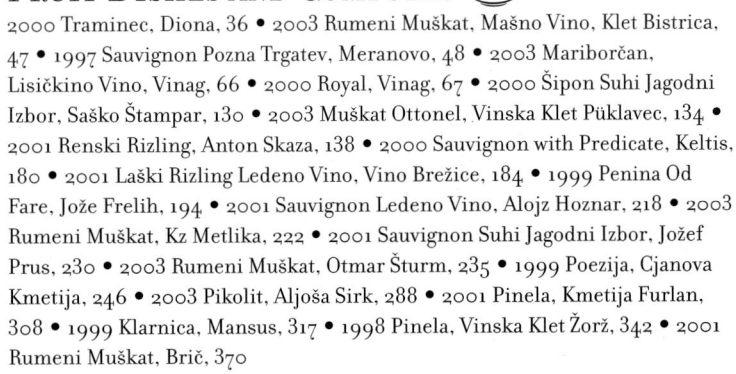

2000 Traminec, Diona, 36 • 2003 Rumeni Muškat, Mašno Vino, Klet Bistrica, 47 • 1997 Sauvignon Pozna Trgatev, Meranovo, 48 • 2003 Mariborčan, Lisičkino Vino, Vinag, 66 • 2000 Royal, Vinag, 67 • 2000 Šipon Suhi Jagodni Izbor, Saško Štampar, 130 • 2003 Muškat Ottonel, Vinska Klet Püklavec, 134 • 2001 Renski Rizling, Anton Skaza, 138 • 2000 Sauvignon with Predicate, Keltis, 180 • 2001 Laški Rizling Ledeno Vino, Vino Brežice, 184 • 1999 Penina Od Fare, Jože Frelih, 194 • 2001 Sauvignon Ledeno Vino, Alojz Hoznar, 218 • 2003 Rumeni Muškat, Kz Metlika, 222 • 2001 Sauvignon Suhi Jagodni Izbor, Jožef Prus, 230 • 2003 Rumeni Muškat, Otmar Šturm, 235 • 1999 Poezija, Cjanova Kmetija, 246 • 2003 Pikolit, Aljoša Sirk, 288 • 2001 Pinela, Kmetija Furlan, 308 • 1999 Klarnica, Mansus, 317 • 1998 Pinela, Vinska Klet Žorž, 342 • 2001 Rumeni Muškat, Brič, 370